QUEEN VICTORIA'S LITTLE WARS

BYRON FARWELL

QUEEN VICTORIA'S LITTLE WARS

W · W · NORTON & COMPANY

New York · London

First published as a Norton paperback 1985
by arrangement with Harper & Row, Publishers

Library of Congress Cataloging in Publication Data

Farwell, Byron.
  Queen Victoria's little wars.
  Reprint. Originally published: New York: Harper
& Row, 1972.
  Bibliography: p.
  Includes index.
  1. Great Britain—History, Military—19th century.
I. Title.
DA68.F37 1985 909.81 85-9002

ISBN 0-393-30235-0

W. W. Norton & Company, Inc., 500 Fifth Avenue, New York, NY 10110
W. W. Norton & Company Ltd., 10 Coptic Street London WC1A 1PU

  2 3 4 5 6 7 8 9 0

TO RUTH
my wife

CONTENTS

Contents

LIST OF ILLUSTRATIONS

List of Illustrations

SOURCE OF ILLUSTRATIONS

The author and publishers wish to acknowledge the following for permission to reproduce photographs: The Tate Gallery, London for No. 1; Radio Times Hulton Picture Library for Nos. 2, 4, 6, 7, 8, 12–15, 17, 18, 20, 22, 23, 24, 26, 27, 33; National Army Museum for Nos. 3, 11, 19, 28, 32, 34; The Mansell Collection for Nos. 10, 16, 21, 25; India Office Library and Records for No. 9. Nos. 29, 30, 31 are from *Chitral* by Sir G. Robertson, Methuen 1898, and No. 5 is from Rait: *The Life and Campaigns of Hugh First Viscount Gough*, Constable 1903. The maps on pp. xii–xiv were drawn by Leo Vernon.

LIST OF MEDALS
USED AS CHAPTER DECORATIONS

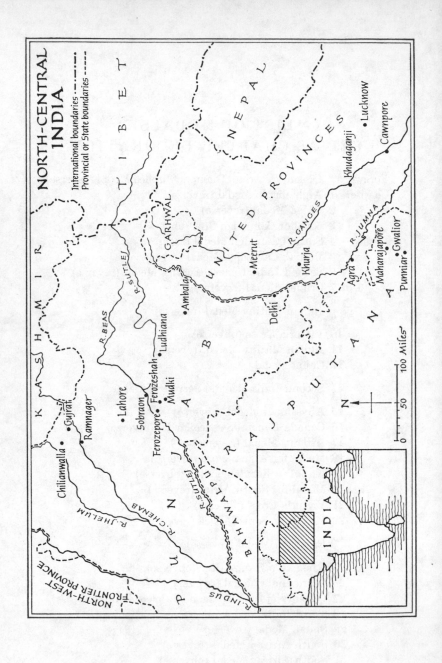

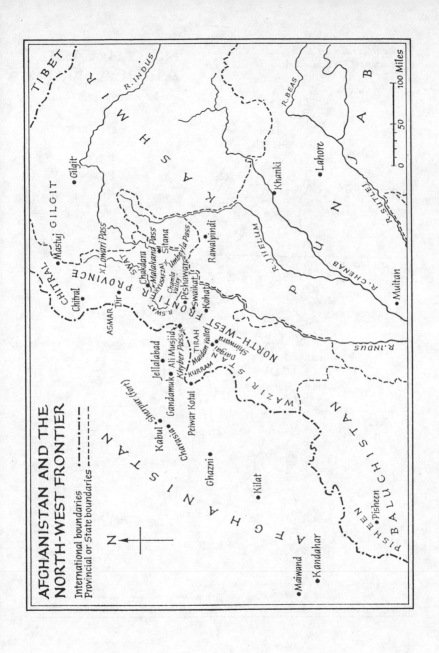

AFGHANISTAN AND THE
NORTH-WEST FRONTIER

International boundaries ·—··—··—
Provincial or State boundaries ————

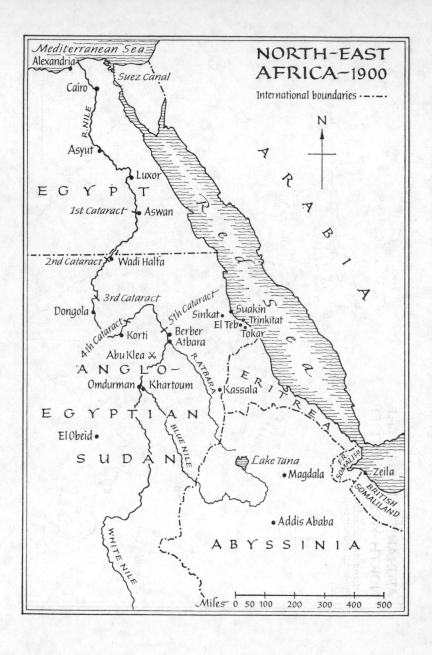

NORTH-EAST
AFRICA-1900

International boundaries ----

Mediterranean Sea
Alexandria

Suez Canal

Cairo

A
R
A
B
I
A

R. NILE

Asyut

Luxor

E G Y P T

1st Cataract
Aswan

2nd Cataract
Wadi Halfa

3rd Cataract

4th Cataract
5th Cataract

Dongola

Korti
Berber
Atbara

Abu Klea

Sinkat
El Teb

Suakin
Trinkitat
Tokar

A N G L O -

R. ATBARA

E R I T R E A

Omdurman
Khartoum

Kassala

E G Y P T I A N

El Obeid

BLUE NILE

Lake Tana

Magdala

FR. SOMALI...

S U D A N

Zeila

BRITISH
SOMALILAND

Addis Ababa

WHITE NILE

A B Y S S I N I A

Miles 0 50 100   200   300   400   500

ACKNOWLEDGEMENTS

I would like to express my gratitude to some of the people who have been helpful to me in the writing of this book. My thanks go to The Marquess of Anglesey, Mr Leo Cooper, Colonel Geoffrey Powell, Major C. J. D. Haswell, Lieutenant-General Sir Brian Horrocks, and Lieutenant-Colonel A. C. M. Urwick.

I want particularly to thank Miss Susan Warner for her excellent research on my behalf. And my wife, Ruth, deserves my deepest gratitude for her advice, criticism and encouragement.

B.F.

Fairfax, Virginia

FOREWORD

THIS is the story of what Kipling called the 'savage wars of peace', and of the men who fought them. Scant attention is paid to the causes of the wars or the political manoeuvrings which preceded the hostilities. They are not of much importance. Reasons for going to war are continually being made available to great nations; the more farflung their interests, the more pretexts for war present themselves. Political leaders can select those which are the most plausible, most appealing, most useful. Vigorous, self-confident, prideful, determined and opinionated peoples, such as the British were in the last century and the Americans in this century, will always provide themselves with armies, and the temptation to use them to enforce national desires is seemingly irresistible.

Although to talk of wars is to speak of battles, no attempt has been made in this book to give a blow-by-blow account of each battle in every war, or even to name every battle. Some famous and fascinating battles and small campaigns have been omitted or barely mentioned. In the case of minor actions, interesting but little-known campaigns have been selected to illustrate aspects of military character or to help describe interesting personalities. Military actions other than those here used might have done as well: the Malakand campaign, ably described by Winston Churchill, could have been used instead of the almost forgotten but more interesting Tirah expedition.

There has been little study of the character of armies, but armies, like individuals, can be characterized. Each nation's army is different; each responds to different kinds of appeals, has characteristic strengths and weaknesses, sets its own standards of conduct, fits into the social fabric of the nation in its own way, and constructs codes of values peculiar to itself. National armies, whether volunteer or conscript, reflect in many ways the character of the nation they represent, and much might be learned of a nationality by a study of its military structure.

The quality and character of an army is determined by its officer corps. Men in the ranks have little influence except in their numbers and their degree of physical endurance. An army – that least democratic of social institutions – is dominated by its officers: it is they who establish its moral and social codes, the standard of discipline, and the degree of inhumanity to be tolerated; they determine its organization, its tactics and strategies, its weapons and clothes, and, most importantly, its attitudes and opinions. As has been often proved, armies can be constructed from the most unpromising of human materials and be successful on the field of battle if they are provided with excellent officers, from subalterns to generals, who have had time to mould their men.

The nineteenth-century British army drew its officers from the ruling classes of Britain – nearly all were the sons of squires, clergymen, civil servants, politicians or other officers – and it developed a sound military caste, a narrow, closed society with its own set of values and standards of conduct. The British developed over the centuries a most curious military organizational structure. In the last century, no one below the prime minister controlled the Empire's army, and even his ability to direct it was doubtful; until after the Indian Mutiny, half of Britain's military strength was owned by a private chartered company. There was a commander-in-chief at the Horse Guards (army headquarters, so called because of its location), but he did not control the forces

outside Britain. There was another commander-in-chief in India,
but he only controlled the Bengal army, not the armies of the
Madras and Bombay presidencies.

No account of any aspect of British imperialism can be told
without mention of India and that peculiar institution: the
Honourable East India Company, familiarly known as 'John
Company'. It was founded at the end of the sixteenth century and
Queen Elizabeth I incorporated it by a Royal Charter on 31
December 1600. It was a decade later before the company established trading posts, called factories, on the Indian mainland. It
was Charles II who gave the Company the power that made it
great: he permitted the Company to acquire territory and build
forts, to raise armies and make war; to coin in its own money; and
to make laws and create law courts.

The first factories were established in Bengal, but by 1640 there
was a settlement at Madras and fourteen years later the town was
made the capital of a separate presidency. In 1661 Charles II
acquired Bombay, a Portuguese possession, as part of the dowry
of the Infanta Catherine, and in 1668 this territory was given to
the Company, becoming the third presidency.

The Company and its agents fought and intrigued with the
Indians and the Moguls, acquiring more and more territory and
wielding ever-increasing power. In 1773 the British government
began to take a direct interest and the appointment of the
governor-general had to be approved by the crown. From this
point on the government began to arrogate to itself more and more
of the power which had been vested in the Court of Directors,
although the Court remained an independent governing body with
vast amounts of patronage until the end. In 1784 Pitt's India Bill
created a Board of Control, which had to approve all policy decisions, and in 1813 the Board of Control was given authority over
the Company's commercial transactions.

The East India Company maintained its own army, composed
of a few 'European' regiments – white men, mostly Irish – and a
growing number of 'native' regiments – mostly high cast Hindus
from Bengal, but later additions included numbers of Sikhs from

Punjab, Moslem Pathans and, of course, the famous Gurkhas. All were officered by Britons. The commander-in-chief of the British army in London had no control over this private army.

In addition to its own army, the Company also hired regular regiments from the British army. These regiments might serve in India for twenty years or more and they were usually brigaded with the Company's regiments on campaigns, but they remained distinct and apart. Certainly in the minds of the officers there appeared a vast difference between officers in 'Queen's' regiments who held their commissions from the Queen, and the officers of 'Company' regiments who did not and were regarded as little better than mercenaries.

All of Britain's armies were, and still are, organized on a peculiar regimental system. Readers unfamiliar with this system should read Appendix I for an explanation; it is essential to an understanding of the workings of the British army and the British military mind. It was faith in the discipline and spirit engendered by this system which time after time led British generals to throw their armies against foes five, even ten, times more numerous – usually with success.

It was British armies – often composed mainly of mercenaries, but always British officered – which built and maintained the British Empire. It seems, therefore, an important task to examine the Victorian officer and the campaigns in which he fought. It seems worth while, too, to examine the thoughts and feelings of the wise, naïve and proud sovereign to whom they gave their allegiance. She had a deep and abiding interest in their activities and their welfare. It was, as she frequently pointed out to her ministers, *her* army; the officers and men were *her* soldiers. She could not direct or control military affairs, but she could and did exert an influence on them.

1

OPENING SHOTS OF THE REIGN

1837–42

THERE was not a single year in Queen Victoria's long reign in which somewhere in the world her soldiers were not fighting for her and for her empire. From 1837 until 1901, in Asia, Africa, Arabia and elsewhere, British troops were engaged in almost constant combat. It was the price of empire, of world leadership, and of national pride – and it was paid, usually without qualms or regrets or very much thought.

Except for the final Boer War, all the military actions were small affairs by today's standards: little wars, military expeditions, rebellions, mutinies, only one of which, the Indian Mutiny, ever posed a threat to the Empire. Britain's little wars did not begin with Queen Victoria, but there were more of them during the sixty-four years of her reign than there had been in the previous two centuries. It was in the Victorian era that continual warfare became an accepted way of life – and in the process the size of the British Empire quadrupled.

It was easy enough to find excuses for all the Victorian wars and campaigns: a frontier could be better defended by extending it; an invasion was called for to protect resident Britons, or British interests. It was necessary to repel a provoked attack; to save an Englishman in distress; to avenge an insult, such as the

1

murder of a British soldier, traveller or envoy (this was known as protecting British prestige); to suppress a mutiny or rebellion by those who did not understand the benefits of British rule and were ungrateful for the blessings of English civilization bestowed upon them; to move into a power vacuum, thus restoring law and order; or to prevent Russia from extending *her* empire.

Naturally, as many of these reasons as possible were mustered to justify any given war or campaign. But these were only the apparent reasons. There are, for all wars, more basic causes than the immediate incidents or the avowed, always noble, reasons nations use as excuses to justify their use of force to impose their will on others. Some of these basic causes were not peculiar to the nineteenth century, nor to the British. Simple possession of power, and the ability to use it, always provides a powerful temptation to exercise it. But there existed among the British people of the last century some peculiar attributes which indirectly led to conflict.

For a small island race, the British have always produced more than their share of able and talented men, but in the nineteenth century there was in many fields a superabundance. The list of eminent Victorians – and they *were* eminent – is staggering, particularly when it is remembered that the population of Great Britain in 1838 was only some nineteen million, less than half its present number and comparable to the present population of New York and New Jersey. And these people concealed behind stiff manners and rigid morals a violent, restless energy which drove them away from the narrow confines of their islands to every part of the civilized world and deep into the vast areas of the unexplored, uncivilized world. Carrying with them their own unbending attitudes, manners, customs and beliefs, they were continually getting into trouble or creating trouble by being in places where they need not have been: the goldfields of South Africa, the interior of China, Tibet and the West Coast of Africa.

Producing a superabundance of leaders, Britain built great armies from more populous but less efficient races and braced them with British officers. But there were more leaders still, and Britons commanded the armies and fleets of other peoples in China,

Argentina, Portugal, Madagascar, Greece, Borneo and Turkey. Britons did not hesitate to exchange their bowlers for turbans, tarbushes or mandarin caps if only they were given men whom they could lead into battle. Lawrence of Arabia was a wonder and a curiosity in this century, but there were hundreds of his countrymen like him who performed similar exploits in the previous century; Lawrence was simply one of the last of the breed, a survivor from an age just dead.

The British people, from prime minister to yeoman, and British soldiers from general to private, were sustained in their international martial activities by an unquestioning and unquenchable conviction that British institutions and British customs, beliefs and doctrines were the best in the world – not only for Britons, but for all the other peoples of the earth as well. And when Britain changed her mind, Britons thought that everyone should: having, for example, given up slavery herself in 1833, Britain energetically set about persuading others to do so, by force if necessary, and her warships prowled the Red Sea and off the Slave Coast, boarding other people's ships and freeing their slaves.

With such well-meaning, hot-blooded, energetic people in the world it is little wonder that it was a century filled with British battles.

*   *   *

When on 20 June 1837 young Queen Victoria ascended the throne the realm was at peace with the world and with itself. But in December of that year there was a rebellion in Canada. William Lyon Mackenzie, a fiery little politician who had been the first mayor of Toronto, labelled his sovereign 'Victoria Guelph, the bloody queen of England' and attempted to create a republic in Ontario. The revolt was quickly suppressed, but Mackenzie and a handful of his followers escaped to Navy Island in the St Lawrence River just below Niagara Falls and began to fortify it. The island was Canadian, but the rebels arranged to have supplies brought to them by an American ship, the *Caroline*. This created an embarrassing situation for both the American and the Canadian authorities. It became an international crisis when on the night of 29 December Captain Andrew Drew and a party of Canadian militia boarded boats and crossed the narrow strip of water that connects Lake Ontario and Lake Erie and stormed aboard the *Caroline*. The ship was set on fire; one American was killed and two were captured. This incident, the now almost forgotten '*Caroline* Affair', nearly started another Anglo-American war. Fortunately, tempers cooled on both sides of the border: there were no further incidents, war was averted, and Mackenzie, after spending a year in an American jail, returned to Canada and eventually became a member of the Canadian parliament, still a radical but no longer a revolutionary.

The Mackenzie revolt, although it provoked the first shots fired in anger in Victoria's reign, caused hardly a ripple in British imperial history. But less than a year later, at the opposite end of the Empire, there was the beginning of a major event in British history: Lord Auckland, Governor-General of India, issued a 'Declaration', which became known as the Simla Manifesto, announcing that British troops would invade Afghanistan. This was the beginning of the First Afghan War, a war which included a most appalling disaster to a British army; a 'signal catastrophe', Sir John Keane called it.

Three years earlier, Dost Muhammad, the Amir of Afghanistan, had written to Lord Auckland, saying 'consider me and my country as yours'. The expression meant no more than 'your obedient servant' at the end of a British letter. But Dost Muhammad soon had reason to consider the British a very literal people. He must also have considered them damnable hypocrites, for Lord Auckland had written him: 'My friend, you are aware that it is not the practice of the British Government to interfere with the affairs of other independent states.' No statesman ever penned a greater lie.

It is difficult for anyone to understand the reasoning behind the extraordinary attitude of the British towards Afghanistan; the Afghans must have found it impossible. While always protesting friendship, the British repeatedly invaded the country and

4

shot at its inhabitants. Although unable to subdue the proud, fiercely independent Afghans, they always feared that Russia or Persia would, and this frequently served as an excuse for meddling in Afghan affairs.

Consider the case of Eldred Pottinger (1811–43) whose actions were so perplexing to the Afghans but so typically British. Pottinger was tall and handsome and possessed all the admired Anglo-Saxon virtues: he was brave, clever, virtuous, adventurous, and he was extremely energetic. When he was commissioned in the Bombay Horse Artillery in 1827 he founded a family tradition of service to India which has continued to the present day. In 1838, disguised as a horse trader, he entered Afghanistan as a spy. On reaching Herat he found that the city was about to be besieged by a Persian army guided by Russian advisers. He at once threw off his disguise, stopped spying on the Afghans and instead became their military adviser. The young man became, at least by all British accounts, the saviour of the city. Lord Auckland praised him as one who had 'by his fortitude, ability, and judgment honourably sustained the reputation and interests of his country'. Although only a subaltern, Pottinger was created a Companion of the Order of the Bath and given a brevet majority.

Lord Auckland, having concluded that the British should not allow 'Russian and Persian intrigue upon our frontiers', decided that he should 'attempt to save Afghanistan' by invading the country with British, Indian and Sikh troops and overthrow its ruler. The plan was to replace Dost Muhammad with a man named Shah Shuja, a more docile Afghan noble who, although unpopular with his own people, had pretensions to the amirship. The British had been keeping him on a dole in India for just such an occasion. The plan sounds fantastic today, and so it sounded to many in London when it was explained: the Afghans were to be persuaded that the British would save them from the clutches of the Persians and Russians by invading their country with Anglo-Indian and Sikh armies – the Sikhs being the most hated enemies of the Afghans – and deposing their ruler, replacing him with a man whom they distrusted and detested!

Acting on this plan, the grandly named Army of the Indus was formed late in 1838 under the command of Sir John Keane and lumbered off into Afghanistan with Shah Shuja. All Indian armies on the march carried in their wake large numbers of transport animals and swarms of servants and camp followers, but the Army of the Indus appears to have had an exceptionally swollen baggage train. Sir John Kaye, first historian of the war and himself a Victorian soldier, justified the excess of camels, tents and luggage: The British officer, he said, 'should not be entirely forgetful of the pleasures of the mess table, or regardless of the less social delights of the pleasant volume and the solacing pipe. Clean linen, too, is a luxury which a civilized man, without any imputation upon his soldierly qualities, may in moderation desire to enjoy.' The fact of the matter was that while the army knew it would be marching through wild and uncivilized country, it did not expect to do much fighting. The officers had been led to believe that Shah Shuja would be welcomed back in Afghanistan and that British bayonets would intimidate his enemies. 'There was no hint', complained General Keane of the country, 'that it was full of robbers, plunderers and murderers, brought up to it from their youth.' The Army of the Indus had to fight its way to Kabul through swarms of outraged Afghans.

The first major obstacle in the path of the army was the great fortress of Ghazni. Here, in July 1839, a technique was developed which was to be repeated many times on other Afghan forts: a gate was blown in with gunpowder and the explosion was quickly followed up with an assault through the breach. It required a great deal of courage and dash, but these were qualities which the British had in abundance.

Less than a month after the fall of Ghazni the Army of the Indus reached Kabul, capital of Afghanistan. It entered the city without a fight, but also without a welcome from the glum inhabitants; Shah Shuja, fat and vain, was installed as Amir of Afghanistan.

The British spent the next few months marching about the country, knocking out pockets of organized resistance and blow-

ing up Afghan forts. Dost Muhammad sought asylum with Nasrullah Khan, the Amir of Bokhara, who welcomed him warmly
and threw him in prison. Nasrullah at this time had a collection
of prisoners so interesting that he must have been the envy of all
his neighbours. Included were several Russians and an Englishman, Colonel Charles Stoddart, military aide to the ambassador
to Persia, who had been sent to try to secure the release of the
Russians. Although they were the feared rivals, the Russians were,
after all, civilized people and, like the British, were playing the
same empire game in Central Asia. Then, too, there was the fear
that the Russians might use the prisoners as an excuse to capture
Bokhara and thus move closer to Afghanistan and India.

The British, of course, now had the best of reasons for attacking
Bokhara themselves, for they could possibly release the prisoners,
thwart the Russians and capture Dost Muhammad. This was discussed in high circles, but unfortunately Afghanistan was still
quite unsettled and the army there had its hands full; for soldiers
and politicians an attack on Bokhara was inconvenient. So instead of an army the British sent another officer, Captain Arthur
Conolly, to plead with Nasrullah. When Conolly, too, was imprisoned, the Russians again tried their luck and sent a delegation
to Bokhara. But Nasrullah must have tired of the game, for he
sent the Russian delegation packing, beheaded his British prisoners, and allowed Dost Muhammad to escape.

The unfortunate Captain Conolly was a nephew of Sir William
Macnaghten, formerly Chief Secretary in India and now Envoy to
Afghanistan. It was an unlucky family. Within a three-year
period, Arthur Conolly was executed in Bokhara, a brother died
of fever while a prisoner of the Afghans, another brother was killed
by a sniper's bullet in Kohistan, and Macnaghten was murdered
in Kabul.

It was Macnaghten who had perhaps done the most to foster the
war in the first place. Now that Kabul was captured and Shah
Shuja was on the throne with a British army standing by to
see that he stayed there, Macnaghten the envoy was the most influential man in Afghanistan, at least as far as the law of Shah

Shuja reached, which was not, in truth, very far. In the mountains and in the all-important mountain passes that led to India it was the Ghilzais who ruled. For centuries rulers of the country had always wisely bribed these wild lawless tribesmen to keep them from attacking those travelling through the passes. But Macnaghten decided to stop these payments, and the next caravan from India was promptly plundered. The routes through the passes, which constituted the British lifeline to India, were effectively closed. The envoy found it all 'very provoking'.

The Afghans openly expressed their contempt for their new rulers, even in Kabul: British officers were insulted by shopkeepers, sentries were killed in the night, lone soldiers had their throats cut, and once an Afghan coolly walked into a tent in the British camp and shot a sleeping soldier. Yet, in spite of repeated warnings of trouble, the British were completely unprepared for the open revolt which broke out in 1841. The British forces at Kabul found themselves besieged in their ill-placed cantonments north-east of the city and in the Bala Hissar, the fort on the eastern edge of town. There were British forces at Kandahar and Ghazni, but they were shut up in their forts as well. The British leaders in Kabul, military and civil, were indecisive and quarrelled among themselves; the commanding general was old and sick. This was particularly unfortunate since only through superior discipline and leadership could the British maintain their tenuous hold on the country, for the Afghans, superb warriors and bred to their trade, were better armed: they used long-barrelled rifles, called jezails, which had a longer range and were more accurate than the soldiers' smooth-bore muskets. Also, as Lieutenant (later General) Vincent Eyre remarked, the Afghans were 'perhaps the best marksmen in the world'.

There were several skirmishes and small battles around the army's indefensible cantonments; an amateurish attempt by the British to play at Afghan intrigue; a parley in which Macnaghten was murdered; and then, at last, the reluctant decision was made to retreat to India. On 6 January 1842 the British force of 4,500 troops, about 700 of whom were Britons, together with several officers' wives and their children and about 10,000 camp followers, left their warm huts and hot breakfasts and marched out of their cantonments towards Jellalabad, about sixty miles east in a straight line, where a British force had established a strong outpost. The weather was cold in the mountain passes, below freezing, the ground covered with snow – and the Ghilzais with their long jezails were waiting for them.

Seven days later, officers of the 13th Regiment on the walls of the fort at Jellalabad saw a solitary horseman riding slowly towards them from the direction of Kabul. Horse and rider were obviously exhausted, but someone made a signal and the rider replied by waving a soldier's forage cap. The gate was thrown open and several officers rushed out to greet Surgeon William Brydon – the sole Briton to complete the march from Kabul. Henry Havelock, one of the officers who ran out to meet him, wrote: 'His first few sentences extinguished all hope in the hearts of listeners regarding the future of the Kabul force. It was evident that it was annihilated.'

A handful of sepoys straggled in later; there were a few other survivors, including a number of the wives and children, who had been given as hostages or were taken prisoner; but most of the army had been slaughtered in the passes by the jezails and swords of the Ghilzais. Kaye said: 'There is nothing more remarkable in the history of the world than the awful completeness, the sublime unity of this Caubul tragedy.' Two months later, when two of her ministers set before the young queen 'the disastrous intelligence from Afghanistan', she was appalled.

Jellalabad was now an isolated post perched on the edge of the enemy's country. It was commanded by General Sir Robert Sale (1782–1845), a man who was personally very brave and who in his forty-seven years of service had seen a great deal of action in India, Burma and Mauritius. But 'Fighting Bob' Sale was now stout, double-chinned and cautious. He was not a strategist and he was uncomfortable when faced with important decisions and heavy responsibilities. Sale had received word of the outbreak at Kabul on 10 November 1841 when he was ordered to take his force there. He had found excuses, many of them excellent – he

9

was encumbered with many sick and wounded – for not going to Kabul. Personal feelings certainly did not influence him, for his wife, daughter and son-in-law were there. Instead he went to Jellalabad, pursued by hostile Afghans, arriving there on 12 November with about 2,000 men: the 13th Light Infantry (about 700 men, nearly half of whom were recruits), some native troops and a few guns.

Jellalabad was a walled town, but when Sale arrived the walls were crumbling and the town's defences were in miserable condition. Sale's men at once began to strengthen the walls, but just as they had them in reasonably good repair, an earthquake shook many of them down again. A week after Dr Brydon's arrival, Sale received orders to retreat to India. He was indecisive and did not know what to do. Knowledge that his son-in-law had been killed and that his wife and daughter were prisoners of the Afghans must certainly have weighed heavily on him. Like many an irresolute commander, he called a council of war. Most of the officers present were in favour of negotiating with the Afghans, who were now all around them, and attempting a retreat to India. There were, however, two strong-minded, determined and able officers, Captain Henry Havelock of the 13th Regiment, and Major George Broadfoot of the Royal Engineers, who argued strongly in favour of holding out at Jellalabad.

In the end they did stay and 'Fighting Bob' Sale won fame as the 'defender of Jellalabad'. Repeated attacks by the Afghans were beaten off, several successful sorties were made and, thanks to the exertions of Broadfoot, the defences were made secure. Food supplies were running low when, on 1 April, a sortie resulted in in the capture of 500 sheep. Equal distribution was made among the troops, but the 35th Native Infantry decided that their European comrades needed the meat more than they did and gave up their share to the 13th Light Infantry. Urged on by his fiery subordinates, Sale was persuaded to make an attack on the Afghan army at his gates. It was a complete success and Sale captured the enemy's camp, baggage, guns, ammunition and horses. The remains of the Afghan army fled towards Kabul.

As soon as the news of the disaster to the Kabul force reached India, an army of retribution was formed and it set out for Afghanistan. It was commanded by Major-General George Pollock (1786–1872), an East India Company artillery officer who had not seen active service since the Burma War of 1824 but who was sound, stolid, unflappable, and the best general available. In the event he proved to be a very good general indeed, although he was inadequately rewarded by his government and history has almost forgotten him.

Pollock began his campaign with a nearly incredible achievement: his army forced the Khyber Pass. It was the first army in history to do so. Tamberlaine had bribed the fierce Afridis who controlled the pass to allow his army to go through; Akbar the Great lost 40,000 men unsuccessfully attempting to force his way through. But Pollock did it. In September 1842 he reached and recaptured Kabul; the British prisoners were freed; General Pollock, under orders to leave in Afghanistan 'some lasting mark of the just retribution of an outraged nation', burned down the Great Bazaar of Kabul, and then marched his army back to India. The uncrushed Ghilzais sniped at him all the way back through the passes, but honour had been restored to British arms and the Afghans were again left to themselves.

Pollock on his victorious march relieved Sale and his men on 16 April and the name of Jellalabad was soon forgotten by most of the world – but not by the 13th Foot (later the Somerset Light Infantry). The name became an inscription on their regimental badge and, until 1959 when the 274-year-old regiment was amalgamated with the Duke of Cornwall's Light Infantry, 17 April was celebrated each year in the regiment as Jellalabad Day. Every soldier learned the story of his regiment's deeds there. Seventy-three years after the 13th left Afghanistan, Arthur Cook, a soldier in the regiment, went over the top during the First Battle of the Somme in an unsuccessful attack on the German positions; most of his comrades were killed or wounded and he came tumbling back into his own trenches alone and feeling, he said, 'like Dr Brydon at Jellalabad'.

2

WAR IN CHINA

1840–54

I N the preceding century and until the end of the wars with
France it had been the Royal Navy which had been the most
important arm of Britain. In Queen Victoria's reign it was the
Army which played the key role in building and preserving the
Empire. Still, the Royal Navy had its part to play, not only in
transporting troops and supplies and sometimes providing naval
brigades to fight side by side with the soldiers on land, but
occasionally taking a direct active role in the growth of the
Empire, as it did in Syria in 1840 when, in conjunction with
Austrian and Prussian ships, it thwarted the expansionist ten-
dencies of Mohammed Ali.

A year earlier a smaller but in the long run far more important
naval operation took place in southern Arabia. In December 1836
a British ship was wrecked and plundered on the coast of Aden,
then an independent sultanate. After prolonged negotiations, the
sultan promised compensation, but he died and his son refused to
honour the agreement. So on 19 January 1839 a military and
naval force under Captain H. Smith in the 28-gun frigate *Volage*
captured Aden, and this small but strategic piece of real estate was
added to the Empire. Captain Smith then sailed off to Hong Kong
where, on 4 September, he fired the shots which began the Opium
War.

War in China

The cause of the Opium War has been attributed simply to the greed of the British merchants in China, but the real causes of the war were cultural rather than commercial: British opium smuggling and the vigorous attempts of the Chinese government to suppress it only sparked the war, which would have taken place sooner or later in any event.

The Chinese and the British were alike in that both regarded their own culture, civilization and way of life as infinitely superior to all others. It was only natural, then, that where the two cultures met there was friction: Chinaman and Briton were astonished at the pretensions of each other; to each, the other was a barbarian. Neither made much of an attempt to understand the other, and doubtless it seems surprising to most Englishmen even today that the Chinese regarded them as inscrutable.

The Chinese wanted foreign merchants to obey Chinese laws, submit to Chinese justice, and to conform to stringent Chinese regulations regarding their export–import business, demands that do not seem unreasonable considering that the foreigners were trading with Chinese in China. The foreign merchants, principally British and Americans, did not like Chinese laws, which they flouted; they thought Chinese notions of justice were unjust, preposterous and barbaric; and they felt unduly constrained by the, to them, peculiar restrictions put on their trading methods. But what annoyed them most was that they were treated, every day, in word and deed, as if they were the inferiors of the Chinese. And the British found this hard to bear. They complained, but they did adjust to the situation. All might have gone on peaceably enough had the Chinese government been strong enough to enforce its rules and had the British government not appeared on the scene in the shape of a series of envoys, consuls and trade commissioners, who were followed in due course by soldiers and sailors.

The war might have been called with greater propriety the Kowtow War, for, as John Quincy Adams told the Massachusetts Historical Society, opium was 'a mere incident to the dispute, but no more the cause of the war than the throwing overboard the tea in Boston harbour was the cause of the North American revolution'. Adams correctly diagnosed the case when he said, 'the cause of the war is the kowtow'.

When the first British official arrived in Pekin in 1792 he refused to kowtow when presented to the emperor. That is, he refused to make the prostrations, face touching the floor, which protocol required in the presence of the Son of Heaven and Emperor of China. It was an attitude much admired at home and was copied by later official British representatives. The British thought the kowtow humiliating; the Chinese regarded their refusal to perform it as inexplicable and decided that it would be better if they simply avoided seeing the ill-mannered barbarians altogether: British diplomatists were not even permitted to meet provincial governors. Consequently, British officials joined the merchants in complaining of the humiliating treatment they received at the hands of the Chinese, and, as the complaints of officials, being addressed to other officials and to politicians, always carry more weight than the cries of mere merchants, there was a good deal of irresponsible talk by responsible men about teaching the Chinese a lesson and putting them in their place.

When Lord Napier (William, 8th baron, 1786–1834) went to China as Chief Superintendent of Trade in 1833 he was not even allowed to stay in the country, except at the Portuguese colony of Macao, and he indignantly wrote home asking for 'three or four frigates and brigs, with a few steady British troops, not Sepoys'. The ships and soldiers were not sent, but there was a growing feeling in England that something would have to be done to defend British prestige in China.

Meanwhile, the harvests continued in the poppy fields of Bengal and the opium clippers, in the season, swiftly and efficiently carried their chests to China, off-loading on the coasts, in the rivers or on islands just offshore. Often accused of being hypocritical, Victorian Britons rarely were, although they often succeeded in honestly deceiving themselves. Regarding the shipment of opium to China, however, they were indeed hypocritical. The East India Company, which then ruled most of India, refused to allow opium to be transported in their own ships, but they encouraged the trade, and for a very good reason: export taxes on opium came to provide more than 10 per cent of India's gross revenue. As to the morality of the business, many Britons tried to justify it by saying that opium smoking in China was really no worse than gin drinking in England (although gin drinking in England had grown out of hand and at best this was a poor excuse).

At Canton, where foreigners were allowed to establish their offices and warehouses (called factories), the opium trade flourished. All the great British trading companies in China indulged in it and the local Chinese officials were easily bribed. Then, in January 1839, the Emperor sent an unbribable mandarin, Lin Tse-hsu, as Imperial High Commissioner to stamp out opium smuggling. Lin gave fair warning, then he struck.

Lin first tried to show the foreigners in little ways that he was indeed serious in his determination to stop the opium trade: in Macao and Canton some smugglers were publicly strangled in front of the British and American factories. An Imperial edict was issued flatly stating that opium smuggling must cease and that stocks now in store must be surrendered. When the foreigners refused to comply with the edict, they were shut up in their factories without Chinese servants or workers, forcing them to cook their own food and clean their own houses. It was considered a great hardship. This incident in May 1839 became known as the Siege of the Factories. It ended when the British, greatly humiliated, gave up 20,000 chests of illegally imported opium. Obviously the British could not go to war over this issue, even though dignity and prestige were involved; a larger issue was needed.

Six weeks after the Siege of the Factories, some British and American sailors started a brawl in a village near Kowloon and a Chinaman was killed. The Chinese authorities demanded that the murderer be given up; the British refused, maintaining, perhaps correctly, that it was impossible to discover exactly who had done the deed. Commissioner Lin withdrew all supplies and labourers from British homes and factories and ordered the Portuguese

15

governor of Macao to expel all the British from his territory. Men, women and children were loaded on British ships, which sailed over to Hong Kong, then a virtually uninhabited island, and anchored. Here floated the entire British colony, a westernized version of the sampan communities commonly found in Chinese ports. It was at this juncture that Captain Smith arrived in the *Volage*, fresh from his successful operations against the Arabs at Aden, and he was presently joined by the 20-gun frigate *Hyacinth*.

Without British officials and the samples of British power on the scene all might have ended peaceably enough, for both the Chinese and the merchants wanted to trade, but now merchants, officials and sailors were delighted by the opportunity to humble the arrogant Chinese and to pay them back for the years of indignity. Chinese were found who were willing to supply the floating British community with food under the protection of the frigates. When the Chinese government sent war junks to stop the trade, Captain Smith drove them off with the fire of the *Volage*. The Chinese then sent a fleet of twenty-nine war junks against the two frigates, and in the battle that followed four junks were sunk and others were badly damaged at no loss to the British ships. The war had begun.

There was the usual debate in the Commons, in which the Palmerston government pointed out that not only had British property been confiscated but British officials had been insulted; Gladstone protested that 'a war more unjust in its origin, a war more calculated to cover this country with permanent disgrace, I do not know and I have not read of '; still, the approval was given for the government to prosecute the war. Troops were sent out from India – the Royal Irish, the Cameronians, men from the Hertfordshire regiment, and some sepoys: 4,000 men in all – and more warships were provided. Captain the Honourable Sir George Elliot was in charge of the naval operations, joining his cousin, Charles Elliot, who was the ranking civil official in China; they were shortly to be joined by Major General Sir Hugh Gough, who took charge of the army. Their orders were to occupy Chusan, blockade Canton, deliver a letter of protest to the chief minister of the Emperor, and force the Chinese government to sign a treaty. All this was done. Chusan was occupied without a fight and British troops were left there to die in great numbers of oriental diseases; eventually a Chinese official was forced to accept the letter from England; then the British set out to capture the Bogue forts on the Bocca Tigris River between Canton and Hong Kong.

A Chinaman at Macao told a British army surgeon: 'Same time you Englishman take that fort, same time that sky make fall down.' But the forts were taken, the sky did not fall, and the Chinese were forced to sign, on 20 January 1841, an agreement known as the Convention of Chuenpi. In it the Chinese agreed to give Hong Kong to the British, to pay them six million dollars, to reopen trade at Canton and to deal with British officials as equals, but both the Emperor of China and Her Majesty's government repudiated the treaty: the Emperor because his representative gave too much and Palmerston because his representative had not got enough.

The British government's policy on China was debated in Parliament and came under attack by Gladstone, ever the champion of the noble savage, who horrified his opponents by maintaining that it was even right for the Chinese to poison wells to keep away the English. But Queen Victoria agreed with her ministers. She took such a keen interest in China that Palmerston sent her a little map of the Canton River area 'for future reference'.

Palmerston was thoroughly disgusted with Elliot, and as for the barren little island he had acquired Palmerston told him: 'It seems obvious that Hong Kong will not be a mart of trade.' But the Royal Family was fascinated by the acquisition of a territory with such a quaint name as Hong Kong, and Queen Victoria wrote to Uncle Leopold to say that 'Albert is so much amused at my having Hong Kong, and we think Victoria ought to be called Princess of Hong Kong in addition to Princess Royal'. But the Queen, reflecting Palmerston's views, was not pleased with Charles Elliot, and in the same letter to King Leopold she expressed her displeasure: 'The Chinese business vexes us very much and Palmerston is

17

deeply mortified at it. *All* we wanted might have been got, if it had not been for the unaccountably strange conduct of Charles Elliot . . . who completely disobeyed his instructions and *tried* to get the *lowest* terms he could.' Clearly, more war was wanted.

The Emperor of China, being closer to the scene, was naturally able to register his displeasure sooner than Palmerston and Queen Victoria. Elliot had not yet learned of London's reaction to the Convention of Chuenpi, but when he saw the Chinese preparing for action he decided to strike first. Captain Elliot moved up the Bocca Tigris River, sending off landing parties to subdue the forts and defeating a squadron of forty war junks sent to stop him. The British did not hesitate to prepare an attack on the great city of Canton itself with its one million hostile inhabitants nor to pit their small force of 2,500 soldiers and 1,000 sailors and marines against a Chinese army of 45,000. They successfully occupied the heights overlooking Canton, the Chinese army retired in some confusion, and the inhabitants began to evacuate the city. At this point, much to General Gough's disgust, Charles Elliot stopped the war and entered into negotiations with the Chinese, who agreed to pay six million dollars and to compensate the merchants for the destruction of their factories if the British would not press the attack on Canton. This deal, generally known as the 'ransom of Canton', was accepted.

Aside from the superior leadership and discipline of the British force, the main reason for the success of the British over such large numbers of the enemy was the inadequate weaponry of the Chinese. The army of the Manchus was not much better armed than it had been when it conquered China more than two hundred years earlier: antique muskets and even bows and arrows were in use. While the sepoys were armed with old flintlocks – which made it almost impossible to fight in the rain – the British marines were equipped with percussion-lock Brunswick muskets which, although invented thirty years earlier, had just been adopted for issue and were far superior to anything the Chinese carried.

There was a pause in the war after the ransom of Canton – and a change of faces on the China station: Charles Elliot, who had displeased his Queen and her ministers by signing the Convention of Chuenpi, was exiled to the newly created Republic of Texas, where he was appointed chargé d'affaires; he was replaced by Sir Henry Pottinger, uncle of the 'Hero of Herat'; Captain George Elliot was invalided home and was replaced by Rear-Admiral Sir William Parker, a veteran sailor who had commanded a frigate under Nelson. Only General Gough remained. A fresh regiment, the 55th Foot (later 2nd Battalion, Border Regiment), newly equipped with Brunswick muskets, was sent out to him from India, and by August 1841 the British were ready to resume the war; an expedition was made ready and sent up the coast to attack Amoy.

It was a bold adventure. As the Duke of Wellington later told the House of Lords:

Little was known of China except its enormous population, its great extent, and its immense resources; we knew nothing of the social life of the country; we knew nothing of its communications than a scanty acquaintance with its rivers and canals; and whether their roads ran along rivers, or in any other way, nobody in this country could give any information, nor could any be acquired.

Nevertheless, Amoy was easily taken with only two killed and fifteen wounded on the British side. Moving further north, Gough took Tinglai, Chinhai and Ningpo; then the British went into winter quarters at Ningpo and Chinhai.

The spring campaign of 1842 was opened by the Chinese, who launched a massive counter-offensive, attacking the British both at Ningpo and at Chinhai. The Chinese were defeated at both places with heavy casualties. No attempt was made to count the bodies of the Chinese left on the battlefields, but old Peninsular veterans maintained that they had not seen so many dead since the siege of Badajoz. The British then moved out to attack the forts guarding the port of Hangchow. There they encountered the strongest resistance they had met within China from Tartar troops, but they captured the forts with a loss of only fifteen killed and fifty-five wounded. It was estimated that the Chinese lost more than 1,200 men, not counting the hundreds of civilians, men and women, who killed themselves rather than fall into the hands of the British barbarians. Shanghai was occupied without a fight in June. There was a last battle at Chinkiang, and then the army stood before the walls of the great city of Nanking.

By now it was obvious, even to the Emperor, isolated as he was at Pekin, that the 'foreign devils' must be appeased, and so three Imperial Commissioners were sent to soothe the barbarians. Pottinger had his treaty terms ready and, as he would not tolerate any discussion, there was nothing for the commissioners to do but sign, which they did in August 1842. This, the Treaty of Nanking, was the first of a series of such treaties, giving special privileges to foreigners, which are known in Chinese history as the 'unequal treaties'; they were to be a source of grievance and humiliation to the Chinese for a hundred years. The Treaty of Nanking gave the British 21 million dollars, the right to trade in five ports – the 'treaty ports' of Canton, Amoy, Foochow, Ningpo and Shanghai – moderate tariff rates, legal jurisdiction over British residents, and other points concerned with trading methods. Opium was not mentioned.

What the British did not get, however, was the respect of the Chinese. Some nationalities respect naked military power, but the Chinese, at least in the last century when the most venerated man was the scholar, did not. Instead, they regarded the British much as the Romans regarded the Goths in the last days of the Empire. So, even after the war was won, the humiliating indemnification paid, and the special privileges obtained, the basic thorn of prejudice remained embedded in Anglo-Chinese relations.

From a military viewpoint, the most remarkable thing about the Opium War is that it was one of those rare occurrences when a war was successfully directed by a committee. There was no supreme commander: Gough, Parker and Pottinger were practically independent agents in China for their own branches of government. That they cooperated so well, the military, naval and diplomatic functions meshing almost perfectly, was undoubtedly due to the great tact and diplomatic skills of Sir Henry Pottinger.

War in China

Queen Victoria was pleased with the turn of events in both China and Afghanistan, and on 25 November 1842 she wrote to Sir Robert Peel saying,

The Queen wishes Sir Robert to consider, and at an *early* period to submit to her, his propositions as to how to recompense and how to mark her high approbation of the admirable conduct of all those meritorious persons who have by their strenuous endeavours brought about the recent brilliant successes in China and Afghanistan.

After the Treaty of Nanking, General Gough returned to India to fight the Sikhs and Mahrattas, but the Royal Navy remained on the China station throughout what historian Edgar Holt called the 'gunboat years'. On 10 December 1846 Palmerston wrote Sir John Davis, then the British plenipotentiary in China, a significant dispatch: 'Wherever British subjects are placed in danger, in a situation which is accessible to a British ship of war,' he said, 'thither a British ship of war ought to be and will be ordered, not only to go, but to remain as long as its presence may be required for the protection of British interests.'

Even when British subjects were not directly threatened, gunboats were needed on the China station to fight pirates. Between 1843 and 1851 the Royal Navy captured or destroyed about 150 pirate junks – at a considerable profit to the sailors who were paid £20 for each 'piratical person' killed or captured. British warships ranged as far south as Borneo in their search for pirates, and in 1845 landing parties even went ashore to destroy pirate lairs. Here they were aided by James Brooke, an Englishman who, acting on his own and without support from his government, carved out a country of his own, Sarawak, becoming its rajah in 1841.

Gunboats were also necessary from time to time to impress the Chinese afresh by seizing a fort or making menacing gestures. After 1851, when the Taiping Rebellion started, the Chinese had too many domestic problems to be over concerned with the foreigners perched on their shores, but the two races did sometimes get in each other's way and the result was often bloody, as it was in

April 1854 when the Battle of Muddy Flat was fought – on absolutely dry ground.

When an Imperial army camped on Soochow Creek near Shanghai and started to molest Europeans as well as Chinese, Rutherford Alcock, the British consul in Shanghai, demanded that the Chinese move their army elsewhere. Although Alcock had practically no force at his disposal, he couched his demand in imperious language: the camp must be moved by 4.00 p.m. the following day. The Chinese did not reply but moved a fleet of war junks up Soochow Creek to defend the camp. Alcock, with typical Victorian audacity, at once put together a tiny army of European civilians from the International Settlement, merchant seamen and a few sailors, including about a hundred men from the USS *Plymouth*. With two field guns and two howitzers, a drum and British and American flags, he marched off for the camp of the Imperial army. The war junks fired on them from Soochow Creek but, as Alcock had rightly anticipated, the Chinese soldiers fled when he brought his own guns into play. The battle was short and ludicrous, but 300 Chinese and four Europeans were killed.

3

SIND AND SIKHS: A NAPIER AND A GOUGH

1843–45

WHILE wars were being fought in the far corners of the Empire, the average Briton in the years between 1838 and 1850 was more concerned with the threat of revolution at home. This was the era of Chartism, when working men began to organize themselves and to demand a 'People's Charter', calling for universal suffrage – universal male suffrage, that is – vote by ballot, annual parliaments and other political luxuries. Some Chartists, though not all, openly advocated revolution. There were, in fact, several small abortive uprisings, 'industrial disturbances', and an attempted general strike, all of which badly frightened the gentry.

In 1843 there occurred in Wales a strange revolt known as the Rebecca Riots. The Rebecca movement started simply as a protest against toll charges on public roads, but the form of the protest was bizarre. Secret societies were formed and bands of mounted night riders attacked toll houses. The captain of each band of raiders was called Rebecca and his followers the daughters of Rebecca, many even dressing in women's clothing. At first the Rebeccaites had considerable success and when toll gates were abandoned they turned to other grievances. But soldiers were sent in, the ringleaders were captured, and the movement was stamped out.

The year 1843 was turbulent and troublesome for Britain's rulers. In addition to the difficulties with the Chartists, the Rebecca Riots, and the war with the Chinese, there was a naval operation to chastise the Borneo pirates, General Gough launched the Gwalior campaign, there was a scuffle with the Boers and Natal was declared a British colony, and General Sir Charles Napier seized Sind.

Sind (or Scinde), lying in the valley of the Indus between India and Afghanistan in what is today Pakistan, was in an unfortunate geographical position in respect to the political needs, or desires, of the British. There had been a series of treaties with the Mirs, as the Baluchi rulers of Sind were called. The first was in 1809; there was a second in 1820; and a third in 1832 when Henry Pottinger (he who seven years later concluded the Treaty of Nanking) negotiated a commercial treaty. With each treaty the British gained something and the Mirs lost a bit of their independence. In 1838, when General Keane wanted to attack Afghanistan by marching through Sind, the Mirs were forced to sign another treaty whereby they gave up an important fort, agreed to pay tribute to Shah Shuja, and to allow British gunboats on the Indus. In 1842, after the British army retreating from Kabul was massacred in the mountain passes, the Mirs thought – or the British thought that they thought – that they could regain their independence. So the British sent General Napier to Sind with the draft of yet another treaty making still more demands on the Mirs.

General Sir Charles Napier (not to be confused with Admiral Sir Charles Napier, or with any of the many other Napiers who appear so frequently in nineteenth-century British military histories) was certainly one of the most extraordinary soldiers and interesting personalities of the nineteenth century. A small man with a slight stoop, he had a beaked nose, a massive forehead, long and straggling iron-grey hair and a white beard. His eyesight was very poor and he wore small steel-rimmed spectacles, making him look more like an eccentric don than a general. This impression was strengthened by his uncouth appearance, which was singularly unsoldierly. He rarely wore a uniform and often appeared, even on formal occasions, looking disreputable. Now sixty years old, he had lived what he himself described as 'a wayward life of adventure'. He had had horses shot from under him, a ship go down beneath him and he had survived many severe wounds and a violent attack of cholera. Lord Dalhousie, who met him a few months later, when he had fought several more battles, exclaimed, 'What a life he has led, what climates he has braved, how rubbed and chopped to pieces with balls and bayonets and sabre wounds he is!'

Born in 1782 he was given a commission in the 33rd Foot at the age of twelve. Such schoolboy commissions were not uncommon in the eighteenth century. Some lieutenants and ensigns were not even of school age: in 1762 John Boscawen Savage, later a major-general, was given a commission in the 91st Foot at the age of two; in 1783 Henry Ellis, who died at the head of his regiment at Waterloo, was given his commission on the day of his birth and was a captain at thirteen.

Charles James Napier (1782–1853) was descended from John Napier, the inventor of logarithms, and he was a great-great-great grandson of Charles II. His paternal grandfather was Lord Napier and his maternal grandfather was the Duke of Richmond. The most colourful member of his family, however, was his mother. She had been proposed to by King George IV, but chose instead to marry Charles Bunbury. Not liking him after a time, she ran off with Lord William Gordon and Bunbury divorced her. Tiring of her noble lover, she married Colonel George Napier, a veteran of the American war and the penniless younger son of Lord Napier. She then contentedly settled down to raise five sons and three daughters, all of whom were completely devoted to her. Charles, the eldest, did not marry until after his mother died in 1826, and then, although only thirty-eight, he married a woman more than sixty years old with children and grandchildren of her own. When she died he again married a woman much older than himself, the widow of a naval captain. Before his first marriage, however, he fathered two illegitimate daughters by a Greek girl named Anastasia.

Charles and two of his brothers, William and George, served in the Peninsular War and all were wounded. Charles, a major at twenty-two, led his men in a charge at Corunna, but his eyesight was so poor that he could not see the French until he was almost upon them. He turned to his men to ask, 'Do you see the enemy plain enough to hit them?'

'By Jasus, we do!' called out a nervous Irish soldier.

The charge was unsuccessful and his men were swept away by the fire of the French infantry. Napier found himself deserted on the battlefield: 'Being armed only with a short sabre, useless against a musket and bayonet, and being quite alone, short-sighted, and without spectacles, I felt cowardly and anxious.' Well he might. He was shot and severely wounded, captured, and then spent fourteen months as a prisoner of war. In 1810 he was back in Spain and at the battle of Busaco he was shot in the face, his jawbone was broken and one eye was injured. In all, he suffered six serious wounds in his first war.

After the Peninsular War he was posted to Bermuda, then regarded as a most unhealthy place, and he took part in raiding operations in Virginia against the Americans during the war of 1812. When Napoleon escaped from Elba, Napier went to the continent as a volunteer and took part in the attack on Cambrai in June 1815. Next he was sent to the Ionian Isles, where he fell in love with Anastasia, became a close friend of Lord Byron, and quarrelled with his superiors. Then he spent ten years, during his prime of life, retired on half pay. In 1839, at the age of fifty-seven, he was given a command in England, where he was involved in suppressing the Chartists, with whom he personally had a great deal of sympathy. Two years later he was sent to India to take command at Poona.

Charles Napier was a hard-swearing, religious, witty, ambitious, quarrelsome man, sentimental, self-critical, given to melancholia. Perhaps his most engaging quality was that he was honest with himself, for he neither under-estimated his own abilities nor minimized his own faults. He had more brains than were really necessary for an early Victorian general: he had a passionate love

of warfare, but his delight in war was marred by a painful aware-
ness of war's cost and of the vanity of his own military ambitions.
Just before going to India he had written to a friend: 'I am too
old for glory now. . . . If a man cannot catch glory when his knees
are supple he had better not try when they grow stiff.' But he did.
No sooner had he arrived in India than he was writing: 'To try my
hand with an army is a longing not to be described, yet it is mixed
with shame for the vanity which gives me such confidence: it will
come and I cannot help it . . .' Then he was sent to Sind and he
wrote in his journal: 'Charles! Charles Napier! Take heed of your
ambition for military glory; you have scotched the snake, but
this high command will, unless you are careful, give it all its
vigour again. Get thee behind me Satan.'

When he arrived in Sind with his proposed treaty he assumed
that the Mirs would not sign it. Ambition combined with opportunity to stir his hot blood: 'I have worked myself to this great
command, and am grateful at having it, yet despise myself for
being so grateful . . . the weakness of man and the pride of war
are too powerful for me.' He began to seize forts and prepared to
conquer the country. 'We have no right to seize Sind,' he said,
'yet we shall do so, and a very advantageous, humane, and useful
piece of rascality it will be.' The word 'humane' seemed an odd
word in such a context, but Napier believed that 'the great
recipe for quieting a country is a good thrashing first and great
kindness afterwards: the wildest chaps are thus tamed'.

Nevertheless, an effort had to be made to convince the Mirs to
sign the treaty and Captain (later General Sir) James Outram was
sent to Hyderabad to try to persuade them. Surprisingly, most of
them did sign, but they were unable to control the wrath of their
own followers. On 13 February 1843 Outram and his party were
attacked by the Baluchis and forced to make a fort of the British
residency, which they successfully defended until they finally
escaped to a waiting river steamer.

Napier, having collected a force of 2,800 men of all arms, only
500 of whom were British, now set off to attack a Baluchi army of
35,000. He told Outram: 'I am as sure of victory as a man who

knows that victory is an accident can be.' But Outram disagreed
with his chief's ideas of humane rascality and told him that he was
unable entirely to coincide with your views. . . . It grieves me to say
that my heart, and the judgment God has given me, unite in condemning the measures we are carrying out for his Lordship as most
tyrannical – positive robbery. I consider, therefore, that every life
which may hereafter be lost in consequence will be murder.

On 17 February 1843 the armies of the Mirs and Napier joined
battle near the village of Miani (or Meeanee) six miles north of
Hyderabad. On the night before the battle Napier wrote to John
Kennedy, a friend:

Not to be anxious about attacking such immensely superior numbers
is impossible, but it is a delightful anxiety. . . . It is my first battle as
a commander, it may be my last. At sixty that makes little difference,
but as my feelings are it will be do or die. . . . God bless my wife and
precious girls. My hope is to live or die worthy of them: no Cabul for
me to make them blush.

Charles Napier's brother William, who had become a famous
military historian, wrote a vivid description of the Battle of
Miani. The enemy were, he said,

thick as standing corn, and gorgeous as a field of flowers . . . they filled
the deep broad of the Fillaillee, they clustered on both banks, and covered the plain beyond. Guarding their heads with their large dark
shields, they shook their sharp swords, beaming in the sun, their shouts
rolled like a peal of thunder, as with wild frantic gestures they rushed
forward . . . with demoniac strength and ferocity.

Well, perhaps it was something like that. In any case the
Baluchis were soundly beaten. Most of Napier's European troops
were Irishmen, and they, to continue Sir William's colourful
language, 'sent their foremost masses rolling back in blood'. It
was indeed a savage affair. Napier described his own feelings and
attitude to his brother Henry: 'I own to you, Henry, being
shocked at myself, but when I saw their masses, each strong
enough to have smashed us, I saw no safety but in butchery: it was
we or they who must die. I urged no man to refuse quarter, and

tried to save one or two in vain.' Near the battle's end Napier saw a soldier of the 22nd Foot about to kill an exhausted Baluchi chief. Napier called out to him to spare the man, but the soldier drove his bayonet into his prey. Turning to Napier he said, 'This day, General, the shambles have it all to themselves.' Only three unwounded prisoners were taken.

The British lost twenty officers and 250 men, the Baluchis an estimated 6,000. Writing of the battle years later Napier said, 'God knows I was very miserable when I rode over the fields, and saw the heaps of slain: and then all my own soldiers stark and stiff as we laid them in a row for burial next day.'

As was the custom, officers who had distinguished themselves were mentioned by name in the general's account of the battle. In Napier's dispatch after the battle of Miani he, of course, gave credit to individual officers for their valour and energy, but he also mentioned the names of non-commissioned officers and even privates and drummers. Never before in the history of the British army had private soldiers been so distinguished. And not only did he single out Europeans such as Private James O'Neil and Drummer Martin Delaney, but he also listed the names of Asiatic soldiers who had performed outstanding services during the battle, and Havildar Thackur Ram and Sowar Motee Sing were also honoured by a 'mention in dispatches'.

After the Battle of Miani most of the Mirs surrendered. One who held back was told by Napier: 'Come here instantly. Come alone and make your submission, or I will in a week tear you from the midst of your tribe and hang you.' Napier believed that 'the human mind is never better disposed to gratitude and attachment than when softened by fear'. There was one Mir, however, who had hung back from the Battle of Miani, although he had been but a few miles away with an army of 10,000. This was Sher Mohammed, called the Lion of Mirpur. Had he come up with his army near the battle's end, or even after it was over, he might well have routed the British army, exhausted from its hard fighting in the intense heat. Instead, the Lion chose to retreat to his den at Mirpur, giving Napier time to rest his men and to bring up reinforcements. Five weeks later he had 5,000 troops, including 1,100 cavalry, and he set off for Mirpur. Sher Mohammed had also collected reinforcements and was waiting for him with 26,000 men near the small village of Dubba. On 24 March Napier attacked and, leading the final charge in person, he drove the Baluchis back, killing 5,000 with a loss of only 270 of his own men.

Napier was said to have sent back a one-word announcement of his conquest of Sind: 'Peccavi' (I have sinned). Of course he did not – no more than did General Pershing cry 'Lafayette we are here!' – but if generals have the wit to win battles there will always be wits to put words in their mouths later.

In June the British decided to forget about treaties and annex Sind. It became part of the Bombay presidency, adding nearly 50,000 square miles to the British Empire; Napier was made its first governor. In England there was considerable debate concerning the propriety of Napier's highhanded action. Lord Elphinstone said, 'Coming after Afghanistan, it puts one in mind of a bully who had been kicked in the street, and went home to beat his wife in revenge.' But the Duke of Wellington himself defended Napier in the House of Lords and declared that he had 'never known any instance of an officer who had shown in a higher degree that he possessed all the qualities and qualifications necessary to enable him to conduct great operations'. The British loved a brave soldier, even if he was a bad commander, but Napier had proved himself both brave and able.

Queen Victoria was pleased by Napier's conquest of Sind and, on 24 June 1843, she approved a GCB for him. At the same time she told Lord Stanley that she was 'much impressed with *the propriety* of a medal being given to the troops who fought under Sir Charles Napier'. Campaign medals had been known in the British Army since 1650, although they were usually issued only to officers. The Honourable East India Company was the first to issue them to all ranks. The first campaign medal to be given to both officers and men by the British government was the medal struck for the Battle of Waterloo. The Queen was much interested in medals and during the course of her reign more than thirty campaign medals were introduced in addition to a growing number of medals for bravery: the Victoria Cross (1856), the Distinguished Conduct Medal (1854), the Distinguished Service Order (1886), and the Conspicuous Gallantry Medal (1874). She also instituted in 1883 a medal which could be awarded to women who nursed the sick and wounded. More than a third of all the medals ever issued to the British army, before or since, were designed during her reign. They were much prized by officers and men alike: Private John Pearman, marching to join Gough's army in the First Sikh War, told how 'all our talk and hope was: "Shall we be in time to get the *medal?*" '

In addition to the honour, glory and medals there was also a more substantial reward for the soldiers in the form of prize money. After the conquest of Sind even the private soldiers got a few pounds, but Napier's share was £70,000. Outram refused the £3,000 that was his share and began a running public feud with Napier that went on for years with no credit to either man. Lieutenant William Hodson, later to win fame as the leader of Hodson's Horse, considered Napier to be 'the best abused man of his day'. Among Napier's most vitriolic enemies was the editor of the *Bombay Times*. Of Napier's prize money, he wrote: 'The Ameer's wife was in labour. Sir C. Napier ordered the prize agents to drag the miserable truckle bed on which she was lying from under her to swell his prize money.' There was just a grain of truth in this statement. One of the Mir's wives was pregnant, though not in labour, and she had indeed tried to save her bed. The 'miserable truckle bed', however, was a rather elaborate affair and contained a considerable horde of gold. Still, Napier had indeed seized it as a prize of war.

Once Sind had been conquered there was no question of returning the country to the Baluchis. Napier felt a deep sympathy for the poor people of Sind and he justified his conquest of the country by maintaining that the common people would be better off under British rule than under the Mirs. This was true, of course, but so perverse is mankind that every nationality prefers to be misgoverned by its own people than to be well ruled by another.

In the nineteenth century the British found this truth too ridiculous to be seriously considered.

As the new governor of Sind Napier violated one of the East India Company's cardinal principles in the ruling of India by daring to meddle with religious customs: he abolished suttee. When the Brahmins protested to him that he was interfering with their religious practices, Napier told them that they could if they liked continue to burn widows, but added that 'my nation has also a custom. When men burn women alive we hang them, and confiscate all their property. My carpenters shall therefore erect gibbets on which to hang all concerned when the widow is consumed. Let us all act according to national custom.'

Napier worked hard at governing Sind, immersing himself in all the problems of bringing British notions of justice, honesty and improvement to the Baluchis. He also managed to supervise his daughters' education. He had not brought his family to Sind, but they were in Bombay and from there Susan and Emily sent their father their arithmetic papers to correct.

Napier was soon ready to begin another campaign, but he was not allowed to conquer the rest of the Indian subcontinent alone: General Hugh Gough was back from China, and it was his turn next. Like Napier, Gough was a controversial old soldier from a military family who had started his career when a boy, had seen much action, had been put on half pay in his middle years and had only obtained an important command when he was sixty. There the similarities end. Gough has been called by the modern writer, Arthur Swinson, 'one of the most incompetent officers ever put in command of troops'. This harsh view was widely held by Gough's critics – and they were numerous – both during his lifetime and since, but not, interestingly enough, by most of the men who fought for him.

Gough was not the most brilliant general Britain ever had, but he was not stupid. The chief charges levelled against him during his tenure as commander-in-chief in India were that his battles were inevitably bloody, and that he placed too much reliance on his infantry and did not make sufficient use of his artillery and cavalry. Against these charges must be set the fact that he had to fight the bravest and best-trained warriors the East India Company had ever encountered in India. Also, if he relied heavily on his infantry, this reliance was not, after all, misplaced; he was victorious.

He was a popular commander, brave and solicitous for the welfare of his troops. Although there were many who were critical of Gough's decisions and his tactics, hardly anyone who came in contact with him was not charmed by his personality and full of admiration for his character. Sergeant P. Keay of the Bengal Artillery wrote of the esteem with which Gough was regarded by his troops, for

when he was present they looked upon success as certain, and it was not as a commander alone that he was respected, but as a kind-feeling and good-hearted old man, who took a lively interest in the welfare of all those who were under him. . . . I don't think that men could ever have been more attached to a commander than they were to old Gough.

Charles Napier said of him: 'Were his military genius as great as his heart, the Duke would be nowhere by comparison.'

Gough was born in Limerick in 1779. He never attended school but picked up his education by listening to the tutoring of his three elder brothers. He was commissioned at the age of fourteen in the Limerick City Militia and first saw action at the capture of the Cape of Good Hope when he was sixteen with the 78th Highlanders (later 2nd Seaforth Highlanders). He transferred to the 87th (Royal Irish Fusiliers) and served with that regiment in the West Indies, taking part in the attack on Porto Rico, the Brigand War in St Lucia, and the capture of Surinam. He was promoted major in 1805 and commanded his battalion when it embarked for Portugal in December 1808.

With the 87th Gough fought in the battles of Talavera, Vittoria, Nivelle and Barrosa and took part in the seige of Tarifa. He was severely wounded in the side by a shell at Talavera, and was wounded again at Nivelle, but he revelled in the glory of war. From his camp before Vittoria he wrote to his wife, a general's daughter whom he had married in 1807 during the brief stay of his regiment in Great Britain, a letter which illustrates his bravery, his vanity and the heavy casualty rate among the men he commanded:

My beloved will rejoice to hear that the opportunity of distinguishing myself and the Corps occurred yesterday, the glorious Twenty-first June. The Battalion out-Heroded Herod, its conduct called forth the warmest encomiums from General Colville, who witnessed a part of its conduct. After the action he said before several officers, 'Gough, you and your Corps have done wonders' . . . I regret to tell you my loss was enormous, but few when I reflect on the tremendous fire we were in for two hours and a half.

After the battle of Talavera he was given a brevet lieutenant colonelcy, the first brevet rank ever given for services performed in the field at the head of a regiment. After the war he was knighted, but it seemed that his career was ended. The battalion he commanded was disbanded in 1817 and he went on half pay. Two years later he was re-employed in the 22nd Foot (Cheshire Regiment) and engaged in suppressing his fellow Irishmen until 1826. Then again, at the age of forty-seven, he was placed on half pay and, although he was made a major-general in 1830, he did not again serve with the army until, at the age of fifty-eight, he was sent to India in 1837 to take command of the Mysore Division of the Madras Army. Three years later he was in China. Gough made the Opium War something of a family reunion, taking with him as officers his son, his son-in-law and his nephew.

At the end of the war in China Gough was created a baronet and appointed commander-in-chief in India (1843). The position of commander-in-chief, like that of the governor-general, was peculiar. In theory the governor-general was the superior of the governors of Madras and Bombay; in fact, his writ ran only in Bengal. A similar situation prevailed in the army: the commander-in-chief had no authority over the troops in Madras and Bombay and had only the Bengal army under his command.

Although Gough was now sixty-four years old, the most strenuous years of his life were ahead of him. In the next six years he was to fight three wars. He was not decrepit; he had all

34

the vigour and stamina required to lead men into battle, and enough vitality left so that when, under protest, he retired at seventy he lived on for another twenty years.

Gough's first Indian campaign was the Gwalior War against the Mahrattas, described earlier by Macaulay as 'a race which was long the terror of every native power'. Gwalior was, or had been, one of the most important Indian states, and as such it had naturally attracted the attention of the British. Clive and Wellington had, each in his turn, fought the Mahrattas and had taken from them all of their lands in Hindustan proper. The Mahrattas were no longer the terror they once were; still, the British found them a thorn in their side and it was now Gough's turn to complete the destruction of their state.

The real cause of the Gwalior War was that the British were afraid that in the anticipated war with the Sikhs the Mahrattas with their army of 30,000 would fall upon the British flank. Lord Ellenborough, the Governor-General, explained the situation to Queen Victoria: 'The continued existence of a hostile Government at Gwalior would be inconsistent with the continuance of our paramount influence in India, by which alone its peace is preserved. It would be inconsistent with the character of our Government in a country wherein, more than any other, character is strength.'

It would indeed have been inconsistent with the character of the British government in India to have allowed Gwalior to survive. And so, in the cause of maintaining influence, preserving peace and upholding British character, Gwalior was invaded. The British always needed a legal excuse, of course, and this was found. In 1843 there were some domestic disputes in the Sindhia family, Mahrattas who had ruled Gwalior for a hundred years, as to who should be the next ruler, the throne having fallen vacant. They had finally settled on a young Sindhia boy, but Lord Ellenborough maintained that the country was badly ruled and disorderly and he justified British interference on the basis of an almost forgotten treaty made in 1804 in which the British promised to assist the Maharaja to maintain an orderly, law-abiding country.

Gough anticipated little difficulty in conquering Gwalior – so little, in fact, that he took a number of ladies along for the trip. In addition to his own wife and his daughter Frances (later married to Sir Patrick Grant), there was Mrs Harry Smith, the wife of his adjutant general, and a Mrs Curtis, wife of the commissary-general. The ladies had an exciting time. In a letter to his son (20 January 1844) Gough described his surprise at the resistance he encountered: 'I thought I should have a mob without a leader, with the heads at variance. I found a well-disciplined, well-organized army, well led and truly gallant.' Although it was indeed a short campaign, there were real battles at Maharajpur and Pannier. At Maharapore the ladies were fired on; their elephants, frightened by an exploding powder magazine, ran away with them; and then, just at the end of the afternoon, as they sat down for a quiet cup of tea on ground captured from the Mahrattas, an enemy mine exploded and blew up the tea tent. Later, Lord Ellenborough gallantly presented each of the ladies with a commemorative medal similar in design to the campaign medal given to the soldiers.

After Gough's Gwalior War it was Napier's turn again, and at the end of 1844 he launched a campaign against the hill tribes of the northern frontier. The tribes had been raiding in Sind, as they had always done, but now the British objected to such disorderliness. Napier moved north with a mixed force to attack the leading hill chief, but his army was temporarily halted by an epidemic which carried away more than half of the 78th Highlanders. The tribesmen, hearing of Napier's difficulties, assumed that they were safe for the time being and calmly went on grazing their flocks in the fertile valleys. They did not yet know the British – nor Charles Napier. He attacked, driving the tribes into the hills and then marching in after them. As the tribesmen tried to avoid a pitched battle, Napier and his men had an arduous experience tramping about looking for them, but at last, in March 1845, the tribes were subdued. Napier returned to Sind, and now again it was Gough's turn to fight.

4

THE FIRST SIKH WAR

1845–46

'The Sikhs have crossed the Sutlej!' On these words 'a shout of defiance ran along the regiment, but as it died away a wail of lamentation was heard along the line of carts occupied by the women and children'. Thus did Captain John Cumming of the 8th Foot describe the reaction in his regiment to the news that the Sutlej Campaign, later known as the First Sikh War, had begun.

The Sikhs were, and are, members of a monotheistic Hindu sect, dissenters from Brahmanical Hinduism, which was founded in the early sixteenth century. Being surrounded by orthodox Hindus and Muslims, they became a militant people, and under their greatest leader, Ranjit Singh (1780–1839), they founded a strong state in the Punjab where the sect originated. Old, one-eyed Ranjit Singh had most of the world's vices, and he flaunted them: among other things, he was a pederast and a drunkard. Emily Eden, sister of Lord Auckland, thought he looked like 'an old mouse, with grey whiskers and one eye'. Although his vices were apparent, she was also impressed by his accomplishments: 'He had made himself a great king; he has conquered a great many powerful armies . . . he has disciplined a large army; he hardly ever takes away a life, which is wonderful in a despot; and he is excessively beloved by his people.' As long

37

as Ranjit Singh ruled, the state prospered, for he knew how to handle the British, when to be their ally and how not to be without provoking them, but when he died in 1839 there was no equally able a man to replace him, and no one strong enough to keep the Sikh army in check.

The oriental customs of polygamy and concubinage made the sons of rulers by different mothers natural rivals for an empty throne, and the Sikh state was disturbed by these usual quarrels when Ranjit Singh died. Complicating matters further was the remarkable Sikh army, the Khalsa, a kind of military fraternity that became, after Ranjit Singh's death, almost a government within the Sikh state, ruled by its own council of five called the Panchayet. It was a splendid army. Its equipment was modern and it had the largest and best artillery park in Asia. The Sikhs made fine soldiers and they had been trained by mercenary European officers, mostly French, but also some Britons, Americans, Germans, Italians and other nationalities. Their drill was patterned after the French army, and even the words of command were in French. The Khalsa also wanted its say in the government.

Sir Henry Hardinge (1785–1856), who had arrived in July 1844 to replace his brother-in-law, Lord Ellenborough, as Governor-General, wrote to the Court of the East India Company in London that he was 'not of the opinion that the Sikh army would cross the Sutlej with its infantry and artillery'. Nevertheless, on 3 December 1845 Sikh troops in force, infantry and artillery and cavalry, crossed the Sutlej, the river which formed the boundary between Sikh and British territories, and marched on Ferozepore. Estimates of the size of the Sikh army vary, but it contained somewhere between 12,000 and 20,000 men. The reasons for the war were complex: the British had long distrusted the Sikhs and wanted the Punjab; they acted in a highhanded manner and tried to dictate Sikh policy; an attack on the Sikhs was openly discussed. When the British started massing troops on the border, garrisoning some on land the Sikhs claimed as theirs, the Sikhs naturally thought the British were going to attack them, so they struck first.

The First Sikh War

The British were not fully prepared – they rarely were. Still, the attack was not completely unexpected. British forces had been concentrated at Ferozepore, Ambala, Ludhiana and Meerut, and on 18 December about 10,000 men were assembled near Mudki, a small village eighteen miles south-east of Ferozepore. Captain Cumming had been in ill-health, so his colonel ordered him to take the women and children of his regiment to safety at Ambala. He did, but then hurried back to Mudki, arriving in time to take part in the battle.

The last British units had just arrived on the scene when, at four o'clock in the afternoon, the Sikh army advanced and opened fire with their heavy guns. Major Henry Havelock, who had been with the 13th Foot at Jellalabad and was later to win fame at Lucknow, had a horse shot under him with the first salvo from the Sikh guns. The country around Mudki was generally flat, but dotted with sandy hillocks and thick jhow jungle behind which the Sikhs concealed their infantry and artillery.

The British hurriedly formed their order of battle: using the same formations which had been used against Napoleon thirty years earlier. Some of the men scarcely had time to get into their uniforms – shakos, scarlet coatees and white cross belts – uniforms which had changed little since Waterloo.

The British guns, though lighter than the Sikhs', won the artillery duel that began the battle, and then the 3rd King's Own Light Dragoons led the 2nd Cavalry Brigade in a spectacular charge that turned the enemy's left flank. Lieutenant George Cookes of the 3rd Light Dragoons, who was no more bloody-minded than his comrades, wrote home afterwards: 'I might have killed several Seiks at Moodkee, but it being my first battle, I was foolishly merciful.'

The British infantry charged after the cavalry and the Sikhs were forced to fall back with heavy losses. They were still fighting when night fell. There was considerable confusion on the battle-field as soldiers groped their way about in the dark and the dust in the jhow jungle. The men were exhausted and nervous from the excitement, tension and bloody fighting. Soldiers in such a condition and in such circumstances – particularly inexperienced soldiers, as most of these were – tend to shoot each other in the dark, and this happened. The soldiers nicknamed this battle 'Midnight Moodkhee'. Some men had lost their units and many regiments did not know where they were and had lost contact with other regiments. As Hardinge said in a letter to Lord Ripon, there was 'a feeling that the army was not well in hand'. Still, from the standpoint of the survivors, it had been a fine battle. Lieutenant William Hodson, who was to win fame as a leader of irregular cavalry and the murderer of the last of the Moghuls, was fighting his first battle, and he wrote home: 'I enjoyed all, and entered into it with great zest till we came to actual blows, or rather, I am half ashamed to say, till the blows were over.' British casualties were not abnormally high: 215 killed and 655 wounded, but among the dead was Sir Robert Sale, the hero of Jellalabad.

There was considerable confusion in the next few days, partly as a result of decisions taken by Hardinge. The Governor-General was himself a soldier, a Peninsular War veteran and former Guards officer who in 1815 had lost his left hand at the Battle of Quatre Bras, two days before the Battle of Waterloo. He had not seen action since. Soldiers and colonial administrators were generally regarded as interchangeable, apparently on the assumption that the command of troops and the ruling of natives required the same skills, or at least the same type of character. But Hardinge had also been a politician, though without losing his army rank, and, in fact, advancing in grade while serving in Parliament, as Irish Secretary and as Secretary for War. He was a friend of the Duke of Wellington, and had been the Duke's second when he fought his famous duel with Lord Winchilsea. Hardinge and Gough had been appointed lieutenant-generals on the same day, although Gough still outranked him, standing just above him on the army list. It was perhaps for this reason that after the Battle of Mudki Hardinge voluntarily placed himself as second in command of the army under Gough. This was not considered an attempt to avoid his proper responsibilities – no one even suggested this, so much did the British love to command in battle – but was generally regarded as a most magnanimous gesture. It was, however, unusual. When Lord Ripon, President of the Board of Control, heard of it he wrote to Hardinge that 'it has a very strange and somewhat unseemly appearance that the Governor-General should be acting as Second-in-Command to the Commander-in-Chief in the field'. Unfortunately – or perhaps it was really fortunate – Hardinge was unable to restrain himself and keep in his self-appointed second place.

At four o'clock in the morning of 21 December, less than forty hours after the Battle of Mudki, Gough marched to attack the now entrenched Sikhs at Ferozeshah, thirteen miles east of Ferozepore. By eleven o'clock the British were in front of the Sikh positions and Gough was ready to attack. Although an additional British column under Sir John Littler, which was to have come up from Ferozepore, had not yet arrived, Gough wanted to attack anyway in order to have plenty of daylight in which to fight, for this was the shortest day of the year. Hardinge thought otherwise and finally said: 'Then, Sir Hugh, I must exercise my civil powers as Governor-General, and forbid the attack until Littler's force has come up.' Here was an extraordinary situation: a governor-general who having made himself the subordinate of his military commander now reverted to his civil rank again in order to overrule a tactical decision of his commander-in-chief in the presence of the enemy. Gough had to comply. When Littler and his men did appear late in the afternoon, Hardinge turned to Gough and said, 'Now the army is at your disposal.' He then reverted to being Gough's subordinate again and was put in charge of the centre of the line.

As at Mudki the battle began with an artillery duel, but this time the British had the worst of it. Littler's infantry, or half of it, launched a savage attack, but was thrown back; later there were complaints that the sepoys did not support the European regiments. Privately, there were worse charges. Lieutenant Hodson wrote to a friend: 'My own regiment received a volley from behind as we advanced; the 1st Europeans fell before our eyes in numbers by a volley from our own 45th Sepoys!! Is not all this disgraceful and cruel to an unparalleled degree!'

Undaunted by Littler's failure, but facing a setting sun, Gough threw his army at the Sikhs and they fought the most savage battle in Anglo-Indian history. Brigades and regiments, Indians and Englishmen, became confused and lost in the gathering darkness, but they did attack, and that night they bivouacked in the Sikh positions.

The British spent a terrible night. After the heat of battle, all were suffering from thirst, but the Sikhs had fouled the wells with gunpowder and corpses. Major Havelock's horse turned away from the water with 'a shudder of disgust', but Havelock and many other soldiers drank it, paying the price later in disease. That night of 21/22 December a sharp cold wind blew across the plain, chilling the untended wounded who lay where they had fallen and cried out in vain for water and blankets. As for the walking wounded, Dr W. L. McGregor, Surgeon of the 1st Bengal European Light Infantry, said: 'During the night of the 21st many a poor wounded European soldier found his way to the rear in search of medical aid.' But he searched in vain. No field hospitals had been set up and there was only such aid as scant medical supplies and the regimental surgeons could provide.

Lieutenant Robert Bellers, acting adjutant of the 50th Foot, wrote in his diary:

No one can imagine the dreadful uncertainty. A burning camp on one side of the village, mines and ammunition wagons exploding in every direction, the loud orders to extinguish the fires as the Sepoys lighted them, the volleys given should the Sikhs venture too near, the booming of the monster gun, the incessant firing of the smaller one, the continual whistling noise of the shell, grape and round shot, the bugles sounding, the drums beating, and the yelling of the enemy, together with the intense thirst, fatigue and cold, and not knowing whether the rest of the army were the conquerors or the conquered – all contributed to make this night awful in the extreme.

Hardinge moved about in the dark among the various regiments: 'My answer to all and every man was, that we must fight it out, attack the enemy vigorously at daybreak, beat him, or die honourably in the field.' The 62nd Foot in Littler's division had lost eighteen out of twenty-three officers and the regiment was largely commanded by its sergeants. Today in the 1st Battalion of the Wiltshire and Berkshire Regiment (the old 62nd) on each 21st of December the colours are turned over to the sergeants to keep for twenty-four hours in honour of this event.

Until daylight came it was impossible for Gough and Hardinge to know if they had won or lost the battle, but dawn showed them that they had indeed captured the entire battlefield, including seventy-three Sikh guns. Hardinge, in a letter to Sir Robert Peel which he read to the House of Commons, described the second day of the battle:

When morning broke we went at it in true English style. Gough was on my right. I placed little Arthur [his son] by my side, in the centre, about thirty yards in front of the men, to prevent their firing, and we drove the enemy, without a halt, from one extremity of the camp to the other, capturing thirty or forty guns as we went along, which fired at twenty paces from us, and were served obstinately. The brave men drew up in an excellent line, and cheered Gough and myself as we rode up the line, the regimental colours lowering to me as on parade.

The Sikh army of the day before was driven from the field, but now a fresh Sikh army led by Tej Singh appeared to do battle. On news of its advance, even old Gough, ever optimistic, was for a moment discouraged. Men and animals were exhausted. All were hungry and thirsty. Many were wounded. There was practically no ammunition left for the guns. Nevertheless, the British pulled themselves together to fight.

Gough ordered the 3rd Light Dragoons and the 4th Bengal Lancers to charge the Sikh cavalry. Both of these regiments were now weak in numbers and their tired horses could hardly be made to trot, yet they charged. The charge was successful and afterwards the cavalry could be seen re-forming. Then, to the astonishment and dismay of the rest of the army, they could be seen moving off with most of the horse artillery for Ferozepore! They had been ordered to do so by a staff officer whose mind had become unhinged. The Sikhs were as puzzled as the British by this move and Tej Singh, fearing a trick or an attack on his rear, began a withdrawal. Havelock exclaimed, 'India has been saved by a miracle.'

The British had won again, but the casualties of the First Sikh War were frightful. Out of less than 18,000 men the British had lost 2,415. Hardinge said, 'Another such victory and we are undone.' Still, old Gough had won again.

Such high casualty rates in an Asiatic war were bound to cause cries of alarm in Britain. Gough was concerned about opinion at home, but for a different reason. By the end of the Battle of Ferozeshah he had lost so many officers that he took the unprecedented step of giving commissions to five sergeant-majors. He was more worried about this than about any of his tactical mistakes or his heavy losses, for he was encroaching not only on the prerogative of the Duke of Wellington, but on the privilege of the Queen herself. However, he defended his action by maintaining that 'I scarcely had an alternative; my losses in officers were so great that it was absolutely necessary'.

Unknown to Gough at the time, he had another enemy in his own ranks. Eight days after the Battle of Ferozeshah Hardinge wrote a private letter to Sir Robert Peel, the Prime Minister and his intimate friend:

It is my duty to Her Majesty, and to you as the head of the Government, to state, confidentially, that we have been in the greatest peril, and are likely hereafter to be in great peril, if these very extensive operations are to be conducted by the Commander-in-Chief. Gough is a brave and fearless officer, an honourable man, and, in spite of differences a fine-tempered gentleman, and an excellent leader of a brigade or a division. He deserves every credit for his heroism in the field. The most devoted courage is always displayed by him, and his merits and his services exceed those of some general officers ennobled by the Crown ... [but] he is not the officer who ought to be entrusted with the conduct of the war in the Punjab. . . . I cannot risk the safety of India by concealing my opinion from you. . . . Sir Hugh Gough has no capacity for

order or administration. . . . His staff is very bad, and the state of the
army is loose, disorderly, and unsatisfactory. At one time I had reflected on the necessity of sending for Sir Charles Napier, and appoint-
ing him to the command of the army in the Punjab. . . . At this extremity of the Empire a defeat is almost the loss of India.

But Gough was not defeated; he was victorious. It was impossible to justify the replacement of a general who won every
battle. The Sikhs had retreated, but not for long. Two weeks later
they were back, raiding in the neighbourhood of Ludhiana.
Sir Harry Smith (1787–1860), another Peninsular veteran, was
dispatched to deal with this menace. On the march to Ludhiana a
part of his force was attacked near Badowal on 21 January 1846.
Private (later sergeant) John Pearman, twenty-seven, of the 3rd
Light Dragoons, has left a vivid account of this minor action.
Although a cavalryman, Pearman had not yet joined his regiment
and he with others in his draft of replacements were on foot and
badly armed: 'The gun I had was deficient of a cock to hold the
flint; the gun of Private Goodwin had no screws to hold on the
lock; the gun of Private Roberts had no ramrod, and several
others were like them. With such arms we were taken into action.'
The march had begun at one o'clock in the morning and about
ten o'clock Pearman thought he saw weapons flashing in the sun
on the column's left front.

'Sergeant-Major Baker, there is the enemy!' he called.

'You be damned!' the sergeant-major replied. He had been
very drunk the night before and he was now about to pay dearly
for his hangover.

The Sikhs' strongest arm was their artillery. Their gunners,
trained by European officers, were skilful, brave and determined.
The Sikh guns now opened on the column. A cannon ball took off
the leg of a corporal of the 80th Regiment and as he lay on the
ground he called, 'Comrades, take my purse!' Pearman thought
his gun would be more useful, so he took it and threw away his
own useless Brown Bess. Stepping over the dead and wounded,
Pearman marched on, 'but had not got far when another ball
struck Harry Greenbank in the head. It sounded like a band-box

full of feathers flying all over us. He was my front-rank man, and his brains nearly covered me. I had to scrape it off my face, and out of my eyes, and Taf Roberts, my left-hand man, was nearly as bad.'

The British tried to continue their march, but the Sikh cavalry hung on their rear, picking off stragglers. The Indian sun was hot and the marching men had no water. One by one they dropped behind, among them Sergeant-Major George Baker.

'For God's sake, George, think of your wife and children!' Pearman pleaded, but the sergeant-major only looked up at him and said simply, 'I can't.'

He was left behind to be slaughtered by the Sikhs.

Seven days later, on 28 January 1846, a clear and beautiful morning, Sir Harry Smith's force won a stunning victory over the Sikhs on the open grassland near the village of Aliwal on the south bank of the Sutlej. Sir Harry, although fifty-seven years old, impetuously charged with the colours of the 50th Foot. Sir John Fortescue, the great military historian, described it as 'a battle without a mistake'. Sir Harry somewhat immodestly described his accomplishment as 'one of the most glorious victories ever achieved in India'. It was, he said, 'a stand-up gentlemanlike battle, a mixing of all arms and laying-on, carrying everything before us by weight of attack and combination, all hands at work from one end of the field to the other'.

In February Gough was reinforced by the arrival of some heavy guns and he moved to attack the main Sikh force. He found them in strongly entrenched positions across the Sutlej from the town of Sobraon on a bend of the river. On the night before the battle the colonel of the 1st Bengal European Infantry talked to all of his officers in the mess and held a solemn ceremony. He asked each officer to shake hands with every other officer, ending all ill-feelings that might exist, for it was certain that by the following evening some would be dead. In fact, five were killed and five wounded.

On the morning of 10 February 1846 the battle began with a two-hour artillery duel which Pearman described as, 'Such a

cannonade and noise as was now taking place, no thunder was
ever equal to. Excitement it was truly.' Then, unaccountably,
the British guns ran out of ammunition. When this was reported
to Gough he said, 'Thank God! Then I'll be at them with the
bayonet!'

Pearman, now horsed and with his regiment, watched the
infantry charge the Sikh positions, be driven back, and then
charge again: 'Oh, what a sight to sit on your horse and look at
those brave fellows as they tried several times to get into the
enemy's camp; and at last they did, but oh, what a loss of human
life. God only knows who will have to answer for it.'

Sir Harry Smith was in the thick of it and he described the
action in a letter to Sir James Kempt:

I carried the works by dint of English pluck, although the native
corps stuck close to me, and when I got in, such hand-to-hand work I
have never witnessed. For some twenty-five minutes we were at it
against four times my numbers, sometimes receding (never turning
round, though) sometimes advancing. The old 31st and 50th laid on
like devils.

Hookhum Singh, a Sikh gunner manning a gun facing the 10th
Foot, has left a description of how the advance of the British
infantry looked from his viewpoint:

Nearer and nearer they came, as steadily as if they were on their own
parade ground, in perfect silence. A creeping feeling came over me;
this silence seemed so unnatural. We Sikhs are, as you know, brave, but
when we attack we begin firing our muskets and shouting our famous
war cry; but these men, saying never a word, advanced in perfect
silence. They appeared to me as demons, evil spirits bent on our destruction, and I could hardly refrain from firing.

At last the order came, 'Fire', and our whole battery as if from one
gun fired into the advancing mass. The smoke was so great that for a
few minutes I could not see the effect of our fire, but fully expected that
we had destroyed the demons, so, what was my astonishment, when
the smoke cleared away, to see them still advancing in perfect silence,
but their numbers reduced to about one half. Loading my cannon, I
fired again and again into them, making a gap or lane in their ranks

each time; but on they came, in that awful silence, till they were within a short distance of our guns, when their colonel ordered them to halt to take breath, which they did under a heavy fire.

Then, with a shout, such as only angry demons could give and which is still ringing in my ears, they made a rush for our guns, led by their colonel. In ten minutes it was all over; they leapt into the deep ditch or moat in our front, soon filling it, and then swarmed up the opposite side on the shoulders of their comrades, dashed for the guns, which were still bravely defended by a strong body of our infantry, who fought bravely. But who could withstand such fierce demons, with those awful bayonets, which they preferred to their guns – for not a shot did they fire the whole time – and then, with a ringing cheer, which was heard for miles, they announced their victory.

Now the cavalry was ordered forward and the troopers swept down the Sikh lines from right to left. Pearman charged with his regiment, the 3rd Light Dragoons, 'whom no obstacle usually held formidable by horse appears to check', Gough said. 'On we went by the dead and dying, and partly over the poor fellows,' Pearman wrote 'and up the parapet our horses scrambled. One of the Sikh artillery men struck at me with his sponge staff but missed me, hitting my horse in the hindquarters, which made the horse bend down. I cut a round cut at him and felt my sword strike him but I could not say where, there was such a smoke on.' The Sikhs, their backs against the Sutlej, fought bravely, refused to surrender, and consequently were slaughtered in great numbers, estimates of their losses being as high as 10,000. It was, as Sir Harry Smith said, 'a brutal bulldog fight'.

General Gough was raised to the peerage, becoming 'Baron Gough of Chinkiangfoo in China and of Maharajpore and the Sutlej in the East Indies', while Hardinge was created Viscount Hardinge of Lahore and Durham. In addition, Hardinge was given an annual pension of £3,000 from the British Government for the lifetime of himself, his heir, and his heir's heir, while the Honourable East India Company gave him a pension of £5,000, it being recognized in the nineteenth century that money was needed to support rank and carry prestige.

The First Sikh War

The Duke of Wellington, who after the Battle of Mudki had
written to Gough suggesting that he subordinate himself in the
war to Hardinge, now wrote to him (9 July 1846) in old-fashioned
but majestic language that must have sounded sweet indeed to
Gough:

Great operations have been planned and undertaken and successfully carried into execution under your command, glorious Battles have
been fought and victories gained, and the War has been brought to a
termination by the destruction of the Army of the Enemy and the capture of all its cannon, by that under your command; and Peace has
been dictated to the Enemy at the Gate of his Capital, upon terms
equally honourable to the Army and to the Nation.

British losses were even higher than they had been at
Ferozeshah. Havelock said: 'I thought I knew something about
war. Now I see that I knew nothing till today.' Among the 2,283
casualties were a major-general, two brigadiers and four colonels,
all killed. Speaking of the 1st Bengal European Regiment (later
Munster Fusiliers), Robert Napier said, 'I saw it stand on parade
at Subathoo in 1845 close on a thousand strong, and after the
battles of the Sutlej Campaign it mustered on parade at Lahore
two hundred and fifty. The rest were killed and wounded.' Other
regiments also suffered great losses: the 31st and the 50th, which
had fought in all four major battles, the 3rd Light Dragoons,
the 9th and the 62nd – all were much reduced; sickness caused by
the hardships of the campaign aided the bullets and shot in
decimating the ranks.

The Khalsa was finally broken, and after the battle at Sobraon
the British marched to the Sikh capital at Lahore. It had been one
of the shortest wars on record. In four major actions in fifty-four
days the Sikhs had been brought to their knees. In terms of pounds
and pence it had also been a most profitable war. It had cost about
two million pounds, but the Sikhs were required to pay one and a
half million pounds and to cede territory which brought in revenue
of at least a half million pounds a year. The new land added to
the Empire was, said Lord Hardinge, 'a fine district between the

Rivers Sutlej and Beas'. The British also took Kashmir away from the Sikhs and sold it to Gulab Singh, of whom John Lawrence said, 'Well known as he is, both in Jullundur and Lahore, nobody has ever yet been heard to say a word in his favour'. Herbert Edwardes called him, 'the worst native I have ever come in contact with, a bad king, a miser, and a liar'. In addition to milking the Sikhs of money and land, the British demanded a reduction in the size of the Khalsa and the right to station a British resident (Sir Henry Lawrence) and British troops in the Punjab. Queen Victoria wrote directly to Hardinge to express her 'extreme satisfaction at the brilliant and happy termination of our severe contest'.

Everyone now thought that trouble with the Sikhs was finished. Almost everyone, that is. Old Charles Napier said: 'This tragedy must be re-enacted a year or two hence: we shall have another war.' As usual, he was right.

5

THE SECOND SIKH WAR

1848–49

THERE was a three-year interval between the First and Second Sikh Wars during which India was comparatively quiet. But there was trouble elsewhere. In China the Bogue forts were seized in 1847 and preparations were made to attack Canton; in South Africa the Fourth Kaffir War broke out in 1846 – there were still more Kaffir wars to follow – and in 1848 there was a scuffle with disaffected Boers; and the first of a series of wars against the Maoris was fought in New Zealand in 1843–48. But the next major action was again in India and once more with the Sikhs.

In July 1847 Hardinge assured Queen Victoria that in India there was 'no native power remaining able to face a British army in the field', and the following January, when he retired from India, he predicted that 'it would not be necessary to fire a gun in India for seven years to come'. Hardinge was a poor prophet. Three months later the Second Sikh War shook the Punjab. Lord Dalhousie, the thirty-five-year-old governor general who had succeeded Hardinge, announced: 'Unwarned by precedent, uninfluenced by example, the Sikh nation have called for war, and on my word, sirs, they shall have it with a vengeance.'

There had been a considerable amount of intriguing among the leaders and would-be leaders of the Sikhs; it was obvious that they had not learned to love the British, nor were they convinced of British invincibility. In the spring of 1848 Patrick Alexander Vans Agnew, twenty-six, was sent with Lieutenant W. A. Anderson to take control of the Sikh province of Multan. There on 21 April both young men were murdered.

Sir Henry Lawrence, the British Resident in the Punjab, was absent on a trip to Europe, but he had appointed a number of exceptional young men as his assistants and had assigned each a district to control: James Abbot in Hazara, Harry Lumsden in the Yusafzai country, John Nicholson at Rawalpindi and Herbert Edwardes in the province of Bannu. All these men lived to distinguish themselves in India.

Lieutenant Edwardes (1819–68) of the Bengal Native Infantry was a slight, delicate-looking young man of twenty-nine who liked to draw and to write poetry. Although he had been in India for only five years he could speak Urdu, Hindi and Persian, and he had served as General Gough's aide-de-camp at the battles of Mudki and Sobraon. When Edwardes, in Bannu, learned of the murder of Agnew and Anderson at Multan he at once began to put together a native army, raising a levy of Pathans and calling for assistance from the nawab of the neighbouring state of Bahawalpur. Taking this force, which he himself raised without money or outside assistance of any kind, he set out in June for Multan, fighting two successful battles on the way and driving the forces of the Sikhs, under Diwan Mulraj, inside the Multan fort. Although reinforced by another young lieutenant with a small native force, he was not strong enough to capture Multan, nor even to besiege it properly. He stayed on the scene, however, until 18 August, when General William Whish came up with an army to invest the place.

Lieutenant Edwardes was a hero and Lawrence, now back from Europe, said that 'since the days of Clive no man had done as Edwardes'. Later the capital of Bannu was named Edwardesbad. But Captain T. H. Stisted of the 3rd Light Dragoons, writing to his mother from India, could not resist a jealous note: 'I was amused at your (and everybody else in England) appreciation of that fool Edwardes' performances.'

When General Whish's force arrived on the scene Multan was properly besieged, but included in his force was a supposedly friendly contingent of Sikhs which, within a week of the opening of the siege, deserted to the enemy, taking ten guns with them. The siege of Multan had to be lifted and Whish's army was itself attacked. Reinforcements were necessary before the siege could be resumed.

At the outbreak of the Second Sikh War Gough, still Commander-in-Chief, had gathered his forces for a major attack on the Sikh army. There was, however, a considerable amount of political manœuvring behind the scenes. Gough preferred a military solution. There was always conflict between the military and the political officers in India, even though the 'politicals', as they were sneeringly called, were usually ex-officers themselves. Gough had no use for them, and in a letter to his son he told how he had ordered his commanders to 'send those attached to them, in irons, to Lahore, if they interfere with my military operations'.

On 22 November 1848 there was a cavalry action at Ramnagar. The battle was remarkable for a particularly unnecessary and disastrous charge by the 14th Light Dragoons under Lieutenant-Colonel William Havelock, Henry Havelock's brother, in which twenty-six officers and men were killed or missing and fifty-nine wounded. Havelock himself was killed so there was no one to give the reason why. Gough wrote: 'Why Havelock charged where he did, no human being can now tell.'

There was a minor battle at Sadullapur on 3 December, but then there was no general action until the following month. On 9 January 1849 Gough noted sarcastically in his diary: 'Heard from Governor-General that he would be glad if I gained a victory.' Two days later he marched. About noon on 13 January 1849, as Gough's army approached the small village of Chilianwala on the left bank of the Jhelum River eighty-five miles north-west of Lahore, it encountered a strong Sikh picket on a mound just outside the village. The picket was driven off, but from the mount Gough and his staff could see a good portion of a formidable Sikh army under Sher Singh drawn up in order of battle: its front in a difficult jungle, its left in a range of low hills, and its right anchored in two small villages. Gough, who hated to begin battles in the afternoon, started to make camp, intending to fight the Sikhs the next day, but the Sikhs opened fire with their artillery and it was obvious that they intended to begin the fight at once. After an hour's shelling by both sides, Gough ordered a division of his infantry to attack the Sikh guns. The division was composed of Indian troops and the 24th Foot.

The history of the 24th Regiment (later the South Wales Borderers) is certainly one of the most interesting stories of any regiment in the British army. Throughout its long history, going back to 1689, it had been an exceptionally courageous regiment, and also exceptionally unlucky. In 1694 it had taken part in the ill-fated descent on Brest. In the War of Jenkins's Ear and the attack on Cartagena it lost more than half its number from disease in the West Indies. In 1756 it was forced to surrender to the French at Minorca. The entire regiment was captured in the American War. Forty-six per cent of the second battalion were casualties at the Battle of Talavera in the Peninsular War – more than any other British regiment engaged. In 1810 about 400 men, nearly half the regiment, were captured by the French while on troopships from South Africa bound for India.

Perhaps it is as well to outline here the story of this gallant but ill-starred regiment after the Battle of Chilianwala. The catastrophe which overtook it in the Zulu War will be described later. In World War I it was in the disastrous Gallipoli campaign, and on 3 December 1917 the second battalion marched out of the lines in France with only two officers, the doctor and seventy-three men. In World War II a battalion was captured by the Germans near Tobruk and, naturally, it was a part of the unfortunate expedition to Norway in 1940 – even the ship carrying them struck a rock and sank.

The 24th had taken no part in the First Sikh War, having arrived in India less than six months earlier. It was nearly at full strength, with thirty-one officers and 1,065 men. Chilianwala was their first battle in India. It was about three o'clock in the afternoon when they began their advance through thick scrub together with two Indian regiments: the 25th Native Infantry on one side, the 45th Native Infantry on the other. Directly in front of them were about twenty Sikh guns which at once began to pound them. They moved rapidly and the order to charge was given when they were still too far from the Sikh positions. As Gough reported in his dispatch: 'This unhappy mistake led to the Europeans outstripping the native corps, which could not keep pace, and arriving completely blown at a belt of thicker jungle, where they got into some confusion.' Later it was impossible to discover who had actually ordered the regiment, alone and unsupported, to charge the Sikh guns, or who had stupidly ordered that muskets were not to be fired and only the bayonet used.

Lieutenant Andrew Macpherson said:

My company was near the centre, we held the Colours and made a good target. One charge of grape-shot took away an entire section and for a moment I was alone and unhurt. On we went, the goal is almost won, the ground clears, the pace quickens . . . the bayonets came down to the charge. My men's pieces were loaded but not a shot was fired, with a wild, choking hurrah we stormed the guns and the battery is won.

The Queen's colours were lost, but Private Perry saved the regimental colours and was later rewarded by promotion to corporal and a Good Conduct Medal. The tattered colours hang today in Brecon Cathedral. Lieutenant Colonel Pennycuik fell near a Sikh gun. His son, fresh from Sandhurst, ran to his side and was shot dead over his father's body. Lieutenant Lloyd Williams received twenty-three sword and lance wounds; his skull was fractured and his left hand was cut off. He survived, retired as a captain and lived for forty years after the battle. Only nine officers came through the battle unscathed: thirteen were killed and nine wounded. Total casualties were 515, nearly half the regiment, of whom 238 were killed. 'This single Regiment actually broke the enemy's line and took large numbers of guns to their front', General Colin Campbell said in his report, 'without a shot being

fired by the Regiment, or a musquet (*sic*) taken from the shoulder.'
But it was, as old Gough said, 'an act of madness'.

It is curious that this infantry counterpart of the charge of the
Light Brigade – both gallant but foolish charges of enemy guns –
should be so little known in spite of its human drama and exotic
setting. Few now know of the Second Sikh War and the Battle
of Chilianwala; fewer still know of the extraordinary charge of the
24th Foot. 'Their conduct', said Charles Napier, 'has never been
surpassed by British soldiers on a field of battle.' In the grounds
of the Royal Hospital at Chelsea there is a stone obelisk which
records the names of the men of the 24th who fell at Chilianwala,
but no great poet wrote immortal lines for men to remember.
There was not even a newspaperman to describe it, for the Second
Sikh War was the last fought by Britain without the benefit of war
correspondents.

On another part of the battlefield other soldiers were acting
out a less heroic role. A brigade of cavalry, consisting of the 9th
Lancers, the 14th Light Dragoons and two regiments of native
cavalry, had been given to Brigadier Pope. In his youth Pope had
been a dashing, brave cavalry officer in the East India Company's
army, but that was long ago and he was now an old man, almost
blind and so infirm that he needed the help of two soldiers to
mount his horse. Also, he knew nothing about commanding large
bodies of men. John Fortescue said that placing fine regiments such
as the 9th and the 14th under his command was like giving valuable
porcelain to a small child. Even Gough himself said that Pope was
'quite unfit for the responsible position to which his seniority
entitled him'. On the battlefield, Brigadier Pope had trouble
getting his men faced in the right direction, and he gave conflicting
orders. His troops had the impression that he did not know what
he was doing – which was probably true. When he finally managed to get his men and horses facing the right way, he halted them,
perhaps to think what he should do next. At that moment some
Sikh cavalry appeared. It was thought that he said, or meant to
say, 'Threes right!' What was understood was: 'Threes about!'
and the troopers wheeled and bolted.

On they galloped, crowding too close together, they overturned four of their own guns, upset wagons and horses. The flight of the cavalrymen was halted by a chaplain, the Rev. W. Whiting. He was attending the sick and wounded at a field hospital when he saw some frightened dragoons fleeing the battlefield. The chaplain stopped them and demanded to know what had happened. 'The day is lost!' cried a dragoon. 'All our army is cut up and the Sikhs have taken our guns and everything.'

'No sir!' the chaplain said. 'The Almighty God would never will it that a Christian army should be cut up by a pagan host. Halt, sir, or as I am a minister of the word of God, I'll shoot you!' Whiting's knowledge of history may have been faulty, but his faith in the British army stopped the rout. He found a sergeant to take charge and formed a rallying point for the retreating cavalry. Gough, with a soldier's view of the hierarchy of the Church of England, proposed that the chaplain be made a brevet-bishop.

The infantry attack on the right of the line was more successful. The 61st Foot (later 2nd Battalion, Gloucestershire Regiment) managed to capture a number of guns, a good supply of ammunition and an elephant. When the colonel of the 61st, a keen sportsman, was congratulated on the splendid performance of his regiment he replied, 'Fine fellows. Fine fellows. Couldn't stop them. Saw game ahead and I couldn't hold them in.'

The Battle of Chilianwala lasted until eight o'clock at night. When it was over, Gough rode along the lines, and everywhere the men he had thrown into battle cheered him. Sergeant P. Keay of the Bengal Artillery in a letter home wrote:

I happened also to be at the General Hospital where the wounded and dying were lying in hundreds, and as soon as they caught sight of his venerable white head, there was such a cheer burst forth that the dullest observer could not have misunderstood for a moment; ay, and that from many a poor fellow who had scarcely a head left upon his shoulders to shout with – it said, as ever cheer could say, 'You will never find us wanting when you require us'!

Under cover of darkness the Sikhs withdrew, taking most of their guns with them as well as three British regimental colours, and leaving politicians, soldiers and historians to debate for years whether the British had won the Battle of Chilianwala or whether it was a draw. Gough, naturally, claimed a victory. 'I am informed that the loss of the Sikhs has been very great', he said in his dispatch. Whatever the Sikh losses, the British had indeed lost heavily: 2,357 men killed and wounded. Havelock described it as 'one of the most sanguinary ever fought by the British in India and the nearest approximation to a defeat of any of the great conflicts of that power in the East'.

When news of the battle and its butcher's bill reached England, people were appalled, for nearly 1,000 of the casualties were Britons and they were unaccustomed to such losses in Asiatic campaigns. Gough, so recently honoured and praised as a hero, was now thoroughly damned for his 'Tipperary tactics'. Queen Victoria described her feelings in a letter to King Leopold: 'The news from India is very distressing, and make one very anxious, but Sir Charles Napier is instantly to be sent out to supersede Lord Gough, and he is so well versed in Indian tactics that we may look with safety to the future *after* his arrival.' Although it had taken only forty-eight hours after the dispatches arrived in London for the politicians to decide that Charles Napier, then in England, should be sent to replace Gough, it had, of course, taken a long time for the news to reach England, and it took a long time for Napier to return to India. Meanwhile, Gough kept fighting and was soon a hero again.

Although Dalhousie fumed, Gough, after Chilianwala, wisely decided to wait for General Whish to capture Multan and join him. Whish, however, had also waited for reinforcements from Bombay. When Dalhousie learned that Whish was to delay his attack he wrote Gough: 'I am afraid to express what I think and feel on hearing this. . . . I declare, on my honour, I had almost as soon have heard that half their number had been cut to pieces.' The attack on Multan was further delayed by a curious bit of military etiquette. The reinforcements sent from Bombay were placed under a general senior to Whish so that when he arrived at Multan he would naturally assume command of the united force.

To Gough it seemed unfair to supersede Whish and he wrote to the Bombay government: 'Do not force me to dishonour a brave soldier, for brave he is.' The reinforcements were delayed while Bengal and Bombay argued over who was to command them. In the end the Bombay government put a more junior officer in charge and the troops marched off to Multan. Had these troops reached Whish in November, as they could have, instead of December, when they did, then Multan would have been taken earlier and Gough would have had Whish's army with him at Chilianwala. Diwan Mulraj finally surrendered Multan on 22 January 1849 and Whish hurried off to join Gough.

With the arrival of Whish's army, Gough now had a force of 24,000 men, strong enough, he thought, to attack the main Sikh army, estimated to be 60,000 strong, at Gujrat, near the Chenab River sixty-eight miles north of Lahore. On 21 February 1849 Gough fought his 'last and best battle', and his report of it to the Governor-General was pure Celtic poetry: He had achieved, he said,

a result, my lord, glorious indeed for the ever-victorious army of India; their position carried, their guns, ammunition, the ranks of the enemy broken, camp equipage and baggage captured, their flying masses driven before the victorious pursuers from mid-day to dusk, receiving most severe punishment in their flight.

And most thankfully he could add that 'this triumphant success, this brilliant victory, has been achieved with comparatively little loss on our side' – 96 killed and 700 wounded. Anaesthetics were used in the field for the first time, and Corporal John Ryder watched in amazement as a man's leg was amputated and the man 'knew nothing of what was going on'.

On 10 March the remainder of the Sikh army surrendered at Rawalpindi, giving up all their muskets, swords and cannon in the presence of the victorious British Army of the Punjab. Dalhousie wrote to Queen Victoria: 'Your Majesty may well imagine the pride with which British officers looked on such a scene, and witnessed this absolute subjection and humiliation of so powerful an enemy.'

The Second Sikh War was over and the Punjab was annexed to British India. It was a splendid end to Gough's long fighting career. He had, with the possible exception of Wellington, taken part in more general actions than any British soldier then living. On his return to England he was created a viscount and given a pension of £2,000 a year for his own life and that of his next two heirs. He was well aware, however, of how close he had come to humiliation and the ruin of his reputation.

Punch commented on the ups and downs of Gough's popularity: 'When Lord Gough met with a reverse, *Punch* set him down for an incompetent octogenarian; now that he has been fortunate, *Punch* believes him to be a gallant veteran; for *Mr Punch*, like many other people, of course looks merely to results; and takes as his only criterion of merit, success.' Thanks to the great distance between the Punjab and London, Gough had had the time to win the Battle of Gujrat, but he bitterly resented the criticism that had been heaped upon him for Chilianwala. To Sir John Macdonald he wrote: 'Thanks to a gracious God for not only covering my head in the day of battle, but for granting me . . . a victory, not only over my Enemies, but over my Country!'

There was booty for all after the conquest and annexation of the Punjab. Sergeant John Pearman received £7 12s 6d as his prize money for the First Sikh War and £3 16s 0d after Gujrat. Queen Victoria acquired the great Koh-i-noor diamond, the 'mountain of light', as a token of submission from the defeated ruler of the Sikhs. Large as the diamond is now (106 $\frac{1}{16}$ carats), it was nearly twice as large when Queen Victoria first received it and before it was inexpertly cut in 1851. Its value cannot be estimated, but Shah Shuja, whose wife once possessed it, said that its true value was good fortune, 'for whoever possessed it had conquered their enemies'. Dalhousie, in sending the diamond to the Queen, said: 'The Governor-General very respectfully and earnestly trusts that your Majesty, in your possession of the Koh-i-noor, may ever continue to realize its value as estimated by Shah Sujah.'

6

OTHER WARS IN OTHER PLACES

1848–54

SIR Harry Smith, the vainglorious hero of Aliwal, missed the
Second Sikh War, for he had been sent to South Africa to be
governor and commander-in-chief at Cape Colony. But he was
energetic and managed to promote a couple of wars of his own:
he fought the Xhosas and declared British sovereignty over a large
part of Kaffraria; then he extended the sovereignty to include the
area between the Orange and Vaal Rivers. This action was bitterly
resented by the Boers who lived there and they revolted. Sir Harry
led an expedition against them and decisively defeated them at the
Battle of Boomplatz (or Boomplaats) on 29 August 1848.

In 1852 Major-General George Cathcart was appointed to succeed Sir Harry at the Cape. He, too, was eager to distinguish himself by fighting with the inhabitants of South Africa. As a young
man he had served as an aide-de-camp in the campaigns of 1813
and 1814 in Germany, and he had been an aide-de-camp of
Wellington during the Battle of Waterloo, but he had not seen
action for thirty-five years and he had never commanded troops
in action. In South Africa he called the first Cape Parliament,
granted the colonists a constitution, and then marched off to fight
the 'Kaffirs'. After subduing them, he turned his attention to the
Basutos, marching against Macomo and Sandilli, their great chiefs,

in the autumn of 1852. He followed them into the mountains, where no British troops had ever gone before, pursuing them relentlessly until they at last surrendered.

In India, the years 1851–54 were full of minor campaigns and military expeditions: there were operations against the Waziris in 1851–52; there was an expedition to the Black Mountains to punish tribesmen for murdering two collectors of the salt tax, and two small expeditions against the hill tribes around Peshawar during 1852; and in 1853 there was an expedition against the Jowaki Afridis. And, of course, in 1854 there was the Battle of Muddy Flat in China. All in all, however, these were comparatively peaceful years for the Empire – except in Burma.

The cause of the Anglo-Burmese difficulty was similar to the cause of the Opium War. Burmese officials had insulted and abused British subjects. This, of course, was not to be tolerated. In a minute on the subject, Lord Dalhousie wrote that the Indian Government, meaning his own, could not 'appear in an attitude of inferiority or hope to maintain peace and submission among the numberless princes and peoples embraced within the vast circuit of empire, if for one day it gave countenance to a doubt of the absolute superiority of its arms, and of its continued resolution to maintain it'. On 15 March 1852 Lord Dalhousie sent an ultimatum to the King of Burma. On 14 April Rangoon was taken by assault.

There had been considerable resistance to the British invasion of Burma and some sharp fighting had taken place in Rangoon, particularly around the beautiful golden-domed Shwedagon temple complex, but the Burmese army had been driven out and fled north. In December Dalhousie imperiously informed the King of Burma that he planned to annex the province of Pegu (Lower Burma), and that if the king objected the British would take over the entire kingdom. On 20 January 1853 Pegu was formally annexed to British India without even the usual treaty. So ended, at least officially, the Second Burmese War. A third war would be waged before the century ended, and between the wars there was a great deal of plain fighting, though not on a scale grand enough to be called war.

Other Wars in Other Places

A subaltern still in his teens, Garnet Wolseley (1833–1913), arrived in Burma a few months after the annexation and here saw his first action. Although born into the British military caste, his family was poor and had not been able to buy him a commission. But his father and grandfather had had honourable military careers and because of this the Duke of Wellington had been persuaded to give him a commission when he was eighteen. He had the proper outlook for a young Victorian officer: the belief that 'marriage is ruinous to the prospects of a young officer', a fierce desire for military glory, and the conviction that all English gentlemen were born courageous.

Military glory is a ridiculous thing; it is also appalling. Yet it fascinates men, and its achievement is thrilling to those who pursue it and survive more or less intact. No man ever sought glory on the field of battle more assiduously than Wolseley. Sent to India, he 'longed to hear the whistle of a bullet fired in earnest', and at first was very much afraid that he would miss the Second Burma War. He need not have worried. Bands of guerrillas and dacoits still harassed the British forces and one of these, led by a chief named Myat Toon, was enjoying considerable success. To the British, Myat Toon was a bandit; to the Burmese he was a national hero. Such differences of opinion usually result in bloodshed. A naval and military force was sent to subdue him – or rather two forces, one military and the other naval; the navy captain and the army colonel, although marching by the same road, did not coordinate their plans. The result was a disastrous defeat. Naturally another expedition was called for to redeem British prestige; this time a larger force under the control of a single officer.

Brigadier Sir John Cheap of the Bengal Engineers was chosen to command this little expedition, which is remembered now only because young Wolseley took part in it. Cheap's force of about one thousand men was made up almost equally of Indian and European troops. Although there were a few European regiments (composed of white Britons) in the army of the East India Company, most of the European regiments in Asia were 'Queen's Army', meaning they were part of the British regular army on

63

loan to the Government of India. 'Queen's officers' tended to take a snobbish view of this distinction, looking down on 'Company officers' and doing everything possible to indicate their own superiority. Wolseley described a difference in dress:

The Queen's Army took an idiotic pride in dressing in India as nearly as possible in the same clothing they wore at home. Upon this occasion [in Burma], the only difference was in the trousers, which were of ordinary Indian drill dyed blue, and that around our regulation forage cap we wore a few yards of puggaree of a similar colour. We wore our ordinary cloth shell jackets buttoned up to the chin, and the usual white buckskin gloves. Could any costume short of steel armour be more absurd in such a latitude? The officers of the East India Company were sensibly dressed in good helmets with ample turbans round them, and in loose jackets of cotton drill. As a great relaxation of the Queen's regulations, our men were told they need not wear their great stiff leathern stocks. This was a relief to the young recruits, but most of the old soldiers clung to theirs, asserting that the stock protected the back of the neck against the sun, and kept them cool. I assume it was rather the force of habit that made them think so.

Thus dressed, General Cheap's force left Rangoon at the beginning of March 1853 in river steamers. The trip up the Irrawaddy was disagreeable: the troops were crowded on the decks of the steamers and exposed to the fury of tropical storms and to swarms of hungry mosquitoes; they also passed a number of rafts fitted with bamboo frames on which were stretched in spread-eagle fashion the corpses of Myat Toon's enemies. After a few days on the river the force landed and started the overland march to Myat Toon's stronghold. There was some skirmishing along the way and Wolseley saw a man killed in action for the first time: 'I was not at the moment the least excited, and it gave me a rather unpleasant sensation.'

On their first day ashore the troops bivouacked 500 yards from a stream where a detachment of Madras Sappers were building rafts while Burmese across the stream sniped at them. Wolseley, unable to resist the sound of the firing, went down to the stream to watch the sappers work and to see how he himself would react under fire. While there, a British rocket section opened up on the Burmese and the scream of the rocket caused some of the sappers' cart bullocks to panic and stampede towards him. As he sprinted for the shelter of some carts, an old soldier, watching him run, called out, 'Never mind, sir, you'll soon get used to it.' Young Wolseley was furious.

For twelve days the British moved forward through the jungle; the food was bad and scanty, and cholera pursued them. At last they reached Myat Toon's stronghold, a fortified village, and a general assault was ordered. Unfortunately the 67th Bengal Native Infantry chose to lie down rather than advance. Ensign Wolseley gave one of the native officers a kick as he ran by him. Included in Cheap's column were 200 men of the 4th Sikhs. Having finally conquered the Sikhs, the British had hastened to enlist these splendid fighters in their own army, and this was the first time they had been in action on the British side. According to Wolseley, 'They were an example of splendid daring to every one present.'

The first attack on Myat Toon's position failed. When volunteers were called for to form a storming party, Wolseley and another young officer quickly offered to lead it. 'That was just what I longed for,' Wolseley said. Many years later, when Field Marshal Lord Wolseley, full of years and honours, was asked if he had ever been afraid during a battle he had to admit that while there was not time to be afraid during the action he was sometimes nervous beforehand: 'I can honestly say the one dread I had – and it ate into my soul – was that I should die without having made the name for myself which I always hoped a kind and merciful God might permit me to win.' Such must have been the only fear of many a young British officer in the nineteenth century. It reflected an attitude that made Britain great and strong.

Collecting a party of soldiers, Wolseley led them cheering down a narrow nullah towards the enemy's defences while the Burmese manning them cried, 'Come on! Come on!' For a few moments Wolseley was in a state of ecstatic excitement. Then he fell in a hole. It was a cleverly concealed man trap and he was knocked unconscious. When he recovered his senses and managed to crawl out, he found that the storming party had melted away and there was nothing for him to do but run back ignominiously. It was not glorious.

A second storming party was called for, and again Wolseley volunteered. Writing of his experiences more than forty years later, he described his emotions as he led this second charge:

What a supremely delightful moment it was! No one in cold blood can imagine how intense is the pleasure of such a position who has not experienced it himself; there can be nothing else in the world like it, or that can approach its inspiration, its intense sense of pride. You are for the first time being, and it is always short, lifted up from and out of all petty thoughts of self, and for the moment your whole existance, soul and body, seems to revel in a true sense of glory. . . . The blood seems to boil, the brain to be on fire. Oh! that I could again hope to experience such sensations! I have won praise since then, and commanded at what in our little Army we call battles, and know what it is to gain the applause of soldiers; but in a long and varied military life, although as a captain I have led my own company in charging an enemy, I have never experienced the same unalloyed and elevating satisfaction, or known again the joy I then felt as I ran for the enemy's stockades at the head of a small mob of soldiers, most of them boys like myself.

This time the attack succeeded, but Wolseley fell when a large gingall bullet passed through his left thigh. He tried to stop the bleeding by putting his hand over the wound and saw the blood spurting between the fingers of his pipe-clayed gloves. Nevertheless, he cheered and shouted and waved his sword, urging his men to charge on. This was Wolseley's last battle in Burma; he was invalided home, promoted to lieutenant, and recovered in time to serve in the Crimea.

The little wars in Asia and Africa seldom seriously engaged the mind of the average Briton. He was aware that fighting was going on more or less continuously on the ever-expanding fringes of the Empire, but except for the officers and a few politicians and merchants very few Britons were interested. Some emotion was occasionally briefly stirred by a spectacular victory or a particularly disastrous defeat, by a daring annexation or by a realization of war's cost, but they were seldom the subject of novels, stories or magazine articles. The wars were too remote, too exotic, the enemies unknown and bizarre. Perhaps the attitude of most people was summed up in a Victorian poet's mock perplexity and genuine ignorance concerning the word 'kotal', a Pushtu word for the highest point in a mountain pass. Having no English equivalent, it was a common word to the British in India, but George Thomas Lanigan thought it a place:

> Alas, unhappy land; ill-fated spot
> Kotal – though where or what
> On earth Kotal is, the bard has forgot;
> Further than this indeed he knoweth not –
> It borders upon Swat.

The Crimea was, at first, as unknown and seemingly as remote as Boomplatz or Swat or Myat Toon's fortified village, but when Britain declared war on Russia and decided to send an army to the Crimea there was tremendous excitement. For this was a European war, close to home and understandable. But was it really a major war?

7

CRIMEA: THE LIGHT BRIGADE
AND ALL THAT

1854-55

On 27 March 1854 Britain declared war on Russia because she did not want Russia to extend her power and influence over Turkey. With France, Turkey and Sardinia as allies, the British landed an army in the Crimea. After the French and British had fought and won the Battle of the Alma they marched to the great Russian fortress of Sevastopol where they sat down for a long winter siege. In October came the Battle of Balaclava and in November the Battle of Inkerman. The siege itself followed the pattern of all sieges: there were trenches, redoubts, masked batteries, attacks, counterattacks, and a considerable amount of boredom, sickness and uncomfortable living. Before the winter was over, a great many soldiers froze to death or died of neglect, being given neither sufficient food nor adequate clothing. Garnet Wolseley said, 'Poor gallant fellows, how nobly, how uncomplainingly they died!' In September 1855, after the French had succeeded in capturing a key position, the Russians blew up the fortress and retired; the allies decided that they, too, had had enough and went home. This was the Crimean War.

The army sent out from England, the Army of the East, as it was called, consisted of five infantry divisions and one cavalry division, but the units were small and the total army amounted to less than 30,000 men. Most British histories of the war not unnaturally concentrate on the actions of the British army, leaving the impression that it was primarily a British–Russian war in which the French got in the way; French histories give a different but equally biased view. In actual fact, both the French and the Turks contributed more men, and only the Sardinians had less than the British. But in action under their over-aged, inexperienced commanders the British soldiers did indeed fight hard and bravely.

Queen Victoria wrote to King Leopold of the Belgians: 'We are and indeed the whole country is, *entirely* engrossed with one idea, one anxious thought – the Crimea. . . . I feel so *proud* of my dear noble Troops, who, they say, bear their privations, and the sad disease which still haunts them, with such courage and good humour.' The Queen took a keen, personal, indeed proprietary interest in her army, as she made clear to the Duke of Newcastle, Secretary for War, in commenting on a letter he had sent to Lord Raglan, the British commander in the Crimea: 'The Queen has only one remark to make, viz. the entire omission of her name throughout the document. It speaks simply in the name of the *People* of England, and of *their* sympathy, whilst the Queen feels it to be one of her highest prerogatives and dearest duties to care for the welfare and *success* of her army.'

Unfortunately, there was not much the Queen could do for the welfare of her troops except sympathize with their plight. The Crimean War was undoubtedly the worst managed war of the century: logistics, tactics and strategy were all badly handled. On the surface it seems strange that the British, who had so much experience fighting in outlandish parts of the world, should have made such a muddle in the Crimea. A partial answer to this puzzle is that most of the senior officers who best knew how to fight – those who had fought in Asia – were not permitted to exercise their talents in this war. Lord Raglan, the one-armed British Commander-in-Chief, had a great contempt for what he called 'Indian officers', meaning the British officers of the Indian army, and would allow few of them to serve under him. He himself had not seen action for forty years, since the Battle of Waterloo, and he had never before commanded troops in the field.

The soldiers were as inexperienced as their officers, for the regiments that fought in the Crimea – the Brigade of Guards, the cavalry regiments of beautifully dressed hussars, lancers and dragoons – were not those experienced in fighting Asiatics in the tangled jungles of Burma, the rocky mountain passes of Afghanistan or on India's hot, dusty plains; more accustomed to the parade ground than the battlefield, most had not been in action since Waterloo. And this army, formed by Wellington, the Great Duke himself, had, as was said, learned nothing and forgotten nothing since.

The uniforms of these home regiments fresh from Britain were impractical in the extreme, but they were gorgeous: hussars, lancers and light dragoons in blue, heavy dragoons in scarlet with gleaming brass helmets, rifle regiments in green and infantry regiments of the line with scarlet jackets, white cross belts and high, heavy shakos. It was, then, a beautifully dressed but ill-trained and ill-equipped little army that the British landed in the Crimea, geared for peace and not for war, and scarcely anyone, from private to commander-in-chief, knew his business properly. The troops were superbly drilled, well-disciplined and imbued with those attitudes towards courage and endurance which win battles, but the men did not know how to care for themselves in the field, a life so different from barracks and parade ground, and their officers were too ignorant to instruct them. The services needed to provide troops in the field with food, clothing, shelter, transport and medical care were inadequate or non-existent. As transport for the entire army, twenty-one wagons were landed.

To understand how this situation could exist it is necessary to look briefly at the muddled organization of Britain's armed might at this time. First of all, there was no connexion whatever between the Army and the Navy; naval officers never commanded troops and military officers never commanded ships or sailors; each service had its own customs, regulations and traditions. When forced to work together, they behaved as allies without a single commander. There was not even a single unified British army. The so-called Commander-in-Chief at the Horse Guards actually had no control over the troops outside Great Britain, and even in England the responsibilities for the various military functions were fractured. Food and transport were the responsibility of the Commissariat, which was not in the Army at all but was a branch of the Treasury. The Medical Department was semi-autonomous, reporting not to the Commander-in-Chief but to the Secretary for War, who was also responsible for the Army's finances, except for the Royal Artillery and the Royal Engineers. These were paid by the Master-General of the Ordnance, who was also responsible for all fortifications, barracks, and certain items of equipment. Over all, however, the size of the Army and its cost were not the responsibility of either the Commander-in-Chief or the Secretary for War or the Chancellor of the Exchequer, but of the Secretary of State for the Colonies. Under such a system, if system it could be called, it was something of an administrative miracle that an army could be put into the field at all.

Most national armies beginning a new war are prepared only to win the previous one, but it is doubtful if the Army of the East could have won the Battle of Waterloo. Its muddled organization and the inadequacy and insufficiency of its equipment were difficulties which might have been surmounted had its officer corps been professionally oriented, but it was not. The few officers who took a professional interest in the arts and sciences of war were regarded as slightly eccentric. Only a few had any conception of, or interest in, logistics or administration of any kind. Most did not even know how to give a clear order or to execute any order not in the drill books. The brave, stupid charge of the Light Cavalry Brigade was the result of a mangled order: the entire brigade – half of the British cavalry in the Crimea – charged in the wrong direction.

Even when orders were clearly given, their recipients often had not an idea as to how they should be carried out. The Duke of Cambridge, who commanded one of the infantry divisions, was astonished to receive an order directing him to march his troops south-east through a forest, and he remarked indignantly that he had received many orders in his day but he had never been asked to march by compass.

Faced with examples of their inefficiency, officers still retained their dignity, their hauteur and even their sense of humour. A Royal Artillery officer received an official letter stating that a Gunner Brown, whom he had reported as dead, had turned up at Woolwich. The Horse Guards demanded an explanation. The artillery officer wrote back that he had known Brown well, had visited him when he was dying and had attended his funeral, adding: 'I know he is dead and am surprised to hear of his return to Woolwich, but am not responsible for his subsequent movements.'

The wars with Napoleon from 1799 until 1815 had bred the generals for the first half of the century; the Crimean War and the Indian Mutiny bred the generation of officers who fought the wars of the last half of the century. Quite a number of the young officers who survived the Crimean War achieved general officer rank, including Garnet Wolseley, John Ayde, Charles Gordon, and Henry Green. One future field marshal, Evelyn Wood (1838–1919), fought in the Crimean War as a midshipman.

Wood entered the Royal Navy as a midshipman in 1852 at the age of fourteen and two years later he was ashore with the naval brigade in the Crimea. That such a young midshipman was included in the naval brigade was due to the fact that his commanding officer was his uncle, Captain Frederick Michell, who, unable to take part in the land operations himself, 'was determined that our family should be represented'.

The 1,400 men of the naval brigade dragged 68-pounder and 32-pounder guns up from the beach to a height overlooking the Balaclava Plain. There for the next few months young Wood helped to work the guns firing at the Russian positions 1,200 yards away. He heard of the charge of the Light Brigade when an officer came into their camp and remarked, 'That was a smart little affair that the cavalry had this morning.' In the prolonged artillery duel between the naval brigade and the Russians, Wood found opportunities to distinguish himself: bringing up ammunition under fire, extinguishing a fire started in the battery by a Russian shell, and taking part in an attack on the Russian positions.

It was dangerous enough in the battery. Once Wood was examining the Russian position through his telescope, steadying his hand by resting his arm on the shoulder of a seaman, when a Russian shell took off the sailor's head. His lifeless body fell on Wood while a sailor named Michael Hardy, who was working a gun beside him, had his chest and face splattered with blood and brains. Wood and the other seamen were stunned, but Hardy kept to his work calling out, 'You bloody fools! What the hell are you looking at? Is he dead? Take his carcass away. Ain't he dead, take him to the doctor.'

In June 1855 Wood, although so sick he had difficulty in standing erect, took part in the ill-fated assault on the redan. There were three attacking columns, each consisting of a storming party of 400 bayonets, a reserve of 800, and a working party of 400. Each column carried ladders and bales of hay or wool to bridge ditches. Just before daylight the column to which Wood was attached crouched in a ditch 500 yards from the redan waiting for the signal to attack. The Russian artillery was already firing into them and a mate next to Wood was killed by a shell. As soon as the signal flag went up at the battery where Lord Raglan was positioned, Wood jumped to his feet shouting, 'Flag's up!' and ran forward. He and the men with him were met by a storm of musket bullets and grape shot. Lord Raglan said later, 'I never had a conception of such a shower of grape', and Captain Garnet Wolseley standing with him was heard to say, 'There is no hope for them.' Describing his view of the assault later, Wolseley said: 'If the ground over which our three British columns advanced upon the redan looked at first like a field made bright with red poppies, it seemed, in the twinkling of an eye, as if struck by a terrific hailstorm that had swept them away, leaving the field strewn with the poppies it had mown down.'

Wood had been armed with a sword, but when this was broken by a bullet he charged on with no weapon at all and with not the

slightest idea of what he would do if and when he reached the
redan. All the naval officers were killed or wounded before they
had gone 300 yards. Wood, wounded in the hand, ran on with a
ladder party, but soon all the men were shot down and there was
no one to carry the ladders. Wood was again hit, this time in the
left elbow by a $5\frac{1}{2}$ ounce ball and was unconscious when an Irish
corporal shook his wounded arm saying, 'Matey, if you are going
in, you had better go at once or you'll be bagoneted.' Jolted into
consciousness by the pain of having his arm shaken, Wood cursed
him roundly. The corporal at once sprang up and stammered 'I
beg yer pardon, sir. I didn't know you were an officer.' The 'Retire' had been sounded and Wood, with the help of the corporal,
made his way back to safety.

He was taken to an Irish doctor who cheerily told him to sit
down: 'I'll have your arm off before you know where you are.'
Wood managed to escape and to get himself carried on a stretcher
by four bluejackets to a hospital. Here, too, the doctors were all
for taking off his arm, but he argued and pleaded with them and
at last they agreed to try to save it. When he was able to be moved,
Lord Raglan himself sent his carriage to take Midshipman Wood
down to the shore where he took a boat out to HMS *Queen*, commanded by his uncle. In reply to a thank-you letter from Captain
Michell, Lord Raglan wrote, a week before his own death: 'I was
very glad to have had an opportunity of being even in the smallest
degree useful to your nephew, whose distinguished career cannot
fail to enlist everybody in his favour.'

Wood returned to England, his arm mended, and, thanks to the
letter from Lord Raglan, he was able to shift from the navy to
the army, obtaining a commission in the 13th Light Dragoons and
returning to the war as a cavalry officer. But in Turkey he acquired typhoid fever and acute inflammation of the lungs, which
leeches, blisters and mustard plasters could not cure. His mother,
told that he was dying, came out to Turkey to bring him home.
But he lived to fight again and again, and to be felled again and
again by enemy bullets, accidents and sickness, for Wood was the
most accident- and sickness-prone officer in the British army. His

experiences in the Crimea were to be but a brilliant beginning to a long military career: before his eighteenth birthday he had been twice mentioned in dispatches, earned the Crimean medal with two clasps, the Legion of Honour, the Medjidie 5th Class, and the Turkish medal. He was also recommended for, but did not then receive, a new medal called the Victoria Cross.

Instituted in 1856, the Victoria Cross was a medal in the shape of a Maltese cross made from Russian cannon captured during the Crimean War. There had not previously been a medal to reward individual acts of heroism. The importance of the award was not at first appreciated; the idea of a medal being available to all ranks of both services without distinction was a novelty opposed by many senior officers. However, it very quickly became, and remains to this day, a most coveted award, bestowing tremendous prestige on its recipients.

Queen Victoria approved the design of the medal in January 1856, suggesting that the motto should read 'For Valour' instead of the suggested 'For the Brave' as the latter would 'lead to the inference that only those are deemed brave who have got the Victoria Cross'. Her suggestion was adopted. The Queen personally decorated the first recipients of the Victoria Cross in Hyde Park on 26 June 1857. She wrote to Lord Panmure in that same month expressing her interest in the initials that should follow the name of those to whom the award had been given, stating that she herself favoured BVC, 'Bearer of the Victoria Cross'. Since the initials VC really stood for 'Vice-Chancellor' and as no one could *be* a Victoria Cross, 'VC would not do', she said. But it did.

The Crimean War marked the end of an era in British military history. Its generals, who had won their spurs in the Peninsular campaigns and at Waterloo, were now obsolete. They had made a hash of the battles and the siege in the Crimea; the charges and the bombardments seemed impressive to the participants, but they were ill-planned and ineffectual. The war did, however, give a baptism of fire to a new generation of young officers who were to fight the many little wars and campaigns of the future in Asia and Africa.

Captain Garnet Wolseley, twenty-two years old and recovered from his wounds in Burma, reached Balaclava with the 90th Light Infantry (later 2nd Cameronians) on 3 December 1855. For him it was the end of 'the misery, the sheer agony' of the dread that he would not reach the Crimea in time to fight. Life in the trenches before Sevastopol was neither pleasant nor dramatic, but Wolseley 'thoroughly enjoyed' his first day there and 'every day that I subsequently spent on siege works afforded me intense pleasure'. He volunteered to work with the Royal Engineers, for 'the engineer was in the post of greatest danger'. To his dowager aunt, Lady Wolseley, he wrote that 'man shooting is the finest sport of all; there is a certain amount of infatuation about it, that the more you kill the more you wish to kill'. Wolseley was not alone in his love of war; Charles Gordon, later famous as 'Chinese' Gordon and the defender of Khartoum but now a subaltern in the Royal Engineers, wrote home to say that in war 'there is something indescribably exciting'.

For a man who delighted in killing, Wolseley had a curious squeamishness: he could not bear to touch raw meat or even to clean a fish, and it always nauseated him to pass a butcher's shop. After nearly nine months in the trenches seeing other men hit by shells, Wolseley's turn came on 30 August 1855, only a few days before the final assault on Sevastopol.

He had been out all night with a working party in the trenches. He and his men had been attacked, driven out of their sap, and then had counterattacked. At dawn he was with a sergeant of Engineers and two other soldiers standing in the sap when a Russian shell burst among them: the sergeant was unhurt, but one soldier had his head blown off and the other lost a shoulder and a lung. Wolseley lay wounded and unconscious amidst the shambles. The sergeant dug him out, brought him to, and helped him to the rear: His left cheek was torn open and the slice of skin laid on his collar; his right eye was sightless and he had many ugly cuts. An Irish doctor patched him up, removing a stone that had lodged in his jaw by putting Wolseley's head between his knees and pulling it out with forceps. He was then carried back to his tent in the Engineers' camp. In a few days he was transferred to a hospital that had been established in an old Russian monastery.

Even Wolseley's wounds could not dampen his enthusiasm for battle and he was heartsick and depressed when he learned that the great assault was to be made upon Sevastopol and he would not be able to take part in it. His orderly, Private Andrews of the 90th Light Infantry, hearing that his battalion was to be part of the assaulting column, begged to be allowed to go back to his unit and join the attack. Wolseley reluctantly allowed him to go. On the day of battle, Wolseley, with one eye sightless and the other inflamed, weak and aching from his many wounds, saddled and tried to mount his pony to go to the front, but he was too weak to climb into the saddle and had to creep back to his cot. He learned from a fellow officer how the British had stormed the redan, held it for an hour, and had then been driven out.

This particular war was almost over for Wolseley, but although left with only one good eye from his wounds in the Crimea and a limp in one leg from his wound in Burma, he had still, at twenty-two, a long army career ahead of him, for physical disabilities were not then regarded as a handicap to military service. When he left the hospital he served for a while as deputy-assistant quarter-master general in the Crimea, and then returned to Aldershot.

Another future general who went to the Crimea as a junior officer was John Ayde. He was in the Royal Artillery, of course, for his father, grandfather and two uncles had served with this arm, and in 1834 at the age of fourteen he was nominated for a cadetship at the Royal Military Academy, Woolwich, where artillery and engineer officers were made. In 1836, after leading his class at Woolwich, he was commissioned a second lieutenant. For the next eighteen years promotion was slow, for the thirty years between the end of the Napoleonic Wars and the beginning of the Crimean War were generally referred to as 'the years of peace' and promotion was by seniority in the artillery. No matter that Britons were fighting in India, Afghanistan, Burma, Syria, China and South Africa; such affairs did not concern officers in the more elegant regiments of the British Army, who had scarcely heard of such units as the 21st Bombay Native Infantry, the 4th Sikhs, or the Madras Sappers, and certainly would not have consented to serve with such outlandish mobs as Pathan levies, the Gwalior Contingent, or the Poona Auxiliary Horse. In 1845, when Ayde was a lieutenant in the Royal Horse Artillery at Woolwich, all three troops were commanded by subalterns over fifty years old who had been present at the battle of Waterloo thirty years before. When sent to the Crimea in 1854, Ayde, age thirty-four, was only a captain.

For those of ability who survived in the Crimea, promotion was rapid. Ayde returned from the Crimea a colonel. Richard Dacre, another gunner, had been a subaltern for twenty years and a captain for fourteen. He began the war as a lieutenant-colonel and finished as a major-general; he died a field marshal and G C B.

Ayde had the privilege while in the Crimea of working closely with Lord Raglan – which accounts, in part, for his rapid promotion. The general in charge of the artillery gave Ayde some advice on how to deal with the commander-in-chief: He was 'never to trouble Lord Raglan more than absolutely necessary with details, to listen carefully to his remarks, to try and anticipate his wishes, and at all times to make as light as possible of difficulties'. Good soldier Ayde wrote: 'These excellent suggestions I did my best to carry out.'

The little war between the great powers was fought almost entirely by the army on the small, curiously shaped Crimean peninsula, but there were a few naval actions around Balaclava and a few others, rarely mentioned, in the Baltic and in the Black Sea. In May 1854 three British steamers bombarded the port of Odessa in retaliation for the Russians having fired on a flag of truce the month before. One of the ships, the paddle-wheel frigate *Tiger*, went aground and was so pounded by Russian shore batteries that she was forced to surrender. Her captain – Henry Giffard, forty-four, son of an admiral, father of a future admiral, and married to the daughter of a major-general – was badly wounded and had to have his leg amputated while the ship was under fire. After his capture he was well cared for by the Russians, but died of his wounds at Odessa. Madame Osten-Saken, wife of Count Dmitri von der Osten-Saken, Sevastopol's commandant, was in Odessa and cut a lock of the captain's hair, which she sent back to his mother. The following spring Ayde and another officer were detailed by Lord Raglan to go out under a flag of truce and deliver to a Russian officer, in addition to some clothes and money for French and British officers taken prisoner, a thank-you letter from Captain Giffard's mother to Madame Osten-Saken. It was a courteous war.

Ayde spent most of his time in the Crimea on staff duty and came through the war unscathed, although his brother Mortimer, an artillery captain, was badly burned when a Russian shell landed in his battery. After the Russians abandoned Sevastopol, Ayde went to Malta for a holiday and then returned to help collect the nearly 2,000 cannon the Russians had left behind.

By the end of the war the British were ready to fight it. The creaking army administrative departments had been oiled and kicked into some reasonable degree of efficiency; a transport department, non-existent at the beginning of the war, was now mobilized and 28,000 animals had been collected; replacements were at last arriving and reserves were stationed in Malta; but a peace treaty was signed in Paris and the machinery for a major war was dismantled.

The Crimea had been a very personal war. The officers, all coming from the same social class in England, knew each other and each other's wives, mothers and relatives. After the Battle of the Alma Lord Raglan had sent for Ayde and asked him to search for his orderly officer, Lieutenant Tom Leslie. Ayde found him lying wounded on the battlefield and arranged for him to be carried back to his tent. When he reported his mission accomplished, Lord Raglan asked him if he knew Leslie's mother. Ayde said he did not. 'A charming woman,' said Lord Raglan, 'I must write to her. How proud she will be to hear that he has a bullet in his shoulder!' He was probably right.

Victorian women of soldier families absorbed much of the spirit of their warriors and were frequently involved in pleading for commissions for their sons, getting their men appointed to regiments of their choice, to staff appointments, or even begging on their behalf that they be sent to the seat of war. As long as they understood their place in the scheme of things, did not marry their men until they had reached at least the rank of captain, preferably major, and did not make scenes when they were left behind while soldier sons and husbands marched off to war, women were tolerated. The women understood, or tried valiantly to understand, the importance of a soldier's honour: her man must come back 'with his shield or on it'. They were jealous of honours and promotions for them, and were proud when they were awarded. They had their opportunities to take care of them when they were stationed in safe billets, or to nurse them if they survived their wounds and returned home to convalesce, but they were not to go near a battlefield nor even to meddle with rear base hospitals like that extraordinary Nightingale woman and her group of nurses, who were at first mocked in the Crimea, being called 'the New Matrimony-at-any-Price Association'. Officers generally kept their women in a safe place, usually in Great Britain, where they could raise sons who would in turn become soldiers.

An exception to the rule was the case of Mrs Duberly. Frances Isabella (Fanny) Duberly, neé Locke, was, when she went to the Crimea in 1854, the twenty-four-year-old wife of Captain Henry Duberly, paymaster of the 8th Royal Irish Hussars, who was seven years older than his wife. He was, as his wife once described him, 'kind and patient and good, indolent, complaining, uninterested and bored'. She was quite the opposite: a splendid rider, witty, ambitious, daring, lively, loquacious and gregarious. He was a stocky, bearish-looking man with a thick beard; she was slim-waisted, golden-haired and pretty. She had a will of iron, but he was tolerant; she had many admirers, but he was not jealous – and so they rubbed along together peacefully enough, and she took good care of him.

Private soldiers were allowed to have wives, with permission, and these were 'on the strength' of the regiment and allowed to live in the barracks with their children, but the number of wives per unit who were allowed to follow their men to war was strictly rationed: one wife per eight cavalrymen and one per twelve infantrymen. These women were permitted to accompany the troops on campaign, where they usually served as washerwomen and sometimes as nurses. Officers' wives, however, were expected to remain at home, although during the Crimean War a number of them installed themselves comfortably in Constantinople and three 'ladies' got to the battlefield, but only Mrs Duberly stayed there. Lady Errol, one of the three, accompanied her husband for a while and shared a tent with him – but there was only one bed. When in her old age she was asked by a grandchild if the bed was comfortable, she replied, 'I don't know, my dear. His Lordship had the bed and I slept on the ground.' Fanny Duberly slept on board ships for much of the time until Captain (later Admiral) Stephan Lushington put some of his sailors to work building a hut for her at Balaclava.

It had taken a considerable amount of enterprise and brashness on Mrs Duberly's part to get to the Crimea. At Constantinople Lord Lucan had issued a direct order for her to be taken off the troopship she was on and put ashore. Captain Duberly was worried, but Fanny wrote in her journal: 'He looks upon the order as a soldier: I as a woman, and – laugh at it.' She stayed aboard the transport because Lord Raglan said he had 'no intention of interfering with Mrs Duberly'. Fanny was not one to allow the war or its generals to disrupt her own plans. As the troops were about to land in the Crimea she wrote to her sister that Henry was sick with rheumatism, lumbago and a bad cold: 'Lord Cardigan intends him to land with the troops, but I don't intend him to do so.'

While the troops fought the battle of the Alma, Fanny stayed on board a troopship and was royally entertained by the captains of the Royal Navy, who found her captivating. Her home was the *Shooting Star* but she was visiting on board the *Bellerophon* when the admiral sent word that he would transport her to Balaclava on the *Pride of the Ocean* if she could be quickly transferred. Fanny was promptly over the side, carrying a ham and some port wine given her by the captain of the *Bellerophon*, but she then insisted on being rowed to the *Shooting Star* to collect her luggage. Meanwhile, the *Pride of the Ocean*, laden with troops, had hove to and was waiting for her. Its impatient captain had decided that he could wait no longer and was putting on sail when Fanny Duberly was set down among the astonished soldiers and sailors with her carpet bags, ham, wine, portable desk and assorted bundles. She went ashore at Balaclava and there she remained until the end of the campaign.

In spite of her contempt for orders and military discipline, Fanny made many influential friends in both the Army and the Navy. On Friday, 8 October 1854 she rode out to the lines on Lord Cardigan's favourite horse, Ronald, which in less than three weeks time was to lead the charge of the Light Brigade. She was lent horses, sent delicacies, entertained, told military secrets, and was always advised in advance when an attack was to be launched so that she could be on hand to see it. She witnessed the successful charge of the Heavy Brigade and the brave, foolish charge of the Light Brigade. Her husband's 8th Hussars were part of the Light Brigade, but Henry was detached on staff duties that day. Her husband was safe, but she had lost many of her friends and admirers in the charge, and when she collapsed on her bed that night she could not sleep: 'Even my closed eyelids were filled with the ruddy glare of blood.' Fanny was not in the lines on 5 November when the Russians caught the British by surprise on the heights of Inkerman, but Henry thought she would like to see the battlefield immediately afterwards. 'I could not go,' she confessed in her journal. 'The thought of it made me shudder and turn sick.' War was not all fun after all, she found, but she stuck it out.

'The longer I live, the greater swell I become,' she wrote to her sister, 'and find myself now much in the position of a Queen – fêted by admirals, asked to meet ambassadors and generals . . .' Being the only lady at the front – young, pretty and greatly admired – gave Fanny Duberly an enlarged conception of her own importance. Thinking that Queen Victoria might not have a plan of the battlefield, Fanny made one and sent it to her. She received no reply. Fanny had high hopes of receiving the Crimean medal, and was bitterly disappointed when she did not. After the war, the 8th Hussars were inspected and congratulated by Queen Victoria, Prince Albert and their three eldest children. Fanny Duberly stood noticeably near by, but she was pointedly ignored by all except the fifteen-year-old Princess Royal, Vicky, who was heard to exclaim, 'Oh, there's Mrs Duberly!' before being hustled away with her parents.

If Fanny was unrewarded by the government and unrecognized by the Queen, she was famous in the Crimea, and even in England, where a number of her letters home had been published. When Prince Albert sent out Roger Fenton to make a photographic record of the war, he naturally took a picture of the famous Mrs Duberly and her husband – and had great success selling prints of the picture to the troops, who called her 'Mrs Jubilee'. But the darling of the troops could not expect to be loved by other men's wives and she did not endear herself to them by her description of the vicious Arab horses of the 10th Hussars which, when loose, 'fly out, fasten on to, and tear each other with a tenacity and venom that I should have supposed only to have existed among women'. After the war, Fanny published a commercially successful book on her experiences. She wanted to dedicate it to the Queen, but Queen Victoria's ideas concerning the place of women in society were not those of Mrs Duberly and permission was refused.

Fanny had two years of dull garrison life in England before again going to war with her husband and the 8th Hussars when they were ordered to India. There was nothing extraordinary about this, however. Regiments of the Honourable East India Company were never sent to England and Queen's regiments were stationed there for so long that it was a common practice for officers to take their wives 'out to India'. There the women had an opportunity to take a more intimate part in their husbands' lives, but they were usually kept safe. Occasionally a woman was killed by natives or, as in Afghanistan during the First Afghan War, was captured and held prisoner. Still, British India was safe. Everyone knew that.

8
MUTINY IN INDIA
1857

On Sunday evening, 10 May 1857, the young wife of Captain
Dunbar Muter sat in her little pony carriage outside the church in
the British Cantonment at Meerut in north-central India. Her
husband was with his men of the 1st Battalion, 60th King's Royal
Rifle Corps, parading them for the evening service, and she was
waiting for him to march his men to church. Listening for the gay
march military bands always played when leading British troops
to divine worship, she heard instead only dull explosive sounds in
the distance. Holiday-making by the natives, she thought.

A man she knew came up to her carriage. There had been
trouble of some sort, he said, that required the presence of the
troops. There would not be an evening service.

'A slight disturbance will not stop the service,' she answered.
'I'll wait a little.'

When the clock struck seven, the hour the service should have
begun, and neither the troops nor the rest of the congregation had
appeared, Mrs Muter decided that perhaps she would go home
after all. Turning her ponies' heads about, she started back. She
saw now that the native lines of the cantonment were in flames.
As she drove in the dusk down the broad street that led to the
bazaar, she found it crowded with men. She saw two unarmed

British artillerymen being chased and stoned by a crowd of Indians. She reached her bungalow safely and found all her servants clustered at the gate. Her house steward at once announced that he could no longer be responsible for her property and returned her table silver. No one was willing to answer her questions: What had happened? What was happening?

One of the servants suggested that she hide. Mrs Muter was indignant. She was, after all, the wife of a British officer in her own house in the lines of a strong and famous British regiment at the great cantonment of Meerut. What need had she to hide? And from whom?

Captain Muter sent a sergeant to find his wife and escort her to the quarter-guard. There she learned to her astonishment that the sepoys at Meerut had mutinied. Her surprise was shared by almost every officer in the British army. In view of the military facts and figures, Meerut seemed a most improbable place for a general mutiny to begin: the European troops there included a battalion of infantry, a regiment of cavalry and several batteries of artillery, while there were only two regiments of native infantry and one of native cavalry.

The mutiny at Meerut was not an isolated event; it was only the beginning of a mass revolt of the Indian troops in the army of Bengal. The British had placed too much confidence in the loyalty of their sepoys and were careless. European troops had been siphoned off to occupy the province of Pegu in Burma and to fight the Persian War, which had just ended.

There were 151,000 men in the Bengal army; there were only 23,000 European troops, 13,000 of whom were in the Punjab and not immediately available to fight the mutineers. Most of the remainder were concentrated at Calcutta, Meerut and Delhi with some scattered in hill stations throughout northern India. In the 900 miles between Meerut and Calcutta there were less than 5,000 European troops and nearly 55,000 sepoys.

With the wisdom given to those who can look back on an event, it can easily be seen that there had been numerous signs that something extraordinary was about to happen. On the morning of that fateful Sunday many of the Indian servants had been absent from the bungalows of their masters, and this had been talked about by those who met at the club for lunch. Everyone at Meerut knew, too, that the Indian troops were uneasy, for the day before there had been a punishment parade attended by the entire garrison at which eighty-five men of the 3rd Native Cavalry were stripped of their uniforms, chained and sent off to serve long prison terms. Their crime was refusal to handle the new cartridges that had been issued.

For several months there had been unrest among all the sepoys of the Indian army because of these new cartridges, which were greased, so frightening rumour said, with the fat of pigs and cows. From barracks to barracks throughout the Bengal army the rumour spread and grew: the British were trying to subvert their religion, for cartridges were normally torn open with the teeth before loading and for a Hindu to eat the fat of the sacred cow or for a Muslim to eat pig fat was an abomination almost too frightful to imagine. Not through malice or design but from sheer stupidity on the part of someone in London, there were indeed some cartridges covered with such grease sent to India. Officers in the Indian army were quick to withdraw the cartridges and, in an effort to placate the sepoys' fears, the Governor-General had issued a proclamation declaiming any attempt by the British to destroy the caste system or to offend religious beliefs, and orders were issued for a new loading drill that would permit the sepoys to tear open the cartridges with their fingers instead of their teeth. But the damage had been done.

Throughout northern India curious things happened. Strange, incomprehensible things. Chapatties (flat griddle cakes of un-leavened bread) were passed from hand to hand, from village to village. No one seemed to know what this meant, not even those caught in the act. To this day, no one knows the significance attached to this passing of the chapatties. In Meerut, a month before the outbreak, a fakir riding on an elephant had been followed through the streets by vast crowds and had created such a disturbance that the police had ordered him out of town, but he had been hidden and protected by sepoys in the lines of the 20th Native Infantry.

Lord Canning, before leaving London to take up his new duties as Governor-General of India, had made a prophetic speech: 'We must not forget that in the sky of India, serene as it is, a small cloud may arise, at first no bigger than a man's hand, but which, growing bigger and bigger, may at last threaten to overwhelm us with ruin.' The small cloud he had envisaged grew in less than twenty-two months into a tornado that first struck in Meerut and soon swept all of northern India.

That the initial outbreak of the mutiny at Meerut was not more successful was due to a fortunate circumstance. The mutiny was timed to begin when all the Europeans would be at church, but, unknown to the plotters, the hour for church service had been changed that day from six o'clock to seven because of the on-coming hot weather. Consequently, when the outbreak occurred the troops were formed near their barracks and their arms instead of being unarmed and unprepared in church. So it was that Mrs Muter and many others escaped what was to have been a general massacre of the Europeans. The mutineers, after killing most of their own European officers and any other Europeans they found unprotected, marched off that night for Delhi, forty miles away, where they were joined by the Indian regiments stationed there. The mutineers, now a rebel army, occupied the ancient Indian capital. They resurrected old Bahadur Shah, a descendant of Timur the Lame, founder of the Mogul Empire, and made him their emperor. Death to the British! Delhi had a large settlement of European civilians in addition to the military establishment. There were few survivors.

The Mutiny of 1857 was not the first mutiny in the Indian army. There had been others before, notably the mutiny at Vellore in 1806 when the sepoys rose and killed their officers. In 1824 sepoys in a regiment of Bengal native infantry had objected to being ordered to Burma and then refused to ground arms on parade; this difference in opinion was quickly resolved when the senior officer present ordered up cannon and blew them away with canister. Never before, however, had a mutiny been so widespread, erupted with such violence and created such alarm. The British reacted quickly and ruthlessly, and in the fierce fighting that followed frightful barbarities were committed by both sides; there was great bitterness and few prisoners were taken.

Perhaps the fury of the British is best illustrated by an extract from a letter written by that valiant English gentleman, John Nicholson, to Herbert Edwardes shortly after the outbreak of the Mutiny: 'Let us propose a Bill for the flaying alive, impalement, or burning of the murderers of the women and children at Delhi. The idea of simply hanging the perpetrators of such atrocities is maddening.'

In no other conflict in the nineteenth century was there ever the slightest doubt that British arms would eventually triumph, but in the Indian Mutiny there were in the first few months grave doubts indeed; there was a very real danger that Britain might lose not only the war but all of India. A sizeable portion of the native army of Bengal, a weapon forged, fashioned and sharpened by the British themselves, was now turned and pointed at their throats. While it was generally believed that native armies needed British officers to lead them, it remained to be proved that the efficient, well-disciplined Indian soldiers would not fight equally well under their own officers.

It is important to remember that the Indian Mutiny was not, as some Indian historians today would have us believe, a national revolution, nor was it even a general uprising of the entire Indian army. Had it been either, the British would have been quickly swept out of India with little chance of ever being able to return. It was, instead, essentially as it was called, a mutiny, and it was confined to the Bengal army. The Bombay Presidency, in spite of its fears, was not actually threatened nor was there any serious trouble in the Madras Presidency. Even in Bengal only about a quarter of the sepoys mutinied, although many who might have were disarmed before they made up their minds to do so.

The British were fortunate indeed that large masses of the population did not rise against them. Naturally there were some princes, princesses (in particular, Lakshmi Bai, the Rani of Jhansi), and would-be politicians who looked on the Mutiny as a splendid opportunity to try to regain their former independence or influence; here as everywhere there were those who found excitement and profit in the breakdown of law and order; and in some places, particularly Oudh, there were sizeable sections of the population who were unhappy with British rule. And, of course, on the North-West Frontier there was always trouble.

In the mid-nineteenth century northern India, with its wild frontiers and its large and populous native states and provinces, was in an almost constant state of turmoil. In the eight-year period from the annexation of the Punjab in 1849 until the Mutiny in 1857 there were no less than twenty expeditions against frontier tribes. These were expeditions led by men such as Colin Campbell, John Nicholson, Neville Chamberlain and William Hodson – and they acquired experience in Indian warfare that was to make them famous during the Mutiny. In Bengal itself there had been little trouble. In 1855–56 there had been a revolt of the Sonthals, but this was a tribe from the northern frontier which in 1830 had been settled in Bengal. None of these disturbances were related to the mutiny of the Bengal sepoys.

The only sizeable section of the population of British India which was disaffected was in Oudh. The British had exercised considerable influence over the independent state of Oudh for nearly a century, but in February 1856 they decided that the rulers were too profligate and formally annexed the entire state. Thanks in part to an unfortunate choice of a chief commissioner for Oudh, the people there were restless and unhappy with British rule when the Mutiny erupted. Still, even here, there was no mass uprising.

The great Indian Mutiny was, then, basically only a bloody internal quarrel within the British forces in India. For all this, it was a spectacular feat of British arms that the Mutiny was, in a remarkably short time, utterly and completely crushed. It was not, however, until Delhi was recaptured on 20 September and Lucknow finally taken on 17 November that the British regained the upper hand and could breathe more easily, knowing that eventual victory was assured.

The rebel Indian troops fought bravely and well, but they lacked, through no fault of their own, leaders in the higher ranks of their army who knew how to command them. There were in the East India Company's army three grades of Indian officers, but the highest, most senior Indian officer, regardless of age, experience or length of service, ranked below the youngest subaltern fresh from England. Thus, the Indian officers lacked experience in high command and no genius emerged from their ranks. The mutineers were deprived of the services of many of the most experienced Indian officers, for they remained loyal to the crown and to John Company's army; in the mutiny of their colleagues and country-men, many remained, in spite of all temptation, British. Even at Meerut, an Indian officer warned Lieutenant Hugh Gough that the sowars in the 3rd Native Cavalry intended to rescue their gaoled comrades and that the gaolers would help them, but when Gough reported this to his commanding officer he was laughed at for believing such a monstrous tale. The descendants in spirit of these native officers, now holding all ranks in the armies of India and Pakistan, are, as Lord Attlee once told the author, the only pukka British officers left.

Lord Canning, the Governor-General, first heard of the Mutiny in a curious fashion. The Lieutenant-Governor of Agra passed on to him a copy of a private telegram which had been sent by the British postmaster at Meerut before the line was cut. The post-master's aunt was in Agra and had planned to visit him. He wired that the cavalry had risen, houses were on fire and Europeans were being killed. 'If aunt intend starting tomorrow evening please detain her.' It was several days before the Governor-General of India could learn more than this of what had taken place in Meerut. Only gradually did the news of what had happened and what was happening in northern India seep out to the rest of the world.

When the news reached London, Palmerston, then Prime Minister, did not immediately grasp the seriousness of the situation and assured the Queen that all would be well. The Queen, however, found the news from India 'most distressing'. As even more distressing news continued to arrive the government and the people became alarmed. The Queen wrote to Lord Panmure, Secretary for War: 'The moment is certainly a very critical one.' She was concerned about the scarcity of troops to man the Empire's bastions and she could not resist chiding her ministers for the hasty demobilization of troops after the Crimean War: 'If we had not reduced in such a hurry this spring, we should now have all the men wanted!'

John Ayde, back now from the Crimea and stationed in Ireland, heard from a neighbour that an extraordinary telegram had been received from India, saying that a native regiment at Meerut had murdered its officers and that Indians were 'passing chew-patties from village to village'. No one even knew what 'chew-patties' were.

The military departments of the government, which had been properly stung by William Russell's series of articles in *The Times* during the Crimean War on their inadequacies and the angry questions in the House of Commons on their stupidities, now moved almost swiftly to meet the emergency in India, and 40,000 men – more than the total force sent to the Crimea – were packed in ships and sent off on the three-month voyage round the Cape to India.

India was a familiar name to Victorians, but the newly arrived officers found the reality of it strange and uncomfortable. The British officers in India had their own long-established customs and way of life, but they were not those of the regular establishment. The newcomers were unaccustomed to the crowds of specialized Indian servants which every British officer stationed there seemed to regard as necessary; the use of bullocks, camels and elephants for transport seemed bizarre; they were unprepared for the vast distances and were perplexed by the curious habits and customs of the people. Being in India as a result of a mutiny of the native army, having heard horrendous stories of Indian cruelty, and blaming the entire Bengal government for coddling the sepoys in the first place, they were contemptuous of the Company's officers and unsympathetic towards the Indians. The supercilious attitude they adopted is well illustrated in a description by Ayde of a sight he saw in Benares:

In one Hindoo temple which we visited, a fanatic, or possibly a lunatic, was seated in a niche. He was quite naked and covered with dust, but, oddly enough, had a fuchsia flower lying on the top of his shaven head. He sat perfectly still, and took no apparent notice of anybody, so that it is impossible to ascertain what object he expected to accomplish by so sedentary and monotonous an existence.

Garnet Wolseley, recovered now from his wounds, though forever sightless in one eye, was on his way to China with the 90th Light Infantry to fight in the *Arrow* War when the Indian Mutiny broke out. He first heard of it after being shipwrecked in the Strait of Bangka in the Java Sea. On being rescued and taken to Singapore, he learned that the 90th, along with other regiments originally destined for China, was to be sent to India.

The 90th reached Calcutta in August and was at once pushed towards the besieged garrisons at Cawnpore and Lucknow. Wolseley, as always, was eager for action and he gave scant attention to the beautiful temples, mosques and palaces or the fascinating life of the Indian people he encountered along the way: 'Our work was with the mutinous sepoys who had been "unfaithful to their salt"', had murdered English women and children, and for their blood we were consequently athirst.'

The troops diverted from the war in China and those sent out from England would all be needed to restore order to India, but they could not arrive soon enough to help in the first great task confronting the government in India: the recapture of Delhi. The British leaders correctly judged Delhi to be the key to the successful suppression of the Mutiny, for not only was it a large and important city strategically located, but it was the very centre of the cancer. Here was the ancient capital of the Moguls, which evoked memories of past Indian glory; here the mutineers had proclaimed their emperor and now guarded him; and here were placed the most fanatic and strongest elements in the rebel army. Although Cawnpore and Lucknow cried for relief, Delhi must be the first consideration of the British commanders. There were no fine regiments from England for this work; it would have to be done by the soldiers of India, Queen's regiments and Company's – and these were few enough for the task.

Frederick Roberts (1832–1914) was a child of the British Army in India. He was born there, the son of General Abraham Roberts, an old Indian army soldier who had led a brigade in the First Afghan War. Frederick Roberts was sent as a child to England to be educated, and returned in 1852 as a cadet in the Company's army. India was, and had to be, his home, for officers in the Indian army were allowed home leave to England only once in a lifetime, and that not before they had served ten years. The Crimean War had been remote to the soldiers in India. Roberts, stationed at Peshawar at the time, never mentioned it in his memoirs; instead he wrote simply that, 'the winter of 1855–56 passed much as the cold weather generally does in the north of India. Our amusements consisted of an occasional race-meeting or cricket match.' In April 1857 Roberts and another young officer moved into a house at Peshawar. 'We were just settling down and making ourselves comfortable for the long hot weather,' he said, 'when all our plans were upset by the breaking out of the Mutiny.'

There was, at Peshawar, a remarkable collection of able and experienced officers at this time, including Herbert Edwardes, the hero of Multan during the Second Sikh War; John Nicholson, of whom Roberts said that his was 'a name to conjure with in the Punjab', and Neville Chamberlain, Commandant of the Punjab Frontier Force and a brilliant leader of irregular horse. Edwardes and Chamberlain were thirty-seven years old and Nicholson was thirty-five, but all had seen a great deal of service. Chamberlain had fought in the First Afghan War, the Gwalior campaign and the Second Sikh War. Nicholson had also fought in the First Afghan War and the Second Sikh War and had been responsible for putting down several tribal revolts; in the district where he was commissioner he was held in great awe by the local population and, to his embarrassment, had even been made a demi-god by a sect that worshipped the great Nikkul Syn. Tall, handsome, brave and able, Nicholson was as admired for what he was as for what he had done; he was that rare phenomenon, a born leader of men. He had a talent for winning ungrudging admiration and gaining respect for his judgment, and no one ever spoke against him. Men, whatever their race, followed him willingly wherever he chose to lead them.

It was this group of officers who conceived the idea of a Movable Column, a body of troops prepared to move quickly in any direction where it might be needed to put down any threat of mutiny in the Punjab. Roberts, to his great delight, was selected to be a staff officer with this force: 'Though the crisis was a grave one, the outlook gloomy, and the end doubtful, the excitement was great.'

9

THE DANGEROUS DAYS

1857

THE prompt and efficient action taken by the officers in the western Punjab undoubtedly prevented the spread of the Mutiny in that direction. Women and children were moved to locations where they could be protected by European troops and many suspect native regiments were disarmed. But it was not easily done.

The British officers of regiments ordered to be disarmed felt it to be a terrible humiliation. Most were proud of their men and had complete confidence in them; few could believe that their own sepoys would mutiny, and commanding officers, striving to avoid this dishonour, frequently argued passionately against the orders. At some disarming parades, British officers angrily threw their own swords onto the pile of muskets. For the commanding officer of the 55th Native Infantry at Mardan the disgrace was too great to bear: he shot himself. At Sialkot, Brigadier Frederick Brind scoffed at the idea that his men would mutiny, refused to disarm them, and was shot and killed by his own orderly.

The disarming of a native regiment was a delicate, dangerous and difficult operation. Where there were European regiments present at a post, native regiments were paraded and ordered to ground arms while being covered by armed British soldiers and often with loaded cannon pointed at their ranks, but in some locations there were no British troops available and the Movable Column could not be everywhere at once. Multan, for example, was garrisoned by two regiments of native infantry, a battery of native horse artillery, and the 1st Irregular Horse (the famous 'Skinner's Horse'), composed entirely of Hindus from the Delhi area. The only Britons, other than the officers and the two British sergeants which every native regiment carried on its rolls, were fifty artillerymen in charge of a magazine in the old Sikh fort. The commanding officer at Multan was Major Crawford Chamberlain, younger brother of Neville Chamberlain and who, like him, had served in both the First Afghan War and the Second Sikh War. Major Chamberlain called together all the native officers, explained the situation to them and asked that the senior officers of each unit give him a written bond that they would be responsible for the conduct of their men. All the native officers in the cavalry and artillery pledged their personal loyalty by signing a guarantee and giving him their signet rings, but the native officers of the infantry regiments pleaded that they could not be answerable for the conduct of their men. Chamberlain knew that for the moment he could trust the cavalry and artillery while the sepoys in the infantry were probably only waiting for the best moment to mutiny.

Knowing that he must disarm his two infantry regiments as soon as possible, he requested that he be sent reliable troops to perform the operation and the 2nd Punjab Infantry and the 1st Punjab Cavalry were dispatched to him. On the evening of their arrival he assembled all of the British officers and told them of his plan for the disarming parade. At four o'clock the following morning, the two regiments of native infantry were marched out as for an ordinary parade. When they had gone a quarter of a mile from their lines they were halted. The Punjabi regiments moved in between them and their barracks, cutting them off from sources of spare ammunition; the European artillerymen took places with the horse artillery, and a selected body of Sikhs of the 1st Punjab Cavalry were positioned behind the guns with instructions to cut down any native gunners who refused to help the European artillerymen work the guns.

Chamberlain rode up to the native infantry regiments, explained the reasons for their being disarmed, and then gave the order, 'Pile arms!'

At once a sepoy in the ranks shouted, 'Don't give up your arms! Fight for them!'

An English officer instantly seized him by the throat and threw him to the ground. The order to pile arms was repeated and, to everyone's relief, the order was obeyed. Multan was saved.

When mutineers, or suspected potential mutineers, were caught they were dealt with most harshly. Roberts was with the Movable Column at Lahore, where the 35th Native Infantry was suspected of being untrustworthy. Spies were put in the regiment, and on the night of 8 June one of them woke Roberts to tell him that the regiment planned to revolt the next day and that some of the sepoys had already loaded their muskets. Roberts awoke Brigadier Neville Chamberlain who at once ordered the regiment to turn out for inspection. Two sepoys were found with loaded muskets. A drum-head court martial, composed entirely of native officers, was at once convened: the two were convicted and sentenced to death.

Brigadier Chamberlain decided that the condemned men should be blown from guns and ordered a parade that day. The troops were formed on three sides of a square, two cannon being on the fourth side. Roberts, who had charge of the prisoners, marched them to the parade ground. There they were quickly lashed over the muzzles of the guns. One prisoner asked if some rupees he had with him could be saved for relatives, but Chamberlain answered, 'It's too late!' The orders were snapped, the two guns exploded simultaneously, and shreds of cloth, bone and bloody hunks of flesh were spewed onto the parade ground in front of the assembled troops. 'It was a terrible sight, and one likely to haunt the beholder for many a day,' said Roberts, 'but that was what was intended.'

There were in India more than 500 states still under their own rulers, although nearly all were more or less under British influence. While a few sided with the mutineers, most remained faithful to the British and many gave them valuable assistance. At Jullundur, in east Punjab, where the sepoys had mutinied and marched off to join the other mutineers at Delhi, Edward Lake, the district commissioner, accepted the offer of the Raja of Kapurthala to garrison the place with his own troops. British resources and prestige were at this time at their lowest in northern India but the British were not humbled. When the Movable Column, under the redoubtable Nicholson, arrived in Jullundur the British officers were disgusted by the attitude of the Raja's troops: 'They swaggered about in swash-buckler fashion, as only natives who think they have the upper hand can swagger,' said Roberts.

While the Movable Column was marching about the Punjab, disarming native regiments and restoring British prestige, a message arrived requesting that all artillery officers not on regimental duty be sent to Delhi, now being besieged by the British. Roberts requested and was given permission to go. He set off at once, his only fear being that Delhi would fall and the fighting would be ended before he got there. He had no need to worry: the British still had three months of hard and bloody work before them. Roberts reached the British lines at Delhi on the night of 28 June, exhausted from days of hard travelling, but he awoke early the next morning, 'scarcely able to believe in my good fortune. I was actually at Delhi and the city was still in the possession of the mutineers.'

'Besiege' was perhaps the wrong word to apply to what the British were doing at Delhi. They had insufficient strength to surround the city, but they had taken up a strong tactical position on a long ridge that ran diagonally north-west of it. This position they were able to hold, beating off all attempts to drive them away, but they were unable to defeat the rebel army or to break through the defences of Delhi. They were, in fact, more often the defenders than the attackers, and Major Charles Reid, in command of the Ghurkas, said: 'The siege is on their part, not on ours.'

At one point there was even talk of abandoning the siege, but reinforcements arrived, morale improved and the siege went on. Included in the reinforcements was the Corps of Guides, a unique body of irregular cavalry and infantry recruited from the 'fighting tribes' of the Punjab. Marching from Mardan at the rate of twenty-seven miles a day in intense heat for three weeks, the Guides reached Delhi on 9 June and went into action with the bayonet within three hours of their arrival: a truly splendid feat by one of the finest units in the Indian army.

In a letter written on the day Roberts reached Delhi, General Sir Henry Barnard, commander of the Delhi Field Force, described to Sir John Lawrence the difficulties of the siege, among them the enemy's superior strength both in numbers of men and in artillery: the mutineers had eight times as many men and four guns to the British one. The British now had 6,600 men, having received small reinforcements from time to time, but the enemy were continually being reinforced by large numbers of mutineers from all over northern India who, as soon as they had mutinied, set off for Delhi. Barnard was concerned, too, over the almost daily losses from the constant fighting: 'You may ask why we engage in these constant combats. The reason is simply that when attacked we must defend ourselves, and that to secure our camp, our hospitals, our stores, etc., every living being has to be employed. The whole thing is too gigantic for the force brought against it.'

In addition to the battle casualties, there was a continual loss from sickness, including cholera: General George Anson, the first commander of the Delhi Field Force, had died of it only ten days after his advanced column had set out from Ambala; now Barnard, too, was stricken, and died just a week after writing to Lawrence. The condition of the troops is illustrated by the 'Daily State of H.M.'s 75th Regiment' for 13 September: the report shows forty-three men 'Fit to turn out', but 396 'On duty'.

Roberts went into action for the first time the day after his arrival, and frequently thereafter. He had been at Delhi only two weeks when he received his first wound, which kept him out of the fighting for a fortnight. In general, the plight of the wounded at Delhi was worse than it had been in the Crimea. There were neither anaesthetics nor antiseptics; the field hospitals were hopelessly overcrowded, and most of the wounded lay on the ground with little shelter from the rain, the fierce sun or the great swarms of black flies. Few of the severely wounded recovered; amputees invariably died.

Roberts was lucky. His wound was not serious and he was able to recover in his own tent, cared for by his own Indian servants. It speaks well of the British as masters that, although the brave little army before Delhi was obviously in a perilous position, nearly all the army's Indian servants, who were, after all, civilians, remained loyal. It speaks well, too, of the Indian servants, who often shared the dangers of their masters. When, at the end of the Mutiny, it was decided to honour the gallantry displayed by all ranks of the 9th Lancers by giving the Victoria Cross to one of them, the men were asked to decide themselves who was the bravest, the most worthy to receive the award. They unanimously chose their regimental *bhistie*, their own Gunga Din, the head water carrier.

After General Barnard's death, General Thomas Reed took command, but he, too, fell ill in less than two weeks' time and had to be evacuated. General Archdale Wilson, although not the next senior, was appointed to succeed him. Within two months' time the Delhi Field Force had had four commanders. One might suppose that the leadership of such a force at such a time would be a dubious honour, but among these vain, brave, self-confident men it was considered a plum and two of the three senior officers whom Wilson had passed over simply quit and left the battlefield. It was understandable to their colleagues; few of their fellow officers blamed them for it, and certainly no one imputed cowardice. After all, fighting was fun but a major command meant honour and glory, an officer's principal pursuit, and to be passed over was, if not a disgrace, a tremendous setback for one's career as well as one's *amour-propre*.

The Dangerous Days

Early in August the British on the ridge outside Delhi learned a bit of what was happening elsewhere in India: on 25 July Henry Havelock, now a general, wrote from Cawnpore saying, 'I have been sent to retrieve affairs here.' He reported that he had defeated rebel armies at Fatehpur on 12 July and at a place called Pandu Naddi on 15 July; he had recaptured Cawnpore on the following day and was now on his way to relieve Lucknow. He expected to reach Lucknow in a week and then march to Delhi. But this was not to be.

Havelock did not tell Wilson what he had discovered when he recaptured Cawnpore. There had been four Indian regiments stationed there, one cavalry and three infantry. While there was a sizeable European civilian population the only European troops were sixty invalid artillerymen. Before the Indian regiments mutinied a few detachments of European regiments arrived, but at the time of the outbreak there on 4 June the total number of Britons able to fight was less than 350 men. From behind puny earthworks this handful held off 3,000 mutineers for three weeks before they were forced by lack of food and water to surrender. Perhaps the men might have fought on to the death, but there were many women and children among them and the Nana Sahib (real name: Dandhu Panth), the rebel leader, promised in writing a safe conduct by river boat to Allahabad. When the small band of British survivors reached the river and were loaded in boats, cannon loaded with grapeshot were run out and fired into them at point blank. Many of the boats were tied to the river bank, all had their rudders tied and none had oars. Only one boat got free and drifted down the river, but most of the people on it were killed when it later came aground. In the end, only two officers and two soldiers escaped to tell the story.

About 125 women and children escaped the massacre at the river bank. They were kept captive, humiliated, and finally, the day before Havelock arrived, every woman and child was butchered. Havelock's men found two huts covered with blood and shreds of women's clothing. In one hut was a row of women's shoes and, across the room, a row of children's shoes with the bloody feet still inside them. A well nearby contained the mangled corpses.

It is perhaps difficult for us today, accustomed as we are to senseless violence, to realize the sensation of horror created in the world by this massacre and the fierce cry for revenge it evoked. Queen Victoria wrote to King Leopold: 'The horrors committed on the poor ladies – women and children – are unknown in these ages, and make one's blood run cold. Altogether, the whole is so much more distressing than the Crimea – where there was *glory* and honourable warfare, and where the poor women and children were safe.' She asked Palmerston to set aside a day for 'National Prayer and Humiliation'. When, a hundred years later, hundreds of European women and children were brutally tortured and killed by mutineers and rebels in the Congo, there was a drive to rescue the survivors, but there was no general cry for vengeance, no demand that the murderers be punished, nor was it even proposed that a stable, civilized government be re-established by Europeans. But in 1857 the British took a quite different view of such events.

Wolseley, who saw the huts and the well at Cawnpore, recorded his reactions, similar no doubt to that of all the soldiers, officers and men:

A more sickening, a more maddening sight no Englishman has ever looked upon. . . . Upon entering the bloodstained rooms, the heart seemed to stop. The horror of the scene was appalling and called up our worst angry passions . . . it awoke in us, the countrymen of these helpless victims, a fiendish craving for the blood of the cowardly murderers. . . . The indignity which had been put upon a proud people by a race whom we regarded as inferior in every sense was maddening. The idea that a native should have dared to put his hands upon an Englishwoman was too much.

New British units arriving in Cawnpore were taken in small groups on a tour of the shambles. Corporal William Forbes-Mitchell of the 93rd Highlanders wrote a description of his visit:

Among the traces of barbarous torture and cruelty which excited horror and a desire for revenge, one stood out prominently beyond all others. It was an iron hook fixed into the wall of one of the rooms. . . This hook was covered with dried blood, and from the marks on the whitewashed walls, it was evident that a little child had been hung on to it by the neck with its face to the wall, where the poor thing must have struggled for long, perhaps in the sight of its helpless mother, because the wall all around the hook on a level with it was covered with the handprints and below the hook with the footprints, in blood, of a little child.

The British took savage reprisals. A gallows was erected in front of the huts where the massacre had taken place and captured mutineers were forced to lick up with their tongues a square foot of the blood on the floor or wall before being taken out and hanged. As the story of Cawnpore spread, the war took on a more savage and cruel character, brutality begetting brutality as it always does.

Captain Wolseley was with his company of the 90th on his way to join Havelock's army when he was ordered to hang a mutineer of the native cavalry regiment that had been stationed at Cawnpore. A year earlier, in the Crimea, it had been impossible to obtain a volunteer hangman from among the troops, although a reward of £20, a free discharge and a return to England was offered; but now every man in Wolseley's company volunteered for the job. 'An all-absorbing craving for ruthless vengeance, that most unchristian of passions, was deep in our hearts,' Wolseley said, 'but had any English Bishop visited that scene of butchery when I saw it, I verily believe that he would have buckled on a sword.'

Even such a staunch Christian as Henry Havelock, who preached Baptist sermons to his troops, had very unchristian ideas concerning the handling of the mutineers: 'There must be no more disbandments for mutiny. Mutineers must be attacked and annihilated; and if they are few in any regiment, and not immediately denounced to be shot or hanged, the whole regiment must be deemed guilty and given up to prompt military execution.' Even so, not all soldiers were eager to take part in the hanging and burning. Lieutenant William Hargood, twenty-three,

of the 1st Madras (European) Fusiliers, recorded his experience
and impressions in letters home as he marched with his unit to
join Havelock:

From Benares, 12 June: In three days we have hung (*sic*) 16 Sepoys.

From Allahabad, 26 June: I am almost tired with soldiering, after
seeing men hanged, and villages on fire – the Natives are the most
cowardly set of brutes possible, they always ran away directly they saw
us.

Cawnpore, 14 August, [young Hargood had been under fire eight
times in the past month]: Fusileers are still distinguishing themselves,
really our dear fellows are splendid, and didn't care a rap for the
enemy's shot, but really war is a dreadful thing, when you see poor
fellows lying shot through every part of the body and cut completely
asunder by round shot.

Hargood died of fever in Lucknow the following May.

While Havelock was marching to Lucknow, the Delhi Field
Force was reinforced by the arrival of the famous Nicholson and
the Movable Column. Having made the western Punjab relatively
safe, he had hurried to Delhi. The main siege train with its heavy
guns was also close at hand, but when it was within twenty miles
of Delhi it was almost captured, being saved only by Nicholson,
who routed a strong enemy force to save it.

When Havelock failed to relieve Lucknow on his first attempt
and fell back on Cawnpore, it was obvious to the officers at Delhi
that no further reinforcements could be expected. If Delhi was to
be taken, it would have to be done by the troops now at hand, so
the decision was taken to attack the city walls in a now or never,
all out assault.

The heavy siege guns, with scanty ammunition available, were
put in place close to the city walls, one battery being only 160
yards away. Shortly after midnight on the morning of 14 September
the troops were turned out and given their orders: wounded
men were to be left where they fell and no prisoners were to be
taken; men could not be spared to tend the wounded or guard
prisoners. The attack was to have begun at dawn, but there were

delays and the sun was high before the four assault columns rose and stormed the walls.

The British succeeded in entering the city, but the fighting was hard and the casualties heavy. The losses were most severe among the officers and, in those days when generals actually did lead their men, many senior officers were killed or wounded. Among those hit was the leader of No. 1 Column, the gallant John Nicholson. Roberts, serving as a staff officer, had been sent into the city by Wilson to discover what had happened to No. 4 Column when he came upon Nicholson alone on a litter, its bearers having deserted him to loot. Roberts stopped to help him and asked if his wound was serious. 'I am dying,' said Nicholson. Wounds and death were common enough, but Roberts was most affected: 'The sight of that great man lying helpless and on the point of death was almost more than I could bear.' Roberts found bearers and a responsible sergeant and sent Nicholson back to the ridge.

Having launched a major attack, there is little more a commanding general can do to further its progress. Information and rumours, true and false, come back to him and it usually takes a strong character to resist doubts, fears, and the eroding of self-confidence that flood over him when the preponderance of the news he hears is bad; then he must resist the temptation to try to change the course of events until the outcome of the attack is certain. General Wilson, ill and exhausted, was for a critical period during this battle in danger of giving way to despair and recalling his troops. Had he done so, the next hundred years of Indian history might have been very different indeed. His chief engineer, weakened by disease and suffering intensely from a wound, told him firmly 'We *must* hold on'. Neville Chamberlain, not yet recovered from a bad wound he had received earlier and scarcely able to move, was propped up in a position near the city wall directing a part of the action; he sent his chief the same advice. The dying Nicholson, when he heard that Wilson was considering retreat, said, 'Thank God I have strength yet to shoot him if necessary!' The stubborn attack went on, though by nightfall the

British held only a portion of the wall on the north side. The city remained to be conquered. Six days of bitter, bloody street fighting followed, but in the end it was the mutineers who grew discouraged. Without senior officers and strong leaders they could not properly coordinate their counter attacks or their defence. As individual sepoys or units grew tired and despondent, they left the battle and the city. By 20 September the entire town was in British hands.

Major William Hodson (1821–58), a wild, brave and brilliant officer, was convinced that to crush the Mutiny completely it was necessary to find and kill or capture the foolish old emperor who had lent his name and support to the mutineers. Hodson was the son of an archdeacon and had the uncommon qualification, for a Victorian officer, of being a university graduate (Trinity College, Cambridge). He first obtained a commission in the militia, but soon after joined the East India Company army, arriving in India just in time to take part in the First Sikh War. After serving with two of the Company's European regiments, he was appointed adjutant of the Corps of Guides. He left the Guides for three years to accept a civil appointment under Sir Henry Lawrence, but then, to his great delight, he was offered command of the unit. Two years later he was accused of misappropriation of regimental funds and of cruelty to the natives. A military court convicted him, but he appealed and was eventually cleared of the charges, but he had lost his command. When the Indian Mutiny broke out he was ordered to raise a new regiment of irregular cavalry. This regiment, known as Hodson's Horse, became famous as a fighting unit and Hodson earned a reputation as a brilliant commander of irregular cavalry.

After persuading General Wilson of the wisdom of his plan, Hodson, taking fifty of his own sowars, set out to find the emperor and soon located him at the Tomb of Humayan, about seven miles outside the city walls. The old man surrendered after Hodson promised to spare his life and, followed by an immense crowd, he was led a captive to his own palace in Delhi. The following day Hodson returned to Humayan's tomb with 100 sowars to capture the three Shahzadahs, princes of Delhi and relatives of the emperor. He found there 'some 6,000 or 7,000 of the servants, hangers-on, and scum of the palace and city'. The princes surrendered voluntarily and Hodson sent them off under guard towards Delhi. He then demanded that the crowd at the tomb give up their arms and they turned over to him more than a thousand swords and firearms. When these had been collected in bullock carts, he rode off to check on his prisoners.

He found the prisoners and their guard not far from Delhi pressed in by a large mob. Hodson dashed in among them at a gallop. He shouted at the crowd: his captives were the villains who had butchered helpless British women and children. Hodson appears to have worked himself into a frenzy. Seizing a carbine from one of his sowars, he ordered the princes to strip and then personally shot each of them in cold blood, one after the other. The horrified crowd drew back in silence. Hodson ordered the corpses to be thrown into a bullock cart and then carried them into Delhi. 'I am not cruel,' he wrote to his brother, 'but I confess I did rejoice at the opportunity of ridding the earth of these wretches.'

Hodson had not promised to spare the lives of the princes and he used the threatening crowd as his excuse, but he was much criticized, particularly in England, for these murders. However, he was not punished and he never regretted his actions. Roberts said that, necessary or not, the act 'cast a blot on his reputation', and he was sorry that 'a brilliant soldier should have laid himself open to so much adverse criticism', but he conceded that at the time there was 'a thirst for revenge' among the soldiers and that 'the shooting of the princes seemed to the excited feelings of the army but an act of justice'.

Although Delhi had fallen much yet remained to be done in northern India. Cawnpore had been retaken, but Lucknow had to be relieved before its defenders suffered the same fate as the British men, women and children of Cawnpore. General Havelock with such force as he had was already moving on Lucknow, and other troops were marching to his support. Four days after the fall of Delhi, Roberts was attached to a column of 750 Britons and 1,900 loyal native troops which marched out of the city towards Lucknow. Tramping through the deserted streets of Delhi in the early morning he saw the dogs and vultures feasting on the corpses that still lay unburned and unburied; the city smelled horribly. Roberts turned his thoughts to Nicholson, for this was the day he was to be buried with all the honours the army could muster. He had already made arrangements to buy Nicholson's horse when his effects were auctioned off, as was the custom when an officer died on active service.

On the road the column encountered sizeable bodies of rebel troops and had to fight its way to Cawnpore. At Khurja, forty-five miles south-east of Delhi, the troops were greeted by a skeleton, said to be of a European woman, propped ostentatiously on a bridge leading to their camp ground. The troops were incensed and ready to destroy the town and its inhabitants, but they were calmed after finding and hanging a few sepoys found in the uniforms of regiments known to have mutinied.

In the camp ground itself a fakir was sitting silently under a tree near the tents. He did not speak a word but pointed to a small wooden plate he had with him. It appeared to be an ordinary plate with the remains of a meal sticking to it, but a careful examination revealed a false bottom in which a note was found. It was from General Havelock, written in Greek characters, saying that he was on his way to relieve Lucknow but badly needed reinforcements. He begged any British commander who saw the note to come and help him.

The column pushed on with all speed towards Lucknow. On its way it received urgent messages from Agra begging for help. The hard-marching column turned aside and tramped to Agra. The British in India were not always militarily wise and forceful, and Agra was an illustration of what could happen when they were not. The locally garrisoned sepoys had revolted and the Europeans and Christian Indians had been gathered into the large old fort of red sandstone built three hundred years earlier by Akbar. By the end of June they were completely cut off, with a force estimated to contain 4,500 mutinous sepoys with eleven guns just outside the town. But the British had a force of 750 men and an English brigadier, and this was considered sufficient to handle the situation. Brigadier Thomas Polwhele led his force against the rebels, used up all the shells for his guns in an artillery duel before charging with his infantry, and then was forced to retreat to the safety of the fort. Colonel G. B. Malleson, the nineteenth-century historian of the Mutiny, said: 'Of Polwhele's battle it only remains to be said that it should stand out in history as a warning of the manner in which Europeans, or I would rather say, the British race, should not fight Asiatics.'

By the time the column from Delhi arrived, the Agra mutineers had left, being unable or unwilling to attack the great, thick-walled red fort. However, just as the troops were making camp they were suddenly attacked by mutineers of the Gwalior Contingent. This was originally a British-officered force of seven regiments of infantry, two of cavalry and five batteries of artillery. The veterans of Delhi, accustomed to sudden attacks, swiftly organized themselves. The mutineers' attack was beaten back and they were driven from the field.

A few days later the column continued its march, reaching Cawnpore on 26 October. The troops were shown the site of the massacre of the women and children, which had been left much as it had been found more than three months before. Roberts, too, found the sight 'quite maddening'. The 93rd (Sutherland) Highlanders had already arrived in Cawnpore. This was the regiment which had been the 'thin red streak tipped with steel' which had repulsed the charge of the Russian cavalry at Balaclava. It was probably the most Scottish of all Scottish regiments. One of its sergeants once described it as 'a military Highland parish', for it had its own Presbyterian minister and its own elders selected from the ranks. This splendid regiment was a welcome addition to the British forces in India. Four days after they arrived, Roberts's column, reinforced by four companies of the Highlanders, pushed on towards Lucknow. The column halted just short of the Alambagh, on the outskirts of Lucknow, where they were joined by additional troops brought up by Sir Colin Campbell, the Commander-in-Chief himself.

Sir Colin was a cantankerous warrior of the old school. He was born Colin Macliver in 1792, the son of a carpenter. He was educated by his uncle, a soldier named John Campbell, who, when Colin was fifteen, presented him to the Duke of York and asked that he be given a commission. 'What! Another of the clan!' roared the Duke. But he gave him a commission in the name of Colin Campbell. Young Colin wanted to protest, but his uncle convinced him that 'Campbell' was a good name to fight under so he kept it until, late in life, he became Lord Clyde. He saw considerable action in the Peninsular Wars and so distinguished himself that he was able to reach the rank of captain in five years without having to purchase a promotion. He fought in the West Indies and finally obtained a regiment, but he was stationed in England for the next twenty years. In 1842 he went to China, where he again saw action, and remained there until he was sent to India in 1846, arriving in time to take part in the First Sikh War. In his journal for 1849 he wrote, 'I am growing old and only fit for retirement', but there were more wars and a lot of fighting yet to do, and more promotions and honours ahead.

He spent three years on the North-West Frontier, leading expeditions against the Momunds and the Swat tribes, but in 1853 he quarrelled with his superiors, resigned his command and went on half-pay in England. During the Crimean War he returned to the service to take command of the Highland Brigade and was promoted major-general: 'This rank', he said, 'has arrived at a period of life when the small additional income which it carries with it is the only circumstance connected with the promotion in which I take any interest.'

Now he was back in India as Commander-in-Chief and with one more war to fight. After pushing forward the troops diverted from the China war, he followed them up and assembled an army of nearly 5,000 men, most of them Britons, at the Alambagh. His force included such Indian army men as Roberts, now a veteran of Delhi and of many a fight with the mutinous sepoys, and young

Crimean veterans such as Wolseley who, though they had yet to fight the rebellious sepoys, considered themselves vastly superior to their Indian army colleagues. It was a colourful army, with turbaned Sikhs, kilted Highlanders, Welch Fusiliers, irregulars such as Hodson's Horse, a contingent of Ghurkas lent by the King of Nepal, and even some sailors from the Naval Brigade, now far from the sea. They were all eager to fight. Most had taken the gruesome tour at Cawnpore, and Corporal Forbes-Mitchell of the 93rd probably expressed the sentiments of all when he said, 'Every man in the regiment was determined to risk his life to save the women and children in the Residency of Lucknow from a similar fate.'

10

THE SIEGE AND RELIEF OF LUCKNOW

1857

THE siege of Lucknow was perhaps not, as it was called, at the time, the greatest siege in history, but it must surely be one of the most curious and fascinating. First of all, there was a period of fifteen days when the future besiegers lived and worked beside those whom they would besiege, both knowing full well that they would soon be at each other's throats. More curious still, those about to be besieged were, during this period, busily preparing an area to be besieged in. Then, after the British had been properly besieged for eighty-seven days, an army arrived to rescue them, fighting its way through the besiegers – and there it stayed, unable to get out. At last old Colin Campbell, the Commander-in-Chief himself, arrived with a second army and Lucknow was really relieved.

Only six weeks before the start of the Mutiny, Sir Henry Lawrence, the brilliant administrator of the Punjab, came to Lucknow as Chief Commissioner of Oudh (now the central portion of Uttar Pradesh), succeeding Coverly Jackson, an incompetent man. Lawrence's headquarters was the Residency, around which were clustered several public buildings, and the homes of some British officials. This area was the heart of British officialdom in Oudh. About a mile away were the barracks of the European troops, Her Majesty's 32nd Regiment, an understrength company of the 84th Regiment and two batteries of artillery. Across the Gumti River, about three miles away, were the lines of three regiments of Bengal Native Infantry: the 13th, 48th and 71st. A mile further on, beyond the race track, was the 7th Native Cavalry; two regiments of Oudh Irregular Infantry, the 4th and 7th, were at a place called Moosa Bagh, about three miles on the other side of the city. In all, there were nearly 7,000 sepoys and sowars and about 800 European troops in and around Lucknow.

Sir Henry Lawrence was one of the first senior officials in northern India to be aware of the discontent among the sepoys and to be disturbed by it. By opening sepoys' mail, employing spies, and talking with loyal Indian officers he tried to follow the course of the approaching storm. On 3 May 1857, exactly one week before the outbreak at Meerut, the great Indian Mutiny almost began at Lucknow.

Lieutenant-Colonel Inglis, forty-three, of the 32nd Foot and his young wife Julia, twenty-three, were driving to church at about five o'clock in the afternoon when Lawrence's military aide rode up in great excitement, telling Colonel Inglis that he and his regiment were needed at Moosa Bagh. Colonel Inglis turned his horses' heads about and raced back, calling to men of the 32nd he saw on the streets to return to their barracks. Within an hour he had assembled the regiment and, leaving a guard for the women and children, he marched to Moosa Bagh. Sir Henry Lawrence had proof that the 7th Oudh Irregular Infantry planned to mutiny.

It was a dramatic evening. Not only were all the European troops, including the artillery, sent to Moosa Bagh, but also all the native infantry. This on the theory that it was safer to have them with the European troops than back in defenceless Lucknow. The 7th, taken by surprise, glumly formed ranks and threw down their arms when ordered to do so. Colonel Inglis's 32nd Foot and the native infantry were drawn up in front of them and the cannon were loaded with grapeshot. The disarming parade might have passed off very smoothly had not someone (not Lawrence, certainly) given the order for the gunners to light their port fires (the long matches used to light muzzle-loading cannon). At this sight the irregulars broke ranks and fled for their lives. It was all very indecorous, but at least this regiment was disarmed.

It was not until 15 May that the British at Lucknow learned of the mutiny at Meerut five days earlier. On 19 May there was a rumour that the 71st Native Infantry would mutiny at two o'clock, but it did not. On the night of 21 May there was a fire in the artillery lines, but the sepoys helped to put it out. Four days later all the women and children, about 500 of them, were sent to the Residency; cartloads of grain, ammunition and supplies were brought in, and preparations were carried forward to withstand a siege.

Lawrence did not attempt to disarm any of the native regiments after receiving news of the mutiny at Meerut for fear it would precipitate the mutiny at Lucknow, but all knew it would happen sooner or later and hastened on with their preparations. A diamond-shaped enclosure containing about thirty-seven acres was made around the Residency and its dependencies, linking together several of the smaller buildings by earthworks. The Residency itself was a large stone building located in the heart of Lucknow on the southern bank of the Gumti River. The mile-long perimeter of the makeshift fortifications was too long to be properly manned by the available troops and the area it enclosed was too small adequately to contain the troops and the large number of non-combatants. Julia Inglis thought it 'all seemed very crowded and uncomfortable'. Unfortunately, there were several tall mosques and temples overlooking this area which, strictly from a military point of view, ought to have been demolished but were not for fear that such a step would add substance to the rumour that the British intended to destroy the Indians' religion.

At nine o'clock on the evening of 30 May the native infantry mutinied. The mutineers did not then attack the Residency, but simply set fire to their own barracks, killed three British officers who got in their way, and marched off. Some of the sepoys, particularly those in the 13th Native Infantry, remained loyal –

at least on this night. The next morning it was discovered that
the mutineers had halted not far from the lines of the 7th Native
Cavalry. The 32nd Foot set out after them, picking up the cavalry
when they reached their lines. The British troops wore themselves
out marching in the sun; the cavalry made a very half-hearted
pursuit, many of the sowars themselves deserting; and a number
of the sepoys of the 13th who had not deserted the night before
took this opportunity of joining the mutineers. The troops
returned to Lucknow with a few prisoners for hanging and went
back to work on the fortifications of the Residency with renewed
vigour.

Anxious days followed as word came of the desperate straits
of the garrison at Cawnpore. Small parties of refugees straggled
in from other towns and stations in Oudh, some were wounded and
some of the women had seen their husbands killed before their
eyes. On 12 June the Indian police force deserted, but they did no
harm to their officers. Everyone was expecting an attack and
nerves were stretched taut. At this time, when each Briton was
worth his weight in gold, the English sergeant-major of the 7th
Native Cavalry quarrelled with the English riding master and
shot him. This was on the 15th. On the same day it was learned
that an officer who had been sent to Allahabad with letters and
dispatches had been murdered by his own men. Two days later
the mutineers were reported to be only fourteen miles from
Lucknow. On 24 June it was learned that Cawnpore had fallen
and its garrison had been massacred.

Every dark face was suspect now, and most of the loyal Indian
troops were disarmed and sent to their homes. Only about 700
were allowed to stay, and this number included some Sikhs,
servants, and about 180 old Indian army pensioners who had come
in from the villages to help their former masters.

Lucknow had been the capital of the King of Oudh, who had
been deposed and was now living on a British dole in Calcutta.
It was not known whether the King of Oudh was loyal or not, but
it was decided that in either case his crown jewels ought to be
taken into custody. A British officer and a detail of Sikhs went

to the royal palace, the Kaiser Bagh, and took away the jewels as well as a cannon and a large supply of arms found stored there.

On 29 June the British sallied out to locate the rebel forces rumoured to be near Lucknow. They found them, and in the ensuing battle the British were soundly beaten. Julia Inglis was in bed with smallpox, but when, the next day, a wounded officer came in with the news, she got out of bed and stood by a window to see the return of the defeated troops: 'The greatest excitement and consternation prevailed,' she said. 'They were straggling in by twos and threes, some riding, some on guns, some supported by comrades. All seemed thoroughly exhausted. I could see the flashes of muskets, and on the opposite side of the river could distinguish large bodies of the enemy through the trees.' Then the news came to the women and children of the fate of their husbands and fathers. It is rare in war that the soldiers' families are so close to the battle. Now, at Lucknow, the battle came to them and soon shells were bursting inside the Residency itself. The siege had begun.

Two days later a howitzer shell crashed into the Residency building and seriously wounded Sir Henry Lawrence in the thigh. The wound was too high for the leg to be amputated and after two days of terrible suffering he died. On the night of his death there was a noisy thunderstorm and rain, but above it could be heard shouting and screaming in the city outside the Residency enclosure as the sepoys plundered the town. 'It was fearful to think how near the wretches were to us,' said Julia Inglis.

John Inglis (1814–62), now specifically charged by Sir Henry before his death with the defence of Lucknow, was the son of the Bishop of Nova Scotia and he had spent his entire military career since he was commissioned at the age of nineteen in the 32nd Foot. He had served with his regiment in the Canadian insurrection of 1837 and in India he had seen a great deal of action in the Second Sikh War. Only six years before the Mutiny he had married Julia Thesiger, whose soldier father became the first Lord Chelmsford, and she and their three children were with him at Lucknow. Inglis was not very clever, but he was not a fool either;

he was an unassuming man, friendly, kind and, of course, brave – the model of a regimental officer.

Inglis's standing orders to his men were: keep under cover, always be on the alert, and never fire unless you can see your man. At the beginning of the siege full rations were issued: a pound of meat and a pound of flour per man per day; there were no vegetables. This allowance was soon reduced to twelve ounces, then to six and, before the siege was over, to four ounces. There was no chivalrous nonsense about the food; the men who were fighting came first. Women were given three-quarter rations and children half. Julia Inglis's description of their hardships sometimes sounds amusing: 'Our ladies were many of them put to sore straits as the siege continued; they had no servants, and had to cook their own food and wash their own clothes.' But the hardships were real enough, and the women rose to the situation: they worked tending the wounded, keeping reports on rations and casualties, and even loading muskets for the men on the firing line while being subjected to an almost constant bombardment. And they saw their men and children die of wounds or from the cholera, scurvy, smallpox and dysentery, all of which were soon among them. There were almost daily losses from enemy shells; among the wounded was Dr Brydon who had been the sole European to survive the march from Kabul fifteen years before. There were, of course, some people who became despondent, and there were several suicides, but in general morale was high and there was even an air of good humour among the besieged. One of the refugee officers whose clothes had been torn off escaping through the jungle amused the garrison by cheerily making himself a suit of Lincoln green out of cloth cut from the Residency billiard table. The mutineers had added to their artillery by improvising mortars out of pipes and lobbing large blocks of wood at the Residency. Seeing these great chunks of wood come swinging through the air, the men would call out, 'Here comes a barrel of beer at last!'

It was an extraordinary group of people assembled at the Lucknow Residency. There were few cowards and many heroes among the defenders. Among the latter was Private Cuney of Her Majesty's 32nd. He was a soldier's soldier and loved fighting for its own sake. Attached to him was a sepoy named Kandial who adored him and followed him everywhere. Private Cuney liked to slip away from the Residency enclosure and go behind the enemy lines. He did this so often, taking only the faithful Kandial with him, without orders, and even against orders, that he became the garrison's expert on the enemy's position. Once he and Kandial attacked a rebel gun emplacement, bayoneting four mutineers and spiking the gun. He was frequently put into the guardhouse for breaches of discipline, but he was always released when there was fighting to be done.

Surrounded, outnumbered, and holed up in half-finished, improvised fortifications with scant chance for reinforcement or relief, it must have seemed to the rebel sepoys that the British were in an untenable position and must soon surrender. In the beginning they made no serious attacks on the Residency and contented themselves with a ceaseless bombardment. Later they took to mining; the British reacted by countermining. Fortunately, the 32nd was a Cornish regiment – it was later renamed the Cornwall Light Infantry – and there were many ex-miners in the ranks; the Sikhs, too, proved good tunnellers. The trick of countermining was to find the enemy's tunnel and choose the proper moment to blow it in. The countermining was not always successful, however, and rebel attacks were almost always preceded by the explosion of a mine under some portion of the Residency's defences.

On 25 July a spy came in with a message from the Assistant Quartermaster-General of Havelock's force that a relief expedition was on the way with 'ample force to destroy all who oppose us'. Time passed but no relief appeared. On 16 August Inglis wrote to Havelock describing his position: the strength of the garrison consisted of 350 able-bodied European men and 300 loyal sepoys; in addition he had 120 sick and wounded, 220 women and 250 children. On 28 August Inglis received a note from Havelock who said he was waiting for reinforcements and expected to reach Lucknow in twenty to twenty-five days. It seemed a long time to wait.

The longer the siege the greater the worry about the loyal sepoys. The English knew that they themselves had the stamina and could find the patience, but they were not so sure that their Indian comrades would be able to stand the strain. There were, in fact, some desertions. On the night of 30 August a party of sixteen – who had originally been the King of Oudh's musicians – together with some of the servants went over to the enemy, leaving their explanations scribbled on walls: 'Because we have no opium', was written in several places. Their needs were ended when the rebels shot them.

At long last relief, or at least help, did come. On 24 September the besieged garrison heard the sound of distant guns and that night Julia Inglis 'could not sleep from excitement and anxiety'. By this time the Residency was a wreck. Walls had been knocked down, roofs had been blown off, and some buildings had completely collapsed under the incessant bombardment, and there were many weaknesses in the undermanned defences. It was feared that the rebels would make a last, violent attack before the rescuers could arrive, but the next day the defenders saw through the smoke of musket and cannon kilted Highlanders fighting their way towards them and above the din of battle they heard the skirl of bagpipes. Julia Inglis was with the other women and at that moment torn between the excitement and joy of their rescue and sorrow and concern for the dying child of a friend. At six o'clock in the evening she heard loud cheers; shortly after she saw her husband walking towards her with a 'short, quiet-looking, gray-haired man, who I knew at once was General Havelock'.

Henry Havelock, now sixty-two years old, had been a subaltern for twenty-three years and was forty-three before he reached the rank of captain. A victim of the purchase system, he once said that he had been 'purchased over by two fools and three sots'. It had taken him thirty years to become a lieutenant-colonel and he had just recently, after forty-two years of service, been made a major-general. He had first seen action in the First Burma War of

1824 and subsequently in the First Afghan War, the Gwalior Campaign, the First Sikh War and the Persian War. He was known as a strict disciplinarian, an earnest Christian, and a good tactician. He was also a teetotaller who regarded drink as the curse of the Army and organized temperance societies among the men in the ranks – men whom their comrades called 'Havelock's saints'. Viscount Canning described him as being 'quite of the old school – severe and precise with his men, and very cautious in his movements and plans – but in action bold as well as skilful'.

In June 1857 Havelock arrived in Allahabad to take command of a column for the relief of Cawnpore and Lucknow. After a series of fights, he reached Cawnpore; although too late to save its defenders, he succeeded in retaking the city on 17 July. He then pushed on towards Lucknow, fighting several successful engagements along the way, but his force became so reduced by casualties and cholera that he was forced to fall back and wait for reinforcements. Shortly after taking this decision he was superseded as commander in Oudh by Major-General Sir James Outram (1803–63) who was given both the civil authority as Chief Commissioner of Oudh and also the command of all the military forces in the province, which included Havelock's column.

'The Bayard of India' Charles Napier once called Outram, before the two men became bitter enemies, and the appellation clung to him until his death and is inscribed on his tomb in Westminster Abbey. Wolseley said of him: 'Of the many leaders I have served under, he possessed the affection and confidence of all ranks more than any other.' He was ambitious but generous; a man of great energy and strong character, he often found it difficult to accept any opinion but his own; he sometimes warred with his superiors and he carried on a paper war with Charles Napier that lasted for years; he took an exceptional interest in the welfare of the soldiers in India and spent much of his own money to create regimental libraries. His entire career was spent in India where he saw action in many little Indian wars, the First Afghan War, with Napier in Sind, and as Commander-in-Chief of the British forces in the Persian War. He had also acquired considerable administrative experience, having served at various times as an assistant commissioner, political agent, and as a resident. Outram reached Cawnpore with reinforcements on 15 September; with him was his military secretary, Robert Napier, who was to achieve fame on another continent later in the century.

In the ordinary course of events, Outram would have taken over command from Havelock, but there now occurred another of those extraordinary situations in which the commander voluntarily relinquished his command. Outram, feeling that Havelock had already laid his plans with care and only needed reinforcements to carry them out, placed himself under his orders so that Havelock could have the honour and the glory of relieving Lucknow. Besides the honour, there was also the commander's share of the prize money, promotion, and a probable baronetcy for the general who led the relief force. It was a noble gesture. Which of them would take the blame if the expedition ended in disaster was not thought of, for defeat was unthinkable. Outram did retain his civil rank as Chief Commissioner of Oudh and stated that he would resume his command of the military forces when Lucknow was relieved. Unfortunately, Outram could not resist giving orders and even countermanding Havelock's orders. He later said of his relinquishment of command that 'It was a very foolish thing', adding that 'sentiment had obscured duty'.

On 19 September the column commanded by Havelock and Outram marched out of Cawnpore. Fighting most of the way, the column arrived four days later at the Alambagh, a large, walled park, the former pleasure gardens of the begums of Oudh, three miles outside Lucknow on the Cawnpore road. It was Outram who drew up the plan for the attack. After giving their men a short twenty-four-hour rest, they made the final push through a storm of grapeshot and musketry fire into Lucknow and the Residency.

11

FINAL RELIEF OF LUCKNOW AND END OF THE MUTINY

1857–58

W HEN Havelock's Highlanders poured into the Residency 'the state of joyful confusion and excitement was beyond all comparison', said Mrs Harris, wife of the garrison's chaplain, 'the big, rough, bearded soldiers were seizing the little children out of our arms, kissing them with tears running down their cheeks, and thanking God that they had come in time to save them from the fate of those at Cawnpore'.

At first the defenders of the Lucknow Residency thought that they would be brought out, but it was soon obvious that the force brought by Havelock and Outram was not strong enough to drive the mutineers from the city and there was not enough transport to carry away the sick, the wounded, and the women and children. The relief force had brought more men, guns and ammunition for the defence of the Residency, but they had brought very little food and the old defenders were already on short rations. It appeared that the arrival of the relief force simply meant they would be starved out sooner. No novelist writing such a story as this would dare invent the solution to the problem which actually occurred. Due to errors in the accounts of the commissariat, it was discovered that there was far more grain than had been thought. Incredibly, no officer had actually examined the stocks available before, and when Colonel Robert Napier (later Lord Napier of Magdala) actually did so, he found a great pit full of grain which Lawrence had prudently hidden away and the existence of which was unknown.

Although still in a dangerous position and outnumbered, the reinforced garrison was now better able to defend itself and even to make a number of sorties to spike enemy guns, capture houses, and enlarge and improve the fortifications. In one of the first of these sorties Private Cuney was killed. He had been on the sick list, but could not resist the chance to fight.

Outram, although wounded, now took command and paid a handsome compliment to Inglis and his defenders of the Residency who had held out for eighty-seven days. He told them that 'the annals of warfare contain no brighter page than that which will record the bravery, fortitude, vigilance, and patient endurance of hardships, privations and fatigue displayed by the garrison of Lucknow'.

For another fifty-three days after the arrival of Havelock and Outram the siege went on – the mining, the shelling, the attacks, the counterattacks, and the deaths from wounds and disease. Meanwhile, old Colin Campbell was bringing up forces for the second relief of Lucknow. By 10 November about 5,000 men, all the troops that could be scraped together, were encamped in and around the Alambagh and eager to attack. As yet, however, no one knew much about the place they were to attack nor about the disposition of the enemy within the city. A rough communications system had been established between Colin Campbell's army and the Residency by means of a visual semaphore, but no one knew the intricate plan of the city with its maze of narrow streets. It was obviously desirable for someone in the Residency to try to break out and advise the relieving army. Thomas Kavanagh, a thirty-six-year-old minor civil servant with a wife and fourteen children volunteered for the task. He must have been well aware of the unlikelihood of succeeding and of the tortures awaiting him should he be captured. Without a word to his wife, he disguised himself as an Indian and slipped out of the Residency. Due to his skill and good fortune, he succeeded in making his way through the enemy lines and reaching Sir Colin Campbell with messages, maps and his own intimate knowledge of the city, enabling the attackers to select a route through the city which involved considerably less street fighting than Havelock and Outram had encountered by taking a direct route. It was a brave deed, and Kavanagh was rewarded by becoming the first civilian ever to win the Victoria Cross. No one knows what his wife thought.

Thanks to Kavanagh, Sir Colin was able to plan a flanking attack; he moved his army to the right, first attacking the Dilkusha Bagh, a large villa in the centre of an extensive park, and La Martinière, an enormous structure originally built as a country residence but converted in 1840 into a school for Anglo-Indian children. On 14 November these were secured after heavy fighting. The following day was spent consolidating these positions and on the 16th an attack was launched on the Sikander Bagh, a thick-walled, castle-like enclosure about 100 yards square (Outram Road now runs through it).

Before the attack began, Colin Campbell rode up to the 93rd Highlanders and spoke to the men. He told them frankly of the danger, but reminded them that the eyes of Christendom were upon them. As Sergeant Forbes-Mitchell remembered his words, he ended with:

We have to rescue helpless women and children from a fate worse than death. When you meet the enemy, you must remember that he is well armed and provided with ammunition. . . . So when we make an attack you must come to close quarters as quickly as possible. Keep well together, and use the bayonet. Remember that the cowardly Sepoys, who are eager to murder women and children, cannot look a European soldier in the face when it is accompanied with cold steel. Ninety-Third! You are my own lads. I rely on you to do the work!

Someone called out: 'Ay, ay, Sir Colin! Ye ken us and we ken you. We'll bring the women and children out o' Lucknow or die wi' you in the attempt!' The regiment cheered.

The British batteries, operating in the open, began the bombardment of the thick walls of the Sikander Bagh and suffered heavy losses from enemy musketry fire. Colin Campbell stationed himself just behind the guns and was wounded in the thigh, but he kept his position. From time to time he turned to call to the High-landers behind him to keep down. Sergeant Forbes-Mitchell heard him cry, 'Lie down, Ninety-Third! Lie down! Every man of you is worth his weight in gold to England today!'

As soon as the guns had made a small breach in the thick walls Sir Colin ordered the charge. The 93rd Highlanders and the 4th Punjab Infantry rose with a yell to the attack. Pipe-Major John M'Leod struck up 'On wi' the Tartan' and the Highlanders, to-gether with the Sikhs, Punjabi Muslims and Pathans of the 4th Punjabis, shouting madly, raced for the breach, each man anxious to be the first to enter it. The reward for the winners of this race was death.

The first man through the small hole in the wall of the Sikander Bagh was Lance-Corporal Donnelly of the 93rd Highlanders. He was instantly killed. The second man was Subadar Gokul Singh of the 4th Punjabis, who was also killed. Sergeant-Major Murray was next, or was it Lieutenant Richard Cooper? No matter, for both were killed. Still the Punjabis and Highlanders came on. A young drummer boy of about fourteen, handsome and fair-haired, had been among the first, and Roberts saw him later, lying on his back just inside the breach. Sergeant Forbes-Mitchell went through with his commanding officer, Brevet Lieutenant-Colonel John Ewart. Forbes-Mitchell was hit by a bullet on his belt buckle, which knocked him down, but he was only stunned and breath-less and soon rose to fight on. Others leaped through the breach and over the bodies of their dead and wounded to charge the rebels inside, driving them from the bungalows inside the garden. There was hand-to-hand fighting with sword and bayonet, the mutineers fighting stubbornly but vainly to throw back the attackers.

Brevet Major Garnet Wolseley's company was employed else-where that day, but late in the afternoon Wolseley went through the breach to look for a missing friend: 'I never before had seen the dead piled up, one above the other in tiers, in order to clear a passage through a mass of slain. Such was the case in the archway leading into that awful charnel-house where lay the bodies of some 2,000 unfaithful Sepoys.'

Roberts, too, saw the piles of dead mutineers inside the Sikander Bagh:

> There they lay in a heap as high as my head, a heaving, surging mass of dead and dying inextricably entangled. It was a sickening sight. . . . The wretched wounded men could not get clear of their dead comrades, however great their struggles, and those near the top of this ghastly pile of writhing humanity vented their rage and disappointment on every British officer who approached by showering upon him abuse of the grossest description.

Neither quarter nor humanity was shown by either side.

Lieutenant-Colonel John Ewart, thirty-six years old and in command of the 93rd Highlanders, had been among the first through the wall and had survived to fight side by side with his men, personally capturing one of the enemy's colours. When the fighting was over he ran back to Colin Campbell just outside the wall and called out, 'We are in possession of the bungalows, sir! I have killed the last two with my own hand, and here is one of their colours!' Old Colin Campbell, wounded himself and worried, looked down from his grey charger on this hatless, dirty, bloody Highland colonel and snapped, 'Damn your colours, sir! It's not your place to be taking colours. Go back to your regiment this instant sir!' Ewart meekly did as he was told. He was recommended for the Victoria Cross for this action, but it was refused him and he received no reward for his gallantry; he was not even mentioned in dispatches. Ewart, a Crimean veteran, was part of a soldier family: his father was a general, and eventually he became a general himself, as did his younger brother; of his four sons, three became army officers. He lived to be eighty-three, although he almost lost his life two weeks after the Battle of the Sikander Bagh when, while fighting the mutinous Gwalior Contingent near Cawnpore, his left arm was carried away by a cannon shot.

Although it was late in the afternoon, almost dusk, when the Sikander Bagh fell, Sir Colin was determined to push on and at once began a bombardment of the enemy's next strong point, the heavily fortified Shah Najaf mosque. The heavy guns of the naval brigade were brought into play, but failed to make a breach in the high walls. Then a rocket battery came up and lobbed a series of noisy rockets over the walls. Meanwhile, Sergeant John Paton of the 93rd went exploring round the wall and found a crack just large enough to admit one man. He reported this to Brigadier Adrian Hope who took fifty men and returned with him. When they worked their way through the opening they saw the enemy fleeing out the back gate in confusion, trying to escape the hissing, crashing rockets.

After gaining possession of the Shah Najaf, a lieutenant of the 93rd Highlanders took a sergeant and a twelve-year-old drummer boy to the dome of the mosque to raise a signal flag to show those in the Residency that the mosque was now in British hands. The little group drew the fire of the enemy but they were rewarded by the sight of the Residency flag being raised and lowered in recognition. They had climbed down again to safety when the little drummer boy, defying the shouted orders of his lieutenant, turned and raced back up the steps to the dome of the mosque. And there, with bullets flying all around him, he waved his highland bonnet and sang – of all things – 'Yankee Doodle'!

Down again, he faced his angry sergeant and lieutenant and their demands for an explanation. It was all very logical, at least to a boy's mind. The 93rd Highlanders had been stationed in Canada for several years and he had been born during this period while his mother was on a visit to the United States. So, as he was really an American, he thought it would be a grand thing if he, the smallest drummer boy in the regiment, could say that he had sung 'Yankee Doodle' under fire from the dome of the tallest mosque in Lucknow. Drummer boys, too, wanted glory and distinction.

The next day, two more strong points – the former mess house of the 32nd Regiment and the Moti Mahal, or 'Pearl Mosque' – were taken by Major Wolseley and his men. Only a bullet-swept open space now separated Sir Colin's force from the besieged Residency. Havelock, Outram and a few other officers braved the bullets and ran across to greet Sir Colin. It was an absurd thing to do, as foolhardy as the feat of the Highland drummer boy. And had these senior officers been called on to explain, their replies would have been no more satisfactory than his: Well, you see we wanted to be able to say that we were the first to greet the commander-in-chief when he reached the Residency.

The defenders of the Residency were now relieved for a second time, but the mutineers still had not been decisively defeated. The British held the eastern end of the town and a line of strong points leading to the Residency, but the mutineers held most of Lucknow. Sir Colin had yet to extricate the besieged garrison with its women and children.

By widening the narrow corridor leading from Dilkusha Park and La Martinière to the Residency, one narrow passage was safely held. Meanwhile the Kaiserbagh was bombarded and ostentatious preparations were made to attack it, deceiving the mutineers into thinking that the British intended to try to take the entire city. During the night, without noise or confusion, the women and children were safely brought out. Julia Inglis said, 'I turned my back on the Residency with a heavy heart, for at that time I fancied a force might still be left there, and that I was bidding farewell to my husband for some time.' She was fortunate to have her husband left alive, for more than half of the 32nd Regiment had been killed or had died of disease, and many of the women from the Residency were now widows and many of the children orphans. An hour's walk brought them to the Sikander Bagh, where the dead had now been buried in a great pit, and then on to Dilkusha Park where tents had been set up for them. Major Wolseley noted that none of the women thanked the soldiers who had fought so hard to rescue them.

At the end of the operation there was a moment when Outram and Inglis jockeyed for the honour of being able to say, 'I was the last man to leave the Residency'. Outram was the senior, but Inglis won when he said, 'You will allow me, sir, to have the honour of closing my own door.'

The extrication of the defenders of the Residency had been a well-planned and brilliantly executed manœuvre, but now Sir

Final Relief of Lucknow and End of the Mutiny

Colin was anxious to disentangle his army from the narrow streets of Lucknow, for he had received word that Cawnpore was under attack and he was concerned not to lose this vital link in his line of supply and communication. Havelock, worn down by anxiety, overwork and illness, died at Dilkusha Park. The British retreated from Lucknow, but left a strong garrison under Outram at the Alambagh; then Sir Colin hurried back to Cawnpore, arriving just in time. On 6 December 1857 he defeated an army under Tantia Topi, the ablest of the rebel leaders, and then started the long process of methodically exterminating the remaining fires of the Mutiny. There was hard fighting in northern India for another two years, but the danger of losing India was past. Lucknow was attacked for a third time and finally captured by Sir Colin Campbell on 16 March 1858 with the help of 10,000 Gurkhas. A wit then coined a Latin pun for Sir Colin: *Nunc fortunatus sum* ('I am in luck now').

Meerut, Lucknow, Agra and Delhi were not the only places where the Mutiny broke out, of course, and there were hundreds of incidents large and small throughout northern India. There was, for example, a 'disturbance' at Rohini on 2 June 1857. A Major Macdonald, commanding the 5th Irregular Cavalry at Rohini, was having tea with two other officers when they were suddenly attacked by three sowars armed with swords. The officers were unarmed but they grabbed chairs and, laying about with them, drove off their attackers. All three were severely wounded and Major Macdonald was virtually scalped, but he immediately launched an investigation into the affair and discovered that his entire unit was bordering on mutiny. Although he was now the only European in town, he staged a trial in which he was chief witness, prosecutor and judge and sentenced his attackers to be hanged. He was in great pain as well as in great danger, but he paraded his sullen men and supervised the execution. When the soldiers deputed to be hangmen held back, he personally adjusted the nooses and hanged all three. Major Macdonald had no authority whatever to do this, but there was no further trouble at Rohini.

At Arrah they laughed at a railway engineer named Vicars Boyle for turning his billiard room, a detached building, into a stocked and provisioned little fort, but fifteen of his civilian friends were glad to join him when mutiny broke out there. With shotguns, sporting rifles and pig-sticking spears they held off an enemy fifty times larger than their small force. In a few days they were reinforced by fifty Sikh soldiers sent to their relief by the commissioner of Patna. It was a small version of Lucknow: there was mining, countermining, and a bombardment by two small cannon of the enemy. A force of 450 men sent to relieve them was ambushed and routed. The tiny garrison of the billiard room at Arrah continued to hold on until finally relieved by Major Vincent Eyre.

Eyre, a forty-six-year-old artillery officer, was an experienced soldier. He had entered the East India Company's military academy at Addiscombe when he was fifteen, and had seen considerable action during the First Afghan War, where he had been wounded and, with his wife and child, had been for a time a prisoner of the Afghans. In July 1857 he was on his way up river with about 220 drafts and three guns when he heard of Boyle's plight. Without orders and on his own initiative, he decided to march to his relief. He was reluctantly joined by another officer, a captain who refused to cooperate without a written order from Eyre, with about 150 men. With this small force Eyre drove off the rebels and rescued the fighting European civilians and the Sikh soldiers.

Julia Inglis survived Lucknow, came under fire again at Cawnpore, and finally reached Calcutta safely and took ship for England; she was shipwrecked off the coast of Ceylon, but survived that experience as well, living on until 1904. Her husband was made KCB and died in 1862. Not long after Julia Inglis left India, Fanny Duberly and her husband arrived there with the 8th Hussars and took part in the exhausting, bloody but less glorious expeditions to stamp out the final sparks of the Mutiny. From Bombay she wrote to her sister, Selina: 'There is plenty of fighting to be done, they say. I hear ladies are forbidden to go further than Deesa. In which case, I shall stain my face and hands and adopt the Hindoo caftan and turban. . . . I ain't going to stay behind.' She did indeed go, undisguised, marching 1,800 miles with the Rajputana Column. Husband Henry began to wilt, and she complained, 'If I had but a *Master* under whom I could work! Instead of a friend I am obliged to support.' Fanny herself was glad to be 'a strong athlete, to fight with and enjoy life'.

It was at Gwalior in the summer of 1848 that Fanny joined a cavalry charge. She and Henry rode out to watch the battle, and when the 8th Hussars and Blake's Horse Artillery started their charge Fanny's horse sprang after them. She did not rein in but called out to Henry, 'I must go!'

'Go along then!' he replied.

And away she went, madly chasing the fleeing rebel cavalry through the dust and heat. Swords flashed, sabred men screamed, and on they rode. Joining a cavalry charge for the fun of it was not particularly unusual for officers. Wolseley once charged with the 7th Hussars just 'to see what the thing was like'. Certainly, though, there were few women who had ever ridden to battle with cavalry, but Fanny Duberly was not the only woman in this particular cavalry engagement. In the course of the fight a trooper of the 8th Hussars cut down a turbaned, trousered rebel officer who turned out to be the Rani of Jhansi. Not much is known about this extraordinary woman except that she was a Mahratta princess with a brilliant grasp of military tactics and strategy and an undying hatred of the British. She probably had no part in starting the Mutiny, but she regarded it as an opportunity to ally herself with Britain's enemies and she fought valiantly and cleverly to the end.

Fanny saw her last battle in India in November 1858 near Mongroulee. She and Henry stayed in India until 1864 and then returned to a quiet life in England. Thirty-two years later she told a nephew, 'I cannot stand dullness for long, and life gets duller and duller as one gets older.' She died in 1903 at the age of seventy-three.

Roberts won a Victoria Cross while a passenger on a cavalry charge. He had joined the squadron of his good friend, George

Younghusband, adjutant of the 5th Punjab Cavalry, when they charged the fleeing mutineers at Khudaganj, near Cawnpore, in January 1858. A group of mutineers had stopped and turned to face the oncoming British cavalry. They fired a volley at Young-husband's squadron and Roberts saw his friend fall, but at that moment he was engaged in saving the life of a Punjabi sowar who was on the point of being bayoneted by a mutineer. He killed the mutineer and galloped after two of the enemy who were making off with a standard. He cut down one man; the other pressed his rifle against Roberts's body and pulled the trigger. The rifle misfired and Roberts cut the man down with his sabre and carried off the standard. Younghusband died of his wound and Roberts won the Victoria Cross.

Evelyn Wood, the midshipman turned cavalry officer, was bitterly disappointed that he had not received the Victoria Cross for which he had been recommended for his services in the Crimean War, but when he sailed from England for India with the 17th Lancers in October 1856 he had high hopes of distinguishing himself in the Indian Mutiny. After a fair passage of forty-two days, his ship reached Cape Town, 'where our spirits fell on hearing that Dehli (*sic*) had fallen, and the confident predictions that the Mutiny would be suppressed before the ship reached Bombay'. True, the great danger of losing British India was past, but there was still work to be done and Wood saw plenty of action in the next two years. Sickness-prone as always, he suffered in India from fever, several sunstrokes, indigestion, ague, toothache, 'intestinal complaints', neuralgia, and an inflammation of the ear that cost him half his hearing. Also, in addition to the usual accidents that happened to officers in the field, Wood had an unusual one: he was badly battered while trying to ride a giraffe. A friendly maharaja had been entertaining a group of British officers by exhibiting his menagerie and Wood, on a bet by a fellow officer, leapt from a balcony on to the back of a giraffe. He did well until he tried to dismount: the giraffe's knee hit him in the chest and knocked him on his back; the animal's hind foot then came down on his face, cutting holes in both cheeks. When he recovered from this, he broke his collar bone by galloping his horse into a tree, slashing his lip and making a mash of his nose.

By December 1859 the Mutiny was over, but many of the mutineers had formed themselves into robber bands that terrorized the countryside. Lieutenant Wood, with only fifteen men and a guide, tracked down such a robber band of eighty men in the Sironji jungles one night and, in a surprise attack on their camp, managed to kill several, confiscate the arms of those who fled, and release three Indians whom the bandits had captured and were holding for ransom. He returned to camp with a toothache. Wood had done braver and more spectacular deeds, but it was for this feat that he was awarded the Victoria Cross he so desperately wanted. He had made an impressive start to his career: a twenty-two-year-old lieutenant with six medals clanking on his breast, including the highest award for valour his country could bestow: few generals could boast more.

In all the accounts of the fighting during the Indian Mutiny, certain facts stand out: the sepoy mutineers were as well armed as the British and generally retained their discipline; they outnumbered their adversaries in every major battle; they were acclimatized to the Indian summer; and they were fighting in their own country against a foreign ruler. The mutineers thus had on their side all the favourable factors needed to win a war except one: leadership. And this was the decisive factor. The British were well aware of this advantage and counted on it; they took their superior leadership at all levels of command for granted and never doubted it. Much lip service was paid to the fine fighting qualities of the British common soldier, but as Wolseley pointed out, 'he must be well led, and as a general rule I believe that leader must be a British gentleman'. Today the British gentleman survives as a quaint anachronism, but in the last century many were bred to be, physically, intellectually and psychologically, ideal leaders of nineteenth-century soldiers, whatever their race or nationality.

12

CHINA AND ELSEWHERE

1858–61

It was fortunate for Britain that the war with China could be postponed and that there were no other major outbreaks of hostilities during those critical months of 1857, for the British regular Army then consisted of less than 176,000 men, of whom about 30,000 were in India when the Mutiny started at Meerut. As the Queen rightly pointed out to Lord Panmure, the Secretary for War, on 29 June 1857:

It will be good policy to oblige the East Indian Company to keep permanently a larger portion of the Royal Army in India than heretofore. The Empire has nearly doubled itself within the last twenty years, and the Queen's troops have been kept at the old establishment. They are the body on whom the maintenance of the Empire depends.

In the following year the size of the Army was increased to nearly 230,000 men, of whom more than 92,000 were in India; never again were the British to have less than 60,000 regular troops in India as long as they ruled there, and not until 1876 did the size of the Army fall below 200,000.

In November 1858 the British Government abolished the Honourable East India Company and transferred its territories and assets to the Crown; it also took over John Company's army. The transfer of government was easily made; it was almost a formality. The India Act of 1833 had closed out the Company's commercial activities and most of the Company's patronage was lost when the Indian Civil Service examinations were thrown open to public competition. The Government had long held most of the real power anyway through the president of the Board of Control. Now a cabinet minister and a council of fifteen replaced the Board of Control and the Court of Directors; the Governor-General's title was changed to Viceroy. There was, however, one aspect of the transfer which created a problem: the transference of the soldiers from the Company to the British army caused considerable discontent among the European troops (Britons) in the Company's army, particularly in the Bengal army, which employed three regiments of European infantry, six battalions of European foot artillery and nine troops of horse artillery. These soldiers maintained, quite rightly, that they had been enlisted by the Company to serve in India and that, as they had not volunteered to serve in the Queen's Army, it was unjust to be shifted about as though they were cattle, without their consent and without being paid the bounty given to men enlisting in the Queen's Army.

As with the discontent among the sepoys, the rebellious spirit among the Company's European troops spread from barracks to barracks across northern India and grew more and more serious. There were other ominous similarities to the sepoy mutiny: an intercepted letter from a European gunner in Meerut contained the idea that the Company's European troops there ought to revolt and march on Delhi, and on the wall of a wash house in Meerut was found scrawled: 'John Company is dead. We will not soldier for the Queen.'

In October 1859 the 5th European Regiment mutinied at Dinapore. The mutiny was temporarily suppressed, but broke out again five weeks later. Although in this instance the ringleader was shot and the regiment disbanded, the authorities were very uneasy about attempting to suppress this mutiny with the same vigour used to put down the sepoys. The Law Officers of the Crown had ruled that the transfer of the troops was legal, but many, including Sir Colin Campbell, felt that the soldiers were being unjustly treated.

It was not at all certain that the regular troops would fight their fellow countrymen. Then, too, the authorities did not welcome the embarrassment of exposing to the Indians the spectacle of British troops fighting each other. In the end it was decided to give the mutinous troops what they wanted, and all who did not wish to transfer were discharged and given a free passage to England. From a total force of about 24,000 Europeans in the Company's army, 10,900 chose to be discharged, of whom more than 6,000 were from the troublesome Bengal army.

The crisis was over and the discharged troops and their dependants were hastily packed in ships and sent home. It was all done a bit too hastily as it turned out. When the clipper ship *Great Tasmania* anchored in the Mersey in March 1860 there was a scandal in Britain. Of her 1,043 passengers, more than fifty had died on the voyage and a hundred were too ill to stand. She had left Calcutta overloaded, with rotten food, insufficient blankets and not enough water. The passengers had only tropical clothing and there was only one doctor on board. There was an outcry in the press and in Parliament and, of course, an official inquiry, but all this was soon forgotten. There were more wars to be fought; Britain needed soldiers; the returning discharged soldiers from John Company's army were destitute; and nearly 3,000 of them soon re-enlisted in Britain to fight in the Queen's Army.

After the great crisis to Empire of the Indian Mutiny of 1857 Britain was free to continue the prosecution of the succession of small wars which expanded British influence and added territories to the realm. Fighting such wars had now become a part of the way of life for Britain and her soldiers. Even during 1857 there had been some minor actions on the Indian frontiers unrelated to the Mutiny. There was an expedition against the Bozdars led by Neville Chamberlain and another against so-called 'British villages' on the Yusafzai border. There were minor actions outside India as well: not many soldiers were in China, but the Navy was there, fighting a series of small boat actions around Canton, and in the Battle of Fatshan Creek in June 1857 about seventy war junks were destroyed. In the Strait of Bab-el-Mandeb, near Aden, the island of Perim was occupied, and in Sarawak there was a revolt of the Chinese against that one-man empire builder, James Brooke, which forced the British raja to swim a creek to escape.

In 1858 there were small expeditions against the Krobos on the Gold Coast, and against the Waziris and 'Hindustani Fanatics' in India. In 1859 there was an expedition against the Dounquah rebels in West Africa and another expedition, under Neville Chamberlain, against the Kabul Khel Waziris on the Trans-Indus frontier. The following year there was still another expedition by Chamberlain to chastise the troublesome Waziris, an expedition to Sikkim, and an insurrection of the Maoris in New Zealand led by a chief named Wirrimu Kingi (anglicized at the time to William King). Some of these small affairs involved a considerable number of troops by nineteenth-century standards. In Chamberlain's 1860 expedition against the Waziris, for example, he commanded 6,796 men, including 1,600 levies, of whom 361 become battle casualties. The war in New Zealand was also more than a few skirmishes.

Many of these campaigns were, like the Mutiny, fought simply to maintain the existing Empire, but conquests continued to be made which added territory to the realm. Until now, Britain's politicians had not taken much interest in the expansion of the Empire. Colonial affairs were looked after by the Secretary of State for War from 1801 until 1854. Sir James Stephen (1789–1859), a civil servant, effectively ruled the colonies for many years and was called 'Mr Mother-Country', but he regarded most colonies as 'wretched burdens which in an evil hour we assumed and have no right to lay down again'. He never visited a British colony. Many, perhaps most, of the upper classes regarded the colonies and the conquered provinces only as a burden upon the exchequer. Still, a sense of imperial destiny was growing and territory continued to be added to the Empire, sometimes for bizarre reasons.

The Third China War of 1860, during which the British again found themselves with the French as allies, was a continuation of the fits-and-starts opium wars, a prolongation of the British–Chinese conflict of ideas and opinions. It is often called the *Arrow* War after the name of the lorcha, or schooner, *Arrow*, which indirectly served as the pretext for starting the war. The Chinese authorities boarded the *Arrow*, a Chinese ship with a Chinese crew, and arrested several of its sailors. The lorcha had once been registered in Hong Kong; its registration had lapsed and the arrested sailors were later released but, no matter, the British decided that the Chinese had again insulted them by boarding a British ship, and declared war. The French discovered that a French priest had been murdered by the Chinese several months earlier and this gave them their pretext for joining the British.

The *Arrow* War has been much written about by military historians, but it was, in fact, a rather simple campaign: the British and French forces started at the mouth of the Pai Ho River and fought their way up to Pekin. It was, however, an exceptionally well-managed campaign, and this was due primarily to the exceptional soldier who commanded it: Sir James Hope Grant.

Hope Grant, the youngest son of a Perthshire squire, was commissioned a cornet in the 9th Lancers in 1826 at the age of eighteen. He remained with the regiment for thirty-two years until he was promoted to major-general. He first saw action in the First China War, where he earned a CB; he also saw considerable action in both the First and Second Sikh Wars, taking part in almost every major battle, and nearly wrecking his career by arresting his own commanding officer for being drunk on the day of the Battle of Sobraon. During the Indian Mutiny he was with the Movable Column, and in command of it after Agra; he was at Delhi and in the first relief of Lucknow; and he took part in many of the lesser expeditions that marched back and forth across Oudh in the mopping up operations of 1858–59. He earned a reputation as a brilliant commander of cavalry and as an acknowledged expert on outpost duties. Wolseley, who served under him in India and in China, described him as 'a tall man of muscle and bone and no unnecessary flesh about him. He had all of the best instincts of a soldier, and was a brave daring man that no amount of work could tire. . . . He was liked by every good man who knew him.'

Everyone admitted that Hope Grant was a splendid officer, but he did have some peculiar characteristics for a soldier: He never learned to read a map; he had difficulty giving orders, expressing himself so badly that his subordinates had trouble understanding what he wanted done – 'puzzle-headed', they called him; and he was an accomplished cello player. Oddly enough, it was his musical abilities that got him to China for his first war. Lord Saltoun, one of the generals in this war, was also a musician, being proficient on the violin; as the voyage to China was long and tedious, Lord Saltoun went to the Horse Guards to see if there was not another officer-musician in the Army. He discovered Captain Hope Grant, who was about to resign his commission because he could not afford 'extravagant living in an expensive regiment'. Lord Saltoun appointed him his brigade-major and the two of them fiddled their way to China.

Although he had attended schools in Scotland and Switzerland, Hope Grant was not well educated. Except for the Bible, which he knew well, he never read books and, in an age when most gentlemen knew how to sketch, he could not draw a line. His brother Francis, however, was a well-known painter and became president of the Royal Academy; it was said, though, that Sir Francis could not tell one bar of music from another.

The names of the principal actors in the Third China War were somewhat confusing: General James Hope Grant commanded the army whilst Admiral James Hope commanded the navy. The chief Chinese general was San-ko-lin-sin, which the British soldiers simplified into 'Sam Collinson'. It was also difficult to know who was on which side. The war was against the Chinese, of course, but most of the fighting was directed against the Tartar and Mongolian troops in the Chinese army. On the British side, as most of the troops were drawn from India, most were Sikhs, others Punjabis, and Pathans. The British had no difficulty recruiting a

Canton Coolie Corps to help them; they rented a camp site at Kowloon from the Chinese governor there, and another Chinese governor rented out mules and drivers to them. During the war a British regiment was sent to Shanghai to help the Chinese governor there fight a local rebellion. It was a curious and confusing war.

The first major action of the campaign was the storming of the Taku forts at the mouth of the Pai Ho River. The engineers, under the direction of Lieutenant-Colonel Gerald Graham, put up a pontoon bridge under fire across a canal behind one of the forts. Graham, who had won the Victoria Cross in the Crimean War, was a large man, six feet four inches tall and well built, who was also exceptionally brave. Tall, brave officers rarely lived long in Victorian wars, but Graham, although frequently wounded, survived to become a lieutenant-general. Wolseley was helping to put the pontoon bridge in place and was bending over a broken section of the pontoon when Graham rode up. Wolseley went over to speak to him and laid his hand on his leg. In a completely normal tone of voice Graham said, 'Don't put your hand there for I have just had a bullet through my thigh.'

There was a great deal of rivalry between the British and the French forces in this war. The British, who had the larger army, considered the French more of a hindrance than a help. The French, always concerned with the outward forms of glory, were careful to have at least a token force at every battle and to make certain that the tricolour flew wherever the Union Jack was hoisted. Once when the British flag flew from a taller pole, the French hastened to erect their flag on a higher pole than the British. The British were incensed when the French looted the large and beautiful collection of buildings known as the Summer Palace, a Chinese Versailles near Pekin, but to teach the Chinese a lesson and to take revenge for the ill-treatment given their envoys, the British burned the place down. There was a considerable outcry in England against this piece of vandalism.

As the heavy guns were drawn up before the gates of Pekin, and only minutes before they were scheduled to open fire, the

Sir Charles Napier

Sir Harry Smith

John Nicholson

Viscount Gough in his famous white 'fighting' coat
which he wore on his campaigns

Two Sikh officers

Captain and Mrs. Duberly in the Crimea, 1855

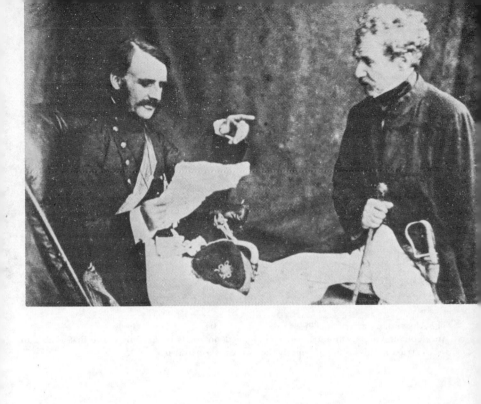

The Abyssinian Campaign 1867–68
An elephant kneels while a howitzer is loaded on to its back. This is the first time guns were carried in this fashion; formerly they were always drawn

· Soldiers on guard at Magdala

The Ashanti War 1873–74
Troops landing on the Gold Coast

Sir Garnet Wolseley receiving news from the front

Chinese capitulated. The Chinese Emperor had fled, but on 24 October 1860 Prince Kung, the Emperor's brother, met with Lord Elgin (son of the Lord Elgin who took the Elgin marbles from Greece) and gave the British all they asked for, including Kowloon and the addition of Tientsin to the list of treaty ports open to foreigners.

It was during this war that the British used for the first time an improved type of cannon: Armstrong's rifled breech-loading 12-pounder. Many of the officers were enthusiastic about the gun. Wolseley said, 'nothing could be better than the accuracy with which our Armstrong guns fired', and Hope Grant sent back a favourable report to the Horse Guards, but at the end of the war the military authorities decided that the old smooth-bore muzzle-loading guns were better – and cheaper. The British could afford to neglect improved weapons for at this stage in history courage, discipline and personal leadership were still the most important factors in war.

In 1861, the year following the Third China War, there were a number of minor campaigns – an expedition to Sikkim and the bombardment and destruction of a village on the Sierra Leone River – and the threat of a larger war with the United States. The British had gone to war with China ostensibly because the Chinese authorities had boarded one of her ships, but the Americans did the same thing and escaped with impunity. On 8 November 1861 an American man-of-war stopped and boarded the *Trent*, a British Royal Mail steamer one day out of Havana, and took off two Confederate envoys bound for London. The *Trent* Affair caused a great uproar. The Royal Navy prepared for action and British troops were sent to Canada.

The threat of war with the United States stirred the breasts of a number of future generals and field-marshals who were now between wars: Garnet Wolseley, Gerald Graham, Evelyn Wood, and Frederick Roberts were all in Britain and eager to go to war with any enemy of the Queen. But only Wolseley had the opportunity of going to Canada, and the *Trent* Affair was finished by the time he reached Halifax. No shots were fired and the Confederate envoys were released. Wolseley now spent a few relatively peaceful years learning to use snow shoes, skating, talking with Indians, enjoying the social life of Montreal and taking trips to the United States, where he visited both the Union and Confederate armies. As for Montreal: 'Altogether it was an elysium of bliss for young officers, the only trouble being to keep single. Several young captains and subalterns had to be sent home hurriedly to save them from imprudent marriages. Although these Canadian ladies were very charming they were not richly endowed with worldly goods.'

Wolseley's views on marriage seem crass, but they were realistic. Most officers found it difficult or impossible to live on their pay and it was considered ruinous to a young officer's career to marry before he was thirty, had reached the rank of brevet major and had obtained a better-paying staff appointment. Roberts broke the rule, marrying when he was only twenty-seven and still a lieutenant, and it caused him to miss the Third China War. His health had broken down after six years in India and on 1 April 1858 he relinquished his post as deputy assistant quartermaster-general on Sir James Hope Grant's staff to Captain Wolseley and took ship for England. There he met and married in May of the following year Miss Nora Bews, whom he took back to India with him. Although Hope Grant was the commanding general in China, the troops were supplied from the army in India and old Colin Campbell, now Lord Clyde, chose the staff officers, disappointing Wolseley, who had hoped to go as quartermaster-general and had to be content with being deputy assistant quartermaster-general, and Roberts, who had hoped to go in the position taken by Wolseley and was not sent at all because Lord Clyde thought it was not right that Roberts's young wife should so soon be parted from her husband.

Evelyn Wood fell in love while in England in 1860 with Miss Paulina Southwell, but did not marry her until seven years later. Lord Southwell, the lady's brother and head of the family, although a good friend of Wood's, objected to the match because Wood was not a Catholic and refused to become one. For four years Wood and Miss Southwell did not exchange a letter; then Wood wrote her one day proposing marriage, explaining however that he had little money and that the proposal was 'on the distinct understanding that she would never by a word, or even a look, check my volunteering for War Service'. The lady accepted, and Wood – at a moment when he did not have fever, 'face ache', tooth ache, 'neuralgia of the nerves of the stomach' or double pneumonia (all of which he suffered while in Britain), and when he had recovered from a hunting accident in which he fell on his head and nearly broke his neck – was married at the age of thirty.

Soldiers in the ranks required permission to marry and only a limited number in each unit were allowed to be married at any one time. General Sir Alfred Horsford, a veteran of the early Kaffir wars, the Crimea and the Mutiny, was a bachelor who believed in a celibate army. He used to tell a story of the days when he commanded a battalion in the Rifle Brigade and a soldier applied to him for permission to marry.

'No certainly not,' Sir Alfred told him. 'Why does a young man like you want a wife?'

'Oh, please, sir,' begged the soldier, 'I have two rings [Good Conduct badges] and £5 in the Savings Bank, so I am eligible and I want to marry very much.'

'Well, go away, and if you come back this day year in the same mind you shall marry. I'll keep the vacancy.'

Exactly one year later the soldier was back and repeated his request.

'But do you really, after a year, want to marry?'

'Yes, sir, very much.'

'Sergeant-Major, take his name down. Yes, you may marry. I never believed there was so much constancy in man or woman. Right face. Quick march.'

The soldier marched off, but as he reached the door he turned about and said, 'Thank you, sir. It isn't the same woman.'

13

THE NORTH-WEST FRONTIER

1855–63

As a result of the conquest of Sind in 1843 and the Second Sikh War in 1848–49 British India was presented with an ill-defined, mountainous border on Central Asia. This was the North-West Frontier. Here in this rugged country the British did battle with hardy and headstrong mountaineers for a century.

The Frontier straddled those areas which were reputed to be under British influence and those which actually were under British administration, the latter being officially called, apparently without tongue in cheek, the 'Administrative Border Line'. Beyond, to the west, was an area supposed to be under the influence of the Amir of Afghanistan. In fact, most of the tribes in the area were not influenced by anyone except their own rulers and mullahs (holy men), and not always by them. History and scenario writers have clothed the North-West Frontier in glamour – the romance of adventure and derring-do, of exotic peoples and forlorn columns of lancers, Sikhs, Highlanders and elephant batteries, led by stiff-lipped British officers in topees looking small and lost in narrow passes surrounded by rocky and precipitous mountains; of tribesmen, with matchlocks ready, crouching in the heat of the hillsides watching their chance to pick off stragglers or to launch a savage attack. This is the conventional picture conjured up by 'the North-West Frontier'. Oddly enough, that is about the way it was.

Even the thick official histories, written by anonymous hands, printed in Simla by the Government of India and encased in forbidding leather covers stamped 'For official use only', cannot hide the excitement and, yes, the romance of the North-West Frontier. Here in the heat of summer and the cold of winter, amid the rocks and scrub of mountain and pass, the nineteenth-century British officer, usually leading mercenary troops of warrior races previously conquered, won his Indian General Service Medal with one or more of the clasps that read 'Umbeyla', 'Hazara', 'Waziristan', 'Relief of Chitral', 'Malakand', 'Tirah', or 'Punjab Frontier'. Here he found scope for his love of action and his military prowess. Here he could find the glory and excitement of battle he sought. Here, under almost medieval conditions, a man could prove himself in the presence of comrades whose respect he cherished, battling a savage but worthy foe.

The men he fought were as bloodthirsty as he himself, and, like him, they were bred for battle. From the most ancient times until the present they have retained their fierce independence, their own customs, and their violent way of life. The blood feud has always been a part of every Pathan's life, even when he comes into contact with civilization and seems to accept it. Perhaps no better illustration of this exists than an event which occurred not long ago on the Frontier.

The British were always eager to enlist the brave and hardy hillmen into their own forces. A number of Pathans did indeed take the Queen's and later the King's, shilling, and they usually proved to be brave and loyal. They were generally put into special units under officers who understood the Pathan nature and Pathan ways. In the South Waziristan Scouts there was a subadar whose family had a blood feud with a jemadar of the Tochi Scouts. Their units frequently served at the same posts and the two native officers frequently met, but there seemed to be an unwritten law among the Pathans that the rules governing feuds were suspended while in British territory. The two men became friends.

Nevertheless, the adjutants of their units always compared notes and saw to it that the two men never took their furloughs at the same time. But one day there was a mistake. The two men went on leave on the same date. Subadar Hajam was a crack shot. Jemadar Akram did not return. This was in 1945.

Reading the long history of the continuing conflict between British and Pathan it is difficult to escape the conclusion that for all the pious sentiments of the Pathan, waging war for his religious beliefs in endless jihads, and the noble reasoning of the British about law and order, the struggle went on because both sides took a keen delight in the martial exercise. There was no conscription; on both sides the men were volunteers. In the twentieth century, when technology began to give the British a decided advantage, they laid down rules for themselves to even the odds: aeroplanes could not bomb unless they first dropped leaflets announcing the time and place of the bombing and, as in a child's board game, certain areas were declared safe for the Pathan, designated places where he could retreat if hard pressed and the British soldiers were not allowed to follow.

Meek, subservient and peaceful races were viewed with contempt by the British, while the warlike tribes who caused them the most trouble won their admiration. The official history compared the tribes on the Frontier: the Bannuchis, for example, are described as 'about the worst specimens of the race on the frontier. Their physique . . . is as degraded as their morals. They are cowardly and unwarlike, and on this account give less trouble than the . . . Waziris, who in appearance and in character are immeasurably their superiors.' And in contrasting the Baloch with the Pathan: 'Both have most of the virtues and many of the vices peculiar to a wild and semi-civilized life . . . the Baloch is less turbulent, less treacherous, less bloodthirsty, and less fanatical than the Pathan; he has less of God in his creed and less of the devil in his nature.' But it was the Pathan the British liked:

There is a sort of charm about him, especially about the leading men, which makes one forget his treacherous nature. . . . For centuries he has been on our frontier at least, subject to no man. He leads a wild, free, active life in the rugged fastness of his mountains; and there is an air of masculine independence about him which is refreshing in a country like India.

John Ayde said of them: 'They are poor but brave . . . and although turbulent and difficult to deal with, still have a great love of their country and cherish their independence, possessing qualities that we admire in ourselves, and which deserve consideration and respect.'

Of all the many races of men the British fought, none were as consistently hostile and none were better fighters than the Pathans. They were, as John Lawrence said of them, 'men of predatory habits, careless and impatient of control'. And, in fact, the British never did control them. In 1947 they passed on their custom of fighting the Pathan to the new state of Pakistan. Today many a Pathan remains, as all his forefathers were, unadministered and untaxed.

The Pathans are a Pushtu-speaking people, divided into many tribes, subtribes and clans. They are of mixed ethnic background, some claiming to be descended from Jews with King Saul as an ancestor; the Ghilzais claim descent from Noah. Since the tenth century they have been militant if not always orthodox followers of Islam. The British attitude towards them was well expressed in 1855 by the Secretary to the Chief Commissioner of the Punjab who wrote a report on the relations between the British government and the Frontier tribes:

Now these tribes are savages – noble savages, perhaps – and not without some tincture of virtue and generosity, but still absolutely barbarians nevertheless. . . . They are thievish and predatory to the last degree. . . . They are utterly faithless to public engagements: it would never occur to their minds that an oath on the *Koran* was binding, if against their interests. It must be added that they are fierce and blood-thirsty. . . . They are perpetually at war with each other. Every tribe and section of a tribe has its internecine wars, every family its hereditary blood-feuds, and every individual his personal foes. . . . Reckless of the lives of others, they are not sparing of their own. . . . They possess gallantry and courage themselves and admire such qualities in others.

Yes, they were faithless to public engagements, bloodthirsty, perpetually at war, possessed courage themselves and admired it in others – just like the British.

Many a British officer learned his trade and made his reputation on the North-West Frontier, and some of them spent their entire careers there. Few, if any, saw more action than handsome Sir Neville Bowles Chamberlain (no relation to the late prime minister). He was a remarkable man. In his day he was famous: Charles Napier called him 'the very soul of chivalry', and Hugh Gough, who saw him in action in the Second Sikh War, called him 'the bravest of the brave'. General Osborn Wilkinson asked rhetorically: 'Is there any one belonging to the last half-century who has not heard of Sir Neville Chamberlain? I should doubt it.' He saw so much action that he sometimes sickened of slaughter, and once during the First Afghan War he wrote that he was 'disgusted with myself, the world, and above all, with my cruel profession'.

Chamberlain was born 10 January 1820 in Rio de Janeiro where his father, a baronet, was consul-general. He had three brothers, all of whom served with distinction in the East India Company's army. Neville was sent to Woolwich when he was fifteen but, as it seemed unlikely that he would pass the examinations, he was taken out and at seventeen commissioned an ensign in the Bengal Native Infantry. He was wounded six times in the First Afghan War, but he escaped the debacle that ended the second phase of that war. In 1843 he took part in the Gwalior Campaign and was present at the battle of Maharajpore. He served in both of the Sikh wars and particularly distinguished himself at the battle of Gujrat.

In 1849 he was appointed assistant commissioner at Rawal Pindi and later in Hazara. In 1852 he was given a long sick leave, but instead of returning to England he went to South Africa and spent a year and a half hunting lions. Refreshed by this experience, he returned to India where, although only a captain in his regiment, he was given local rank of brigadier, the command of 11,000 Punjabi irregulars, and the task of guarding 700 miles of the Frontier. He led a busy life.

In the spring of 1855 he led an expedition into Meeranzie; in August another against the Orakzais. The next year he led a second expedition into Meeranzie. Then came the Mutiny and Chamberlain led the Movable Column before turning it over to John Nicholson and joining the army before Delhi as adjutant-general. There he received a musket ball in his shoulder when he leaped his horse over a wall lined with mutineers. He recovered in time to take part in the storming of the city.

He was again back on the North-West Frontier in August 1858 when he 'nipped in the bud a dangerous conspiracy among Sikh troops at Dera Ismail Khan', and the following year he led an expedition against the Kabul Khel Waziris. In 1860 he led still another expedition, this time against the Mahsuds, with a force composed entirely of natives, some of them tribal levies. In between these expeditions there were many smaller frays.

In 1863 Chamberlain was called upon to lead his last expedition. Although only forty-three years old, he was worn out by constant active service, aching wounds and recurring malaria. He had no zest for another expedition. To his younger brother Crawford he wrote, 'If "duty" *really* requires the sacrifice I cannot repine, but . . . I have no wish for active service.' It was to be a difficult campaign, however, and Chamberlain was unquestionably the most able man to lead it.

Punitive expeditions against the Pathan hill tribes were usually small affairs and the campaigns short. From 500 to 1,500 troops were sent into the hills for a few weeks. They killed some tribesmen and burned a few villages. The tribesmen would retreat deeper into their mountains and lick their wounds or promise to behave and pay their fine of rifles. All would then be peaceful in that area for a while until the Pathans could steal enough rifles or enough money to buy them; then they would again swoop down to the plains to steal cattle, kidnap wealthy merchants or attack mud forts. This was the classic pattern, but this expedition was more complex in its plan of operations and the political situation was more than usually intricate.

The root of the trouble had begun about fifty years earlier when a holy man – Frederick Roberts called him a 'religious adventurer' – named Sayyid Ahmed Shah Brelwi, originally from Oudh, came back from a pilgrimage to Mecca and began to preach war against the infidels in the Yusafzai villages on the northern border of Peshawar. In 1829 he and his followers even captured Peshawar itself from the Sikhs, although two years later they were driven back into their hills. Sayyid Ahmed was killed, but the sect he had founded, called Mujahidin, survived and flourished in and around the village of Sitana, which was located in a rugged mountain area on the west side of the Indus River about 75 miles north-west of Peshawar. Followers of the sect were called, at least by the British, the Sitana Fanatics or, after they left Sitana, the Hindustani Fanatics. 'Their ordinary occupation', according to John Ayde, 'consisted of incursions into the plains of Eusafzye [Yusafzai] and in robbing and murdering peaceful traders in our territories.'

In 1853 Colonel Frederick Mackeson led a force of 2,000 irregulars and levies against them but failed to break up the sect. During the Mutiny they welcomed every fleeing sepoy and sowar and built up a sizeable stock of arms and ammunition. In 1858 Sir Sydney Cotton led a 5,000-man expedition against them. He blew up their forts and drove them out of Sitana, but they reformed and retreated to the village of Malka on the north side of Mahaban mountain. By the summer of 1863 their numbers had increased and their raiding parties were larger than ever. On the Frontier it was widely believed that Russian intrigue was behind their troublemaking, but this is doubtful.

The British now decided that the Fanatics must be punished and their stronghold at Malka destroyed. This was easier said than done, for Malka was located deep in the mountains and it was not easy to get there. It was the 'politicals' who dictated the campaign. Sir Hugh Rose, the Commander-in-Chief, was against it;

Chamberlain did not want to go and was particularly disturbed by the thought of taking troops into the mountains in winter. But all objections were overruled. An inadequate force, consisting mainly of native troops with insufficient supplies and insufficient transport, was sent off in the late season of the year to march through mountainous Frontier country inhabited by tribes with whom the British had no quarrel but from whom they concealed their intentions.

Chamberlain's base of operations was to be the Chamla valley, but to reach this valley it was necessary to cross a belt of mountains. There were three passes: one was unknown; one (the Daran Pass) was controlled by unfriendly tribes and was thought to be impassable for artillery; and only the third, the Umbeyla (also spelt Ambala, Ambela, Umballa, Umbeylah, Ambeyla and Umbela) was thought to be practicable. The Umbeyla Pass was in the land of the Bunerwals, a large and powerful tribe capable of mustering 10,000 fighting men.

On the Frontier the Bunerwals were generally regarded as a superior breed, representing the Pathan at his best. Austerely religious, they lived simply and kept to themselves. They had a reputation for being trustworthy and truthful, and for honouring the laws of hospitality. It was the territory of these brave and hardy people which the British intended to invade in order to reach Malka. As the Bunerwals were known to be unfriendly to the Fanatics, the politicals reasoned, somewhat naïvely, that they would not mind if the British army tramped through their country.

The plan was to march the expeditionary force towards the Daran Pass and then, when about six miles from its entrance, abruptly change direction and make for the Umbeyla 'in order not to alarm the frontier tribes'. The Bunerwals were not told of the plan until the British were at the entrance to the pass. Then a proclamation was issued saying that no harm was meant to them and that the army simply wanted to march through their country. However, as Major H. R. James, Commissioner of Peshawar who later joined the expedition as political officer, said 'Even supposing that the proclamations actually reached their destination, was it likely that a brave race of ignorant men would pause to consider the purport of a paper they could not read when the arms of a supposed invader were glistening at their door?'

The Bunerwals were alert and soon alarmed. The Hindustani Fanatics sent messages to them saying that if the heathen British ever got into their country they would never leave. Considering the history of the British in India, it is not surprising that the Bunerwals believed the Fanatics and not the British.

On the morning of 20 October 1863 Chamberlain and the Yusafzai Field Force entered the pass. The little army consisted of five battalions of native infantry, the Corps of Guides, the 4th and 5th Gurkhas, the 11th Bengal Cavalry (Probyn's Horse), the 71st Highlanders (later Highland Light Infantry), the 101st Royal Bengal Fusiliers (formerly a European regiment in the East India Company's army and later 1st Battalion, Munster Fusiliers) and some mountain batteries. In all, about 6,000 men. On the 22nd a reconnaissance in force was made and there was a first skirmish with the Bunerwals. The campaign had begun.

14

THE UMBEYLA CAMPAIGN

1863

On 23 October Chamberlain wrote in his dispatch: 'The Bonair people [Bunerwals] having taken a hostile part against us is extremely serious, and has altered our whole position and probably our plan of operations.'

Two days later Chamberlain's force was pinned down and unable to move forward. In another dispatch he warned:

There appears to be reason to believe that the Bonair people have applied to the Akoond of Swat for aid, and should they succeed in enlisting him in their cause – which is not improbable, as they are his spiritual followers – the object with which this force took the road to the Chumla Valley would be still more difficult of attainment.

It was only too true. The Akhund of Swat soon planted his standard on near-by Guru Mountain and rallied the tribesmen for miles around. The Akhund, now a venerable seventy years old, was a Muslim holy man who had attained a tremendous influence over the Pathans on the Frontier by his piety and his teachings. He was not a hothead or a religious fanatic, and he normally held himself aloof from worldly affairs; in the past he had exerted a moderating influence over the violent tempers of the tribesmen and he was no friend of the Hindustani Fanatics at Malka. Now, however, he felt that the British, by invading the territory of the

Bunerwals, had gone too far. At his call the Pathan tribesmen slung bags of food over their shoulders, picked up their weapons and set off for the Umbeyla Pass to fight the British. Even tribes with blood feuds agreed to forget their differences and join forces against the invaders.

The position of the Yusafzai Field Force at the crest of the pass was precarious. Not only was it unable to go forward, but its line of retreat and communications was threatened by what the official report described as 'a mischievous gathering of our own subjects'. Chamberlain, unable to move, could only try to strengthen the position in which he found himself and to call for reinforcements, while daily the numbers of hostile tribesmen around him increased.

The British camp was located on a small plateau protected by pickets stationed on two heights, one of which, called the Crag, was the key to the entire position. Originally it was only large enough for twelve men, but it was eventually enlarged to accommodate 300 men and a battery of guns. The tribesmen, experienced hill fighters, were fully aware of the Crag's importance and there was bitter fighting for this small piece of ground.

At eight o'clock on the morning of 13 November Major Charles Brownlow, commanding the picket on the Crag, was relieved by Lieutenant J. P. Davidson and a detachment of the 1st Punjab Infantry. He was glad of the relief, for he and his men had spent forty-eight sleepless hours fighting the Pathans and strengthening the defences. Major Brownlow was an able officer who had seen much service on the Frontier, but Lieutenant Davidson was young and inexperienced. Davidson had not been long on the Crag when he sent word to Major Charles Keyes that he needed reinforcements. Keyes sent off thirty men under a native officer, but he soon saw soldiers rushing down the hill: They 'appear to have been seized with an unaccountable panic', he said. He was able to halt some of them and to form a firing line which temporarily checked the enemy's advance on the lower picket. But the Pathans had captured the Crag.

Two counterattacks failed and the Pathans launched a furious assault on the lower picket, which Major Keyes was trying to hold with a handful of men from behind breastworks. But help was on the way: Captain T. E. Hughs, commanding the Peshawar Mountain Train Battery, had already swung his guns towards the Crag and was bringing down an accurate fire on the tribesmen there; Lieutenant-Colonel Alfred Wilde, in command of the Guides, was hurrying forward with three companies of Guides infantry; and Chamberlain himself was on his way with the 101st Bengal Fusiliers. They arrived just in time to save Keyes and the lower picket.

The Pathans were held, and then driven back. Chamberlain ordered Lieutenant-Colonel F. O. Salisbury, commanding the Bengal Fusiliers, to retake the Crag at whatever cost. Three companies of the Guides infantry made an assault on the enemy's flank while the 101st Bengal Fusiliers stormed up the narrow and precipitous path to the Crag. It was retaken.

The Umbeyla campaign was, as Major Frederick Roberts put it, 'an admirable school for training men in outpost duty'. Unfortunately, young Lieutenant Davidson was unable to use the experience he had gained, for he was killed defending the Crag. He was not blamed for losing the Crag; his honour was saved. According to the official report, he 'behaved in a most heroic manner' and had tried 'in every way to recall his men to their sense of duty'. The common soldier's duty was sometimes a hard thing to face and there was something of the 'Birkenhead drill'* in outpost duty here. One British soldier relieving another on picket duty asked

---

* On the night of 26 February 1852 the *Birkenhead*, an iron paddle-wheeled troopship carrying drafts for several regiments stationed in South Africa as well as a number of women and children dependants, struck a rock in Simon's Bay, near Cape Town. The troops were mustered on deck and calm order was maintained as the lifeboats were lowered. Unfortunately, there were not nearly enough. As the last boat pulled away the remaining troops stood quietly in ranks with their officers until the ship broke and sank. Out of 630 passengers and crew, 438 were drowned. King Frederick William of Prussia was so impressed with this example of perfect discipline that he ordered an account of it written by a survivor to be read to every regiment in his army. Kipling wrote: 'To stand and be still to the Birken'ead drill is a damn' tough bullet to chew.'

what the orders were for that post and was told: 'Why the orders is, you're never to leave it till you're killed, and if you see another man leaving it, you're to kill him.'

Many of the troops in the native regiments were handicapped by being armed with Brunswick rifles sighted for only 250 yards. Some even had smooth-bore muskets that had first been issued in the Peninsular War. Most of the tribesmen, on the other hand, had locally made but superior rifles which were effective at 400 yards. The British troops supplemented their armament by making their own grenades – soda water bottles filled with gun-powder – an early Molotov cocktail, here called 'Umbeyla pegs'.

Meanwhile, back in the Punjab, the authorities who had sent out the Yusafzai Field Force became alarmed by the unexpected developments in the Umbeyla Pass. Sir Robert Montgomery, Lieutenant-Governor of the Punjab, drafted an order for the withdrawal of the force, but General Hugh Rose, although he had been against the idea of sending out the expedition in the first place, thought it would be disastrous to British prestige on the Frontier if the force retreated. He ordered up reinforcements, and soon there were clouds of dust all along the great northern road from Lahore to Peshawar as cavalry, infantry and artillery moved towards the Umbeyla Pass.

Although by 19 November there were 166 wounded and 286 men sick in the British camp, it was reported that 'the health of the troops was good and the weather mild'.

On the following day the Crag was for the third time captured by the Pathans. Its loss was due to 'the unaccountable conduct of an officer on the left of the picquet, who suddenly ordered the troops in his part of the position to retire'. Chamberlain himself led the 71st (Highland Light Infantry) and those famous Frontier fighters, the 5th Gurkhas, in a counterattack. The sweeping of the slums of Glasgow and the hardy little mountaineers from Nepal recaptured the Crag at a cost of 27 killed and 110 wounded. Among the latter was Chamberlain, who received his ninth and last wound near the crest of the Crag.

The Umbeyla Campaign

It is the curious custom of the British to give their greatest honours to their brave and faithful servants long after their active days are over, thus making the honours seem more a reward for physical durability than for worthy deeds. During his active career Chamberlain received only brevets, mentions in dispatches and a CB for all his fighting, his many wounds and his heroism. He was now only forty-three years old, but he was burnt out by war. After the Umbeyla Campaign he never again saw action, but he lived long enough to reap a harvest of honours: he was made KCSI in 1866, GCB in 1875, and, at the age of eighty, he was made a field-marshal. Ten years after leaving the Umbeyla Pass, and still a handsome man, he married. Eight years later he retired from active duty to live out the last twenty-one years of his life in peace, far from the North-West Frontier, in Southampton. Before he left India, however, he gained fame of a different sort by inventing the game of snooker.

While the fighting was going on in the pass, Major James, the political officer, was carrying on continuing negotiations with the tribal leaders. After the British had captured the Crag for the third time, James was able to persuade some sections of the Buner tribe to return to their homes, but in spite of these losses and some desertions, the tribesmen continued to increase their forces: fresh reinforcements from distant tribes continued to arrive on the scene, called by the great Akhund of Swat. James's negotiations were made difficult by a lack of coordination between the politicals and the military. Major James had promised the Swat leaders that no troops would enter Swat, but General Rose, unaware of this agreement, decided to create a diversion by sending troops to the Swat frontier and threatening the Malakand Pass. To the tribesmen, this was another proof of British duplicity.

At the end of November Chamberlain, too badly wounded to command, was replaced by John Garvock, who had been made a major-general only eight months earlier. Garvock was a protégé of Sir Harry Smith, having served on Smith's staff in the First Sikh War, the South African War of 1848, and the Kaffir War of 1850–52. This was his first experience as a commander in action.

Garvock's tenure as commanding general was intended to be brief; Sir Hugh Rose had decided that he would assume command himself and Garvock was instructed not to attack until Rose arrived on the scene. Garvock ignored these orders and was rewarded with a KCB.

Early in December the Yusafzai Field Force in the Umbeyla Pass was reinforced by the 7th Fusiliers, the 3rd Sikhs, the 93rd (Sutherland) Highlanders and the 23rd Punjab Infantry – all excellent regiments. The total force now consisted of about 9,000 men. Garvock, on the advice of Major James, decided not to wait for Rose but to advance out of the Umbeyla Pass into the Chamla plain.

On the morning of 15 December, 4,800 troops assembled at the base of the Crag and moved forward in two columns for an attack on the village of Lalu. The first objective was 'Conical Hill', a formidable enemy stronghold, its sides rocky and precipitous, its crest strongly held behind stone breastworks.

Two of Sir John Rose's staff officers, Colonel John Ayde and Major Frederick Roberts, had arrived at Umbeyla and they were now spectators at the battle. Roberts watched as the 101st Bengal Fusiliers scaled Conical Hill and stormed the enemy's positions there. 'It was a grand sight,' he said. The village of Lalu was a mile and a half further on and the British troops raced towards it, the Guides infantry and the 23rd Sikhs reaching there first as the enemy fled. Back at the camp, however, those who stayed behind had to beat off a Pathan attack. By the end of the day the British had lost sixteen killed and sixty-seven wounded; enemy losses were estimated at 400. The way through the pass was now open.

So far the campaign had been an infantryman's war; there was little scope for cavalry in the Umbeyla Pass. But now the 11th Bengal Cavalry, 400 sabres under Colonel (later general) Dighton Macnaghten Probyn, VC, advanced rapidly towards the Chamla Valley.

Probyn was an exceptionally fine cavalry commander and an experienced Frontier fighter. He was tall and handsome but, as Osborn Wilkinson said of him: 'With all his reckless dash and daring there was no swagger about him. . . . He was singularly courteous, soft and gentle in his address to all.' He had served on the Trans-Indus Frontier in 1852–57, took part in operations in the Bozdar Hills in 1857, and had played a distinguished role in the Mutiny, where he had been at Delhi, had taken part in the relief of Lucknow under Colin Campbell and was present at the battle of Cawnpore, winning his Victoria Cross for a series of daring exploits. Just three years before the Umbeyla Expedition he had commanded the 1st Sikh Irregular Cavalry in China. Probyn's career had a curious ending for a dashing cavalry commander: he became Controller and Treasurer of the Household of H.R.H. the Prince of Wales. This battle in the Chamla Valley was to be his last, though he did not know it as he led his sowars and their jingling horses down from the pass in the clear December air.

The approach to the village of Umbeyla was covered by a low ridge of hills on which the enemy now appeared in force. It was a set battle piece and called for the kind of fighting at which the British excelled. The enemy's left flank was soon overrun by the infantry and around this end of the line of battle swept Probyn's Horse, galloping into the valley beyond, not stopping until it reached the village. The villagers had fled, but Probyn fired the huts and houses. The infantry moved relentlessly forward and, in spite of several determined counterattacks, carried the field. Over the fertile Chamla Valley there hung the smoke of musket, cannon and burning homes, and beneath it lay the dead and wounded, Pathan and Indian and British.

Opposing the British this day had been mostly tribesmen under the influence of the Akhund of Swat or the Hindustani Fanatics. The Bunerwals in whose land the battle raged had already had enough and had abstained. On the following day their chiefs came in to the British camp and simply asked what was required of them. Someone, probably Major James, had a brilliant idea: the Bunerwals were told that they themselves must destroy Malka and expel the Hindustani Fanatics. They agreed to do this, but to be certain that the work was done, it was decided that there must be some officers on the scene.

On 19 December six officers, including Colonel Ayde and Major Roberts, set off from Umbeyla in the rain with a small escort of Guides cavalry. They were supposed to be accompanied by 200 Bunerwals, but only about sixty came. Malka was not in Buner territory but in the land controlled by the smaller Amazai tribe. The Bunerwals reasoned, probably rightly, that it would be better to persuade the Amazais then to try to intimidate them with a show of force, but the British officers and their Guides escort were in a dangerously uncomfortable position.

There were, of course, no roads and they had to travel over difficult country. They made only eight miles the first day, stopping frequently while the Bunerwals argued fiercely with bands of angry men along the way. On the second day they reached Malka. The Amazais did not conceal their hatred and gathered in scowling knots, pointing at the English officers and talking excitedly among themselves. 'The force found themselves in the presence of strong tribes, certainly not over well pleased with their visitors, or the errand on which they had come.' This was Roberts's understatement of their position.

Nevertheless, the village was burned by the Bunerwals while the British officers sat on their horses and watched. The deed done, the party started back. Angry Pathans were all around them. Colonel Reynal Taylor, in charge of the mission, remained calm, even when surrounded by gesticulating tribesmen who wanted to murder them.

At one point it looked very serious indeed, but the situation was saved by an old one-armed Bunerwal chief. Raising his one arm for silence he said, or so it has been translated: 'You are hesitating whether you will allow these English to return unmolested. You can, of course, murder them and their escort; but if you do you must kill us Bunerwals first, for we have sworn to protect them with our lives.'

No one wanted to start a blood feud with the Bunerwals and the old chief's speech had a quieting effect. The party started back, but they were followed by angry tribesmen, and the British officers, looking up at the hills around them, saw them fill with bitter armed men. In one narrow defile a wild Amazai waving a standard rushed at them, but he was pulled back by one of his fellow tribesmen. Roberts later said, 'If he had succeeded in inciting anyone to fire a single shot, the desire for blood would quickly have spread, and in all probability not one of our party would have escaped.'

This was exactly what Sir Hugh Rose thought would in fact happen. He was furious when he learned that such a small party had been sent with so little protection to Malka. Roberts's wife overheard him say, 'It was madness, and not one of them will ever come back alive.' Poor Mrs Roberts spent several anxious days before she learned that her husband was safe.

The British army, having marched into the mountains and done what they had set out to do, now turned and marched back again. And so the campaign ended. It was only another minor Frontier affair: 15 British officers, 34 British soldiers and 189 native troops killed; 24 British officers, 118 British soldiers and 541 native soldiers wounded. It was all over in less than three months.

No medal was issued for this campaign, but the survivors were issued a clasp to their India General Service Medal inscribed 'Umbeyla'. Although John Ayde called it 'a very interesting campaign', the rest of the world forgot the incident, except perhaps the Akhund of Swat and his followers.

English-speaking people found in the sound of 'the Akhund of Swat' something both poetic and amusing. Curiously, the most lasting result of the campaign was to make the Akhund and his country famous as symbols of outlandish peoples and remote places no one had ever heard of and ordinary people had no interest in. They were far away and funny. Of the many poems, perhaps the best known is Edward Lear's *The Akond of Swat*:

> Who, or why, or which or what
> Is the Akond of Swat?
> Is he tall or short, or dark or fair?
> Does he sit on a stool or a sofa or a chair, or SQUAT,
> The Akond of Swat?

George Thomas Lanigan wrote a mock threnody when the Akhund died. Across the Atlantic the Akhund of Swat seemed even more remote, and the American poet Eugene Field asked:

> Now the Ahkoond of Swat is a vague sort of man
> Who lives in a country far over the sea;
> Pray tell me, good reader, if tell me you can,
> What's the Ahkoond of Swat to you folks or to me?

As the frontiers of Empire expanded, Britain's soldiers were called to ever more curious places and the fighting seemed more and more remote to those who never left England and who were more concerned about Parliamentary Reform, the Corn Laws and the perennial Irish Question. These odd little wars hardly seemed real, and certainly those who stayed at home made little attempt to understand them. They were, they said contemptuously, 'Foreign Office wars', 'Colonial wars'; or not real wars at all but simply 'nigger smashing'.

15

AFRICA

1863-68

THE years 1863–66 were busy ones for the British Army: In addition to the Umbeyla Campaign, the Doaba Field Force carried on operations against rebellious peoples in the Peshawar valley, while on the North-East Frontier there was an expedition to remote Bhutan; in New Zealand the Second Maori War began; there was an insurrection of freed slaves in Jamaica in 1865, and in the same year there was an expedition into the interior of Arabia from Aden to punish some disorderly tribes; in 1866 there was a fracas on the American–Canadian border when armed Irish-. American Fenians tried to invade Canada from the United States. The Royal Navy was active, too, and there were fights with the Japanese when a combined fleet of British, American, French and Dutch ships bombarded and destroyed the Nagato batteries in the straits of Shimonoseki in retaliation for the Japanese practice of firing on all foreign ships that approached their shores.

In the first thirty years of Queen Victoria's reign most of the little wars were fought in Asia, but as the century progressed the fighting shifted more and more to Africa. When Queen Victoria mounted the throne in 1837 Africa was still the dark continent, its rivers unexplored, its tribes unknown and its potentials unrealized. By 1867 explorers such as Burton, Speke, Grant, Livingstone,

Barth and Baker had found that Africa could be penetrated, and their discoveries created a tremendous interest in the continent; politicians, diplomatists and merchants began to consider its opportunities; representatives of various European government were sent there, and then, of course, there was soon a need for soldiers.

The west coast of Africa had been known to Europeans for centuries, and natives of this area supplied the slaves for the New World, but little evidence of European civilization was to be found there. A lack of good harbours, the prevalence of disease-carrying insects, the uncomfortable climate and the inhospitable jungles just behind the coast all combined to make this part of the world unpopular with Europeans. Most of the slave-hunting and gold-gathering was done by the Africans themselves, who sold both to European traders perched in little forts and 'factories' (trading posts) stationed at irregular intervals along the coast.

No one ever had a good word to say about the coastal Africans, the middlemen in the slave trade, who adopted the worst aspects of European culture and lived in fear of the more virile and vigorous tribes in the jungle behind them. But on the Gold Coast the Fanti tribe had for generations served as a thin layer of quaking humanity between the warlike British and the equally warlike Ashantis. The Ashantis were a large, brave, bloodthirsty, well-organized tribe, living just inland from the coast in what is today called Ghana. Their capital was Kumasi, 125 miles from the coast, where the King of the Ashantis ruled from a stool of gold. The Ashanti nation was expanding in all directions, just as the British in their larger sphere were expanding their Empire, and it was inevitable that the two would clash in an unequal struggle.

Although there had been several minor fights in 1806, 1811 and 1814, the first employment of British troops against the Ashanti warriors came in 1823 when Sir Charles Macarthy, the British governor at Cape Coast Castle, launched a punitive expedition against them. When the two armies came close, Sir Charles ordered the band to play 'God Save the King' while he stood at attention in the jungle, confidently expecting the Ashantis to join him. Instead they attacked, and Sir Charles's West Indian regiment and Fanti allies were soundly defeated. Sir Charles was killed and his skull was taken to Kumasi where in future it was displayed annually at the Yam Festival.

Wars with the Ashantis were to go on into the twentieth century, but in the numbering of them the one started by Sir Charles is generally ignored and the numbers started with the 'war' of 1863–64. Because the British were militarily weak on the Gold Coast, it was the custom to return to the king of the Ashantis all runaways from his domains, but in 1862 Governor Richard Pine refused to return a slave boy and an old man who had stolen a gold nugget. The Ashanti king was patient and tried to reason with the British governor, but at last, failing to get satisfaction, he sent his warriors into the British protectorate in April 1863 and burned thirty villages. Pine wrote to the Duke of Newcastle, Secretary for the Colonies, describing the situation and adding,

I will not conceal from your Grace the earnest desire that I entertain that a final blow shall be struck at Ashanti power, and the question set at rest for ever as to whether an arbitrary, cruel and sanguinary monarch shall be for ever permitted to insult the British flag, and outrage the laws of civilization.

Pine needed British troops to crush the Ashantis and begged Newcastle to send him some, but the Government was not yet concerned enough to act and Pine was left to carry on his war with the West Indian troops he already had. West Indian regiments were used on the west coast of Africa because they were considered best able to withstand the climate. Pine sent six companies to the Pra River, the border between the British Protectorate and Ashantiland, where they built stockades and a bridge and then returned to the coast, having unaccountably lost all their guns and most of their ammunition and stores. In the 'First' Ashanti War neither side fired a shot at the other. Real war came to the Gold Coast ten years later.

On the other side of the continent trouble was brewing between Britain and another strong African kingdom. In January 1864 the

Emperor Theodore of Abyssinia, King of Kings and Chosen of God, imprisoned Captain Charles Cameron, Her Britannic Majesty's Consul to the Abyssinian court, and had him tortured on the rack and flogged with a hippopotamus hide whip. The cause of Cameron's troubles and the war that followed – involving 62,000 men – was an unanswered letter.

The Emperor Theodore was of humble origin. He began his career as a scribe, but soon discovered that banditry was more profitable. He was so successful at this trade that he was crowned emperor at the age of thirty-seven. Unfortunately, he was a madman, but the imbecility of the civil servants in the Foreign Office in London made it difficult to determine who was the more demented. The Emperor had written a letter to Queen Victoria, telling her that he wanted to send a delegation to England to explain how Islam was oppressing good Christians such as the Abyssinians and suggesting that he form an alliance with the Queen against his Muslim neighbours. His letter reached London early in 1863 but someone in the Foreign Office mislaid it, or it was forgotten, or no one could think of an appropriate answer – in any case it was not answered. Angered by this slight, Theodore imprisoned the British consul.

When news of Cameron's predicament reached England, the Foreign Office dug up the Emperor's letter and wrote a reply, which included a statement that the Queen would be grateful if Theodore would release her consul. For obscure reasons, the letter was given to a Turkish Assyriologist named Hormuzd Rassam to deliver. He encountered some difficulty getting to Abyssinia, or in screwing up his courage to go there, and the letter, dated 26 May 1864 was not handed to the Emperor until sometime in January 1866. When Rassam finally arrived he was warmly welcomed by the Emperor – and then joined Cameron in prison.

The situation became odder. Theodore sent another letter to Queen Victoria, this time asking for skilled workmen, some machinery and a munitions manufacturer. Incredibly, a civil engineer and six artisans were actually recruited and got as far as Massawa before the British Government came to the conclusion that somehow things were not all that they ought to be in Abyssinia. The engineer and artisans were halted, and after sitting idle in Massawa for six months were sent home.

In 1850 Palmerston, during a debate in the House of Commons, had said: 'As the Roman in days of old, held himself free from indignity when he could say *civis Romanus sum*, so also a British subject in whatever land he may be, shall feel confident that the watchful eye and the strong arm of England will protect him against injustice and wrong.' A Briton who had stumbled into trouble in an outlandish country could not always feel so confident, even when the Empire was its mightiest. Still, there was a general feeling in Britain that a British subject should be protected and, if need be, rescued wherever he might be. And so, in July 1867, the Secretary of State for India telegraphed the Governor of Bombay to ask how long it would take to mount an expedition to Abyssinia. In August the cabinet decided on war, and in September the Government sent Theodore an ultimatum and prepared for war. The man selected to lead the expedition was another Napier.

In the military history of the nineteenth century it is easy to get lost among the Napiers. There were the Peninsular War Napiers: a set of brothers, three of whom became generals. There was Charles, the conqueror of Sind; William, the historian of the Peninsular War; and George, who became governor of Cape Colony. There was also a fourth brother who was a naval officer and also an historian. Sir William Napier the historian is not to be confused with William Napier the naval captain, who was almost the same age, or with his son of the same name who became a general and married his cousin, the daughter of Charles Napier. Then there was the Napier who was not really a Napier at all: General Edward Delaval Hungerford Elders Napier, whose father was Lieutenant Edward Elders but whose mother later married Admiral Sir Charles Napier, took the name of his stepfather. There was also a General Mark Napier and a General Thomas Napier. In the Navy there was also, in addition to Admiral Charles Napier, an Admiral Henry Napier. Both the Army and the Navy were full of other, less distinguished, Napiers. Even contemporaries became confused. When in 1867 Evelyn Wood, then in Ireland, learned that a General Napier was to lead an expedition to Abyssinia, he hurried to London to offer his services, but was disappointed to 'learn that the expedition's commander was not General Sir William Napier, whom he knew, but General Sir Robert Napier (1810–90) whom he did not know. (Although an engineer, Robert Napier should not be confused with his contemporary of the same name who won distinction as a marine engineer, building in 1860 one of the earliest ironclad warships.) This Napier, unrelated to any of the others, was now about to win his peerage and become Lord Napier of Magdala, not thereafter to be mistaken for yet another Lord Napier (Francis, 9th baron, 1819–98), who was Governor of Madras.

Robert Cornelis Napier's middle name commemorated the storming of Fort Cornelis in Java in 1810, an action in which his father, an artillery major, had been mortally wounded. Born the same year in Ceylon, he was sent to England to be educated and graduated from Addiscombe at sixteen. Two years later he sailed for India as a lieutenant of Bengal Engineers. He was interested in botany, geology, poetry, and painting, particularly landscape painting, and he had ample opportunity to indulge in these pursuits for he did not see active service until the First Sikh War in 1845. Although he started his fighting career rather late in life for a nineteenth-century British officer, he more than made up for it in the years that followed.

In the First Sikh War he fought at Mudki and Ferozeshah and had his horse shot under him in both battles. At Ferozeshah he charged on foot with the 31st Regiment and was severely wounded, but he recovered in time to take part in the battle of Sobraon. In the Second Sikh War he was present at the siege of Multan and the battle of Gujrat. In 1852 he commanded a column in the First Black Mountain Hazara Expedition on the North-West Frontier, and the following year he was with an expedition against the Jowaki Afridis in the Peshawar district. During the Indian Mutiny he was with Outram and Havelock in the first relief of

Lucknow and later took part in the final capture of Lucknow. He saw considerable fighting while chasing rebel bands in Oudh and Gwalior during 1858–59 and he commanded a division in the China War of 1860. He was commander-in-chief of the Bombay army when he was called on to lead the expedition into Abyssinia in 1867.

Napier's married life, like his fighting career, began somewhat late, but once begun it was exceptionally productive. He was nearly thirty when he first married and his wife lived for only nine years, but in that time she bore him six children: three sons (all of whom became soldiers) and three daughters. When he returned from the China War, Napier, then fifty years old, remarried. His wife, the daughter of a major-general, gave him nine more children – six sons (three of whom became soldiers) and three daughters. All but one of these fifteen children survived childhood.

Napier had apparently learned sometime during his career that generals are usually only mildly censored for overspending, but that they are never forgiven for losing battles. He warned his superiors in London and India that the Abyssinian expedition would be expensive, but they preferred not to believe him. What was envisaged in London was simply a dash into the wilds of Abyssinia, to snatch from the hands of a barbarous king his European prisoners, and then a quick return. The Duke of Cambridge wrote to Napier telling him that 'what is desired here is that a flying column or a succession of flying columns should be pushed forward and operate to the front, so as to make a dash if possible and finish the business before the rains set in'. But the Duke and the other officers at the Horse Guards were unfamiliar with the rugged terrain of Abyssinia, which was ill-suited to a mad dash strategy. Napier wisely did not attempt it. Instead he laid elaborate plans for moving his army into the heartland of the country, and he prudently provided sufficient supplies to maintain them while they were there. The expedition eventually required the services of 13,000 British and Indian troops, hordes of servants and workers, 291 ships of all sizes and 36,000 camels, horses, elephants and donkeys.

The great lesson the British ought to have learned twenty years earlier from the Crimean War – that logistics are as important as the number and quality of the fighting material sent – seems to have been taken to heart by Napier, and he did his best to impress on his superiors the complexities of the transport and supply problems he faced. That he won the war was due to such success as he had in overcoming the objections of his superiors and to his skill in working out the difficult logistic problems involved.

Methods of waging war were changing, and the Abyssinian War of 1867–68 was a transitional war in terms of military science. Some of the troops were armed with breech-loading rifles and some with smooth-bore muzzle-loaders; some were dressed in the new khaki uniforms and some in the traditional red or blue coats; for transport there were locomotives and elephants, steamers and sailing ships. To provide fresh water on a desert shore, condensers and water pumps of the latest design were ordered from the United States, and, for the first time on a British military expedition, there was a photographic unit to reproduce maps in the field.

As Wood had discovered when he applied to join the expedition, it was Napier's intention to fight the war primarily with troops from India. There were Sherwood Foresters, Dragoon Guards and Royal Artillery, as well as a Naval Brigade with rockets, but most of the troops were from Indian regiments: Bengal cavalry, Madras sappers and miners, Bombay native infantry, and a regiment of the Sind Horse. There was, however, one interesting European regiment which was to play a prominent role in the fighting: the 33rd Foot, later the Duke of Wellington's (West Riding) Regiment. Although a Yorkshire regiment, it was, as were many of the English regiments, filled with Irishmen. The men of the 33rd were noted for being an exceptionally tough, hard-swearing, hard-drinking lot, and difficult to manage. Also in the regiment were ninety Germans, most of whom spoke little or no English. These were the remnants of a British foreign legion which had been raised for service in the Crimean War but had not been used and had ended up in South Africa instead. Now, for obscure reasons, they were made a part of Her Majesty's 33rd Foot in Abyssinia.

Africa

An unknown young war correspondent named Henry M. Stanley found the army and its activities all very colourful and exotic. Landing at Annesley Bay, near Zula, the point on the African coast where the army was disembarking, he found a 'most extraordinary and novel sight'. It was, he said, 'as if a whole nation had immigrated here and were about to plant a great city on the fervid beach'. Besides the British and Indian soldiers, there were Africans, Turks, Arabs, men of many races, dressed in their exotic costumes and speaking dozens of tongues, all struggling to get the supplies ashore, construct a base camp, build a railway and move the army inland.

Stanley, who three years later was to win fame by finding David Livingstone in the heart of Africa, was not the only newspaper correspondent with the Abyssinian expedition, but such people were still regarded with suspicion and general contempt. Gentlemen sometimes wrote for the press, but newsmen were rarely gentlemen.

Napier divided his army into two unequal divisions. The first was the smaller, but this was the 5,000 man striking force: the second was responsible for maintaining the long line of communications and for putting the first division within striking distance of Magdala, the Emperor Theodore's stronghold. Major Frederick Roberts, after his part in the Umbeyla Expedition, was delighted to find himself selected to go to Abyssinia, but he was disappointed to learn that his job was the difficult and unglamorous one of seeing that men and supplies were expeditiously offloaded from the ships. Although he did not see any action, Napier thought so well of him and of his work that he recommended him for a brevet lieutenant-colonelcy and gave him, rather than one of the fighters, the honour of carrying his final dispatches to London.

Thanks to good planning and fine staff work – exceptionally good by Victorian standards – the striking force was within twelve miles of its goal by 8 April 1868. The fortress of Magdala was perched on a nearly inaccessible mountain range. There are three heights that dominate this range and the Arogee plain below. The closest of these to the advancing army was a flat-topped mountain called Fahla, and there Theodore established his first line of defence. It was from here that he watched with fury in his heart the lines of British and Indian troops tramping into the heartland of his country.

Osborn Wilkinson referred to the Abyssinian War as 'that most extraordinary and faultless campaign'. But well planned though it was, it was not a faultless campaign, for the biggest battle of the war was fought because on 9 April Napier allowed his unguarded baggage train to pass into the Arogee plain directly under the Abyssinian guns on the heights of Fahla. Napier saw the error just in time. As the Abyssinians swarmed down the slopes towards the baggage train, he ordered the 23rd Punjab Pioneers to move to their defence. The Naval Brigade brought its rockets into play and the first major battle of the war was begun. The Abyssinians charged with considerable élan, but the breech-loading Snider-Enfield rifles of the British were more than a match for the double-barrelled percussion muskets of the Abyssinian warriors. By the end of the day there were 700 Abyssinian dead and an additional 1,200 wounded on the field of battle. On the British side, only twenty men were wounded, two fatally. As Henry M. Stanley rolled up in his buffalo robe by the camp fire that night he heard the sounds of animals around him: 'In ravenous packs, the jackals and hyaenas had come to devour the abundant feast spread out by the ruthless hand of war.'

King Theodore now decided to open negotiations. He sent a delegation, which included some of the European prisoners, to discuss what terms he could get. Napier, although anxious about the fate of the prisoners, set forth harsh conditions: the prisoners must be released, Magdala given up and Theodore himself must unconditionally surrender, though he was promised fair treatment. King Theodore was enraged when he heard these terms and threatened to execute all his European prisoners. When he had calmed down he decided to release them, to see if this would satisfy Napier.

When the prisoners, and even the European artisans Theodore

had employed, were safe in the British camp, Napier was much relieved and wrote to his wife: 'It is not easy to express my gratitude to God for the complete success as regards the prisoners.' There were forty-nine prisoners in all, or perhaps fifty (depending on how one counts), for the day after their arrival in Napier's camp a Mrs Moritz gave birth to a son. He was christened Theodore.

The soldiers were unimpressed by the prisoners they had come so far to rescue. 'I must say, I think they are a queer lot, taken as a whole,' said one of Napier's aide-de-camps. 'The rag-tag and bob-tail they have with them in the shape of followers etc., are wonderful to behold. They have about twenty servants of each sort, and the idea of being able to move with less than three mules for baggage seems to Mr Rassam as utterly impractical.'

Napier sent the former captives to the rear and prepared to assault Magdala. Theodore had watched with despair the relentless march of Napier's column towards him. Perhaps to prove to himself that he was not really powerless, he spent a night killing hundreds of Abyssinian prisoners, some of whom were thrown, still in chains, over a precipice.

Magdala was a fortress perched on an eyrie rising 300 feet above a plateau. On three sides there were unscaleable, precipitous cliffs but on the eastern side the land rose in three terraces, each covered with batches of straw-thatched conical houses. The attack on the fortress began at nine o'clock on the morning of 13 April 1868, led by a company of Royal Engineers and the 33rd Foot. As they moved up the difficult slopes, thousands of women, children and unarmed Abyssinians came streaming down.

The only practical plan of assault on the fortress itself was a frontal attack up a narrow path and through the main gate. Had the fortress been resolutely defended the British would have had a difficult, if not impossible, task and would certainly have suffered terrible losses. As Napier said later, 'If simply old women had been at the top and, hiding behind the brow, had thrown down stones, they would have caused any force a serious loss.' But fortunately Theodore was now completely demoralized and only a few hundred uncertain followers remained with him. Even so, the British found it difficult enough.

The assault plan was good and seemed practicable. First, two companies of the 33rd Regiment were to storm up the narrow path to the foot of the cliff and then fan out and direct a hot fire on the wall's defenders while a company of Royal Engineers and a company of Madras Sappers and Miners passed through them, rushed up the path to the walls with scaling ladders and powder charges, blew in the gate and scaled the walls. Six companies of the 33rd would then quickly follow, charging through the gate and over the walls. The rest of the troops were to be in ready reserve behind them. In the event, all went exactly according to plan – except that when the sappers reached the gate it was discovered they had forgotten to bring powder charges and scaling ladders!

The sappers set to work on the gate with crowbars, but the gate was massive; it would not move. Some of the 33rd started around the right side of the wall to try to find another way into the fortress. A tall private named Bergin asked a drummer boy to give him a lift up the twelve-foot-high wall. Private Bergin was too heavy for the drummer, so they reversed roles and Bergin heaved Drummer Magner to the top of the wall with the help of his rifle butt under the boy's buttocks. Magner then reached down and helped Private Bergin up. While Bergin opened fire on every black face in sight, Drummer Magner helped up more men of the 33rd. Young Ensign Walter Wynter, carrying the regimental colours, described how he got to the top of the wall: 'It was a tough pull up, but I was hardly ever on my feet as the men took me and the colours in their arms and passed us on to the front . . . I shall never forget the exhilaration of that moment, the men firing and shouting like madmen.' This was the last time the 33rd ever carried its colours into battle.

There was little serious resistance after this, and both the Queen's and the regimental colours were soon flying from the highest point in the fortress and the men of the 33rd quickly discovered Theodore's large stock of arrack. It seems almost incredible that in this capture of what ought to have been an impregnable fortress only two officers and thirteen other ranks were wounded. The Emperor Theodore shot himself with a pistol which had been sent to him in happier days by Queen Victoria. Napier ordered the destruction of Theodore's fifteen smooth-bore cannon and the walls of Magdala's fortress. The fortress was never rebuilt. One enormous mortar, Theodore's pride, was too heavy to be destroyed so it was simply toppled off its carriage – and there it has lain to this day.

The army now began the long march back to the coast. By 18 June 1868 all the men and animals had embarked at Zula, and by the end of the next day there was not a British soldier or ship to be seen. And so, as the *Illustrated London News* said, 'the military expedition to Abyssinia, so reluctantly determined upon, so carefully organized, so wonderfully successful, has come to a close'. The Abyssinians were left to stew in their own juice – which they did. For years afterwards, minor princes and chiefs battled for supremacy in the power vacuum left by Theodore's death.

In England there were some complaints about the cost of the expedition: Parliament had voted £2,000,000 for the war, but it had cost £8,600,000. Disraeli, however, said that 'money is not to be considered in such matters: success alone is to be thought of'. The cost in human life was astonishingly small: only thirty-five Europeans were killed and 333 badly wounded or seriously ill. Losses among the Indian troops were somewhat higher, but not much.

Among the loot brought back by the conquering army was the Emperor Theodore's gold crown. Sixty-eight years later, in 1936, George V returned it to Abyssinia and presented it to Haile Selassie. A number of scholars had accompanied the expedition and there was more cultural loot than usual, including more than 500 valuable manuscripts. Also brought back to England was the Emperor Theodore's ten-year-old son, Alamayu, who was sent to Rugby. He died eight years later.

As was the custom, Napier was sounded out as to the nature of the reward he would like and he indicated that he thought a

peerage would be in order. There was some discussion in high
circles about the propriety of this, particularly as Hope Grant
had not been ennobled for winning the China War. But Disraeli
told the Queen that

History will place the Abyssinian expedition in a higher and more
enduring position than the China War. So well planned, so quietly
and thoroughly executed, the political part so judiciously managed,
the troops so admirably handled during the long, trying march, the
strength of Anglo-Indian organization so strikingly demonstrated in the
eyes of Europe, wiping out all the stories of Crimean blundering – the
Abyssinian expedition stands apart, and merits, Mr Disraeli thinks,
perhaps an exceptional reward.

Robert Napier received not only his peerage, but a cornucopia of
other honours as well: he was made a Knight Grand Commander
of the Star of India and a Knight Grand Cross of the Bath; he
was thanked by Parliament and granted a pension; he was given
the freedom of London and made an honorary citizen of Edinburgh; he was appointed honorary colonel of the 3rd London
Rifles; Oxford gave him an honorary degree and the Royal Society
elected him a Fellow. Soon after he was made Commander-in-
Chief in India. He fought no more battles, but he lived on to
become a field-marshal and he died in 1890 of influenza in London.

No sooner had the Abyssinian War ended than trouble broke out
anew in one of the farthest corners of the Empire: in New
Zealand in 1868 the Third Maori War began.

William Fitzherbert, New Zealand's Colonial Treasurer, speaking at a dinner in his honour in London, said, 'Remembering
what sacrifices England has recently made to liberate some twenty
Europeans from captivity in Abyssinia, I can never believe that
she will remain indifferent to the agony of a young colony where
not only men, but women and children, are exposed to the brutal
tortures of the cruel Maoris.' But she did.

There had been intermittent fighting with the Maoris for more
than a decade; in fact, since colonists first began arriving in numbers on these beautiful but remote islands. The three numbered

Maori wars were merely periods of exceptional activity and crisis in a running struggle as Europeans, mostly British, wrested the land from the natives: the intelligent, brave and warlike Maoris. These almost-forgotten wars are among the most disgraceful episodes in British imperial history for they sprang from stark, naked, unabashed greed.

The cause of the fighting was always the same: land. The Europeans wanted it and were even willing to pay for it, but most of the Maoris simply did not want to part with it. The Maori, of whatever tribe, always had a special affection for his tribal land; it was his most treasured possession. 'The blood of man is the land,' said a Maori proverb. By the Treaty of Waitangi the colonists had guaranteed the Maori the undisputed possession of his lands for as long as he wanted them. But the ever-increasing number of colonists – rising from 59,413 in 1858 to 218,637 in 1867 – also wanted land.

Disputes about land always ended in fighting. There were atrocities. Soon it was war. The New Zealanders called on the mother country for help, but, far from offering support, the British government announced that in accordance with a self-reliance policy it had established in respect to colonies it intended to withdraw the one Imperial regiment in New Zealand: the 18th Foot (later the Royal Irish, disbanded in 1922). There were screams of terror from the New Zealanders.

The British Government had not favoured the idea of colonizing New Zealand in the first place, and the Colonial Office had strongly disapproved of the policy adopted by the New Zealand colonial government of confiscating the Maoris' land. The colonists now outnumbered the Maoris and they were considered big enough to take care of themselves. Lord Granville put the matter succinctly and bluntly: 'the present distress of the colony arises mainly from two circumstances: the discontent of the natives consequent on the confiscation of their land, and the neglect by successive governments to place on foot a force sufficiently formidable to overawe that discontent'.

In spite of the uproar concerning the announced withdrawal of the 18th Regiment, it was, after some delay, withdrawn. In spite of the colonists' fears, when the last detachment of the regiment left New Zealand on 24 February 1870 the Maori wars ended. The colonial forces did, after all, defeat the Maoris. The fighting continued until the Maoris had been decimated and the Europeans had taken all the land they wanted. But even when the fighting ended the New Zealanders still lived in fear, while the Maoris still lived with the fading hope that they would one day regain their land. As late as 1928 a Maori was quoted as saying: 'We have been beaten because the *Pakeha* [European] outnumbers us in men. But we are not conquered or rubbed out, and not one of these *Pakeha* can name the day we . . . sued for peace. The most that can be said is that on such and such a date we left off fighting.' Today the Maoris are on the increase, and they are now, finally, as numerous as they were 100 years ago, but they have less than a sixteenth of their original land holdings. Their hopes and the New Zealanders' fears are ended. All live in peace under a socialist government.

16

WOLSELEY: RED RIVER AND ARMY REFORM

1870–73

SOME years are more eventful than others. Some seem more full of history's milestones; they contain more beginnings and endings. The year 1870 was such a year, for in it a remarkable number of extraordinary things happened. The end of an era was marked by the deaths of Charles Dickens, Alexandre Dumas and Robert E. Lee, and by the conclusion of the war little Paraguay fought with the combined forces of Brazil, Argentina and Uruguay. But 1870 was above all a year of beginnings: John D. Rockefeller founded the Standard Oil Company and B. F. Goodrich started his rubber company; Henry M. Stanley set out to find Livingstone in the heart of Africa; Heinrich Schliemann started digging in the ruins of Troy; the Americans began the construction of Brooklyn Bridge; compulsory education began in England; and in the United States, with a population of only 38½ million, 22 per cent of whom were illiterate, four important universities were founded. It was also the year in which Wagner wrote *Die Walküre*, diamonds were discovered in the Orange Free State, the Vatican Council proclaimed the Dogma of Infallibility, and Italy was at last unified.

Most of these happenings were more important to future generations than the Franco-Prussian War of that year or the question of who would sit on the throne of Spain, but they did not seem so at the time. The crushing defeat which the Prussians inflicted on the French, the downfall of Napoleon III and the siege of Paris.were the events watched with the closest attention by the civilized world. The ease with which the Prussian army marched into France was a frightening sight to the British and alarmed them – as it was to do again in 1914 and again in 1940 and may yet again. Fear of a war on the continent caused British politicians and soldiers to look at their own army and to make comparisons with the new weapons and methods of the Prussians. Many thought that the army needed some drastic reforms.

Throughout the great British Empire all was relatively calm in 1870. Only in Canada was there trouble: an army of Irish-American Fenians attacked Canada from Vermont and a half-breed in Manitoba led a rebellion and tried to form a republic.

After the Irish famine of 1848, millions of Irish fled to the United States. Unlike most other immigrants, they brought their politics with them, becoming even more Irish and more politically minded in the new world than they had been in the old – and hating the British even more. The Fenian movement, dedicated to the establishment of a republic in Ireland, was popular among Irish-Americans, although not so popular in Ireland itself. It is difficult to understand how the Fenians reasoned that they could free Ireland by attacking Canada, but attack they did – and more than once.

On the night of 31 May 1866 a body of 1,500 Fenians, many of them jobless Irish-American veterans of the Civil War, crossed the Niagara River from Buffalo and landed at Fort Erie. There were some ill-fought battles between them and Canadian militia before they were defeated and returned home. In May 1870 there was another invasion of Fenians, this time from Vermont into Quebec. They were soundly beaten in a battle on the Trout River, not far from Montreal. Again, the survivors retreated to the United States. Fortunately these affairs did not draw either the British or the American governments into rash acts which might have led to a major conflict. The Fenians had to be delicately handled by the

American government because of the sympathy they generated among the strong Irish voting block, but the British understood the position of the American politicians and serious repercussions were avoided.

More serious than the threat of the Fenians was a curious revolt which took place in the wooded wilds of western Canada. The Hudson's Bay Company claimed sovereignty over vast, ill-defined areas of North America. In November 1869 the Company surrendered all of its rights in the area known as Prince Rupert's Land to the Dominion of Canada for £300,000. On 15 July 1870 this was declared a province of Canada: Manitoba. Unfortunately, a number of the inhabitants of this new province, principally the French-speaking people living in the Red River Area, did not want to be Canadians.

John Macdonald, Canada's first prime minister, called the inhabitants of the Red River Settlement 'miserable half-breeds'. Many were indeed half-breeds. Called Métis, they had a strong French and Roman Catholic culture and they resented being taken over by British, English-speaking, mostly protestant Canadians. One of them, a man named Louis Riel, who had received some education and had lived for a time in the United States, organized a 'National Committee' to oppose the Canadian government. He and a small group of men seized Fort Garry, a Hudson's Bay Company fortified station on land that is now a part of the city of Winnipeg, and turned back the Canadian lieutenant-governor who had been sent out to govern the province. According to Garnet Wolseley, it was the French Catholic priests who were to blame for the revolt. He claimed that they 'openly preached from their altars resistance to the Canadian government', and that Riel's rebel flag had been made by local nuns.

Riel dispatched a delegation to Ottawa to demand that the Métis be allowed to retain their customs, language and religion, and these demands, which were supported by the French Canadians from Quebec, were granted by a sympathetic government. In the meantime, however, Riel had not only established himself in power but had exercised that power by executing a British-

Canadian surveyor. When this became known, British Canada was incensed and it was decided that a military expedition must be sent to quell the rebellion. Colonel Garnet Wolseley, then the quartermaster-general in Canada, was selected to lead it.

Wolseley was given an adequate force to deal with the rebellion: a battalion of the 60th (King's Royal Rifle Corps), two battalions of Canadian militia, and some Royal Engineers – in all, about 1,400 men. He also had four 7-pounder guns and an able assistant: Captain Redvers Buller (1839–1908), who had served in India and in the China War of 1860. Wolseley later said of him: 'I think he was the only man with us of any rank who could carry a 100-pound barrel of pork over a portage on his back. . . . Full of resource, and personally absolutely fearless, those serving under him trusted him fully.'

It was while in Canada that Wolseley began to compile a list of 'the best and ablest soldiers I knew'. This was the start of what was to be known as the 'Wolseley ring' or 'Wolseley gang'. Buller's name went on the list as did that of another young officer: Lieutenant William Butler (1838–1910), a tall, strong, intelligent Irishman from Tipperary who had served in Burma, India and the Channel Islands, where he met and became a friend of Victor Hugo. He was in Ireland on leave when he heard of the Red River Expedition being formed. He at once wired Wolseley: 'Remember Butler 69th regiment.' Wolseley's staff was filled, but he gave Butler a special assignment: he sent him through the United States and up into the Red River country to find out the situation and then come down river to meet Wolseley's advancing forces and report. Butler not only got to Fort Garry, but interviewed Riel himself, and then came down to meet Wolseley on 4 August 1870 at Fort Frances. Wolseley said of him: 'In genius and in inventive power, as it can be employed in all the various phases of war, he is second to none.' Butler also admired Wolseley, believing that he possessed 'the best and most brilliant brain I ever met in the British army'.

This was Wolseley's first independent command, and it was marked by the careful preparation before the start that was to characterize all his campaigns. His route from Toronto would be ninety-four miles by rail to Collingwood, on Georgian Bay; then by steamer across Lake Huron and through St Mary to Lake Superior and up to Thunder Bay, a total distance of 535 miles. Then the real journey would begin. The route at first was overland, forty-eight miles to Shebandowan Lake, and then by boat for 310 miles, with seventeen portages, some of more than a mile, on Rainy River to Lake of the Woods, north across Lake of the Woods to Rat Portage, where the Winnipeg River runs into the lake, and up that beautiful, dangerous and difficult river, making about thirty portages, nearly 300 miles, to Fort Alexander on Lake Winnipeg. Then, finally, down the Red River to Fort Garry. In all, about 650 miles from Thunder Bay, through land known only to Indians and the employees of the Hudson's Bay Company.

From Thunder Bay all supplies would have to be transported with the expedition, as few provisions could be obtained along the way. Each boat was to carry eight or nine soldiers and two or three Indians or Canadian voyageurs (men skilled in the use of canoes and small boats) as well as supplies, ammunition and sixty days' provisions: salt pork, beans, preserved potatoes, flour, biscuit, salt, tea and sugar. No liquor, for 'it was a strictly teetotal undertaking', Wolseley said. Among the supplies were entrenching tools, cooking pots, blankets, tin plates, boat builder's tools, white lead for patching holes in the boats, and axes. The standard axe issued to the British army at this time was of ancient design; the Canadian woodsmen laughed when they saw them. Wolseley thought the pattern might have been handed down from Saxon times. He wisely purchased serviceable double-wedge American axes for his expedition.

Wolseley also provided 'mosquito oil' and 'veils' for his men to protect them from the black flies, mosquitoes and sand flies they would encounter. His men seldom used either for the purposes intended, but the veils came in handy to strain the scum from lake waters and the mosquito oil was burned in lamps.

The trip was long and arduous and they had an unusual number of rainy days, but the men thrived on the exercise and the fresh air. Boats overturned, but no one was drowned. Wolseley himself travelled in the lead of his brigade, descending the Winnipeg River in a birch-bark canoe manned by Iroquois Indians whom he considered 'the most daring and skilful of the Canadian voyageurs'. He found the experience exhilarating. By 20 August all of the regulars of the brigade had reached Fort Alexander. Their clothes were in tatters, but they were bronzed and healthy; there was not a sick man among them.

On 21 August the battalion of regulars set out in a fleet of fifty boats on Lake Winnipeg for the mouth of the Red River. Three days later they landed at Point Douglas, just two miles above Fort Garry on the left bank of the Red River, and at once advanced to the attack through a heavy rain and deep mud. The fort consisted of a high stone-walled square with a circular tower at each corner; the wooden houses of the village of Winnipeg were then a half-mile north. When all were in position, Wolseley's troops stormed the fort. The result was anticlimactic. The place was deserted. Riel, forewarned, had fled to the United States – to return fourteen years later, start another rebellion and be hanged for his pains.

It was a most successful campaign in every respect: it had accomplished its objective, not a life had been lost, it had exercised the troops, several good officers had gained invaluable experience, and it had not cost much money – the campaign expenses came to less than £100,000. Wolseley, who had noted that when he was at Fort Garry he had been as far from a telegraph office as Caesar had been from Rome when he landed in Britain, attributed the success and economy of the expedition to 'the fact that it was planned and organized far away from all War Office influence and meddling'.

All his life Wolseley railed against abuses, inefficiencies and anachronisms in the army and strove mightily to develop a modern professional army. He was able to do a great deal towards this end, but it was a civilian who never served a day in the Army and who had an intense dislike of all violence who was responsible for the most far-reaching reforms ever made in the British army.

Wolseley: Red River and Army Reform

Edward Cardwell (1813–86) was a brilliant man. At twenty-two he took a first class both in mathematics and in classics at Oxford. He first entered parliament in 1842 at the age of twenty-nine, where he attached himself personally and politically to Sir Robert Peel. He served in a number of cabinet posts – President of the Board of Trade, Chief Secretary for Ireland, Chancellor of the Duchy of Lancaster, and Colonial Secretary – until in 1868 he became Secretary of State for War in Gladstone's first cabinet, a post he held for more than five years, during which he took up the British army, shook it soundly and scraped off much of its long-accumulated moss.

Among 'Cardwell's Army Reforms' were the abolition of the system of purchasing commissions and promotions, the introduction of short service for soldiers, the formation of a veteran reserve, the abolishment of flogging in peacetime (it was completely abolished as a punishment in 1880), the linking of regiments to counties, the withdrawal of Imperial troops from self-governing dominions unless they were paid for, a retirement system for officers, improvements in the military education of all ranks, and, perhaps the most difficult task of all, he brought the Commander-in-Chief under the control of the War Office.

The Duke of Cambridge, grandson of George III and the Queen's first cousin, had been a major-general since the age of twenty-six and was Commander-in-Chief of the army from 1856 until 1895, and he was bitterly opposed to all change in any form. In his one war, the Crimean, he had shown himself to be brave but over-excitable. He did not understand strategy or even tactics, but he was an acknowledged expert on close-order drill. He believed discipline, the regimental system and esprit de corps to be the foundation stones of the British army and he regarded Cardwell's reforms as a threat to these fundamentals. He was supported by most of the senior generals and by many other officers who had a vested interest in the existing system, who honestly believed that reforms would be ruinous to the army, and who insisted that the army must follow the precepts of the great Duke of Wellington in spite of the existence of improved weapons which

185

demanded changes in tactics, strategy and military organization to exploit them and the need to provide defence against them.

On 1 March 1869 the Queen wrote to Cardwell 'on some things connected with the Army which give her considerable uneasiness'. One of the principal points in her letter was the question of the status and prestige of the Duke of Cambridge:

> She cannot shut her eyes to the fact that a disposition exists in some quarters to run down the C-in-C. and generally to disparage the military authorities as obstacles to all improvements in our Army administration.
>
> So far from this being the case, the Duke of Cambridge has always acted most cordially, as the Queen is sure Mr Cardwell will have already found, with successive Secretaries of State, in promoting and giving effect to all well-considered measures of improvement; and ever since he has been at the head of the Army he has deserved the Queen's entire confidence, and is entitled to her best support.
>
> Anything that could tend to lower his position in the eyes of the public, would, the Queen feels, be a misfortune as regards the public service: and she is confident that Mr Cardwell will give his sanction to no measures likely to have that effect. The Queen is led to say this now, feeling very strongly on the subject, before Mr Cardwell makes his statement in the House, lest in admitting the advantage of having the military and civil departments of the Army under the same roof, he should inadvertently commit himself to what the Queen would feel herself bound to resist, as likely to produce the effect she so much deprecates – she means the removal of the military departments of the Army from the Horse Guards to Pall Mall. Such a step could not fail to damage the position of the C.-in-C.

At this time Cardwell assured her that he would 'lend no countenance to any attempt which shall be made to disparage [the Duke's] authority'. As for moving the Duke out of the Horse Guards, he had not even thought of it. Yet, some sixteen months later, on 28 June 1870 the Queen reluctantly signed an Order in Council which made the Duke a subordinate of Cardwell and he was moved out of the Horse Guards.

The Queen was somewhat more successful in imposing her will on the navy, for in June 1869 the First Lord of the Admiralty was able to assure the Queen that as soon as the orders could be printed they would be sent out directing that in future 'moustaches should not be worn without beards'.

In 1871, in spite of a tremendous political uproar, Cardwell was able to abolish the purchase system in the army. The system, which applied to infantry and cavalry officers below the rank of major general, had many obvious disadvantages: it held down many poor officers of merit and, perhaps worst of all, it permitted rich men of little merit to succeed, the prime example being Lord Cardigan (the fool who led the charge of the Light Brigade at Balaclava) who purchased regiments as though they were toy soldiers.

It is perhaps more necessary today to explain the advantages of the system. There was, of course, the argument that officers had to be gentlemen and gentlemen were more likely to be found among those who had money. But a stronger argument was the vested financial interest of every company and field grade officer in his rank. It was, after all, his pension fund. He had usually purchased each step of his rank, selling his old rank as he moved up, so that when he retired he could get back all, and often more, than he had paid. There was an official price list, but officers in the most desirable regiments could sometimes obtain more than double the approved sum. Then, too, the system was not inflexible. Some deserving but poor officers managed to advance without purchase: Hope Grant, for example, obtained both his majority and his lieutenant-colonelcy without purchase. To abolish the purchase system was expensive, for the Government had, in a sense, to buy back the army from its officers.

While the Duke of Cambridge and his generals were against Cardwell and his reforms, the Secretary for War had the backing of Gladstone and also of a small group of brilliant and literate young officers – all under forty – each of whom was to win fame before the end of the century: Colonel Garnet Wolseley, who returned to London after his success in Canada, and was soon damned by the Duke of Cambridge as a 'radical Cardwellite', Major George Colley, Major Robert Biddulph, Captain Henry

Brackenbury and Captain Evelyn Baring. They fought a great political campaign.

As Baring rightly said, 'the abolition of the purchase system was the keystone of army reform'. Once that stone was removed, the entire wall of the Wellington-type army came tumbling down and a flood of reforms followed. Cardwell put all branches of the army under three heads: the Commander-in-Chief, the Surveyor General and the Financial Secretary. Cardwell also agreed to a suggestion of the Queen that the right to appoint officers in the militia be taken from the lords-lieutenant and be vested in the Commander-in-Chief.

The British army did not have a general staff until the twentieth century, but Cardwell did change the staff structure. Formerly, every general officer had two key staff officers of equal importance who gave orders in his name: the quartermaster-general and the adjutant-general. At the War Office, Cardwell subordinated the quartermaster-general to the adjutant-general.

From 1815 until 1847, when the army was under the Duke of Wellington, soldiers enlisted for twenty-one years. In 1847 the term of service had been reduced to twelve years. Recruiting difficulties aside, the trouble with the long service enlistments policy was that it failed to provide a trained reserve. Cardwell introduced 'short service' – six years of active duty followed by six years in the reserve – and when he did this all old soldiers shook their heads. Now Cardwell had done it. The army was surely ruined.

The cavalry was too politically and socially powerful for Cardwell to do much with it except to increase its strength from 8,762 to 10,422, but the infantry was drastically reorganized on new principles into what were called 'linked battalions'. Line regiments of infantry had been known by their numbers until Cardwell gave them homes. Most regiments of the line were assigned a county; they had their depots there and took the name of the county. Under the Cardwell system, each regiment was to have two regular battalions, usually one at home and one abroad which were from time to time rotated, and one to three battalions of militia. Thus, the 6th Foot became the Royal Warwickshire Regiment and by 1885, when the system was well ensconced, it had its first battalion in Plymouth and its second battalion in Bengal; its third and fourth battalions were the first and second Warwick Militia. The system worked. It facilitated recruiting and it ensured that battalions sent overseas were largely composed of trained men.

Cardwell did more for the army than give it a better organization and administration; he increased its size and gave it more and better weapons. More than a decade earlier, in 1861, Prince Albert had urged Palmerston to equip the army with breech-loading arms. Now at last the infantry was given modern Martini-Henry rifles. Although European armies were rapidly exchanging their muzzle-loading cannon for breech-loaders and the British themselves had proved the value of the new breech-loaders in the China War of 1860 and in the Abyssinian War, the artillery experts insisted on returning to muzzle-loading guns and, incredibly, this was done. Cardwell could not improve the weapons, but he added about 5,000 men to this arm and increased the number of horsed guns from 180 to 336.

It took more than a decade to bring about all the army reforms. During the years when Wolseley and Cardwell were most busy changing the features of the army, the Empire was at peace – almost. The calm was broken only by some minor campaigns such as the expedition against the Lushais in 1871–72 when soldiers went into the hills of southern Assam to rescue little Mary Winchester, who had been carried off by the Lushais, and to punish the tribesmen for their raids on tea plantations. But then, early in 1873, a mail steamer from West Africa brought disturbing news of trouble with the Ashantis on the Gold Coast.

17

WOLSELEY IN ASHANTILAND

1873–74

THROUGHOUT the last half of the nineteenth century cabinet ministers and civil servants tried to rid Britain of her unprofitable colonies on the African west coast, but they were always prevented from doing so by traders who wanted protection of their interests and by humanitarians who wanted Britain to stop the slave trade and to bring the benefits of intellectual enlightenment, Victorian moral standards and material progress to the Africans. Politicians and bureaucrats complained that the cost of attempting this was too high and that very little of European civilization rubbed off on the natives. Certainly the possession of Gold Coast, Sierra Leone, Lagos and Gambia was not worth the small amount of trade that was carried on in those places. And there was always some kind of trouble. Countless small expeditions were undertaken against one tribe or another, but these were generally launched by officers on the spot using the available West Indian troops, local levies and sometimes sailors off ships on the West African station. Rarely was it necessary to bring in troops from England or other parts of the Empire. But no local force could cope with the fierce Ashantis, and again in 1873 they were causing trouble.

A large Ashanti army, said to number 12,000 men, crossed the Pra river and invaded the British protectorate. They cut a wide swath of destruction and, in June 1873, they moved on Elmina, a coastal fort which the British had recently acquired from the Dutch. Although the fort was inadequately manned by detachments of marines, sailors and West Indian troops, a determined Ashanti attack was beaten off. The Government now reluctantly decided that the proud, barbarous Ashantis must be humbled and their army whipped. As white men died rather quickly on the Gold Coast, the politicians hesitated to commit British troops, hoping that friendly tribesmen under competent British officers could throw back the invaders. In July *The Times* and the *Daily News* advocated sending 'Chinese' Gordon, but on 13 August the Government selected Wolseley to be Administrator and Commander-in-Chief on the Gold Coast.

One month later, when Wolseley and thirty-five carefully selected officers boarded what Wolseley described as 'the most abominable and unhealthy craft I ever made a voyage in' to take them to the Gold Coast, he already had a carefully worked out plan for his campaign. He would first do what he could with levies of coastal Fantis, but he had little hope of succeeding with them. The Fantis were generally unwarlike – cowards, in fact – and he knew that they would have to be strongly reinforced by British regulars. He had already requested that two battalions be specially equipped and kept ready to join him when he needed them. From his studies he had concluded that in the pestilential climate of West Africa military operations could only be undertaken with safety by European troops in the months of December, January and February, the dry season. He therefore planned to make a dash into the country, smash the Ashanti army and make a quick return.

Wolseley's fears about the unhealthiness of the Gold Coast were well-founded. Of the 130 English officers and men in the country at the time of his arrival, only twenty-two were fit for duty. Total British troops in the country – some marines and the 2nd West Indian Regiment – amounted to about thirty officers and 770 other ranks, one-fifth of whom were sick. The country had a bad reputation as 'the white man's grave'; one officer scheduled to go there asked an experienced friend what kit he should take and was told: 'A coffin. It is all you will require.'

None of the officers with Wolseley was dismayed by the difficulties and dangers of fighting savages in a deadly climate; like Wolseley himself, they looked forward only to opportunities for distinguishing themselves. They were an extraordinary group. All were brave: two had won the Victoria Cross and two more would win it before their careers were ended. They were also exceptionally brilliant and literate: instead of the usual shipboard games and the relaxations of shipboard life they read piles of books on West Africa, pored over maps and lectured to each other. Eleven of them eventually reached general officer rank and there were others who obviously would have had they lived long enough. All were relatively young (under forty) and all had been hand-picked by Wolseley, himself the youngest general in the British army. This was the 'Wolseley gang'. Some thought Wolseley's staff was too good for the task at hand and Augustus Anson said he was 'using the finest steel in our army to cut brushwood'.

Wolseley's chief of staff was Lieutenant-Colonel John McNeill (1831–1904), a future major-general who had seen much action in the Indian Mutiny, had won the Victoria Cross in the Second Maori War, and had taken part in the Red River Expedition. Wolseley considered him 'daring, determined, self-confident and indefatigable'. Unfortunately he was to be put out of action in the first battle of the war. Wolseley was standing by a gun that was in action when McNeill came through the bush towards him. His arm was covered with blood and all the muscles and tendons of his wrist had been sliced and stood out like the threads of an unravelled rope. 'An infernal scoundrel out there has shot me through the arm!' he exclaimed indignantly. McNeill had to be sent home, but he survived to fight again in Egypt and in the Sudan.

Wolseley's private secretary was another future major-general: Lieutenant John Frederick Maurice (1841–1912), now on his way to his first war. Maurice is best known today for his writings on military doctrine and history, and it was through one of his first literary efforts that Wolseley heard of him. The second Duke of Wellington offered a prize for the best essay on how a British army could best meet a continental army in the open field. Although Wolseley himself had entered the contest, young Maurice, then a subaltern instructor at Sandhurst, won with a brilliant essay.

Wolseley's military secretary was Captain (later General) Henry Brackenbury (1837 1914), who had served as an artillery officer in the Indian Mutiny and had written a series of articles in support of Cardwell's army reforms. Brackenbury was an ugly man with a pasty face, a straggling moustache and a large, red nose. In common with many officers of stylish regiments, he affected the lisp whereby all r's were pronounced as w's, regiment being pronounced 'wegiment' and his own name becoming 'Bwackenbaywee'. He was an excellent, energetic staff officer and was to write the most complete account of the Ashanti War.

Another military writer on the staff was Captain Robert Home (1837–79) who was Commanding Royal Engineer for the expedition. He possessed an exceptional brain, and was unduly proud of it. Wolseley claimed that 'he had an ineradicable repugnance to admit he was unable to give detailed answers to all questions, on all subjects, whether great or small, that any one put to him'. He doubtless would have become a general but at the age of forty-one, already a colonel, he died of typhus. It was said that Disraeli cried when he learned of his death.

Redvers Buller had returned from Canada to England and was enrolled in the Staff College when Wolseley began to select his staff for the Ashanti War. Buller left the course without finishing it and went to West Africa. William Butler was still in Canada when he heard of the impending Ashanti campaign, but he at once sent off a cable to Wolseley and hurried to England where he found orders for him to join the staff at Cape Coast Castle on the Gold Coast. He reached there on 22 October 1873, just twenty days after Wolseley.

Lieutenant-Colonel Evelyn Wood, able and daring, and accident prone as always, also accompanied Wolseley. He had recently broken his ankle in a hunting accident and his doctor had accidentally given him an overdose of morphine, but he considered himself fit enough for the Ashanti War. Wood's soldier servant wanted to go with him, but when Wood applied for him the application was rejected because 'Mr Secretary Cardwell considers that the climate is particularly fatal to the constitutions of Europeans'. The concern for the soldier was commendable, but no such concern was shown for the officers for whom a campaign was a plum. When young monocled Arthur Eyre applied to go, Wood endorsed his letter of application with a curt, 'the son of a good soldier, his mother is a lady', and young Eyre, only surviving child of a widow, went to the Gold Coast and was shot through the bladder, dying a painful death.

Lieutenant-Colonel George Pomery Colley (1835–81), later a major-general, had been appointed an ensign in the 2nd Foot at the age of sixteen and had subsequently served in South Africa and in the China War of 1860. He was an accomplished artist and a keen scholar with a wide range of interests. He had just had time to complete the writing of a sixty-page article on 'Army' for the ninth edition of the *Encyclopaedia Britannica* before leaving for the Gold Coast.

There were others as well: Lieutenant-Colonel George Greaves, Lieutenant-Colonel Durand Baker and Major Baker C. Russell, all of whom became generals, and Captain C. Barnett, who became a lieutenant-general. Kofi Karikari, the king, or asantehene, of the Ashantis, had to match wits with some of the finest military brains Britain ever produced. He did not have a chance.

To Wolseley's disgust, a great number of war correspondents came out to cover the war, including all the most famous ones: Winwood Reade for *The Times*, G. A. Henty for the *Standard*, and Henry M. Stanley, fresh from his success in finding Livingstone, for the *New York Herald*. Wolseley abhorred war correspondents, 'those newly invented curses to armies, who eat the rations of fighting men and do no work at all'.

One of Wolseley's first acts on reaching the Gold Coast was to demand the assistance of the coastal tribes and he summoned the chiefs to come to him. Some of the most important, fearing the Ashantis more than the British, failed to show up. One replied, 'I have got smallpox today, but will come tomorrow.' The chief of

Ampeene cut off the head of the messenger, and the chief of Essaman sent back an insolent message: 'Come and get me!' Wolseley decided to do just that.

In his *Soldiers' Pocket Book*, a famous but controversial work, Wolseley had recommended that generals give false information to war correspondents in order to deceive the enemy. Following his own advice, he told the newsmen that he was going to move east and then set off down the coast to attack Essaman. He left on the night of 13 October, exactly two months from the day he had been given his command in London.

Leading a force of about 500 West Indian troops, Hausas, and British sailors and marines, he marched off at dawn from Elmina to attack disaffected coastal villages. By noon he had fought a small battle at Essaman and dispersed the hostile natives, but the Europeans were exhausted and Wolseley thought he had done enough for one day. Wood, however, wanted to go on to Ampeene, another five and a half miles down the coast, and he was allowed to proceed with the bulk of the force. After a difficult march through soft sand under a burning sun, he reached Ampeene, only to find that the enemy had fled.

There were small skirmishes as Wolseley and his officers did what they could with the forces available to them locally. However, as Wolseley had suspected, there was little he could do with his Fanti allies, whom he characterized as 'too cowardly to fight their own battles and too lazy, even when well paid, to help those who were risking their lives in their cause'. Wolseley may have been somewhat confused as to who was fighting for whose cause, but one thing was certain: the Fantis had no stomach for fighting Ashantis. In November Wolseley called for three battalions of British troops from England and these were sent out under the command of a Highlander named Archibald Alison, a veteran of both the Crimea and of the Indian Mutiny, where he had lost an arm fighting under Colin Campbell.

So that the European troops would have to spend as little time as possible in the inhospitable climate of West Africa, elaborate preparations were made to get them in and out quickly. The first transports landed in December and by 19 January 1874 the bulk of the troops were camped at their advanced base at Prahsu, seventy miles from the coast, where a bridge 200 feet long had been thrown across the Pra River. Thanks to Wolseley and the energy and efficiency of Major Home, the troops marched in comparative comfort. Working under enormous difficulties, Home had constructed seven stations at roughly ten-mile intervals, each with huts for 400 men, a hospital, storage sheds and a water purifier. Two of these stations also had a bakery and four had abattoirs. A native porter was assigned to every three soldiers to help them carry their equipment, which included veils, respirators and cholera belts. The scarlet coats and rifle green uniforms, even the Highlanders' kilts, were replaced by suits of grey homespun.

The troops had been given courses on how to stay healthy in the bush, and each man was given a dose of quinine before the start of each day's march. So efficient was Wolseley that his name passed into the language for a time: 'All Sir Garnet' meant that all was in perfect order.

Wolseley's force consisted of about 4,000 men: Black Watch, Rifle Brigade, Welch Fusiliers, West Indian troops, 250 sailors, some Hausa artillery, and two regiments of local levies commanded by Wood and Russell. The goal was Kumasi, capital of the Ashanti nation. The original plan was to have two subordinate columns of Africans led by British officers converge on Kumasi, but in the end it was only the main column which reached there in time to fight. Wolseley told his European troops: 'Soldiers and sailors, remember that the black man holds you in superstitious awe. Be cool, fire low, fire slow and charge home.'

The local regiments raised by Wood and Russell contained companies of men from a variety of West Coast tribes and it was often extremely difficult for their officers to maintain any sort of discipline. As his soldiers refused to beat their own tribesmen, Wood employed men from a different tribe to do the flogging, picking men of a tribe who most disliked the tribe of the man to be flogged. Perhaps Wood's best men – or at least the least useless

– were the Hausas, but they, too, caused him trouble. One day at Prahsu he received a letter from Butler:

My Dear Colonel, – The King of Accassi's Queen has been carried off by the Haussas and her chastity is in danger. Express messengers have arrived to announce her detention at Prahsu when tending plantains. Please do what you can to save Her Majesty's honour – or the plantains – for I cannot make out which is rated at the highest figure by the King. I am *en route* to Iribee. Yours in haste,

W. Butler

By 24 January 1874 Wolseley's main force was within thirty miles of Kumasi. The King of the Ashantis sent conciliatory messages, but Wolseley demanded 50,000 ounces of gold, the release of all Fanti prisoners, and important hostages such as the Ashanti queen mother, the heir apparent, and the sons of important chiefs. These demands the king could not fulfil, nor did Wolseley want him to, for he was bent on reaching Kumasi and doing battle.

Wolseley pushed on, and near the village of Amoaful the Ashantis waited for him, the warriors concealed in high undergrowth among tall trees in the traditional Ashanti horseshoe-shaped line of battle. On the morning of 31 January British scouts were ambushed. Two companies of the Black Watch were pushed forward and the battle began.

The Black Watch (42nd Highlanders) saw the heaviest fighting, but all units were engaged as the Highlanders advanced in the centre and the Ashantis tried to envelop the British flanks. The British formation was a large square, but it was a confused jungle battle: units lost contact with each other, the square formation could not be maintained, and the Highlanders complained that the Naval Brigade fired on them.

Wolseley set up his headquarters in a village roughly in the centre of the square and from here he received the reports of his commanders and their requests for reinforcements. He tried to direct the battle, though there was little he could do except pace up and down. H. M. Stanley noted, however, that he retained a 'calm, proud air', even when, early in the afternoon, some

Ashantis broke through and attacked the headquarters. Then surgeons, wounded, guards, staff officers and war correspondents seized their weapons to beat them off.

Colonel Wood was up front and at one point saw that he was being fired upon from several directions. Thinking that the Highlanders were shooting in his direction by mistake, he called out, 'Forty-second. Don't fire this way!' Young Lieutenant Eyre rushed into the bush to investigate. There was a report of a musket and Eyre soon returned. He told Wood quite calmly, 'There are no 42nd men there. The fellow who fired at us is black, and quite naked.'

Shortly afterwards, Wood was wounded. Naturally. Wood never in his life served in a campaign in which he was not injured, if not by the enemy then by himself. This time the head of a nail fired from a musket entered his chest just over his heart. The surgeon thought he would die, but three weeks later he was back in service with his regiment.

The Ashantis finally retreated, but slowly and in good order. The Highlanders captured Amoaful and the village rang with their wild Scots cheers and the wail of their bagpipes. Wolseley pushed on slowly towards Kumasi. The Ashantis broke up into small marauding bands and continued to harass the British line of communications. The Fanti bearers were so terrified by the sight of Ashanti warriors behind the lines that they refused to carry supplies to the front. This caused some delay, but Wolseley put his troops on short rations and pushed on.

There was another battle near the village of Ordahsu and then, late in the afternoon of 4 February, Wolseley's army, led by the Black Watch, entered Kumasi. It was an empty city. The next day the soldiers wandered around, savouring the sights of a barbarous capital where the evidence of human sacrifice was visible in the thousands of skulls piled up in a sacred grove. All the loot left by the fleeing Ashantis was auctioned off; the town was burned; and the palace of the king was blown up by the engineers.

While the king and his golden stool had not been captured and there was no treaty or formal surrender of the Ashanti forces, still it had been a very successful and brilliantly organized expedition. Losses among the troops were only 18 killed by the enemy, 55 killed by disease and 185 wounded – and only £800,000 spent. Major-General Wolseley returned to London and a shower of honours: GCMG, KCB, the thanks of Parliament, a sword of honour from the City of London, and honorary degrees from Oxford and Cambridge. He also received £25,000 from a grateful nation.

18

ROBERTS'S WAR

1878-79

I N the last quarter of the nineteenth century little wars came ever more frequently. There were so many campaigns, military expeditions, revolts suppressed and full-scale wars that no one has ever counted them all. British history books simply ignore most of them. Even at the time, punitive excursions, field forces and minor expeditions were so commonplace that most Britons never knew of them. In the five years following the end of the Ashanti War of 1873-74 there was much fighting in India, Malaya, Afghanistan and southern Africa. In India alone there were no fewer than fourteen military expeditions mounted against such frontier tribes as the Afridis, Utman Khels, Mohmands, Wazirs, Zaimukhts, Marris and Bhitannis. The number of troops employed on these expeditions varied from 280 to 7,400 men. In 1875 British troops were brought in from Hong Kong and Calcutta to conquer the independent state of Perak in the Malay Peninsula and add it to the British Empire. And in what was then called Kaffirland, or Kaffraria, there was another Kaffir war and numerous disturbances calling for military expeditions: the insurrection of Langalibalele was suppressed; Kreli, a Galeka chief in the Transkei, attacked tribes protected by the British and had to be defeated and deposed (the Transkei War); there was the rise of the Gaikas

200

under their famous chief, Sandilli; in Basutoland a chief named Moiroso had to be overcome after he entrenched himself on a mountain and began to make predatory raids; the Transvaal was annexed to the Empire and the Boers were again troublesome. And as if all this was not enough, there was another 'Eastern Crisis' in 1878 and British forces, including Indian troops, were sent to Malta. By 1879 Britain was engaged in two serious little wars at the same time: one in Zululand, where Cetewayo, King of the Zulus, appeared threatening, and the other in Afghanistan.

As was the case in the First Afghan War, the second one was divided into two parts, the first of which was marked by great success. But as the Afghans had a disconcerting habit of not knowing when they were defeated, the second half of the war proved more difficult for the British.

In July of 1878 Wolseley was appointed Lord High Commissioner for Cyprus, which the British had just taken over from the Turks. It was a tame post and he felt uncomfortable in it. When he heard of the impending war in Afghanistan he longed to go, but his application was denied. 'I feel like an eagle that has had its wings clipped,' he wrote in his private journal. Wolseley could not have all the glory, and the hero of the Afghan War was to be a hitherto almost unknown Indian officer, Frederick Sleigh Roberts, known affectionately to his soldiers as Bobs Bahadur.

The Second Afghan War provided Roberts with his first real experience as a commander in battle. As a subaltern he had seen much active service during the Mutiny, winning the Victoria Cross, and he had served on the Umbeyla expedition of 1863, in the Lushai campaign of 1871–72, and in the Abyssinian War, but for most of his career he had been a staff officer with little opportunity for displaying his talents as a commander. He advanced from assistant quartermaster-general to quartermaster-general in Bengal, where his most arduous duties were to prepare for the reception of the Prince of Wales when he visited India in 1875–76 and to arrange for an elaborate durbar to announce on 1 January 1877 that Queen Victoria would henceforth be called the Empress of India in addition to her other titles. Then, in March 1878, he was appointed to the command of the Punjab Frontier Force. He was the right man in the right place at the right time.

Trouble with Afghanistan started – as it had started in 1839 and would again in 1919 – because the Afghans wanted to be left alone and the British, fearing that if they did not influence Afghan policy the Russians would, wanted to meddle in Afghan affairs. The threat of Russia seemed very real to the British. Pushing out their frontier in central Asia, the Russians had annexed Tashkent in 1865, captured Samarkand in 1868 and conquered Khiva five years later. In 1877 they sent a mission to Afghanistan which was warmly received by Amir Shere Ali, third of the seven sons of Dost Muhammad and now the ruler of Afghanistan. The British became greatly alarmed and wanted to send a mission themselves, but Shere Ali would not permit it.

The two main instruments used by the British for controlling the affairs of an Asian country for which no pretext could yet be found for conquering were the offer of a subsidy and a demand that a British resident or envoy or mission be stationed at the court. These tools were successfully used with the native states of India, the subsidy being substantial and the presence of a resident seeming, at first, innocuous. Somehow this did not work in Afghanistan. Shere Ali, whom Lord Lytton described as 'a savage with a touch of insanity', refused to allow a British mission even when his subsidy was cut off, and then, horror of horrors, in August 1878 he signed a treaty with the Russians.

The British then decided that they would send a mission to Kabul whether the amir liked it or not. A mission was formed and set out under an armed escort. It did not get very far. At Ali Musjid, a fort in the Khyber Pass, the advance guard was threatened with attack if it proceeded further and it was thought prudent to return to Peshawar. An ultimatum was then sent to Shere Ali: he must apologize for the indignity to British pride caused by turning back the mission and he must allow them to have a mission in Kabul – otherwise they would invade. Not expecting a favourable reply, the government of India began to assemble an army. No expense was spared to make the invasion of Afghanistan a success. The army was divided into three field forces: the largest was the Peshawar Valley Field Force, consisting of 16,000 men and forty-eight guns under Lieutenant General Samuel Browne (1824–1901), an experienced soldier whose battles are now forgotten but whose name is known to the officers of many nations, for he was the designer of the Sam Browne belt; the second was the Kandahar Field Force under Major-General Donald Stewart (1824–1900) with nearly 13,000 men and seventy-eight guns; the smallest, with 6,300 men and eighteen guns, was put under Roberts, who although only a major in his regiment was given the local rank of major-general.

It was expected that most of the fighting would be done by Browne's force at the Khyber Pass and he was given the best troops. Roberts, the junior general, was given the third best selection. Originally, all of his troops were native, that is to say Indians and Gurkhas, except for the 2nd battalion of the 8th (Liverpool Regiment), which was composed largely of young and unacclimatized soldiers. Four of his six native regiments were made up of Muslim sepoys who did not like the idea of fighting their co-religionists in Afghanistan, and Roberts feared that they might mutiny. His best unit was the 5th Gurkhas. Before starting out, however, he asked for and received some additional artillery, some Sikhs and part of the 72nd (Seaforth) Highlanders. His transport facilities were inadequate and badly organized and most of his animals were in poor condition. Nevertheless, when the British ultimatum went unanswered, forward elements of Roberts's force crossed over into Afghanistan at three o'clock on the morning of 21 November 1878.

As the column moved down the Kurram valley, Roberts heard that the Afghans had installed themselves in force at the Peiwar Kotal. And so they had. When Roberts saw the Afghan position, he had 'a feeling very nearly akin to despair'. The pass was narrow and at the head of it the enemy had strongly fortified a mountain rising 2,000 feet above it. It seemed impregnable, and eight regular regiments of the Afghan army and hordes of local tribesmen were there waiting for them.

Roberts camped just out of artillery range for several days while he sent out reconnaissance parties and studied the situation. When he decided what he should do, he told his plan to only two other officers, for he knew that while he had very little intelligence of the enemy, they knew his every move. In a daring and dangerous gamble, he set off with the bulk of his force on a night march round the left flank of the mountain. The previous day he had put his men to work making gun positions in the front and giving every sign that his attack would come from this direction. At daylight the remainder of his men in the valley did indeed attack from that quarter, but he had been successful in bringing Gurkhas, Highlanders and Sikhs round the left side of the mountain, taking the Afghans completely by surprise. They bolted and ran.

To have outwitted the wily Afghans was no small feat. Night marches in the presence of the enemy are always difficult, even for modern armies; to have made a night march over such difficult terrain to attack a strongly entrenched enemy of superior numbers in his own territory was an incredible piece of daring. An addition to Roberts's laurels was the fact that losses were exceptionally light: two officers and eighteen men killed; three officers and seventy-five men wounded. The Viceroy passed on to Roberts a message from the Queen:

I have received the news of the decisive victory of General Roberts, and the splendid behaviour of my brave soldiers, with pride and satisfaction, though I must ever deplore the unavoidable loss of life. Pray inquire after the wounded in my name. May we continue to receive good news.

'Peiwar Kotal Day' is still celebrated each year by the 5th Gurkhas.

Roberts, after giving his troops a few days' rest, pushed on to the end of the Kurram Valley, fighting minor battles and capturing towns and small forts. His biggest difficulties were lack of sufficient transport and having too few troops to subjugate the tribesmen completely. But successful generals usually get what they ask for and Roberts soon received reinforcements: 2,685 infantry, 868 cavalry and 13 guns. These were placed along his line of communication. A few months later he was given the magnificent 92nd (Gordon) Highlanders. The junior general now had a fine command. However, like many heroes, particularly if they are generals, he was fired on from the rear.

Roberts's attitude towards newsmen was quite different from Wolseley's: 'I consider it due to the people of Great Britain that the press correspondents should have every opportunity for giving the fullest and most faithful accounts of what might happen while the army was in the field.' He took special pains to see that the newsmen were given as much information as possible. However, there had been an unfortunate incident in which some Afghan prisoners had broken loose and attacked their guards; some of the prisoners were shot to prevent their escape. The correspondent for the *Standard*, a man named Macpherson, presented this affair as a massacre. All correspondents submitted their stories to Roberts before they were sent, but Macpherson altered some of his after Roberts had signed his approval. Roberts sent him back to India; then he found himself accused of 'burking the press' as well as committing atrocities. There were questions about his conduct in the House of Commons. To his wife, Roberts wrote that 'whatever is said you must not let it trouble you, it will not trouble me *in the least*', though one suspects that it did. But war correspondents had not then the power they now have and all ended well: Roberts was given a KCB and the thanks of both houses of parliament.

Shere Ali fled towards Russia and died a few months later in Turkestan, leaving Yakub Khan, his son, in charge. Negotiations were opened with the new ruler and on 26 May 1879 a treaty was signed at Gandamuk in which the Afghans agreed to live 'in perfect peace and friendship' with the British; to cede the districts of Kurram, Pishin and Sibi to them; to allow a British envoy in Kabul; to permit British subjects to trade with Afghans; to permit a telegraph line to be erected from Kabul to India; and to allow Britain to dictate Afghan foreign policy. The British promised to protect them.

With the signing of the Treaty of Gandamuk the Second Afghan

War ended – or so thought the British. Actually, only the first phase of the war was over. Part Two was about to begin. In July 1879 Roberts entertained Major Cavagnari, then on his way to Kabul with a small military escort of Guides to be the British envoy and plenipotentiary. Major Pierre Louis Napoleon Cavagnari was a naturalized Englishman, a rare type in the British officer caste, but he came from a military family: his mother was Anglo-Irish and his father had been one of Napoleon's generals. He was educated in England and came to India as an ensign of native infantry at the age of seventeen in time to see action during the Indian Mutiny. Like many Indian army officers, he found more rapid advancement in the political service. As deputy-commissioner for Kohat and later for Peshawar, he had taken part in many negotiations with hill tribes on the North-West Frontier and he had just been knighted for negotiating the Treaty of Gandamuk.

People had mixed feelings about Cavagnari. Lord Lytton, the viceroy, spoke of his 'open-mindedness and intellectual quickness'. Robert Warburton called him 'a beau-ideal of a chief', and said 'it was a great feat and honour to serve under such a man'. Colonel H. B. Hanna, however, thought him 'a man of rash and restless disposition and over-bearing temper, consumed by the thirst for personal distinction'. Now thirty-eight years old, he was on the most important assignment of his life – and his last.

At a final dinner in camp before parting, Roberts was asked to propose a toast to the health of Cavagnari and his party. He found that he could not, for he was too depressed. He had a feeling that Cavagnari would not return. He thought that peace had been concluded too soon, before 'we had instilled that awe of us into the Afghan nation which would have been the only reliable guarantee for the safety of the Mission'. As many Europeans had learned before and many have learned since, not all other races attach the same importance to signed agreements. Less than two months later, Cavagnari and all the Englishmen with him were murdered in Kabul.

After the Treaty of Gandamuk most of the army of invasion had been dismantled: Browne was left with only two brigades and most of Stewart's army had marched back to India. Only Roberts's forces remained in the field to police the newly acquired Kurram Valley. Roberts himself was in Simla preparing to take a vacation in England when the news reached him of the fate of Cavagnari and the Kabul mission. He at once hurried back to his command. Fresh reinforcements were sent to him, and his army, renamed the Kabul Field Force, prepared to advance on the Afghan capital.

It took some time for Roberts to collect supplies and a sufficient number of transport animals to move, but on 27 September 1879 he turned over the command of the Kurram Valley to a brigadier and set off for his most advanced camp at Kuchi with one squadron of the 9th Lancers, the 5th Punjab Cavalry and elements of the 5th and 28th Punjab Infantry. While on the march he was met by a detachment of twenty-five men from the 92nd (Gordon) Highlanders, who had come from Kuchi to warn him that his column could expect to be attacked. Soon after he was indeed attacked by about 2,000 Afghans. In the sharp engagement that followed, Roberts was struck by the bravery and leadership shown by a colour sergeant of the 92nd. His name was Hector MacDonald and during the course of the action one of his men had called out to him, 'We'll make ye an officer for this day's work, Sergeant!' And another added, 'Aye, and a general too!' Roberts gave MacDonald a battlefield commission and he in due course became a major-general and played an important though little remembered part in British history.

Another future general who took part in this obscure and now almost-forgotten battle was Lieutenant Ian Hamilton, an infantry subaltern in the same regiment who found himself in the cavalry pursuit when the Afghans broke. He never forgot the experience and years later he described it:

The dust clouds in the Chardeh Valley – 5th Punjab Cavalry – red pugarees – blue swords flashing; the galloping line, and I also galloping. . . . Nearer, nearer, every stride nearer! Those dust clouds of the Chardeh Valley, flecked here and there with a flicker of moving colours, the foothills speckled with puffs of white smoke. Wonderful! A big jump and I nearly fall off. My horse has leaped over a dead tribesman. Then in the thick of it. Afghans in little knots, or else lying on their backs whirling their big knives to cut off the legs of our horses, a hell of a scrimmage in fact, until the *sowars* got to work in couples, one with sword uplifted, the other pulling his carbine out of the bucket and making the enemy spring to their feet and be cut down or be shot as they lay. Dust, shouts, shots, clash of steel . . . only a nameless little skirmish and yet it is a favourite picture amongst the many that come back to me in my dreams.

Amir Yakub Khan had been quick to deny that he had been responsible for the death of Major Cavagnari and his mission. He had exchanged several letters with Roberts and had sent high-ranking Afghan emissaries to beg him not to invade his country. Finally, the Amir himself came to Roberts's camp at Kuchi.

I cannot say that I was favourably impressed by his appearance [Roberts said]. He was an insignificant-looking man, about thirty-two years of age, with a receding forehead, a conical-shaped head, and no chin to speak of, and he gave me the idea of being entirely wanting in that force of character without which no one could hope to govern or hold in check the warlike and turbulent people of Afghanistan. He was possessed, moreover, of a shifty eye . . . and from the first I felt that his appearance tallied exactly with the double-dealing that had been imputed to him.

Roberts found the presence of Yakub Khan an embarrassment, particularly since the amir kept sending and receiving messages which Roberts was too gentlemanly to intercept. Although the amir did everything he could think of to delay his advance, Roberts left Kuchi for Kabul on 30 September, his forty-seventh birthday. Ahead, in Afghanistan, where Roberts's father had found honours in the First Afghan War, lay the glory every British officer longed for. The importance of a nineteenth-century military enterprise, and thus the prestige of the general commanding, could usually be judged by the percentage of British troops involved. Roberts had a first-class force at his disposal: 192 British officers commanding 2,558 British and 3,867 native other ranks, and the bulk of the native troop were Gurkhas and Sikhs, superb soldiers.

The Kabul Field Force encountered comparatively little opposition until they had reached a point about twelve miles from Kabul. There Roberts found the enemy in force occupying a ridge at a place called Charasia, south-west of the city. It was obvious that the enemy intended to attack, but Roberts attacked first, feinting to the left and lunging with Gurkhas and Highlanders to the right. The battle began on the morning of 6 October 1879 and by 3.45 p.m. his troops had possession of the entire ridge and had killed more than 300 Afghans. The British casualties were eighteen killed and seventy wounded. Two Victoria Crosses were won on this battlefield. The infantry fired 41,090 rounds and the artillery fired 238 shells, both shrapnel and common shells with percussion fuses. Also used in this fight were two Gatling guns, the first rapid fire (by crank) machine guns. Although invented by Richard Gatling, an American, in 1862, this was the first time they had been used in action. Roberts was not impressed. They fired only 150 rounds and one jammed. They were probably not properly used; the most efficient deployment of machine guns was not learned until thirty-five years later.

Having won the battle of Charasia, Kabul was now open to Roberts and his army. He was elated: 'At last I was at Kabul, the place I had heard so much of from my boyhood, and had so often wished to see! The city lay beneath me, with its mud-coloured buildings and its 50,000 inhabitants, covering a considerable extent of ground.' But he was now faced with a variety of political and diplomatic problems and he lacked confidence in his own abilities to cope with them. Among the instructions given to him was that his punishment of the individuals responsible for the murder of Major Cavagnari was to be 'swift, stern and impressive'. He was also instructed to leave 'a memorial of the retribution exacted from the city in some manner and by some mark that will not be easily obliterated'. Roberts appointed a military commission to find the murderers and try them. Some plausible Afghans were selected and on an appointed day British soldiers, bayonets fixed, stood in double lines near the blackened, ruined residency Cavagnari had occupied. A row of gallows was in front and on each was an Afghan with a noose about his neck. These were, or were thought to be, the ringleaders of the mob that had killed Cavagnari, and on a signal they were set swinging. Thus, Colonel G. J. Younghusband said, they were 'brought to justice by the strong resistless power of British bayonets . . . for a sign throughout the length and breadth of Asia of the righteous fate that overtakes those who disgrace the law of nations'.

Corpses on gallows made a fine mark of retribution, but they are not very lasting. Roberts thought that a more permanent mark might be the destruction of the Bala Hisar, the great fortress at the end of a ridge of hills that overlooks the city of Kabul. But the Bala Hisar was full of gunpowder and arms, and before these could be removed Roberts was overtaken by swiftly moving events in Afghanistan.

19
FROM KABUL TO KANDAHAR
1879-80

WELL aware of the unfortunate positioning of the British
cantonment when the British first occupied Kabul in the First
Afghan War, Roberts was careful to select for his force a defensible camp. Previous rulers of the country had started to build a
large walled area to the north of the city. This fortified area, called
Sherpur, was in the shape of a parallelogram, with walls twenty
feet high on the south and west sides and three gates protected by
circular bastions. The east side was the weakest with walls only
seven feet high and uncompleted. The Bimaru ridge was on the
north side and it was necessary to hold the entire ridge to protect
Sherpur. The total perimeter was four and a half miles long.
Sherpur was made the cantonment for the British forces and
Roberts strengthened it by constructing six towers; he also dug
trenches and gun pits on Bimaru ridge. It was well that he did this
for the British were soon to have need of a fortified refuge.

No one could pretend that the British were welcome in Afghanistan. They were hated, and they knew it. Roberts said, 'not a
single Afghan could be trusted'. A line of communication was
established with India through the Khyber Pass, where the
British now had an army of more than 11,000 men, but in December
1879 the Afghans, aroused by religious leaders, again took the

field against the invader. Several enemy armies were advancing on Kabul and Roberts developed a complicated plan to meet and defeat them. His objective was to 'break up the combinations by dealing with the enemy in detail, and prevent them getting possession of the city and the Bala Hissar'. Unfortunately his plan miscarried. In the opening battle Roberts was himself almost killed by a tribesman who attacked him with a knife. He was saved by a trooper from the 1st Bengal Cavalry. Watching his men being driven back, he said: 'I realized, what is hard for a British soldier, how much harder for a British commander, to realize, that we were over-matched, and that we could not hold our ground.'

Roberts heliographed to Brigadier Herbert MacPherson, whose brigade was deployed on a ridge above the city, to ask if he could determine the strength and direction of the enemy. He replied that large masses of Afghans could be seen approaching from the north, south and west. A young signal officer added: 'The crowds of Afghans in the Chardeh Valley remind me of Epsom on the Derby day.' Roberts decided, very reluctantly, to withdraw his forces into Sherpur. He supervised the withdrawal and watched with great anxiety.

It is comparatively easy for a small body of well-trained soldiers, such as those of which the army in India is composed, to act on the offensive against Asiatics, however powerful they may be in point of numbers. There is something in the determined advance of a compact, disciplined body of troops which they can seldom resist. But a retirement is a different matter. They become full of confidence and valour the moment they see any signs of their opponents being unable to resist them, and if there is the smallest symptom of unsteadiness, wavering, or confusion, a disaster is certain to occur.

The withdrawal into Sherpur was made in good order and without serious loss and Roberts breathed more easily. He had prudently stored there enough food for his men to last four months, food for his animals for six weeks, plus firewood, medical supplies and ammunition. On the night of 14 December the Afghan forces occupied Kabul and the Bala Hissar, and Roberts was besieged at Sherpur.

During the first week of the siege Roberts was left alone to strengthen his position while the Afghans looted the city and carried away gunpowder from the Bala Hissar. Yakub Khan having been sent to India, the Afghans were led by a man named Mohammed Jan who declared Yakub Khan's eldest son, Musa Khan, to be the amir. The Afghan force was estimated by the British to be about 100,000. Although this figure seems improbable the British were obviously badly outnumbered. Brigadier Charles Gough was on the way with reinforcements – 1,500 British infantry and Gurkhas and four guns – but on the night of 22/23 December the Afghans attacked Sherpur, advancing over the snow-covered ground on the south and east sides. Roberts's defences were good, his men well placed and resolute, and he had had advance knowledge of the enemy's plans; the Afghans were beaten off. By one o'clock on the afternoon of 23 December the fighting was over and the great Afghan army melted away. When on the following day a force was sent out to escort General Gough's brigade into Sherpur, not an enemy was to be seen.

For a couple months all was quiet. Sir Donald Stewart had moved his force to Kandahar, but on 30 March 1880 he moved towards Kabul, leaving behind a garrison under Major General James Primrose. Stewart fought a battle on 19 April but reached Kabul on 5 May with a force of 14,000 troops, 38 guns and 12,500 camp followers. While the army continued its uneasy occupation of Afghanistan, there was a political debate as to what was to be done with the country. It was Roberts's recommendation that it be broken up and its parts be put under separate rulers. The Afghans, however, were not yet ready to stop fighting. In early August word was received that a British brigade had been nearly annihilated by Afghans under Ayub Khan at a place called Maiwand in southern Afghanistan and that General Primrose was besieged in Kandahar. Out of a force of 2,476 men at Maiwand, 934 had been killed (310 of these were European) and 175 men were wounded or missing. It was a major disaster.

Roberts, although now holding local rank as lieutenant-general, was inferior in rank to Stewart and was no longer the senior commander in northern Afghanistan. But fortunately for him, Stewart sent him with an army for the relief of Kandahar. Fortunately, too, a fine army could quickly be put together from the troops available: 92nd (Gordon) Highlanders (651 men), 72nd (Seaforth) Highlanders (786 men), 2nd battalion of the 60th Rifles (616 men), 9th Lancers (318 men), plus Gurkhas, Sikhs and excellent Indian cavalry, a total of 9,986 men divided into three brigades of infantry and one of cavalry. There were also 8,000 followers, 2,300 horses and gun-mules, and 8,000 transport animals (Afghan and Indian ponies, mules, donkeys and camels). Roberts deliberately refrained from taking any wheeled artillery, his guns being limited to three batteries of mountain artillery; as there were no roads, he wanted to press on as fast as he could, and he feared that heavier artillery would slow him down.

The British defeat at Maiwand had focused the attention of Britain on Afghanistan. Roberts was the shining white knight off to the relief of his countrymen besieged by ferocious natives in Kandahar. It is not always easy to understand why some campaigns and battles excite little interest and remain unknown while others catch the popular imagination and history remembers the deeds and the men. Stewart's earlier fighting march from Kandahar to Kabul had almost passed unnoticed, but Roberts's march in the opposite direction was followed with intense interest in Britain, and the 'march from Kabul to Kandahar', a phrase which somehow conjures up all the romance of the nineteenth-century Asiatic war, has gone down in history as a major event. Roberts, a good professional soldier with little romance in his soul, was delighted by his command and his mission, but he had no idea of the fame that would accrue to him by his march on Kandahar when he set out from Kabul under a blazing sun on the morning of 9 August 1880.

Today one can go to Ghazni by motor car in less than two hours over the seventy-five miles of road built by the Americans, but it took Roberts six days, pushing men and animals as fast as he could, and he estimated the distance travelled as ninety-eight miles. Roberts's father had been awarded a CB for his part in the capture of Ghazni forty-one years earlier. Now there was no need to blow in the gates; they were opened to him. He did not linger at Ghazni, but pressed on across the rugged land to the south, reaching Kelat on 23 August. Here he rested his troops for a day and then moved on.

On the 25th he received a message from General Primrose saying that the Afghans, hearing of his approach, had lifted the siege and were entrenched near by at a place called Mazra, which was described as 'beyond the Baba Wali Kotal in the valley of the Arghandab.' To Roberts, the country there was 'extremely difficult and easily defensible'. Roberts now knew that he need not push his army so fast: for the time being Kandahar was safe. He would have a tough fight when he arrived and his troops had better be in good shape to fight it – and so had he.

Much to his disgust, Roberts himself was not in fighting trim. He had come down with a fever and had to be carried along on a doolie, 'a most ignominious mode of conveyance for a General in service; but there was no help for it, for I could not sit a horse'. Roberts had been unwell from the beginning of the war, suffering from 'torpidity of the liver and aggravated dyspepsia'. He had continuous pain in his chest and a feeling of weariness. Throughout the march to Kandahar he suffered from violent headaches, constant nausea, pain in his back and loss of appetite – none of which held him back.

The 4,000 man garrison turned out to cheer when, on 31 August, Roberts's army marched into Kandahar. Roberts was shocked by 'the demoralized condition of the greater part of the garrison'. In his estimation, this sizeable force, situated behind thick walls thirty feet high and with fifteen field guns, had not really been in any danger at all. 'For British soldiers to have contemplated the possibility of Kandahar being taken by an Afghan army showed what a miserable state of depression and demoralization they were in.' The Royal Artillery and the Bombay Sappers and Miners had exhibited 'unfailing good behaviour and creditable bearing'; as for the rest, 'they never even hoisted the Union Jack until the relieving force was close at hand'.

Roberts now had 940 sick men with his force. Many simply had sore feet, but others had suffered from the extremes of temperature: bitterly cold nights and day time temperatures that rose to 105°F. Nevertheless, he reported to India that 'the troops from Kabul are in famous health and spirits', and he hastened to attack the Afghan positions. On 1 September his army won a great victory over the Afghans, capturing Ayub Khan's camp and all his artillery. Again, 'Highlanders and Gurkhas, always friendly rivals in the race for glory', bore the brunt of the fighting. British losses were forty killed and 210 wounded, eighteen of whom died later of their wounds; Afghan losses were uncounted, but at one spot on the battlefield there were the bodies of about 600 tribesmen.

The British now withdrew their armies from Afghanistan. Abdur Rahman, a nephew of Shere Ali, mounted the throne as amir and the British no longer insisted on a mission in Kabul. It had been proved once more that the British could defeat the Afghans in open battle but they could not hold the country. Except for the glory won by the soldiers, no object was achieved.

Roberts returned to India and not long after to England and a shower of honours: he was thanked by the Queen, the Duke of Cambridge and both Houses of Parliament; he was given the GCB, two swords of honour, an honorary degree and a baronetcy. He was also given £12,500, but he was rather bitter about this as it was only half what Wolseley had received for his short Ashanti campaign which, according to the *United Services Gazette*, had resulted only in the 'capture of a royal umbrella'.

A special 'Kabul to Kandahar' medal was struck (it became known as the Roberts Star) and was presented to all who had taken part in the march. The Queen even gave one to Roberts's horse, Voronel, which also received the Afghan campaign medal with four clasps. Voronel was not the only animal to be decorated for his part in the Second Afghan War. When, in June 1881, the 66th Regiment, newly redesignated the 2nd Battalion of the Royal Berkshire Regiment, marched to Osborne to be given their campaign medals, a small white mongrel dog named Bobbie also went along, and Queen Victoria personally presented him with an Afghan medal. Bobbie, owned by a sergeant but the pet of the entire regiment, had served throughout the Afghan War and had been with the 66th at the disaster of Maiwand where ten officers and 275 men of the regiment were killed and two officers, thirty-one men and Bobbie were wounded. He was lost on the battlefield during the retreat, but several days later he rejoined his regiment at Kandahar, fifty miles away. Only eighteen months after receiving his medal, Bobbie was run over and killed by a hansom cab in England. The regiment had him stuffed, and he can still be seen in a glass case in the regimental museum at Reading, his Afghan medal suspended by its red and green ribbon from his neck.

20

ZULUS
1878–79

T H E first phase of the Second Afghan War had just ended and
Roberts was busy consolidating the newest bits of annexed
territories when in South Africa another British army began
another campaign: the invasion of Zululand.

In this second half of Queen Victoria's reign Britain found it
increasingly difficult to win her small wars; her enemies, though
still mostly savages, proved more ferocious; more money, men and
blood were required to subdue them. This is not to say that
Britain was yet in danger of losing any war, but as the price of
victory grew increasingly higher she became more reluctant to
pay the price. As the scale of the wars increased and communications improved, politicians and the British public became ever
more involved and concerned with them. The war correspondent
became a familiar, though often still resented, figure on the battlefield, bringing to an increasingly literate British public the exciting
happenings on the fringes of its Empire.

This awakening at home to the extent, glory, cost and responsibility of empire gave rise to two quite opposite attitudes:
jingosim and what might be called moralism. There was much
wavering between the two views so that at different times one or
the other might predominate. Strange though it may seem today,

for most of the time the jingoist attitude held sway over these empire-proud people. The officers in the army and navy were jingos almost to a man; Wolseley once described himself as 'a Jingo in the best acceptation of that sobriquet'. The term 'jingoism' came from the lyrics of a popular music hall song that well expressed the view of many, often most, of the British people:

> We don't want to fight,
> But by jingo if we do,
> We've got the ships,
> We've got the men,
> We've got the money too!

Disraeli was the chief exponent of jingoism, pushing a 'forward policy' of empire, while the opposite attitude was held by moralists with a 'noble savage' approach to empire whose chief spokesman, Gladstone, was Disraeli's great enemy. Gladstone spoke of that 'most wanton invasion of Afghanistan' and related the savage Afghans, Zulus and other hostile tribesman to poor British farmers and, as most of his listeners were as ignorant of those far off people as he was, he was rather successful in gaining acceptance of his views. In a speech he gave in Scotland on 26 November 1879 he begged his audience to 'remember the rights of the savage, as we call him. Remember that the happiness of his humble home, remember that the sanctity of his life in the hill villages of Afghanistan, among the winter snows, is as inviolable in the eye of Almighty God as can be your own.' And a few days later (5 December) at Glasgow, he denounced the Afghan war as a crime against God and claimed that money voted to relieve famine in India had been diverted to throw Afghan 'mothers and children from their homes to perish in the snow'. In the same speech he attacked the policy of fighting the Zulus, claiming that ten thousand Zulus had been slaughtered 'for no other offence than their attempt to defend against your artillery with their naked bodies, their hearths and homes, their wives and families'. These sentiments were echoed by the Aborigines Protection Society, then an organization of some influence, which pronounced the Zulu War 'morally indefensible'.

Morality was not all on one side, however. Redvers Buller spoke for the soldiers and doubtless many civilians when he said in a speech: 'Now I am certain that when the history of the Zulu War comes to be written, nobody will doubt that it was a righteous war. It was a war of civilization against barbarity.' It was firmly believed by nearly all Englishmen that British rule was the best rule; that it was the rule of law and order; that peace, trade, Christian virtues and good government followed in the wake of British armies; that in spite of the cost in blood and money, the heavy responsibilities and expense involved in ruling distant lands, British rule was indisputably the best rule for everyone; and that it was for the best interests of the inhabitants of conquered lands to submit to it. There was, of course, some truth in the arguments of both sides. Although the Afghans and the Zulus were both warlike, savage peoples, the invasion of their territories was indeed 'morally indefensible'. On the other hand, where Britain stayed to rule she did bring law and order and undoubtedly ruled the country better (by European standards) than any native ruler could be expected to do.

The politicians in London were rarely familiar with the vast lands they governed. They had not firsthand knowledge of the countries, peoples and problems. Neither Disraeli nor Gladstone had ever seen more of the Empire than was to be found in the British Isles. The educated upper classes of England, while intensely proud of their Empire and well aware of the importance it gave them in the world, were scornful – as, incredibly, they still are – of the colonials and the soldiers who built and maintained it.

Until the Berlin Conference of 1885 which divided Africa among the European powers, expansion of the Empire rarely proceeded from conscious, deliberate policy initiated in London. How then did the Empire manage to grow? The answer lies in the difference in viewpoint between the Government in London and their agents, soldiers and diplomats, their consuls and proconsuls in Asia,

Africa and the widely scattered colonies and protectorates around the world. Part of the answer also lies in the slowness of communication, but even when telegraph lines were strung and cables laid the men in London had not the habit of giving operational instructions on day to day activities, and those on the Empire's frontiers had no inclination to accept such instructions. Consequently London knew only what their soldiers and diplomats told them, and the knowledge of the politicians and civil servants in London was always well behind the course of events initiated or caused by the Briton on the spot. And he, knowing that his government had the power and ability to expand, believing firmly that British rule was the best rule, and not being faced himself with the fiscal and political problems of the home Government, had little incentive to moderate his imperialistic views or to restrain his ambitions. Still, those responsible in London did their best.

Even among the greatest admirers of Empire there was a feeling at all stages of its growth that it was large enough, that it did not need to be bigger. The chief check on expansion was, or was thought to be, the budget. British politicians, representing as they did the moneyed classes, were extremely cost conscious. The expenses for each campaign were carefully reckoned: estimates were made beforehand and the cost of each little war in pounds, shillings and pence was exactly calculated. Politicians, civil servants, taxpayers – all were against increased expenditure and did their best to prevent costly military campaigns and the acquisition of additional colonies and protectorates which were always expensive to maintain. But lack of money rarely prevented additional acquisitions, for the fact was that the politicians had little control over events on the Empire's frontiers.

While everyone agreed that British influence was necessary to increase trade and to bring the great benefits of British civilization to the unenlightened, the view from London was that such influence ought, whenever humanly possible, to be exerted by indirect means without the expense of actually ruling. They wanted only that native rulers should keep order in their countries, rule justly, and permit Britons to roam through their lands, exploring, trading and preaching. It seemed a simple and reasonable demand. To ensure this all that was needed was a capable Englishman at the right hand of the ruler to advise him. Thus Britain preferred residents, agents, missions, administrators, envoys and the like to actual governors. Even substantial subsidies to primitive rulers were preferable to the expense of actually ruling a country. But Asian and African rulers were autocrats. They had to be. They found it difficult enough to keep order among their turbulent peoples and they could rarely see how a foreigner at their elbow without direct responsibility for executive decisions would assist them to keep their thrones. Also, being human, they were not always as wise, just and virtuous as the British wanted them to be. Thus Britain often found it difficult to exert the influence she wished. To the man designated as resident or envoy and given the responsibility for exerting the desired influence it obviously seemed easier to rule directly rather than to cajole, threaten, bribe and flatter native rulers. Besides, this required skills which many proud Britons found repellent and demeaning to exercise.

In the struggle between those in London who wanted to influence and the men in the field who wanted to rule, it was the latter who usually prevailed. All the Queen's men in the Foreign Office, the Colonial Office, the Horse Guards, and Parliament – and, in its day, the Court of Directors of the Honourable East India Company – were unable to restrain their agents in the field. It was all too easy for the Briton on the frontier, reinforced by subordinates of like opinions and ambitions, to convince his superiors in London that the local ruler, or the chieftain just across the border, was ruling badly, was unable to keep order in his realm, was being influenced by Russia or some other European power, was planning to attack the colonists, and so on; a few incidents, such as border encroachments or insults to British representatives, could usually be provided to prove the point, to obtain the reluctant permission of London and so depose the native ruler, institute direct rule and widen the boundaries of Empire.

The dilemma in London caused by these conflicting pressures

were well described by a Colonial Office official, E. Fairfield, in a memorandum of 4 August 1885. He was describing African policy, but his remarks were equally applicable to Asia and other parts of the world.

When we lean to the policy of controlling all sections of the population, and regulating their mutual relations, we find that a huge bill has been run up. Then the advocates of retirement and retrenchment have their day, until it is perceived that retirement and retrenchment have involved the abandonment of some weak and friendly tribe to the mercy of the Africander, or the triumph of anarchy among the natives themselves. Then there is a cry for a resumption of responsibility.

Expansion of the Empire in Asia was always easier to effect politically because of the peculiar geographical and political position of India, and, in particular, the unique position of the Indian army, which did not come under direct control of the Horse Guards. Huntingdon summed up this position in 1878:

The Indian Army is not limited by an annual Vote of Parliament. It is not voted by Parliament at all. . . . In fact, it may be described as a non-Parliamentary Army, as compared with the Army which is maintained at home and in the other Dependencies of the Crown.

Thus, the Indian army, being less subject to the control of the politicians in London, was used more and more outside India, in China, Burma and even Africa. In consequence of its almost constant employment, it was perhaps a better army than the home army, though no one at the Horse Guards would ever have admitted this. Had the Indian army been used in Zululand the events of that war would probably have been quite different, but as the Indian army was then occupied in India and Afghanistan, the Zulu War was fought by imperial troops from England with the aid of hastily raised colonial and African contingents.

The South African pot had been boiling for many years. The source of the turmoil was a three-sided struggle among peoples of radically different interests, each of whom strongly believed in living his own way of life and who found the other two interfering with it. In the vast, sparsely populated land of South Africa one might have thought that there was room for Afrikaner, British colonial and Bantu, but seemingly there was not. The three groups jostled and pushed and fought each other and, as is usual in such cases, the weaker group was subdued first; this was made easier because the various African tribes were divided by language and customs and fought among themselves. The proud Afrikaners, fleeing the hated British, made their great treks northwards by ox cart, avoiding the coasts, seeking the vast open spaces beyond the Orange River, beyond the Limpopo, beyond the Vaal, and they collided with the African tribes they found there. The British, too, had fought Gaikas, Bapedis, Basutos and other tribes, but the struggle with the Zulus was the biggest, most difficult and most memorable of all the South African native wars, for they were here fighting against an exceptionally well-organized savage army, which opened the war by delivering them a resounding defeat the moment they stepped inside the frontiers of Zululand.

Ostensibly, the campaign against the Zulus was undertaken because of alleged encroachment by them on British territory and because Cetewayo, their great chief, was said to misgovern his tribe. The real reason was that the presence of the large well-trained Zulu army was a standing menace to the British colonists in Natal, who knew that the Zulus could overwhelm them if they chose. They therefore demanded, and eventually received, imperial troops to crush them. Cetewayo was sent a twelve-point ultimatum listing humiliating and impossible demands, one of which was that he should break up his army. The Zulu nation was based on a military caste system and it is doubtful if the king could have forced compliance on his people even had he been inclined to try.

A British army was assembled and it prepared to invade Zululand. The man chosen to lead it was Frederick Augustus Thesiger (1827–1905), who had just become the second Baron Chelmsford on the death of his father. A handsome man with a rounded spade beard, he had a reputation for being a perfect gentleman. He had been commissioned at the age of seventeen and gazetted to the Rifle Brigade, then stationed in Halifax. He later served with the Grenadier Guards in the Crimea and he had been in India during the final days of the Mutiny with the 95th (Derbyshire Regiment). During the Abyssinian War he had served as Napier's deputy adjutant-general, and then had spent five years as a staff officer in the East Indies. At a time when many officers were beginning to ask whether British infantry ought not to adopt some new tactics to meet the conditions of warfare brought about by improved weapons, he had argued that the old double line of soldiers was still the best and could withstand any attack. He was soon to learn that British infantry tactics were not always good enough to hold off an attack by men armed with assegais. He arrived in South Africa in February 1878 with the local rank of lieutenant-general and immediately took charge of the war against the Gaikas which was then in progress. He had little chance to display his military abilities, however, for this war was soon won for him by Colonel Evelyn Wood and Major Redvers Buller.

On 11 January 1879 Lord Chelmsford had about 5,000 European troops and 8,000 armed Africans perched on the borders of Zululand. The Zulu army was estimated to be 40,000 strong, but Chelmsford's request for more men had been refused; it was thought in London that his force was quite large enough to destroy an army of savages. Although he wanted more men, he was obviously not frightened by the Zulus for he divided his force into three nearly equal parts and planned a three-pronged invasion. Commanding the centre column himself, he placed his right column under Colonel Charles Knight Pearson and his left under Evelyn Wood. The columns were to unite at Ulundi, Cetewayo's capital, about sixty miles away. Chelmsford led his force across the Buffalo River at a fording place called Rorke's Drift, and on 22 January his main force was camped some ten miles away near a hill called Isandhlwana and his patrols were out looking for Zulus. He received a report from one of his scouting parties that contact had been made with the enemy. Support was requested and Chelmsford himself moved out with about half of his force, leaving behind six companies of the gallant but unlucky

24th Regiment (later South Wales Borderers), a couple of guns, some colonial volunteers and some native contingents (Natal Kaffirs) to guard his camp.

Brevet Lieutenant-Colonel Henry Burmester Pulleine, commanding officer of the 1st battalion of the 24th, was left in charge. He was an officer with twenty-four years' experience, but this was his first war. Indeed, except for a bit of service during the Indian Mutiny (no battle honours) and a brief affair with savages at Little Andaman Island in May 1867 in which a detachment of the regiment took part, the 24th had not been in action for thirty years, since the Second Sikh War in 1849 when it made the gallant but disastrous charge of the guns at Chilianwala.

Chelmsford left before dawn and first light found Pulleine busy arranging his outposts. About eleven o'clock news arrived from an advanced vedette – about three miles from the camp – of the approach of large masses of Zulus. An hour later Pulleine had another report from the vedette: a Zulu impi (war party or field army) in three columns had approached an outpost and there had been some firing, but the enemy now appeared to be going off in another direction and were not thought to be headed for the camp. Then a mounted colonial stumbled upon the main Zulu impi hidden in a long ravine. There were thousands of them, stretching along the ravine for as far as the eye could see. As he dashed back to report his discovery, the Zulus rose to attack, moving at a trot towards the camp.

When Pulleine learned of the Zulu army bearing down on him he prepared his defences, but he had no notion that the enemy consisted of the largest, best disciplined and bravest army of blacks in African history. Had he drawn his forces in close to the camp and massed his firepower he might have had a chance. Instead, he distributed them about the landscape. The Zulus broke through his defences, yelling and stabbing with their sharp assegais. The Natal Kaffirs fled, and they were pursued and cut down by the Zulus; the twenty-one officers and 534 men of the 24th Regiment stayed, fought, and died. There were no wounded or missing.

Zulus

Of the 1,800 men at Isandhlwana (950 Europeans and 850 Natal Kaffirs), only 55 Europeans and about 300 Africans escaped. The camp, with its transport, arms supplies and equipment, was looted. All the wounded, including the severely wounded Zulus, were killed. Then, having finished their bloody work, the Zulus vanished. It was the most crushing defeat the British army had suffered since the First Afghan War. In the understatement of the century, Lord Chelmsford said, 'We have certainly been seriously underrating the power of the Zulu army.' They had indeed.

The invasion of Zululand came to an abrupt halt after the disaster of Isandhlwana. Pearson's force had successfully beaten off an attack while laagered at a place called Ginginhlovu (pronounced by the British soldiers as 'Gin, gin, I love you'), but it was for a time unable to move and had to be relieved. Only Wood's force, which had won a victory over the Zulus at Kambula, was still mobile and able to fight.

The outlandish name of Isandhlwana rang through the British Isles. There was astonishment and dismay at the disaster. When Queen Victoria first heard of it she wrote in her journal: 'How this could happen we cannot yet imagine.' Osborn Wilkinson said of the Zulus: 'I suspect that hardly a soul imagined that they were capable of displaying such reckless bravery and utter contempt of death in the face of the havoc-dealing fire of disciplined troops.'

Six months later, reinforced by 10,000 troops hastily dispatched from England, Chelmsford again assumed the offensive and set off once more for Ulundi. This time he was successful. The Zulus had also been surprised at Isandhlwana. They were unprepared for the tough discipline of the British army and for its tremendous firepower. They had paid dearly for their victory. Too dearly. 'An assegai has been thrust into the belly of the nation,' Cetewayo is reported to have said. 'There are not enough tears to mourn for the dead.' In the end, Zulu assegais and Zulu bravery proved no match for the rifles, cannon and equal bravery of the British. On 4 July 1879 Ulundi was captured and burned. Cetewayo escaped, but the Zulus were defeated and their power effectively broken forever.

Before the final battle at Ulundi it was decided in London to supersede Lord Chelmsford, and, over the strenuous objections of Queen Victoria, Wolseley was selected to replace him. In answer to the Queen's comments on Wolseley, Disraeli told her: 'It is quite true that Wolseley is an egotist and a braggart. So was Nelson.' The Queen finally said that she would 'sanction' the appointment, but she 'would *not approve* it'. Wolseley set out for South Africa, but Chelmsford, like Gough in the Second Sikh War, won the final battle before his successor had time to arrive on the scene. Wolseley praised Chelmsford for his victory – publicly – but privately referred to 'that failure Chelmsford' and he resented the award of a G C B 'upon poor, incapable Chelmsford'. And, of course, he was bitter that the course of war was not delayed long enough to give him the opportunity of finally defeating the Zulus.

Lord Chelmsford never fought another battle, although he lived for another twenty-six years and rose to the rank of full general. He died while playing billiards in the United Service Club.

21

INCIDENTS IN THE ZULU WAR

1879

In many ways the Zulu War was like other small wars the British had fought: it began with an initial defeat and ended in victory; it was fought against savages on the Empire's fringes; and the simple strategy and tactics employed, so well suited to disciplined Victorian soldiers, were not unlike the means used to win other small wars in other parts of the Empire. But the Zulu War was memorable for a number of interesting small events: tragic, humorous, disgraceful and gallant.

The officers of the 24th Regiment who were commanding troops at Isandhlwana stayed and died with their men, though all of them had horses and could have tried to escape. The only officer of the 24th to leave the battlefield was Lieutenant Teignmouth Melvill, and he was ordered by Pulleine to try to save the Queen's colours of the 1st battalion. He got as far as the Buffalo River, but was drowned trying to cross at a place that came to be called Fugitives' Drift. The colours were later found and returned to the regiment. In a little ceremony at Osborne on 28 July 1880 the Queen decorated these colours with a wreath of immortelles. Ever after, the staff of the Queen's colours of the 1st battalion of the 24th carried a silver wreath on it.

After the battle of Boomplatz in 1848 the Queen had noted

that, as usual, there was a higher percentage of casualties among the officers than among the other ranks. She wrote to Lord Grey: 'The loss of so many officers, the Queen is certain, proceeds from their wearing a blue coat whilst the men are in scarlet; the Austrians lost a great proportion of officers in Italy from a similar difference in dress.' The Queen was probably right. Still, many officers continued to go into battle wearing blue patrol jackets. In at least one instance their blue coats saved their lives.

There were some civilians with Chelmsford's army, mostly transport and supply people, so the Zulu warriors had been told by their chiefs to concentrate on the soldiers, who could be distinguished from the civilians by their red coats. One of the few soldiers to escape from Isandhlwana was thin, square-jawed Lieutenant Horace Lockwood Smith-Dorrien, nineteen years old, who lived to command the British Second Division in the retreat from Mons in 1914. He, like the other four officers who escaped, was wearing a dark coat that day. All red-coated officers were killed.

Smith-Dorrien did not have a command; he was serving as transport officer. As usual, transportation of supplies was one of the army's major problems and there was a need for more animals than South Africa could supply. Every ox, mule and horse in the country that was for sale or hire was swept up by the army, and Chelmsford was forced to look outside the country for more. A British officer in the American Far West trying to buy animals for the Zulu War would be a theme too improbable for the producers of Westerns, but one British officer found himself buying mules for Chelmsford in Texas.

Part of the tide of Zulus which swept away the six companies of the 24th Regiment at Isandlhwana lapped at the little post at Rorke's Drift a few miles away on the same day. Here was enacted one of the most incredible dramas in the history of the British army. The story has been brilliantly told in detail by Donald Morris in *The Washing of the Spears*, but it deserves to be retold here for it describes an outstanding example of the type of courage so often displayed by ordinary officers and men of Queen Victoria's army.

Rorke's Drift had been churned into a muddy quagmire by the passing army and the continued movement of oxen and supply wagons. A mission station-farm was located about a quarter of a mile from the drift on the Natal side of the river and this had been turned into a field hospital and supply centre. On the morning of 22 January there were thirty-six men in the hospital, together with a surgeon, a chaplain, and one orderly; eighty-four men of B Company of the 2nd Battalion of the 24th Regiment and a company of Natal Kaffirs were there to guard the crossing; there was also an engineer officer who helped wagons to cross the river, and a few casuals.

Neither of the two regular officers entitled to hold a command (the surgeon-major did not count) was regarded as outstanding. At least neither of them had ever done anything remarkable in their careers up to this point. The senior of the two was black-bearded Lieutenant John Rouse Merriot Chard, the Royal Engineer officer. Commissioned at the age of twenty-one he had served for more than eleven years without ever seeing action or receiving a promotion.

Lieutenant Gonville Bromhead was in charge of B company of the 24th at Rorke's Drift. His brother, Major Charles Bromhead was in the same regiment, as was natural, for members of the Bromhead family had served in the 24th Regiment for more than 120 years. Charles was regarded as a brilliant officer; he had been in the Ashanti War with Wolseley and was now on staff duty in London. But Gonville, thirty-three years old with nearly twelve years of service, had been a lieutenant for eight years; he was not so bright and was almost totally deaf. He ought not to have been in the army at all. That he was left behind and assigned to the dull job of watching the river crossing was probably due to the natural reluctance of Pulleine to allow him to command a company in battle.

It was about the middle of the afternoon before Chard and Bromhead learned from two volunteer officers of the Natal

Kaffirs of the disaster at Isandhlwana and of their own danger. There were no defences at all at Rorke's Drift, but Chard decided that it would be impossible to bring away all the sick and injured men in hospital so they must do what they could to make the mission defensible. Using wagons, biscuit boxes, bags of mealies and existing walls, they managed to enclose the house, barn and kraal. Fortunately, the buildings were of stone, as was the wall around the kraal, but the house, now being used as a hospital, had a thatched roof, making it vulnerable. All the sick and injured who were well enough to shoot were given rifles and ammunition and Chard counted on having about 300 men to defend his little improvised fort.

A few refugees from Isandhlwana reached Rorke's Drift, but most continued their flight. The mounted natives who had been stationed at the drift and the native contingent with Chard all fled, together with their colonial officers and non-commissioned officers. Chard was left with only 140 men, including the patients from the hospital, to man his 300 yard perimeter. Late in the afternoon a man came racing down the hill in back of the station shouting 'Here they come, black as hell and thick as grass!' And a Zulu impi of 4,000 warriors now descended on Rorke's Drift.

The soldiers were still carrying biscuit boxes and mealie bags to the walls when the Zulus, with their black and white cowhide shields and with assegais flashing in the sun, came running into view. Boxes and bags were dropped, rifles and cartridge pouches were seized and the soldiers ran to man the barricades. Rifles crashed as the defenders fired into the black masses of Zulu warriors that swept down on them. The Zulus had a deadly open space to cross and took terrible casualties – but they came on in waves. The soldiers could not shoot fast enough and as the Zulus swept around the walls of the hospital there were hand to hand fights along the makeshift barricades, bayonets against assegais, the Zulus mounting the bodies of their own dead and wounded to grab at the rifle barrels and jab at the soldiers.

The men of the 24th had already been enraged before the Zulus arrived by the sight of their native allies and colonial volunteers deserting them. One soldier had even put a bullet into the retreating back of a European non-commissioned officer of the Native Contingent. They were in a fighting mood, and now with the Zulus upon them they fought with a frenzy.

Some of the Zulus who were armed with rifles crouched behind boulders on the rocky slopes behind the mission and fired at the backs of the defenders on the far wall. Fortunately their shooting was erratic, and they did little damage. The steady marksmanship of the soldiers was better; one private downed eight Zulus with eight cartridges during the first charge. The soldiers had found plenty of ammunition among the stores in the barn and the chaplain circulated among them distributing handfuls of fresh cartridges.

There was wild, vicious room to room fighting when the Zulus broke into the hospital; the sick and wounded, together with a few men from B Company, held them off with desperate courage until they set fire to the thatched roof. Meanwhile, Chard was trying to withdraw his men into a narrower perimeter encompassing only the barn, kraal and the yard in front of the barn. Into this area the men who had escaped from the hospital, the freshly wounded and Chard's remaining effectives retreated and continued the fight. It was dark now, but the Zulus still came on and by the light of the burning hospital the fight went on.

In rush after rush the Zulus pressed back the soldiers. The kraal, which had been defended by bayonets and clubbed rifles when there was no time to reload, had at last to be abandoned. Rifles had now been fired so often and so fast that the barrels burned the fingers and the fouled guns bruised and battered the shoulders and frequently jammed. The wounded cried for water and the canteens were empty, but Chard led a sally over the wall to retrieve the two-wheeled water cart that stood in the yard by the hospital. It was about four o'clock in the morning before the Zulu attacks subsided, but even then flung assegais continued to whistle over the walls.

It seems nearly incredible that even brave, disciplined British soldiers could have sustained such determined attacks by men equally brave and in such numbers. But they did. By morning, Chard and Bromhead had about eighty men still standing. Fifteen had been killed, two were dying and most were wounded. When dawn broke over the hills, the soldiers looked over the walls and braced their tired, wounded bodies for another charge. Their faces were blackened and their eyes were red; their bodies ached and their nerves were stretched taut from the strain. But the Zulus were gone. Around them were hundreds of black corpses; a few wounded Zulus could be seen retreating painfully over a hill; the ground was littered with the debris of battle: Zulu shields and assegais; British helmets, belts and other accoutrements; broken wagons, biscuit boxes and mealie bags, and the cartridge cases of the 20,000 rounds of ammunition the defenders had fired. Chard sent out some cautious patrols, but there were no signs of the enemy in the immediate vicinity. The soldiers cleared away some dead Zulus from the cook house and began to make tea.

About seven-thirty the Zulus suddenly appeared again. Chard called his men and they manned the walls, but the Zulus simply sat down on a hill out of rifle range. They, too, were exhausted, and they had not eaten for more than two days. They had no desire to renew the fight. Besides, the leader of the impi had disobeyed the order of Cetewayo by crossing the Buffalo River into Natal and he was doubtless considering how he would explain to his chief the costly night of savage fighting outside the boundaries of Zululand. While Chard and his men grimly watched, the Zulus rose and wearily moved off over the hills.

Later in the morning, some mounted infantry rode up and soon after Chelmsford appeared with what was left of his main force. He had hoped that some portion of his troops had been able to retreat from Isandhlwana to Rorke's Drift, but he found only the survivors of those who had been left there. With the remnants of his column and the handful of men from Rorke's Drift, he sadly retreated into Natal.

Eleven Victoria Crosses were awarded the defenders of Rorke's Drift: the most ever given for a single engagement. There might have been even more, but posthumous awards were not then made.

Both Chard and Bromhead received the medal. There were many Welshmen in the 24th (which later became the South Wales Borderers), and among the eighty-four men of B Company there were five men named Jones and five named Williams; two of the Joneses and one Williams won the Victoria Cross. Private Williams's real name, however, was John Williams Fielding; he had run away from home to enlist and had changed his name so that his father, a policeman, would not find him.

Private Frederick Hitch, twenty-four, also won a Victoria Cross and survived his years of service to enjoy the wearing of it as a commissionaire. The bad luck of his regiment seemed to pursue Hitch and his medal, even to the grave. One day while Hitch was in his commissionaire's uniform and wearing his medals a thief snatched the Victoria Cross from his chest. It was never seen again. King Edward VII eventually gave him another to replace it, but when Hitch died in 1913 this one, too, had disappeared. Fifteen years later it turned up in an auction room; his family bought it and it is now in the museum of his old regiment. Mounted on his tomb in Chiswick cemetery was a bronze replica of the Victoria Cross. In 1968 thieves stole that.

Lieutenant Chard finally received his first promotion – to brevet major, becoming the first officer in the Royal Engineers ever to skip the rank of captain. He was also invited to Balmoral where Queen Victoria gave him a gold signet ring. He served for another eighteen years in Cyprus, India and Singapore, but he received only one more promotion. In 1897 cancer of the tongue caused him to retire and he died three months later.

Bromhead was also promoted to captain and brevet major, though he never rose any higher. He, too, was invited to Balmoral by the Queen, but being on a fishing trip when the invitation arrived he missed the occasion. He died in 1891 at the age of forty-six in Allahabad, still in the 24th Regiment.

Bromhead and Chard were fortunate in a sense when their moment for glory arrived: fighting with their backs to the wall, they had only to show the kind of stubborn bravery and simple leadership for which the British officer was conditioned and which he was best equipped to display. No great decision or military genius was required of them. But this is not to detract from their feat of courage and the British army was rightly proud of them.

Chard and Bromhead achieved a certain degree of fame, but there was another subaltern who became better known in Britain, though for quite different reasons: he once chose to be prudent rather than heroic. His fate was tied to the Prince Imperial, Louis Napoleon, only son of Napoleon III and the Empress Eugénie and the great hope of the French Bonapartists, who already called him Napoleon IV.

The Prince Imperial had been educated in England and had attended Woolwich, although he was not given a commission. After Isandhlwana, when reinforcements were being shipped out to Chelmsford, he begged to be allowed to go fight. Although Disraeli thought it would be 'injudicious', the Empress Eugénie enlisted the support of the Queen on her son's behalf and he was at last permitted to go to war as a 'spectator'. Chelmsford was told to look after him. The Prince wrote his will – the only document he ever signed as 'Napoleon' — and, taking the sword carried by the first Napoleon at Austerlitz, he sailed for Durban. There he donned the undress uniform of a British lieutenant and with a valet, a groom, and two horses – one of which was named 'Fate' – he proceeded to the front to join Chelmsford's staff.

He was a lively, popular young man and eager to see action. He went out on a few patrols and worried his commanders by his dash and daring. The Duke of Cambridge had told Chelmsford: 'My only anxiety on his conduct would be, that he is too *plucky and go ahead.*' After one experience with the Prince, Buller refused to take responsibility for him. The Prince told Wood: 'I would rather fall by assegai than bullets as it would show we were at close quarters.' Chelmsford finally ordered that the Prince should remain in the camp unless he went out with a strong escort.

Chelmsford's columns were now beginning to move into Zululand and the Prince was given the task of sketching the ground over which one of them travelled. One 1 June the Prince asked if he could extend his sketch to cover the ground they would be covering

Upper Bala Hissar from the Gateway above the Residency, Kabul

General Roberts and his staff inspecting captured guns after the defeat of Ayub Khan at Kandahar, 1880

The last of the men retreating from Majuba Hill, 1881

Sir George Colley

The scene immediately after the capture of Tel-el-Kebir , 1882

Queen Victoria distributing the Egyptian war medals to officers and men of the expeditionary force, Windsor Castle, 1882

The Nile expedition for the relief of General Gordon. Towing the armed steamer *Nasaf-el-Khair* over the second cataract, beyond Wadi Halfa. Note the soldiers on the foredeck and rocks semaphoring

Fighting near Gilgit on the North-West frontier. A mountain battery on its way to the front, 1891

Ethel St. Clair Grimmond, 'the heroine of Manipur,' wearing her Royal Red Cross

An elephant battery ready to move off *c.* 1890

Chitral 1895
Sher Afzal and his advisers

Lieutenant Henry Harley,
Lieutenant B. E. H. Gurdon,
Captain Charles Townsend and
Surgeon-Major George Robertson *(seated)*

Chitral Fort

View at Dargai. Tirah Expeditionary Force in the foreground, 1897

General Cronje with Lord Robert's ADC and other members of his staff, 1900

Lord Roberts's and his family

on the following day. The ground had already been gone over by a patrol and no Zulus had been seen, but orders were given that a dozen troopers accompany him. It was then that another staff officer, Lieutenant Jahleel Carey, apparently on an impulse, asked and obtained permission to go with the Prince.

Lieutenant Carey, son of a clergyman, was an exceptionally religious officer and devoted to his wife, two daughters and his mother. He had been commissioned in the 3rd West Indian Regiment and had taken part in a minor expedition to Honduras in 1867. Three years later he went on half pay in order to go to France with an English ambulance unit. He had now served fourteen years in the Army and had passed through the staff college. He had transferred to the 98th Regiment (North Staffordshire) and was soon to be gazetted captain. This was a fateful day in his life.

Not all of the troopers assigned to go with the Prince appeared – they reported to the wrong place – but Lieutenant Carey and the Prince took the seven men that did report and set off. A light rain was falling as they rode out of camp. Major Francis W. Grenfell saw them and called out to the Prince, 'Take care of yourself, and don't get shot!' The Prince waved and replied that Carey would take good care of him.

It is not clear who was, or ought to have been, in command of this little party. Technically, of course, the Prince had no authority and Carey, as the only commissioned officer, was in charge, but the Prince seems to have given most of the orders and the soldiers obeyed him. Shortly past midday they halted at a deserted kraal, pulled thatch from a roof to build a fire, and made coffee. The kraal was, they knew, only temporarily deserted, ashes by one of the huts were still warm, but no lookouts were posted and no member of the party seemed anxious. Carey and the Prince discussed the campaigns of Napoleon Bonaparte as they rested and drank their coffee. About 3.30 they prepared to move on. The horses were saddled. The men stood by their horses' heads. The Prince gave the preliminary order, 'Prepare to mount!' Each left foot was put in a stirrup. Then the order, 'Mount'. And at that moment there was a crash of musketry and about forty Zulus

237

ran screaming towards them. Most of the troopers gained their saddles and their horses carried them away, but the Prince's horse shied and dashed off before he could mount. For a hundred yards he clung to a leather holster attached to the saddle; then a strap broke and the Prince fell beneath his horse.

The horse trampled on his right arm, but he leapt to his feet, drew his revolver with his left hand, and started to run. The Zulus were behind him running faster. One hurled an assegai that pierced his thigh. He stopped, pulled it out and turned on his pursuers. He fired two shots, but missed. Another assegai struck him in the left shoulder. He tried to fight with the assegai he had pulled from his thigh, but, weak from loss of blood, he sank to the ground. In a few moments he was overwhelmed. When found, his body had eighteen assegai wounds.

Of the Prince's escort, two had been killed and one was missing. Lieutenant Carey and the four remaining men had been carried off by their frightened horses at the first volley but they stopped and came together in a depression about fifty yards from where the Prince was killed. None had fired a shot at the Zulus. To Carey it seemed foolhardy to return to look for the Prince when they were so obviously outnumbered. He led his men back to camp.

When Lieutenant Carey entered the officers' mess he was greeted for the last time by a cheery remark from a fellow officer: Major Grenfell called out, 'Why, Carey, you're late for dinner. We thought you'd been shot.'

'I'm all right,' Carey said glumly, 'but the Prince has been killed.'

The word soon spread through the camp. Chelmsford was shaken. All those responsible knew the importance of the tragedy, not only to the world at large but to their own careers and reputations. The wretched Lieutenant Carey sat down that night and wrote the whole story to his wife: 'I am a ruined man, I fear. . . . But it might have been my fate. The bullets tore around us and with only my revolver what could I do. . . . I feel so miserable and dejected!' He had reason for feeling sorry for himself. It was probably true that there was little he could have done to save the

Prince and that he probably would have been killed himself had he tried. But he did not try. And for this he was condemned by every officer in Zululand; indeed, by every officer in the British army. He tried to find excuses for himself. Apparently he came to believe in his own blamelessness and to resent the scorn of his fellow officers. He demanded a court of inquiry to clear his name. The court met and recommended that he be court-martialled. At his trial Carey maintained that he had not been in command of the party but had only accompanied the Prince to correct his sketches. He did everything possible to shift the blame for the disaster onto the victim. He did not succeed. The court found him guilty of misbehaviour in the face of the enemy.

The news of the death of the Prince Imperial created a sensation in England. Queen Victoria heard of it on the forty-second anniversary of her accession to the throne while at Balmoral castle. The newspapers were soon full of it. It was the biggest story of the year and was given more coverage in the press than the defeat at Isandhlwana, and far more than the gallant defence of Rorke's Drift.

Carey was sent back to England where he found considerable sympathy among civilians who did not understand the soldiers' code and who thought that Chelmsford and the Duke of Cambridge were more to be blamed than he. Carey, in his talks with the many reporters who interviewed him, put more and more of the blame on the Prince. In spite of everything, Eugénie pleaded with Queen Victoria not to allow him to be punished and the Queen reluctantly wrote to the review board to ask them to drop the charge, which they did. Carey was ordered to report to his regiment, but he was still not content. He felt that he would be completely vindicated only if Eugénie received him. He wrote time and time again requesting this, but, unknown to him the text of the letter he had written his wife immediately after the fight admitting his cowardice, had been sent to Eugénie. He wrote and talked so much that at last the Empress released the letter to the press. Carey was ruined.

When he rejoined his regiment Carey found himself a pariah. No one spoke to him. Officers turned their backs when he approached them. He had disgraced his regiment and the army, and he was never forgiven. Oddly enough, he did not resign but endured this social hell for six years until he died in Bombay.

Soldiers and civilians obviously had different views of the affair. For the most part the soldiers kept their mouths shut, but Wolseley, writing to his wife, expressed the views of many officers when he said: 'He was a plucky young man, and he died a soldier's death. What on earth could he have better? Many other brave men have also fallen during this war, and with the Prince's fate England as a nation had no concern. Perhaps I have insufficient sympathy with foreign nations; I reserve all my deep feeling for Her Majesty's subjects.'

A month after the Battle of Ulundi, Cetewayo was captured and sent off to England. There on 14 August 1882 he was presented to Queen Victoria. She recorded the meeting in her journal: 'Cetewayo is a very fine man in his native costume, or rather no costume. He is tall, immensely broad, and stout, with a good-humoured countenance, and an intelligent face. Unfortunately, he appeared in a hideous black frock coat and trousers. . . .' Cetewayo could not wear his necklace of lions' claws for it had been appropriated by Wolseley, who broke up the necklace, had the claws suitably mounted, and presented them to the wives of important men.

Cetewayo was later returned to Zululand and reinstated. The Queen thought this a mistake, but, as she told Sir Henry Ponsonby, 'Cetewayo is unscrupulous, as might be expected, but he is not a fool; and I do not think he will with his eyes open come into collision with us again.' She was right.

The British army went away to fight elsewhere and the Zulus were left to try to recover from their disaster. They never did. Eighteen years later Zululand was annexed to Natal. In 1906 the Zulus made a last attempt to be free, but their revolt was quickly suppressed. The Zulus still exist, one tribe among many in the Republic of South Africa, and they still make their distinctive black and white cowhide shields and their sharp assegais – tourists like them.

POOR SIR GEORGE COLLEY

1881

SOUTH Africa was becoming more and more turbulent. There had been the war against the Gaikas in 1878, then against the Zulus in 1879; now there were two other wars in rapid succession. No sooner had Wolseley taken over from Chelmsford and tidied up the Zulu War by capturing Cetewayo than he turned to the disorderly state of affairs in the Transvaal, an area between the Vaal and Limpopo rivers inhabited by about a million Africans and 40,000 Boers. The British fought first one and then the other.

From a well-fortified base in the middle of 250 square miles of sand, rocks and thorn bush Sekukuni, chief of the Bapedi tribe, led his warriors on periodic raids against other tribes and Boer farms. Wolseley led a small expedition against him, defeating the Bapedis and capturing their stronghold. He then led Sekukuni through the streets of Pretoria in a triumphal parade. This done, Wolseley returned to England – there to find himself caricatured as 'the modern major-general' in Gilbert and Sullivan's *The Pirates of Penzance.*

The next war in South Africa was brief, disastrous for British arms, and destined to have a long-range effect upon the history of that part of the world. Under the pretext that there was anarchy in the Transvaal, Britain had annexed the little Boer republic in 1877 and two years later declared it a crown colony. But its Boer inhabitants had a bitter hatred of British rule. They desperately wanted to pursue their own way of life, which was based on a devout faith in a strict Calvinist religion, a firm belief in white supremacy, an intense love of land, and strong feelings of personal independence. To obtain this the *voortrekkers* had left Cape Colony and British rule to move north into the wilderness beyond the Vaal River. British imperialism overtook them, but they were determined to fight for their independence. In December 1880 they revolted, declared themselves free, established a republic and took up arms against Britain. It was the first successful revolt against British rule since the American revolution, and it was the first and only time in the nineteenth century when the British chose to lose.

In every battle – Bronkhorstspruit, Ingogo River, Laing's Nek and Majuba Hill – the Boers beat the British, acquiring in the process a somewhat exaggerated concept of their own powers, considerable though they were, and a hearty contempt for the British army. This was not surprising, for the undeniable fact is that a group of South African farmers did indeed humble the proud and mighty British army and forced – or so it seemed – the British Government to agree to their demands and give them their freedom.

What happened? Gladstone's Liberal party had been indignant when Disraeli annexed the Transvaal, but when Gladstone came to power in 1880 he neglected to free the Boers and even failed to grant them self-governing status within the Empire. He forgot about the Transvaalers until they broke into open armed rebellion, then hastily gave them their independence. It was too late – or too soon, depending upon one's point of view.

The British frequently began wars by losing the first battles, but in the Transvaal peace was made so swiftly – the war lasted only three months – that the army did not have a chance to redeem itself for its initial defeat and much of the onus of the lost war fell on the British generals. It was all very well to win battles against Africans and Asians – 'natives' – but now the British army was fighting against other Europeans, or at least men of European descent, and the British came off second best. It was true that the Boers were a hardy, intelligent, highly motivated people fighting in their own country with modern weapons, but on the other hand they were not professional soldiers and they were loosely organized under amateur generals.

The man who led the British army to the series of defeats in the Transvaal War (also called the First Boer War or the First South African War) was not an incompetent, but a man generally considered to be one of the most brilliant officers in the British army. Major-General Sir George Pomeroy Colley, forty-six, came from an old and wealthy Irish family. He was appointed an ensign at the age of sixteen and two years later he was serving as a lieutenant in South Africa. He first saw action in the China War of 1860, being present at the capture of the Taku forts and taking part in the march on Pekin.

Colley had a keen mind and he made up for his meagre formal education by private study. He learned Russian and studied chemistry and political economy. When he attended the Staff College after the China War he made an extraordinary record: he not only completed the two-year course in less than ten months, but he obtained the highest marks ever made on his examination papers. Later, as a major, he served as professor of military administration and law at the Staff College. He was remarkable in other ways, too, for not only was he a Victorian soldier who read books, but he exercised a talent for drawing and painting as well.

He was a lieutenant-colonel when he went to fight in the Ashanti War. He became a favourite of Wolseley's and one of his best friends. Wolseley said of him: 'He was a man in a thousand, with an iron will and of inflexible determination.'

As a colonel, he served in India, first as military secretary and later as private secretary to Lord Lytton, the viceroy. Then Wolseley took him to South Africa as his chief of staff, but he arrived too late to take part in the conquest of Zululand. On 24 April 1880, on Wolseley's recommendation, he was appointed Governor of Natal and High Commissioner for South East Africa.

Colley's responsibilities included the problems of Zululand and the Transvaal, but he had not yet had time to devote to the situation in the Transvaal when the Boers there revolted; he was as surprised as his superiors in London by what occurred. In fact, he was in the process of withdrawing troops from the Transvaal in compliance with orders from London to reduce military expenditures in his area.

Much of the blame for the start of the war must fall on Colonel Sir William Owen Lanyon, thirty-nine, the Administrator of the Transvaal. He, too, was a Wolseley protégé, and had served as his aide-de-camp during the Ashanti War. Colley trusted his judgement. Unfortunately, Lanyon badly under-estimated the depth of the Boers' feelings and, worse, he underrated their ability and their determination to make their grievances known and attended to. Less than a week before their open defiance of British rule, Lanyon reported that the Boers were 'incapable of any united action, and they are mortal cowards, so anything they may do will be but a spark in the pan'. Just a few months earlier Lanyon had been knighted for his services in South Africa.

When, on 16 December 1880, the Boers proclaimed their independence there were only 1,760 British troops in the Transvaal, mostly infantry, scattered in seven garrisons around the country. The troops were not happy in these isolated forts on the veld and there were a disturbing number of desertions, the disaffected soldiers running off to the near-by Boer republic of the Orange Free State. The opening moves of the war saw the beginning of the pattern which was to become so familiar in the great South African War eighteen years later: British troops besieged in garrison towns, and columns of other British troops marching to their rescue.

The first battle of the war took place on 20 December near the little town of Bronkhorstspruit (then called Bronker's Spruit) when 264 officers and men of the 94th Regiment (Connaught Rangers), marching from Lydenburg to Pretoria, were halted on the march by a Boer commando and ordered to turn back. The lieutenant-colonel in command was given two minutes to reply to the demand. He refused to surrender and was killed by the Boers' opening shots. Nearly a thousand Boers were concealed around the halted British column; when they opened fire all the officers went down at once and in the brief fight that followed nearly the entire column was annihilated. The British thought this tactic very unfair.

If the military and civil authorities in South Africa underrated the Boers, the Queen did not. In a letter to Gladstone written six days after the disaster of Bronkhorstspruit she said; 'The Boers are a dangerous foe and we shall have to support Sir G. Colley strongly.' The Boers were undisciplined, badly organized and short of artillery and ammunition, but their military advantage lay in their mobility, their marksmanship and their skilful use of concealment, in all of which the British were as deficient as they had been a hundred years earlier fighting the American colonists. Expecting the British to send an army into the Transvaal, the Boers moved over the border into Natal and put 2,000 men in commanding positions at Laing's Nek, the only real pass in the Drakensberg range by which an army could enter the country from Natal. Colley, who was trying to put together an army from the meagre resources available to him, was not disturbed when he heard what the Boers had done: 'Very good natured of them,' he said. 'They will thus give me the opportunity of meeting them close to my base.'

On 10 January 1881 Colley marched out of Pietermaritzburg with an army of about a thousand troops whom he considered 'as queer a mixture as was ever brought together'. Considering the many queer mixtures of troops the British had put into an army in the previous fifty years, Colley's force was not as odd as he thought, but it did consist of twelve companies of infantry from four different regiments and 120 mounted infantry (most of whom could not ride), a naval detachment and six guns. Many of the soldiers were young and half-trained, but there were also some fine units, such as the Gordon Highlanders, who had recently distinguished themselves in Afghanistan, and the 60th Rifles. It was, however, an inadequate force to meet a Boer army twice its size and strategically placed. Colley had obviously accepted Lanyon's appraisal of the Boers' resolution and capabilities.

On 28 January Colley was in a base camp at Mount Prospect, just three miles from Laing's Nek, and from here he launched an attack on a spur of the mountain range from which he hoped to turn the Boer position. The attack, spearheaded by 480 men of the 58th Regiment was a failure. The 58th suffered 160 casualties, including all its officers. Total British casualties were 83 killed and 111 wounded. The Queen found this news 'most distressing'.

Colley then decided to wait for reinforcements, but on 7 February the Boers started a flanking movement to cut him off from supplies and reinforcements. The next day Colley himself set off with five companies of the 60th Rifles and three dozen mounted infantry to escort the mail wagon part way back to Newcastle and make sure the route was clear. It was ridiculous, of course, that the commander of the army should give himself such an assignment, but Victorian generals could rarely resist temptation when there was a chance to see action. Perhaps it was natural in an army where bravery was more esteemed than strategy.

Eight miles from camp, just after crossing the Ingogo River, Colley encountered a much stronger force of mounted Boers. The battle lasted from noon until about six o'clock in the evening, the British clinging to the top of a hill and beating off the attackers. Under cover of darkness Colley was able to make his escape, but he had sustained 150 casualties, half of his party.

In two weeks of action Colley had lost two battles and a third of his men had been killed or wounded. To his sister he wrote: 'I have to look cheerful, and I dare say I am thought callous . . . but sometimes it is hard not to break down. However, reinforcements are now arriving, and I hope it will not be long before I have force enough to terminate this hateful war.'

The Boers were well entrenched on both sides of Laing's Nek, but on the left front, looking from the British camp at Mount Prospect, there was a sugarloaf-shaped mountain, an extinct volcano 6,500 feet above sea level and 2,500 feet above the camp;

its crest appeared to be undefended by the enemy, who apparently regarded it as inaccessible. It was called Majuba Hill. To Colley this mountain seemed to be the key to the nek. If he could seize it he would be able to rout the Boers or force them to fight from a very disadvantageous position, though he thought that by merely occupying the summit he would force the Boers to retire from their positions.

At 10.00 p.m. on Saturday, 26 February, Colley led 490 soldiers and 64 sailors on a night march, or rather climb, to the top of Majuba Hill. Among the small group of officers with Colley were at least four who survived the next day's battle to become knighted generals, and three of them famous ones. Perhaps tainted by the fate of Majuba Hill, the names of all three were to be associated with tragedy and failure.

Lieutenant-Colonel Herbert Stewart, thirty-eight, had served most of his career in India, where he had made a good record but had seen little action. At the end of 1878 he had been sent to South Africa and took part in the last half of the Zulu War and in the Basuto War that followed soon after. Wolseley had marked him down as a good officer and made him his military secretary in Natal. Stewart had joined Colley as his chief staff officer less than a week before.

In the two companies of Gordon Highlanders that climbed Majuba Hill that night were two twenty-eight-year-old subalterns of very different backgrounds: Lieutenant Ian Hamilton and Lieutenant Hector Macdonald. Hamilton's father had been an officer in the Gordon Highlanders before him and his mother was the daughter of a viscount; Macdonald's father had been a poor crofter in Scotland. Hamilton had had a public school education and had graduated from Sandhurst; Macdonald had been a draper's assistant before running off to enlist in the army at the age of eighteen, and he had served nine and a half years in the ranks before being given a battlefield commission in the Second Afghan War. Macdonald's moment in history came in 1898 when commanding a brigade of Egyptian and Sudanese soldiers, he saved Kitchener's army from destruction at the battle of

Omdurman. Hamilton's great opportunity did not come until 1915 when Kitchener gave him an army and orders to take the Dardanelles. Hamilton had a long life, dying in 1947 at the age of ninety-four, but for the last thirty-two years of his life he was known as the man who had commanded the disastrous Gallipoli campaign.

At this point in their lives, however, it is doubtful if any of the officers had any thoughts of the future that extended beyond the next twenty-four hours. The night march was the first stage of an arduous and daring enterprise and officers and men alike were excited by their coming adventure. As the men, each loaded down with seventy rounds of ammunition and three days' rations, stumbled along in the moonless night, they heard dogs barking at O'Neill's farm, a deserted homestead between the lines, and feared that the enemy would be alarmed. But they reached the base of the mountain safely and at once began to climb its steep sides. Just before four o'clock in the morning Major Thomas Fraser (another future major-general) and two African guides reached the top. As Colley had suspected, it was deserted. An hour later the rest of the party arrived and Colley sorted out the men by companies and placed them around the perimeter or in the reserve in the centre of the saucer-shaped mountain top. So far, so good.

The top of Majuba Hill was certainly a commanding position. To the north Colley could look down on the camp fires of the Boers in their laagers about 2,500 yards away and as dawn broke the troops had a splendid panorama of the Drakensberg range. Colley felt very secure. He remarked to Lieutenant-Colonel Stewart, 'We could stay here forever.' This feeling of confidence – over-confidence, as it turned out – was shared by his men. In spite of orders to stay concealed, the soldiers were soon shaking their fists and shooting at the Boer camp below them. There was a considerable amount of long range firing, but at 9.30 a.m. Stewart signalled to the base camp at Mount Prospect: 'All very comfortable. Boers wasting ammunition. One man wounded in foot.' To the British on the mountain top it seemed that consternation had seized the Boers. They could see them driving in their oxen and inspanning their wagons, and Colley thought they were preparing to abandon their position.

It should have been obvious to any subaltern that the first thing to be done on reaching the summit was to entrench. In fact, Lieutenant Ian Hamilton requested permission to do so. Colonel A. D. Macgregor, Colley's ADC, also suggested entrenchment, but Colley, of whom Wolseley had said that he 'would always work as long as there was anything important to be done', refused to give the order, saying that not much was needed as there was only rifle fire from the enemy. Then he went to sleep. It was the sort of very stupid mistake that very brilliant men sometimes make. In this case it was fatal.

The Boers, far from being frightened by the British occupation of Majuba Hill, were only angry that the British were fighting on Sunday. Among the many volunteers for the force to drive the British off, only 180 expert marksmen were selected. Under the cover of about a thousand rifles firing from below, the Boer volunteers, divided into two assault groups, began to climb the mountain.

Lieutenant Hamilton rushed up to General Colley, who had stationed himself in the centre of the mountain top, and reported that about a hundred Boers had reached the summit. Colley thanked him politely and Hamilton ran back to the fight. He was soon back to report 200 Boers on the hill. Colley was undisturbed. The next time he reported about 350 of the enemy were on the hill and asked for reinforcements. Neither Hamilton nor Colley appears to have been overcome with excitement:

'I do hope, General,' said Hamilton, 'that you will let us have a charge, and that you will not think it presumption on my part to have come up and asked you.'

'No presumption, Mr Hamilton,' said Colley calmly, 'but we will wait until the Boers advance on us, then give them a volley and charge.'

The fourth time Hamilton came back – to report even more exaggerated numbers of the enemy – he found Colley asleep. Hamilton can be forgiven for thinking there were more Boers involved in the attack than there really were for their fire was accurate and deadly. The British had no time for formal volleys and charges. The Boers crept up on them and then mowed them down. Of the eighteen men with Hamilton, thirteen were soon casualties and Hamilton's kilt and coat were cut by bullets. Lieutenant Hector Macdonald, who was trying to hold part of the west side of the mountain with twenty men, soon found himself left with only one private.

Hamilton, a crack shot, picked up a rifle, but before he could fire it a bullet shattered his left wrist, making him a cripple for life. Turning in pain and despair, he saw the line giving way and Gordon Highlanders fleeing with the rest. Colley was awake now, shouting orders. A bullet struck him in the head and he died instantly. Macdonald tried to fight with his fists, but he was overpowered and made a prisoner. The actual battle lasted only an hour; by 1.30 p.m. it was all over.

Hamilton clutched his broken, bleeding wrist and ran with the rest until he was hit in the back of the head by a spent bullet or a piece of rock kicked up by a bullet and fell unconscious. He awoke to find two young Boers, about fourteen years old, turning him over and removing his equipment. A Boer with a large black beard then appeared, chased off the boys, and appropriated Hamilton's sword, his father's claymore. Finally the Boer commander had him brought up to identify Colley's body. This done his hand was tied up in a bandana and he was turned loose. For a while he carried water to the wounded, and then he stumbled down the hill. He was found by a British patrol unconscious beside a stream.

It was little wonder that the Boers did not fear the British. Only 180 Boers, mostly young farm boys, had assaulted a seemingly impregnable position held by 554 regular soldiers and sailors commanded by one of the British army's brightest generals and had completely routed them. British casualties were 93 killed, 133 wounded and 58 taken prisoner; Boer losses were said to be one killed and five wounded. Majuba Hill was the last time the British army carried its colours into battle.

Poor Sir George Colley

The day after the battle, at Windsor Castle, Queen Victoria wrote in her journal: 'Dreadful news reached me when I got up. Another fearful defeat, and poor Sir G. Colley killed . . .'

Evelyn Wood, who had joined Colley only a week before as second in command, now took charge of the army in Natal. The Queen sent him a telegram: 'Most deeply grieved and distressed by the terrible news received today. My heart bleeds for the many valuable lives lost. Deeply lament Sir G. Colley. Pray don't expose yourself unnecessarily, your life is precious. Saw Lady Wood on 26th. Anxious to know how wounded are doing?'

The War Office ordered Roberts out to take charge of the Transvaal War, but Majuba Hill was the last battle of the war. Wood wanted to continue the fight, as did the Queen, who wrote in her journal: 'I do not like peace before we have retrieved our honour.' On 9 March she sent a telegram to Lord Kimberley, the Colonial Secretary, saying: 'I find an impression prevails that we are about to make peace with the Boers on their own terms. I am sure you will agree with me that even the semblance of any concessions after our recent defeats would have a deplorable effect.' But on orders from London Wood arranged a prolonged armistice which lasted until a peace treaty was signed. When Roberts reached South Africa there was nothing for him to do but get back on the ship and go home.

The immediate result of capitulating to the Boers was satisfactory: there was peace between Britain and Boer in the Transvaal and the Boers were free to continue their running fight with the local Bantu. But the long term result was tragic: the Boer conviction that the British could be defeated on the battlefield and made to yield to political demands led directly to the bloody South African War that closed the century.

Wood was blamed, unfairly, by many civilians and soldiers for making peace and not ignoring his orders and attacking the Boers. Even four years later, Wolseley had not forgiven him and told his wife:

I have always regarded the peace made by Wood as infamous, and I have no doubt whatever in my own mind that it would never have been

251

made if General Roberts had not been sent to supersede Wood. This fact drove Wood to make an end to the war, *coûte que coûte*, before Roberts could arrive to supersede him. Such is the whole story but, of course, because the Queen likes Wood she believes that he made the terms he did because he was forced by the Government to make them. When a general is desired by his Government to do anything that he regards as infamous it is his duty to resign and say why he resigns.

All was not well in the Empire, as the Queen told Lord Granville, the Foreign Secretary: 'Great Britain's star *is NOT in the ascendant since the last 6 or 7 months?*' Indeed it was not. If one were forced to say, as in a school examination paper, at what exact moment in history the mighty British Empire first began to crumble, it would perhaps not be far wrong to point to that Sunday afternoon in February 1881 when British soldiers, fleeing from Boer farm boys, ran down the steep slopes of Majuba Hill.

23

WOLSELEY VERSUS ARABI
AND THE QUEEN

1881–82

No sooner was peace made in South Africa than war was declared in North Africa. The French had just conquered Tunisia; now the British took Egypt. It was Britain's fifth war in Africa in five years, but there were more to come: British soldiers and explorers were to paint red great patches of the map of the continent from the Cape to Cairo.

British interference in the affairs of Egypt began in 1875 when Disraeli negotiated the purchase of shares in the Suez Canal and British influence grew ever stronger over the next decade. The ruler of Egypt, who owed nominal allegiance to the sultan of Turkey, was the Khedive Ismail, a spendthrift who brought the financial affairs of his country to a position where, in 1876, Egypt was no longer able to pay her debts or even the interest on the money she had borrowed in Europe. Ismail attempted to throw off the ever growing influence of the European powers, particularly France and England, but the French, with British support, pressured the Sultan of Turkey to depose him and put his son, Tewfik, on the throne in his stead. Tewfik, knowing who was buttering his bread, agreed to permit France and Britain to appoint controllers-general of Egyptian finance. These officials, acting on behalf of Egypt's European creditors, so controlled the Egyptian economy that by 1880 two-thirds of the country's entire revenue was being paid to her creditors.

In 1879 there was a revolt in the Egyptian army, but it was quickly suppressed. Two years later there was a more serious rebellion, one which threatened to overthrow the Khedive and throw out the foreigners. Colonel Ahmed Arabi was a nineteenth-century Nasser born before his time. He began by presenting a series of demands to the Egyptian government, each of which was granted, until in January 1882 he succeeded in dismissing the prime minister, making himself minister of war and putting through a new constitution. His rallying cry was 'Egypt for the Egyptians' and he was supported not only by his fellow army officers, but also by Egyptian landowners, who did not like the efficient tax collecting methods of the controllers-general; by Muslim religious leaders, who hated the growing power of the Christians; and by many intellectuals, who resented the influence of foreigners in Egyptian affairs.

In May British and French fleets were threateningly anchored in the harbour of Alexandria; Arabi, however, refused to be intimidated and began to fortify the waterfront area. On 11–12 June there was rioting in Alexandria and about fifty Europeans were killed. To the British this was a clarion call for action, but the French decided to wash their hands of the whole affair and sailed away. On 10 July the British admiral, Frederick Beauchamp Paget Seymour, began what Wolseley later called 'that silly and criminal bombardment of Alexandria'. It lasted for ten and a half hours; then landing parties destroyed the fortifications and seized the town. In London Gladstone and his cabinet decided to send an army to destroy Arabi.

The war that followed, being managed by the ever-efficient Wolseley, now a lieutenant-general and Adjutant-General of the Army, was short, neat and successful: 'all Sir Garnet'. It went exactly as he planned. It was the most brilliantly devised and executed campaign of the century. Not only did Wolseley work out a plan for winning the war, but he developed a campaign for winning the heart of his Queen. Arabi was easily overcome; the Queen proved more difficult.

Queen Victoria did not like Wolseley and he knew it and was embittered. 'I have done my best for my country,' he wrote to his wife, 'and if my country's sovereign does not appreciate my services, I cannot help it.' The strained relations were primarily the result of the running quarrel between Wolseley and the Duke of Cambridge.

Wolseley and the Duke both had a love affair with the army; it was the great passion of their lives. But they had quite different views on how their mistress could best be served. The Duke loved the army as it was; he did not want to see it changed in any way. He once said that while he was at the Horse Guards there was change only at the right time; the right time he explained was only when change could no longer possibly be avoided. Wolseley saw that much was outdated in the army and that although many improvements had been made there was still much that ought to be changed, and he was a passionate advocate of reform.

Within the army, both had their supporters, although if a poll had been taken it is probable that the Duke would have had more than Wolseley, and even among those who favoured reform there were many who still admired the Duke. The advocates of reform, however, were more vocal and literate; it was Wolseley's speeches and articles condemning what he called 'pipeclay prejudices' at the Horse Guards that most infuriated the Duke, who thought it unseemly to air the army's affairs in public. On the other hand, the Duke had the ear of his cousin the Queen, and knew how best to influence her: Wolseley argued for promotion on merit, but the Duke implied that this innovation, being the system used in the republican French army, would probably lead to revolution in England. The Queen had complete confidence in the Duke.

Queen Victoria turned her partisanship into a personal dislike of Wolseley, whom she did not really know. The Duke and Wolseley, however, each of whom thought the other dead wrong on almost every issue, had a personal respect for each other's character and abilities and they did as well as two stubborn and self-confident men could to get along with each other. Although Wolseley saw the Duke as the chief stumbling block to army reform, he never openly attacked him; the Duke thought Wolseley a radical, but he gave the Queen a fair appraisal of his abilities. When the time came to select the leader of the expedition to Egypt, the Duke wrote a 'Private and most confidential' letter to the Queen on 20 July 1882:

> I have reason to think that Mr Childers [H. C. E. Childers, Secretary for War] will propose Sir Garnet Wolseley for the chief command if an expedition is sent . . . and I do not think it would be advisable to oppose the selection, as I am satisfied that the public will feel pleased with the appointment, and I further think that Wolseley is very decidedly as able a man for the field as we have got. I therefore would suggest that you would graciously *accept* the submission if made.

Even on campaign in South Africa Wolseley had been worried about the feeling against him at court and was constantly corresponding with people in England about it. Redvers Buller once said: 'Soldiers have nothing to do with politics and I think the less they know about them the better.' Wolseley knew better – and Buller himself was to learn too late how wrong he was. Wolseley had tried to win the Queen to his views by implying that Prince Albert would have agreed with him, but the Queen was not impressed. Writing to his wife from Pretoria on 20 March 1880 he had summed up the matter:

> My letters show me that the formidable party against me is in the ascendant, and will crush me if it can. The Queen's private secretary tells me Her Majesty is offended because I said in a letter I wrote to him that we have never had any substantial reforms in the Army since the Prince Consort died, and that were he living now, Army Reform would be in a very different position. This is certain, for Prince Albert was a very sensible man, and took his own view. The Queen very naturally adopts the Duke of Cambridge's outlook, and because he dislikes the modern views I hold on military subjects, Her Majesty assumes I am a Radical. I detest Radicals; men of Mr Gladstone's stamp are abhorrent to my instinct.

Wolseley versus Arabi and the Queen

Wolseley admired Disraeli, and the feeling was mutual. Disraeli once told Lady Bradford: 'Sir Garnet has not disappointed me. He is one of those men who not only succeed, but succeed quickly. Nothing can give you an idea of the jealousy, the hatred, and all uncharitableness of the Horse Guards against our only soldier.' Our only soldier. It was a flattering phrase, but not one which would reduce the jealousy. There was, after all, 'England's other general': Roberts.

Thanks to Wolseley's great abilities and the Duke of Cambridge's honest character, Wolseley was given command of the army assembled to crush Arabi. The Egyptian campaign was a popular one with the jingos and everyone with any military pretensions at all wanted to go, even the Prince of Wales. On being appointed to lead the expedition, Wolseley, who always attached great importance to the selection of his officers, was besieged by applications from officers who wanted to accompany him and pressure was applied on all sides, and even on his wife. He managed to take most of the officers he wanted, but he also had to take others whom he did not want, and his army of 40,000 was top-heavy with no less than eighteen generals. With help from the politicians he was able to turn down the Prince of Wales, but in an effort to please the Queen he did take on her third son, Arthur, the Duke of Connaught (1850–1942), and gave him command of the 1st Guards Brigade. The elite Guards were popularly believed to consist of the finest soldiers Britain possessed; their officers were of the bluest blood in the realm; but in fact, no Guards regiment had seen action since the Crimean War and the Life Guards had not heard a shot fired in anger in sixty-seven years, since Waterloo. Now, under the Duke of Connaught, they were to be shipped to Egypt.

For Wolseley, happiness was leading men into battle, and he thought a general had no greater favour to bestow than to give an officer a command. Queen Victoria admired soldiers and she too knew the importance of a command, but she was also a mother, and she wrote in her journal: 'When I read that my darling, precious Arthur was really to go, I quite broke down. It seemed like a dreadful dream. Telegraphed to him. Still, I would not on any account have him shirk his duty. Went with a heavy heart to bed.'

As a young man Wolseley had proved his physical courage, but it took courage of a different sort to give this appointment to the Queen's son. It was a great personal risk, and he knew it. If he kept the Duke of Connaught and the Guards safely behind the lines he would be criticized both within and outside the army and, indeed, from a military standpoint he was forced to employ them, but if the Queen's favourite son was killed Wolseley's career would be finished. Fortunately, he still had that which, in addition to ability, all good generals must have: luck.

In spite of the royal and political pressures put on him, and over the strong objections of the Duke of Cambridge, Wolseley managed to take with him almost all of the 'Wolseley gang', which included most of the officers who had served him well in the Ashanti War. Even Colonel Lanyon, whose faulty analysis of the Boers' discontent and under-estimation of their abilities and determination had done so much to bring on the Transvaal War, was included and, as base commander at Ismailia, proved himself a better soldier than colonial administrator.

The appointment for which Wolseley was most criticized at court and at the Horse Guards was that of Sir Baker Creed Russell, who was given a brigade of cavalry and the temporary rank of brigadier. Russell was an able and distinguished officer. As a subaltern he had been at Meerut when the Indian Mutiny started and he was in many a fight throughout that war. He had been with Wolseley in the Ashanti War and in the campaign against Sekukuni in the Transvaal. When Wolseley gave Russell the brigade in place of Sir Henry Ewart of the Life Guards, who had never seen a battle, he received a critical letter from the Prince of Wales himself, who, said Wolseley, 'was furious at my making Baker Russell a brigadier'. Still, Wolseley kept the appointment and, as he told his wife,

I reminded the Prince that although Colonel Ewart, whom Russell superseded, had become a full Colonel before Russell, it was because he belonged to a corps in which the officers were given privileged rank; that he had never seen any service, whilst B.R. had been made Major, Lieutenant-Colonel, and full Colonel for distinguished service in three campaigns, and had entered the service and gone through his first campaign before Ewart had been gazetted into the Army at all.

That redoubtable old war horse, Evelyn Wood, was also in Egypt, but he saw very little action. Wood had been a part of the original Wolseley gang, but since the Transvaal War armistice, he had been in disfavour with his old chief. Wolseley also considered him a possible rival, for Wood was one of the Queen's favourite generals. After the Zulu War the Queen had called Wood and Buller 'our two most distinguished men', and she wrote to Disraeli urging him to talk with Wood when he returned to England:

Sir E. Wood is a remarkably intelligent man; not only an admirable General with plenty of *dash* as well as prudence, but a man of what is now called *Imperial* views, loyal and devoted to Sovereign and country, and who takes *in all* the *difficulties* of the position. He is most agreeable as well as amusing, very lively yet *very discreet*.

Disraeli did meet Wood and was most impressed with him. He had, Disraeli told the Queen, 'a mind rich with practical conclusions, which will be ever ready to assist him in the conduct of affairs and the management of men'. Wood also admired and was admired by Gladstone, proving that he had those political qualities so helpful to a soldier who aspires to become a field-marshal.

When, in August 1882, Wood embarked with his brigade to go to Egypt, the Queen came on board to say good-bye: 'She embraced my wife, and was very gracious to me. She had honoured me with a long private interview in July, when I was commanded to Windsor, and treated me with a condescension for the memory of which I shall be ever grateful.' This ability to charm the Queen and her ministers did not endear him to his old chief: 'I am forced to leave Wood behind in Alexandria,' Wolseley told his wife. 'He will fume, but I cannot help it. . . . He can write dispatches home about the doings there, but I am afraid he will miss the big coup here, and I am very sorry for him.' Wood did indeed fume. According to Redvers Buller, Wood was 'eaten up with personal vanity', an uncharitable remark from a man of whom only a few months earlier Wood had said, 'I have not known a better friend, nor a better soldier, than Redvers Buller'.

Buller, tall, big-boned and ponderous, was again with Wolseley. He had not been long in England after his return from South Africa, but he had managed to marry a widow with four children and was on his honeymoon when the army for Egypt was being assembled. He quickly left his bride to join Wolseley, who put him on his staff as chief of intelligence. Buller was a splendid field soldier, brave and possessing great powers of endurance, but he was never noted for his brains or imagination and Wolseley had cause to complain of the work of his intelligence department. To Childers he wrote: 'Those employed to collect information are such wild people when any estimate of the enemy's strength is called for, that it is difficult for me to give you any statement that would be worth your hearing.' Buller's idea of intelligence work was to go see the enemy's front lines himself. This he did, and he managed to get into the major battle of the war at Tel-el-Kebir and was awarded the KCMG for his efforts.

William Butler was also on the staff as assistant adjutant and assistant quartermaster-general. He was an Irishman with a quick brain and a sharp tongue. When he came to write his autobiography at the end of his career, he said, 'When I look back over forty-seven years of service, the thing that astonishes me is the entire absence of the thinking faculty in nine out of ten of the higher-grade officers with whom I was associated.' But Wolseley, said Butler, had 'the best and most brilliant brain I ever met in the British army'. Butler's admiration for his chief seldom flagged and Wolseley rewarded him in campaign after campaign – Canada, the Gold Coast, South Africa and Egypt – by giving him plenty of hard work, danger and honours, all of which he craved.

Hugh McCalmont was not particularly bright, but he had been with Wolseley on the Red River Expedition, in the Ashanti War

and in the Transvaal; he had also served as a military attaché in
Turkey, where he had accompanied the Turkish army in the field
during their campaign in Armenia, and had been on the staff of
General Charles MacGregor when, at the end of the Second
Afghan War, he had made a march through the hostile Mari
country. An experienced soldier was McCalmont, and now he was
for the fourth time on campaign with Wolseley, serving as brigade
major for the 1st Cavalry Division.

They were a battered lot, these stout Ashanti veterans serving
their one-eyed chief. Besides Maurice, still recovering from
wounds received while storming Sekukuni's stronghold in the
Transvaal, and Wood, now growing quite deaf and his body still
holding the nail fired into him from an Ashanti's musket, there
was Archibald Alison, who had lost an arm in the Indian Mutiny
but was now a major-general, and John McNeill, his hand crippled
by an Ashanti bullet but serving now on the staff of the Duke of
Connaught. Also present was Herbert Stewart, recently released
by the Boers after his capture on Majuba Hill and now on the
staff of the cavalry division. He was the newest member of the
Wolseley gang. Wolseley first met Stewart in Zululand and he had
become his closest friend in the army.

The only member of the Wolseley gang who was missing –
besides poor Colley, of course, and Robert Home, who had died of
typhoid fever in Bulgaria two years earlier – was the ugly and
brilliant Henry Brackenbury. He had gone with Wolseley to
Cyprus and had stayed on there after Wolseley left to organize the
military police force and reform the prisons on the island. He had
rejoined Wolseley in Zululand as his military secretary and had
taken part in the operations against Sekukuni. Then he had a
series of postings, none of which lasted very long: private secretary to the Viceroy of India, military attaché in Paris, and then
to Ireland as under-secretary for police. In this last post he
had quarrelled with the authorities; he was put on half-pay
and refused permission when he applied to join Wolseley in
Egypt.

In addition to his trusted friends, Wolseley also had a number of officers who, although not members of the Wolseley gang, had seen much active service. He wanted all the experienced fighters he could get. For his chief of staff he selected, over the objections of the Duke of Cambridge, Sir John Ayde, an artillery-man whose grandfather, father and two uncles had also served in the Royal Artillery, as did his eldest son. He had seen action in the Crimea, the Indian Mutiny, and the Umbeyla campaign. Although fourteen years Wolseley's senior, he did not object to serving under him and served him well, though he did not agree completely with his plan for the campaign.

Another experienced soldier whom Wolseley was happy to have with him was a goateed officer with the curious name of Drury Drury-Lowe, who had spent almost his entire military career with the 17th Lancers (known as the 'Death or Glory Boys') in which Evelyn Wood had also served as a subaltern when he left the navy at the end of the Crimean War to join the Army. Drury-Lowe had served in the Crimean War, the Indian Mutiny and the Zulu War. Now Wolseley put him in command of a cavalry brigade.

One old warrior who wanted to get into the fight was Sir Henry Havelock-Allan, son of General Henry Havelock. Havelock-Allan (the last half of the name was added to obtain a legacy from a cousin) was first in action during the Persian War of 1857. He then saw much service during the Mutiny, where he was several times wounded and won the Victoria Cross, and in the Maori War of 1863–66 in New Zealand. In addition to this active service, he had taken leaves of absence from the British army to see the Franco-Prussian War in 1870 and the Russo-Turkish War of 1877. Just before the Egyptian Campaign he had retired from the Army as a lieutenant-general, but he turned up at Wolseley's headquarters in Egypt and wanted an assignment. Havelock-Allan was a brave soldier, but on his way out to India for the first time in 1848 he had suffered a bad sunstroke and thereafter and with increasing frequency he had what were called 'periodical fits of mental excitement and eccentricity'. He was slightly insane.

Wolseley versus Arabi and the Queen

Just before the battle of Tel-el-Kebir, Wolseley, writing to his wife, said:

Havelock is still here as mad as ever: I received a letter from him yesterday, begging to have it sent home as it was a request to be re-employed, etc., etc., in his usual strain. I am extremely sorry for him, and feel for him very much, but still feel that he can never be employed again: he is not sane enough to argue with.

He never received another appointment, but he managed to find a soldier's death fifteen years later when, as a Member of Parliament, he went to see the fighting on the North-West Frontier and was killed by an Afridi bullet.

Although Wolseley managed to keep Havelock-Allan out of his army, he was forced to take a number of officers in whom he had little confidence. One of these was the Duke of Teck, the Queen's cousin. He had served in the Austrian army and was present at the battle of Solferino, but, according to Wolseley, he was 'quite an impossible human being, just like a spoiled child'. He kept packing and unpacking his kit and was constantly complaining about his quarters and the hardships of the campaign. He was on Wolseley's staff but Wolseley could think of nothing better to do with him than to put him in charge of the foreign military officers who were observing the war.

Another unwanted officer was Major George Fitzgeorge, eldest son of the Duke of Cambridge by a morganatic marriage to an actress. Wolseley thought him a 'horrid snob and I dare say quite useless'. The Duke had asked that he be taken along and Wolseley found a place for him, but said later that 'he took precious care never to expose his useless carcass to danger'.

There were other officers whom Wolseley had selected, or at least had approved of, but who did not give him satisfaction. One of these was Sir Edward Bruce Hamley (1824–93). He appeared to have many of the qualities which would recommend him to Wolseley: he was literate, a military student, and he was intensely disliked by the Duke of Cambridge. So Wolseley made him a division commander. He had written poems, literary criticisms, a two-volume novel and many articles, but he was best known for his writings on military subjects and his great book on strategy, *The Operations of War*, which he completed in 1866, was the most widely read book of its kind by a British soldier in the century. It had been praised by Moltke, Sherman and *The Times;* until 1894 it was the sole text for the Staff College entrance examination. He had served as a professor of military history at the Staff College and he enjoyed tremendous prestige as a strategist. 'Hamley expected his pupils to accept his deductions as well as his facts and did not encourage original research', according to Wood, who had been one of his students. 'As a soldier at the Staff College, Hamley was a civilian; as a civilian in his literary club, he was a soldier,' said Butler, adding, 'and equally in college or club he was an autocrat.'

On joining Wolseley in Egypt Hamley, who felt 'if I call myself a strategist, I ought to behave as such', proceeded to give his commander his opinions on how the war should be fought. Wolseley at once put him to work drawing up elaborate plans for an attack on the Egyptians at Aboukir Bay, near where Nelson had defeated Napoleon's fleet in 1798. Soon everyone knew, including the enemy, that Aboukir Bay was to be the point of attack. Then Wolseley left Hamley and his division and quietly sailed off with the rest of the army to seize Port Said, Ismailia and the Suez Canal.

He left Hamley a note telling him that the Aboukir Bay plan was 'a humbug and that my real destination is the Canal'. Hamley the strategist was furious. Although he later saw action with a part of his division at Tel-el-Kebir, he never forgave the man who had deceived and humiliated him. Wolseley and his gang were busy with their pens for years defending themselves against his attacks. Wolseley called him an 'angry man with an exaggerated opinion of his own capacity as a commander'. Being neither a friend of Wolseley and his clique nor of the Duke of Cambridge, who hated all theoreticians, the Staff College and all who were associated with it, Hamley had no more future in the army. He spent the rest of his life sulking and, as a biographer said, 'he was widely regarded as an ill-used man'.

The other infantry division commander, Lieutenant-General Harry Smith Willis, had not been on active service with the British army since the Crimean War. Except for one three-year period in which he was in charge of a military district in Britain, Willis had not even held a command during the past twenty-three years. On 28 August 1882, when Arabi sent out a force to attack General Graham, Willis sent Wolseley in Ismailia a frantic telegram: 'Enemy advancing on Mahsama. Fear Graham has been defeated.' But Wolseley knew Graham, and he knew Willis; he refused to believe the message and went to bed: 'Willis is a very plucky fellow personally but an alarmist,' he said.

Gerald Graham, about whom Willis was so concerned, was one of Willis's brigade commanders, and an excellent one. On 28 August Graham, with about 2,000 men, had indeed been attacked by about 10,000 Egyptians, but Wolseley's confidence in him was not misplaced. As he said later in his report: 'General Graham's dispositions were all that they should have been, and his operations were carried out with that coolness for which he has always been so well known.' With some help from Drury-Lowe's cavalry, Graham drove off the enemy.

Wolseley's deception, which began the campaign and which so infuriated Hamley, also deceived the war correspondents (to his great delight), the Duke of Cambridge, the enemy, and all but four of his own officers. On 10 September 1882 his army was marching westward across the desert towards Cairo and the Egyptians were, as he had predicted, preparing to make a stand at a place called Tel-el-Kebir, a village sixteen miles east of Zagazig on the Sweetwater Canal and the railway line, about half way between the Suez Canal and Cairo. The first stage of the campaign had been a brilliant success, but Wolseley had his worries and from his camp twenty-two miles from Ismailia he wrote to his wife:

The poor Guards Brigade marched all through the heat of the day, and came in in the evening very tired and bivouacked for the night. I went down from my camp to see them, and met the Duke of Connaught.

He is really one of the most active Brigadiers I have, and is very keen. I am distressed in my mind as to what I shall do, for I want to shove the Foot Guards into a hot corner, and they want this themselves, and they are the best troops I have, but I am so nervous that no injury should befall the favourite son of the Queen that I am loath to endanger his life. This is a serious matter for me, for I have determined to move out from here on Tuesday night to attack the enemy's fortified position on Wednesday morning a little before daybreak. I am so weak that I cannot afford to indulge in any other plan, and it requires the steadiest and the best troops to attain my object – and then I may fail – oh God grant I may not! – I know that I am doing a dangerous thing, but I cannot wait for reinforcements; to do so would kill the spirit of my troops, which at present is all I could wish it to be. I hope I may never return home a defeated man: I would sooner leave my old bones here than go home to be jeered at. Ayde doesn't like my plan, I can see. . . . Everything depends upon the steadiness of my infantry. If they are steady in the dark – a very crucial trial – I must succeed. Otherwise I might fail altogether, or achieve very little. You can fancy that this responsibility tells a little upon me, but I don't think any soul here thinks so. By this hour Wednesday we shall know all. How inscrutable are the ways of God, and how ignorant we are of what the next hour may bring forth, joy or sorrow, victory or failure.

Wolseley was impressed by the Egyptian fortifications at Tel-el-Kebir, which contained about seventy guns, some of them excellent breech-loading Krupps. The defences were manned by the main force of the Egyptian army: about 25,000 troops and some bedouins. Wolseley thought these fortifications would be 'a very hard nut to crack', particularly since the area in front of them was smooth desert, giving the Egyptians a clear field of fire. For four days before the attack he and his staff went over the ground in front of the Egyptian positions. One result of this careful reconnaissance was the discovery that the Egyptians did not man outposts at night. Wolseley therefore resolved to make a night march, which he described as 'a new thing, I may say, in our military annals'. He forgot about Roberts's night march to attack the Peiwar Kotal. Still, a night march on an enemy position was then a rare and risky thing. There was always the danger that the troops would move too far or not far enough or in the wrong direction; soldiers in the dark, being unable to see their comrades or their officers, were, or might be, unsteady. This was Wolseley's great worry.

Before the attack began, each commander was given a sketch and was shown exactly where his unit was to go and told what it was to do. In the dark early morning of 13 September the troops began to move across the trackless desert to their assigned positions – 17,401 men and sixty-one guns, led by a navigator from the Royal Navy. Each man carried 100 rounds of ammunition and two days' rations. The operation was carried out almost silently – a drunken Highlander was quickly subdued – and almost smoothly – the Highlanders not quite getting in their proper positions. Concern for the safety of the Duke of Connaught probably led Wolseley to put the Duke's brigade in the second line. In the first line to lead the attack were the brigades of his most experienced and trustworthy brigadiers, Graham and Alison.

Just at dawn the Highlanders of Alison's brigade charged the Egyptian lines. Willis was still fussily deploying troops and for a while the Highlanders were unsupported. The Egyptians were taken by surprise but, unfortunately for the Highlanders, they struck where tough Sudanese troops were holding the line. These were the finest and fiercest troops in the Egyptian army. The first line of Gordons and Camerons was driven back, but it was steadied and the second line of Highlanders was brought up to support it.

Graham's brigade, though making a late start, successfully negotiated the first line of the Egyptian entrenchments. On the right flank, Drury-Lowe's cavalry, starting 2,000 yards from the enemy's front lines, began their advance, while on the left flank the Indian brigade swung in towards the enemy's rear. Graham's brigade broke through the inner defences and the Egyptians began to flee, only to be caught or run down by the British cavalry. The Highlanders, supported now by artillery, also broke through. Two hours after the battle's start it was all over except for the pursuit of the Egyptians to Cairo fifty miles away. The 'butcher's bill' for the battle was fifty-seven killed, 382 wounded and thirty missing, about half the casualties being Highlanders.

Thanks to Wolseley's military genius, the entire war was finished in less than two months from the time the decision was taken in London to send an expeditionary force to Egypt. Wolseley now expected a reward. He had personally kept the Queen informed and he had made a point of praising her son's efforts, but when, on 15 September, he arrived in Cairo he found a letter from the Queen which he considered 'as cold-blooded an effusion as you have ever read'. He thought that all his efforts to please had failed and he told his wife bitterly: 'All the Royalties may go to Scratch!!' But he had made more of an impression than he thought. Not only had the Queen been pleased by his generous praises of the Duke of Connaught, but the Duke had written letters to his mother full of glowing praise of Wolseley. The Queen wrote of this to Lord Granville and the Duke of Cambridge. To Granville she said:

Dear Arthur's great modesty and his great appreciation of Sir G. Wolseley are very gratifying.

If only this *really* great General behaves with tact and good taste when he returns, and does not make injudicious speeches! His friends should warn him against this!

The Duke of Cambridge answered the Queen with an honest and accurate appraisal of Wolseley:

Wolseley is a very pleasant man to deal with, when he likes it, and I am not at all surprised therefore at Arthur's liking him as a Chief. His great fault is that he is so *very ambitious*, and that he has only a certain number of officers in whom he has any real confidence. If we could, on his return, only modify these two feelings, he would be twice the value he is to his country whilst indulging in these views. I think a little hint from you on these points at the proper time, perhaps given through a third person, McNeill or somebody of that sort, might do him a world of good.

Wolseley certainly was ambitious and he did have confidence only in a select group of officers. Whether these constituted such serious faults as the Duke implied is debatable. In any case, the Queen took the Duke's advice and had Sir John McNeill write to Wolseley, who gave a spirited and not very humble reply back directly to the Queen. Nevertheless, Wolseley was rewarded, though not quite as well as he had hoped. Only the year before, when he returned from South Africa, the Queen had refused to give him a peerage; now she consented, though he was only made a baron and he wanted to be a viscount. He was also given a grant of £30,000 (he wanted £35,000) and promoted to full general (he wanted to be a field-marshal).

It was the intention of the British government to withdraw its soldiers from Egypt as soon as possible, but British troops were to remain on Egyptian soil until 1956, when the British tried to repeat Wolseley's feat and failed. The campaign against Arabi was the last war for most of the Crimean veterans, but Wolseley and his gang were to take part in one more expedition, again in Egypt.

24

THE SUDAN I: HEROES IN DISTRESS

1883–84

WHEN Britain conquered Egypt no one quite realized that she had also acquired all Egypt's problems, nor did anyone quite understand the full extent of Egypt's responsibilities. There was, for example, the Sudan: Egypt's pride, and one of her major problems. The Sudan now became a thorn in the foot of the British lion; a thorn that was to remain and fester, troublesome and perplexing, for the next sixteen years.

The Sudan was a million square miles of desert, swamp, rock, thorn and scrub where, under its blistering, baking sun, lived a medley of savage and uncongenial tribes, fierce, tough and uncompromising. Since 1822 Egypt had ruled there after her fashion – which was badly – and had tried to exploit this land and its peoples. There was, however, little to exploit. The Sudan's principal export was slaves, Blacks caught in the primitive south of the country and used as soldiers or sold as slaves throughout the Arab world. But Egypt was under great pressure from the European powers, particularly Britain, to suppress the slave trade. The vast country proved extremely difficult to govern; even when Europeans were employed to rule, it proved an almost impossible task to establish and maintain order among the wild and turbulent tribes in the north and the primitive and fearful tribes in the south.

The Sudan I : Heroes in Distress

During Arabi's revolt, when Egyptian leaders were concentrating all their attention on the internal problems of Egypt proper, there arose in the Sudan a religious leader who called himself El Mahdi, the Messiah. This man did what no one else before him had been able to do: he united the tribes under his banner and persuaded or forced them to accept his rule. Starting with a small group of followers, he inflicted a series of defeats on Egyptian troops sent to capture him. After each victory El Mahdi gained new adherents to his cause and soon he and his followers, called by the British 'Dervishes', were in almost complete control of all the Sudan west of the Nile.

Britain's politicians tried hard to avoid any responsibility for the problems of the Sudan, but they found it impossible. They compromised by doing as little as they could and this proved too little in the end and only magnified the problem. In the nineteenth century Britain always had such a surplus of officers who wanted to fight that all of her little wars could not satisfy their ambitions. Sometimes the British government would in effect loan out its officers. It was this policy which brought her to grief in the Sudan.

William Hicks (1830–83) had not been a particularly distinguished soldier. He had entered the Bombay army in 1849 at the age of nineteen and had served throughout the Indian Mutiny and in the Rohilkand campaign. Except for service under Robert Napier in the Abyssinian War of 1867–68, his entire career had been spent in India. He was retiring from the Army as a colonel when, in February 1883, he was given command of the Egyptian army in the Sudan. The British government, trying to maintain the fiction that there was still a sovereign Egyptian state, pretended that Hicks was no longer working for Britain but only for Egypt. Except to provide Hicks with a handful of other European officers, Britain gave no further thought to the Sudan.

Hicks Pasha, as he was now called, being a general in the Egyptian army, won some small victories over the Dervishes south of Khartoum. Then, gathering all of the force available, he marched off into the desert with 10,000 men to fight the main army of El Mahdi. His command consisted of poor fighting material, many of the soldiers being the remnants of Arabi's defeated and demoralized army, and some being brought to the Sudan in chains. After weeks of marching across the wastes of Kordofan the hot, thirsty, tired army encountered the Dervishes at a place called Kashgil. The Dervishes were waiting for them – in ambush. There Hicks Pasha and his army were annihilated: 10,000 men disappeared in blood under the swords and spears of the fanatic followers of El Mahdi. England was horrified and astonished. Lord Fitzmaurice told the House of Lords that there had not been such a complete destruction of so large an army since 'Pharaoh's host perished in the Red Sea'.

Hicks had been recommended for his command by another British ex-officer, Valentine Baker (1827–89), a man who had had a curious career. He was born in Enfield, England, the son of a rich merchant who had large estates in Jamaica and Mauritius. At the age of twenty-one he went with his elder brothers, John and Samuel (later Sir Samuel Baker, the great African explorer) to establish an English settlement in Ceylon at a place in the hills 115 miles from Colombo. Valentine soon decided that he did not want to be a pioneer farmer and joined the Ceylon Rifles as an ensign. Four years later he transferred to the 13th Lancers and distinguished himself fighting in the Kaffir War of 1855–57. During the Crimean War he saw more action at the battle of Tchernaya and during the siege of Sevastopol.

In 1859 he obtained his majority and exchanged into the 10th Hussars. The following year, at the age of thirty-three, he was given command of the regiment. Valentine Baker was a keen, serious student of military science. He wrote pamphlets and books on national defence and the organization of British cavalry, and he brought his own regiment to a high state of efficiency. Not content to remain unoccupied in England, he went as a spectator to see the Austro-Prussian War and the Franco-Prussian War, and he travelled and explored in the remoter parts of Persia and Russia. In 1874 he was appointed assistant quartermaster-general at Aldershot.

In 1875 Valentine Baker, now forty-eight years old and married

The Sudan I : Heroes in Distress

to a squire's daughter, appeared to be a happy man leading an interesting life and in the middle of a successful career. As *The Times* later said in his obituary, 'his career might have been among the most brilliant in our military service'. Might have been. On 2 August 1875 he was convicted of 'indecently assaulting a young lady in a railway carriage' and sentenced to a year in prison and a fine of £500. His career and his reputation were in ruins. He was, of course, dismissed from the army, 'Her Majesty having no further occasion for your services'.

Good officers who assaulted young ladies in railway carriages were not banned from the Turkish army, and Valentine Baker, after his release from prison, went to Turkey and was at once made a major-general. The British attitude towards the Turks at this time was one of universal bitterness and outrage. In the summer of 1876 the British government and people were horrified by the 'Bulgarian atrocities', and when a few months later Russia declared war on Turkey, British sentiment, if not pro-Russian, was definitely anti-Turk. But Valentine Baker, the social outcast, had long thought that Europe's greatest danger was from Russia's military pretensions, and he threw himself into the struggle on behalf of the Turks. For the Turks the war consisted of a series of defeats and retreats, but Baker distinguished himself by fighting brilliant rearguard actions and was promoted to the rank of lieutenant-general.

The British, after destroying Arabi's army, then set about rebuilding it again, but on British lines. Valentine Baker was offered the command of this army, but by the time he arrived in Cairo to take up his post the British authorities had changed their minds; the offer was withdrawn. Since a number of British officers were to be seconded to the new Egyptian army, it was felt that many might refuse to serve under a man who had been ignominiously dismissed from the British army. Instead, he was offered the command of the gendarmerie. Baker, whose dream it was to reinstate himself in the British army, was bitterly disappointed. Nevertheless he accepted the post, believing that this semi-military organization would eventually see active service.

He was right. Six weeks after the defeat of Hicks Pasha, Baker and his gendarmerie landed at Suakin, the Red Sea port in the eastern Sudan.

After the defeat of Hicks Pasha the army of El Mahdi swelled to a vast host. Few Sudanese now doubted that he was indeed the messiah and they hurried to swear allegiance to him and to take up arms in his cause. In the eastern Sudan, along the Red Sea littoral, an able Arab called Osman Digna had been converted to Mahdiism and had raised an army among the tribesmen. He had then laid siege to the Egyptian garrisons at Tokar and Sinket, not far from Suakin. Baker's gendarmerie was sent to protect Suakin, the Sudan's only seaport, and to prevent it from falling into Osman Digna's hands.

Before leaving Cairo Baker had been carefully instructed, both verbally by Lord Cromer and in writing by Sir Evelyn Wood, to act with the utmost caution. It was felt that he had too few men to engage in offensive action and the gendarmerie was too ill-trained. He was told not to fight at all except under the most favourable conditions. His written orders ended with: 'My confidence in your prudence enables me to count upon your conforming to these instructions.' The confidence was misplaced. Valentine Baker had never been prudent.

Five weeks after landing at Suakin he collected such a force as he could muster – the gendarmerie, a few Black Sudanese troops and a handful of European officers – and moved it down the coast to Trinkitat preparatory to marching to the relief of the beleagured garrison at Tokar twenty miles away. In ordinary circumstances 3,500 troops ought to have been adequate for the task. Unfortunately for Baker, the Egyptians, who constituted the bulk of his force, were the most unpromising and unwilling soldiers in the world, and he had not had time to train them or to infuse in them anything resembling a fighting spirit. They were frightened to death of the Dervishes. The Sudanese troops were Blacks from the swamps and forests of the southern Sudan; slaves or descendants of slaves trained as soldiers, they were brave, well disciplined and on whichever side they fought, whether for El Mahdi or the British, they invariably did splendidly. But Baker had too few of these splendid Blacks when he set out to relieve Tokar. Nevertheless, on 31 January 1884 Baker telegraphed Cairo that he had 'every chance of success'.

Valentine Baker marched westward with his 3,500 men formed into a marching square and almost immediately encountered small parties of Dervishes who retreated before him. Then, at a place called El Teb, Osman Digna's Dervishes struck. Baker sadly reported the result in a telegram to Cairo on 6 February 1884:

On the square being threatened by a small force of the enemy, certainly less than 1,000 strong, the Egyptian troops threw down their arms and ran, carrying away the Black troops with them, and allowing themselves to be killed without the slightest resistance. More than 2,000 were killed. They fled to Trinkitat. Unfortunately, the Europeans who stood suffered terribly.

More details followed, and it made sickening reading to the officers in Egypt and England. Valentine Baker's Egyptians had been well armed with rifles and they carried with them four Krupp guns and two Gatling machine guns; the Dervishes had clubs and spears. When the Dervishes attacked, the Egyptian square instantly collapsed into a struggling, surging mass of camels, mules, falling baggage, terrified Egyptians and confused Blacks, fanatic Arabs and resolute British officers. The Egyptian gendarmerie, shrieking madly, were in a state of abject terror: men tried to hide behind each other; some terrified Egyptians knelt in the sand and begged for mercy, while the Dervishes seized their hair and slit their throats. One Dervish was seen to pick up a rifle and, being ignorant of how to shoot it, used it as a club to crush the skull of its owner. The Egyptian officers were as cowardly and as frightened as their men. In all, ninety-six officers and 2,225 men were killed and all the guns were lost.

It was impossible for anyone in England or Egypt to understand what was happening in the Sudan. How could two well-armed Egyptian armies, led by British officers, be wiped out by untrained and ignorant savages? How indeed. A few days after

Valentine Baker's defeat at El Teb came the news that Sinkat had fallen. The defeats and disasters in the Sudan seemed to be, whether the politicians liked it or not, the fault of the British. To redeem Britain's falling reputation the British cabinet decided to accept Wolseley's suggestion to send a force of regulars for the relief of Tokar. The Queen, who had been pushing Gladstone to accept Wolseley's plan, was delighted and telegraphed Gladstone from Osborne: 'I am glad that my government are prepared to act with energy at last. May it not be too late to save other lives! The fall of Sinkat is terrible.'

On 28 February 1884 a force of 3,000 British regulars and a naval detachment – no Egyptians this time – landed at Trinkitat. They were commanded by Gerald Graham, tall, brave and ever-calm, with stout Redvers Buller as his second in command and Herbert Stewart in command of the cavalry. This was a team obviously hand-picked by Wolseley. Graham had known Wolseley since they had served as subalterns in the Crimea, where Graham, a lieutenant in the Royal Engineers, was twice wounded and won his Victoria Cross. Standing six feet four inches tall in his stocking feet, and of massive proportions, 'his appearance at once impressed one with a sense of physical grandeur and power', according to Colonel R. H. Vetch, his biographer. He was a handsome man, with blue eyes, dark hair and strongly marked eyebrows. Wolseley and Graham had both served in China in 1860 and Graham was one of Wolseley's best brigadiers in the Arabi rebellion of 1882.

In spite of his great size, Graham was known for his gentleness: 'A man with the heart of a lion and the modesty of a young girl,' Wolseley once said. At the age of thirty-one he had married the widow of a vicar who already had four children, one an invalid. He was a voracious reader, in both English and German; he loved poetry and knew much of Heine by heart. He was, however, as even the admiring Colonel Vetch admitted, 'somewhat slow in assimilating both facts and theories', and Wolseley once told his wife, 'Graham is not exactly brilliant'.

This brave, gentle giant, now a lieutenant-general, had come with an army to the eastern Sudan to relieve the beleaguered

Egyptian garrison at Tokar. No sooner had he landed at Trinkitat, however, than news reached him that Tokar had fallen. He was too late. Nevertheless, Graham's orders had been to go to Tokar and so he went. At El Teb, where Valentine Baker had been so disastrously defeated, 6,000 Dervishes descended on him in a wild charge. 'They seemed not to dream of asking for quarter', Graham said in his dispatch, 'and when they found their retreat cut off, would charge out singly or in scattered groups to hurl their spears in defiance at the advancing lines of infantry, falling dead, fairly riddled with bullets. . . . I am also informed that the women of the tribe were present with hatchets to despatch our wounded.' Under the disciplined fire of the British troops more than 2,000 Dervishes fell dead in the sand; British casualties were only 189, among them the unfortunate Valentine Baker who was severely wounded in the face.

After this victory Graham marched on unopposed to Tokar and there being nothing to do there, marched back again. The following month he set out with a force of 116 officers and 3,216 men to find Osman Digna's camp and encountered the Dervishes in force at a place called Tamai. Many of Osman Digna's men were frizzle-haired Beja tribesmen whom the British soldiers called 'fuzzy-wuzzies'. It was here at Tamai that the fuzzy-wuzzies, in Kipling's words, 'bruk a British square'. Graham described what happened in his dispatch: a large number of Dervishes, who appeared suddenly from a ravine, were cleared by a charge of the Black Watch,

but at this moment a more formidable attack came from another direction, and a large body of natives, coming in one continuous stream, charged up to the edge of the ravine, charged with reckless determination, utterly regardless of all loss, on the righthand corner of the square formed by the 1st York and Lancaster. The Brigade fell back in disorder and the enemy captured the guns of the Naval Brigade, which, however, were locked by officers and men, who stood by them to the end.

The square was reformed. The fuzzy-wuzzies were cut down in great numbers. The battle was won. But to this day the Black

Watch are sensitive to the charge that they allowed the square at Tamai to be broken; to call out 'broken square!' to these Highlanders – as Welsh soldiers sometimes do – is to start a fight. Graham himself, who at one point was completely surrounded by the enemy, attached no blame to any regiment for the broken square: 'Our losses were very grievous, many brave men of the Royal Highlanders and York and Lancaster devoting themselves to certain death in noble efforts to maintain the honour of their regiments.' Total British losses were 221 officers and men killed or wounded.

These two battles had made a most satisfactory little campaign. The British army had shown that the Dervishes were not really invincible and the British public were delighted to hear at last of victories in the Sudan, but Gladstone referred to the campaign as simply a 'frightful slaughter of most gallant Arabs in two bloody battles'. It was true that not much of lasting value had been accomplished. Lord Cromer, Britain's proconsul in Egypt, had not been in favour of further military action once Tokar had fallen, and he later summed up the results: 'It had been shown, not for the first time in history, that a small body of well-disciplined British troops could defeat a horde of courageous savages. But no other important object had been obtained.' Graham's forces were withdrawn in April and May, much to the distress of the Queen, and most of the area outside of Suakin was quickly taken over by Osman Digna.

While Graham was fighting in the eastern Sudan, Charles 'Chinese' Gordon, colourful, erratic and eccentric, was making his way up the Nile to Khartoum. He was another British officer who had made his reputation outside the British army. As a major in China he had been given the command of a private army of Chinese soldiers raised and supported by the foreign merchants in Shanghai to fight the Taiping rebels. He was so successful that he was made a mandarin. After leaving China, he had spent a number of years on routine military assignments in Britain before being loaned out to Egypt, serving first as Governor of Equatorial Province in the southern Sudan and later as Governor-General of the entire Sudan. Then, after quarrelling with his Egyptian superiors, he returned to England and the British army. Gordon spent the next few years on assignments for which he was ill-suited. He went to India as private secretary to the Viceroy, but resigned five days after arriving in Bombay. He served for a while in the Mauritius where he was in command of the Royal Engineers and while there he was promoted to major-general. He was sent to South Africa to deal with discontent among the Basutos but as he sided with the Basutos he was soon returned to England. Now once again he was on his way to the Sudan. The British felt that if anyone could handle El Mahdi and clean up the mess in the Sudan it was Gordon. The British press had clamoured for his appointment and when it was made Britons cheered. There were a few people who knew Gordon and were doubtful, but most people were convinced that this one man, without any troops other than the worthless Egyptian soldiery already in the Sudan, could work a miracle. Gordon thought so himself. The British had already decided, reluctantly, to abandon the Sudan and Gordon's mission was, ostensibly, simply to withdraw the Egyptian garrisons and officials. But most people, including Gordon, thought that he would be able to water down the fanatic fire of Mahdiism and restore order. It was an impossible task.

Gordon managed to evacuate a few hundred Egyptians, but by March he was besieged in Khartoum. He might still have escaped, for he still had some small Nile steamers, but he refused to leave. On 28 May 1884 Berber fell to the Dervishes and his last chance to escape was gone; gone too was all hope of speedy relief. Gordon had not been long in Khartoum when the hopelessness of his position became apparent even to the politicians in London.

Now began a great debate as to what should be done. The alternatives were clear: either Gordon was to be left to his fate, or an army must be sent to his rescue. Gladstone tried to continue the illusion that the Sudan was really no concern of Britain's. Besides, he said, the Sudanese were 'people struggling to be free, and they are struggling rightly to be free!' and he was definitely against 'a war of conquest against a people struggling to be free'. This, of course, was a somewhat different argument than the one he had used when he sent Wolseley to crush Arabi. It was, naturally, ridiculous to sacrifice the lives of so many other soldiers in an effort to save the life of one eccentric general, but Gladstone's views were unpopular. The Queen's view – and, as usual, she reflected the sentiments of most of her subjects – was simply expressed in a letter of 25 March to Lord Hartington, the Secretary for War: 'Gordon is in danger: you are bound to try to save him.' To Sir Henry Ponsonby, her Private Secretary, she wrote; 'If not only for humanity's sake, for the honour of the Government and the nation, he must not be abandoned.'

The debate went on for weeks. There was a public subscription for a relief expedition and a large meeting in Hyde Park to protest against the Government's procrastination. Gladstone tried to tell the House of Commons that Gordon was 'not surrounded, merely hemmed in', but on 14 May 1884 Gladstone's Government escaped a vote of censure by a narrow majority of twenty-eight. Two days later the Queen told Ponsonby in a much underlined letter:

The conduct of the Government in this Egyptian business is *perfectly miserable*. . . . The Queen feels *much* aggrieved and *annoyed*. She was never listened to, or her advice followed, and *all* she foretold *invariably* happened and what she *urged* was done when *too late*! It is dreadful for her to see how we are going downhill, and to be unable to prevent the humiliation of this country.

Meanwhile, Wolseley was urging Hartington to act swiftly for he saw that time was running out. In June he told him that 'Time is the most important element in the question, and indeed it will be an indelible disgrace if we allow the most generous, patriotic, and gallant of our public servants to die of want or fall into the hands of a cruel enemy because we would not hold out our hands to save him.' Wolseley had developed a plan based on his experiences on the Red River for an army to reach Khartoum by way of the Nile. At long last, on 23 August, Hartington told the Queen that he was going to send Wolseley 'temporarily to assume the command of the troops in Egypt, not necessarily of an expedition if it should be despatched, but to direct and superintend the preparations and the organization of the force'. Under steady pressure from the Queen, the Army, the press and the public, the Government was slowly being pushed towards a relief expedition. As Wolseley had warned Hartington, 'the English people will force you to do it whether you like it or not'. And so they did, but it was not until 19 September that Wolseley received the order to proceed to the rescue of Gordon. Now began a race against time.

25

THE SUDAN II: TOO LATE!

1884–85

WHEN Wolseley went to Egypt to try to save the beleaguered Gordon, he took with him most of his 'gang': Stewart, McCalmont, Buller, Butler and Brackenbury. Wood was already there as sirdar (commander-in-chief) of the Egyptian army, and he was buying camels and preparing a base at Wadi Halfa, the southernmost point still held by Egypt.

After the defeat of Arabi's army and the conquest of Egypt, the Egyptian army had been virtually disbanded. Early in 1883 Evelyn Wood had been given £200,000 and told to create a new army of which he would be the sirdar. To help him, he selected twenty-five British officers who were seconded to the Egyptian army and given ranks two grades above their rank in the British army. The men selected turned out to be a remarkable group of officers; a dozen of them reached general officer rank. Included in the original group were Reginald Wingate, Hector Macdonald, H. S. Smith-Dorrien, Archibald Hunter, C. Holled Smith, Leslie Rundle and two who were elevated to the peerage: Grenfell and Kitchener.

The Nile campaign to rescue Gordon was a military expedition which began and ended in controversy. The distance between Cairo and Khartoum is about 1,200 miles as the crow flies, but further as the Nile flows or the camel walks. The first major problem was to move an army this distance, up the Nile and around its cataracts, through sand and rock and hostile Arab tribesmen. Everyone had a theory as to the best way to do this and tried to tell Wolseley what he should do, but, as usual, he had his own ideas, and some were so original that they shocked not only the Horse Guards but the British public as well. One scheme was to select the best officers and men from the Guards and form them into a camel corps. 'The principle is unsound,' thundered the Duke of Cambridge, but units of camel cavalry and camel-borne infantry were created. Wolseley also decided that no liquor would be carried; instead, he ordered tons of jam and marmalade. The War Office protested. Men could not be expected to fight on jam instead of rum. But Wolseley had his way and the Queen thought it an excellent idea.

The most controversial of all Wolseley's ideas, but vital to his plan of the campaign, was that the Nile and its cataracts could be negotiated by specially built whale boats manned by skilled boatmen such as Canadian voyageurs. Men and supplies could thus be moved into the Sudan, perhaps even to Khartoum. 'A more wicked waste of money has never been perpetrated,' said the *Army and Navy Gazette,* 'a more silly quackery was never devised by any public department than . . . that monstrous armada of boats, that unfloatable flotilla for the Nile!' The Admiralty, which thought it knew something about boats, considered the whole idea ridiculous. For a start, said the admirals, it would take three months to build enough of them. Wolseley assigned to the energetic Butler the task of getting the boats designed and built; in less than a month nearly 100 were assembled and ready to be shipped to Egypt, and forty-seven British companies were working feverishly to produce 400 more. The boats were thirty feet long, six and a half feet wide and two feet three inches deep; each was equipped with oars and a mast. They were designed to carry twelve men with food and ammunition for 100 days.

Much time had been lost by the politicians. Now every hour counted and the key to success lay in the quick and efficient use of the Nile 'whalers' – or so it seemed to Butler, who was in charge of the whole boat operation and who considered the expedition to be 'the grandest and the noblest work in war tried in my time'.

When Butler arrived in Cairo on 25 September he went straight to the railroad station to see the boats move out for Assuit on the way to Aswan. He noted with satisfaction that at this point not one had been damaged. He was a week ahead of his estimated time schedule but he was jealously guarding every hour. Butler saw the basic problem of the expedition as this: 'We cannot afford to lose one hour; we are two months too late at this work; it is a race against famine; there is still a certain margin of time left; in what manner can that narrow balance be best used.' When he learned that the train with his previous boats was delayed for three days by the shipment of eighty railway wagons of food for the Egyptian army, he was furious and wired headquarters at Wadi Halfa: 'Would it not be better to send the Egyptian army back to the beans and lentils, than to send the beans and lentils forward to the Egyptian army?'

Butler reached Aswan at dawn on 7 October. From here it was 600 miles to Khartoum. Thirty-two of the boats arrived at noon and by the end of the day they were anchored at the foot of the First Cataract. Early the next morning they started the ascent of the cataract, the boats' first test. By evening all had passed unharmed to Philae on the other side. The boats now started to arrive in great numbers at the end of the railway line and by 18 October there were 130 at the foot of the Second Cataract. Boatmen, too, had arrived from Canada. Unfortunately, not all of them were voyageurs. Some were lumberjacks, lawyers and businessmen with little knowledge of boats, but all were ready for an adventure on the Nile.

Late in life, when the trials of Egypt and its river were behind them, Butler said: 'The Second Cataract of the Nile has lived in my memory since October 1884 as a spot in the world where I suffered mental tortures of the acutest kind – that which results from seeing terrible disaster ahead and being powerless to prevent it.' It was here that he was ordered to allow sixty to seventy native craft to go through ahead of his boats. 'This decision cost us a loss of ten days,' he wailed. Eventually the boats were rowed, hauled, portaged through the first three cataracts and up the Nile with their men and supplies, but for Butler 'it was one long, unbroken nightmare'.

For the troops this novel method of transport seemed quixotic and Ian Hamilton said later that they looked as if they were 'Boy Scouts dressed up like Red Indians and let loose in a flotilla of canoes'. Hamilton said: 'My company took their seats in eleven small boats to struggle hundreds of miles up the Nile in order to save Gordon; a vague and typically British adventure – just like a fairy tale.'

For Butler it was a nightmare, for Hamilton it was a fairy tale, for Wolseley it was a time of intense frustration and worry such as he had never known. The great planner's plans, which had always been so perfect in the past, were now going awry. The troops were not always at the embarkation points on time, boats were required to carry heavier loads than they were designed for, and there were countless unexpected delays. Buller, his chief of staff, forgot to order coal for the steamers running between Aswan and Wadi Halfa and Wolseley swore that this cost him three weeks delay until a contract was negotiated with Thomas Cook and Company. Wolseley raced up and down the banks of the Nile on a camel complaining of the delays. He complained, too, of his camel, a gift of the Khedive. He hated camels and this one made disgusting noises which reminded him of Brackenbury.

Butler, subjected to his chief's complaints, felt that the difficulties of his task were not understood and his efforts not appreciated. He laid much of the blame for his troubles on Wood's new Egyptian army, 3,000 of whom were by November echeloned along the Nile between the Second and the Third Cataracts and had to be supplied by the same river route Butler was using for the expeditionary force. The Egyptian army, said Butler, was used 'to lessen our supplies, block our way, and be all but useless to us in any way'.

Wood's version of what happened at the cataracts is somewhat different from Butler's. According to him, his 2nd Egyptian Battalion carried 609 out of 700 whalers around the First Cataract and in October his troops 'worked from daylight to sunset throughout this month passing supplies, and later troops, up the river'.

When Butler reached the head of the Third Cataract on 27 November he received what he considered 'the cruelest check of all my life': he was ordered by telegraph from Wolseley not to go further south. He was to stick to his whale boats while others dashed across the desert to whip the Mahdi and save Gordon. He sent a long complaining telegram to Wolseley and then went back to work, cursing everyone who stood in his way or who did not work as hard or as fast as he did. 'Late sleepers and starters, the modern soldier and officer. The breed is falling off,' he wrote bitterly in his journal.

It was such a frustrating time for everyone that there was even friction among the stoutest members of the Wolseley gang. Wood called General Earle 'a Sergeant-Major that is quite useless'; Wolseley said that Buller belittled 'everyone who may possibly enter the lists with him in the military race for distinction'. Butler complained of Wood and Buller and told his wife: 'I had suffered so much from what I must always regard as unjust treatment at the hands of my "best friends" that I could only go on day after day working, and lying down each night with the hope, which work done gives, that it would all come right in the end.'

Wolseley had other problems besides offended officers. The telegraph line kept breaking and the operators were inefficient. Eight thousand camels had been bought, but many were inferior and there were not enough; he needed at least 2,000 more. An Egyptian army major named Horatio Herbert Kitchener was out front employing Arabs to carry messages in and out of Khartoum and Gordon was sending out conflicting and sometimes abusive messages. Gordon was not pleased with the information he was getting: 'There is a lot of "I hope you are well", etc.; men like

Kitchener . . . might be expected to have more brains than that.'
Many of the messages sent to Khartoum could not be read anyway as Gordon no longer had the cypher books. One of Gordon's
messages said that he could only hold out until 15 December; this
gave Wolseley less time than he had counted on.

Wolseley brooded because he had written three letters to the
Queen and had not received any acknowledgement; then he
received a blistering reply from her for a comment in one of his
letters in which he had said that he hoped to wipe out the disgrace
of 'General Wood's ignominious peace', a reference to the treaty
with the Boers signed by Wood after Majuba Hill. The Queen told
Wolseley he was being unjust. When the troops were not arriving
fast enough and Wolseley offered £100 to the battalion which
could march the fastest from Sarras to Korti, he was again censored by the Queen, who thought that her troops should not be
bribed for doing their duty. Wolseley began to feel very sorry for
himself. In a letter to his wife he wrote: 'My dear child, what a
host of enemies I have! Do you suppose it is only the usual number
that a successful General has, or is there something about me that
makes men bear me ill-will?'

All was not completely bad, however. By the time the troops
reached the Sudan the weak soldiers had been weeded out and the
remainder, according to McCalmont, were 'lean, bronzed and
muscular, ready and fit to go anywhere and do anything'. Also,
there arrived on the scene one of the most colourful characters in
the British army: Colonel Frederick Gustavus Burnaby (1842–85).
In appearance he was most un-British: he had a swarthy com-
plexion and stood six feet four inches high. He had a high thin
voice and a forty-six-inch chest. In his youth he was thought to
have been the strongest man in Europe and he is said to have once
carried a small pony under his arm. He had joined the army as a
cornet in the household cavalry when he was sixteen, but he had
such a passion for gymnastics and muscle-building that he
ruined his health. To regain it he took to travelling. He travelled
in Central and South America, and Central Asia, hardly places
one would normally choose to go for one's health, particularly in

the last century, but that was his excuse and that is what he did. He was *The Times* correspondent in Spain during the Carlist War and he visited Gordon in the Sudan in 1875. A linguist, he spoke French, German, Spanish, Russian, Italian and some Turkish. His experiences in Central Asia were written up in a successful book, *A Ride to Khiva*. A trip through Asia Minor resulted in another popular book. As a 'visitor' to the Russo-Turkish War he commanded the 5th Brigade of the Turkish army at the battle of Tashkesan. In Turkey he had known Valentine Baker and the two of them were once poisoned in the home of a Greek archbishop. He had at one time stood for parliament, but had been defeated. Burnaby was passionately interested in ballooning and had made nineteen ascents, on one of which, in 1882, he crossed the English Channel.

Without leave he went to Egypt and was with his friend Valentine Baker in the Eastern Sudan. As a volunteer with Gerald Graham's expedition, he cleared out a stone building at El Teb with a double-barrelled shotgun. Saying that he was going to Bechuanaland, Burnaby, now forty-two years old, went to Korti and joined Wolseley, who was delighted to see him. It was illegal, but Wolseley put him on his staff.

On 5 January 1885 Herbert Stewart arrived in Korti. 'It is a comfort to have such a man to work with,' Wolseley told his wife. 'He is always cheery – always prepared to undertake any job, no matter how unpleasant it may be, and the very best Staff Officer all round I have since poor Colley's death.'

At Korti Wolseley was only 200 miles from Khartoum, but it was 200 miles of desert, for the Nile here swings north-east in a giant loop and by this route the distance to Khartoum is twice as far. It was Wolseley's plan to strike across the desert at the open end of this loop and capture Metemma, near present day Shendi, and only 100 miles by Nile or desert to Khartoum. It was for this purpose that he had turned the Guards into a camel corps. This was the Desert Column – 1,800 men, with Herbert Stewart in command. Burnaby was also sent, to take command should anything happen to Stewart. On 30 December 1884 advanced elements of the Desert Column had moved out of Korti; it was followed eight days later by Stewart and the main body of the force. No sooner had they left than Wolseley was consumed with anxiety:

> As long as Stewart is safe I don't mind, but a stray bullet might any moment rob me of all confidence in the success of the operations he is now entrusted with. Only fancy how all the *Generals of the Old School* would rejoice, and yet howl, if any serious repulse were encountered here; their hatred of me is only equalled by my contempt for them.

On 17 January 1885 ten thousand Dervishes led by one of the Mahdi's best generals struck Stewart's column near some wells at a place called Abu Klea, forty-five miles from Korti. Winston Churchill described this battle as 'the most savage and bloody action ever fought in the Soudan by British troops'. Stewart's men were in the traditional square when the Dervishes crashed into them. At one point the square broke, but the lines closed again and all the Dervishes who had penetrated the square were killed. The Dervishes lost about 1,100 men; British casualties were nine officers and sixty-five other ranks killed and nine officers and eighty-five other ranks wounded. Among the killed was the dashing Colonel Burnaby.

Wolseley learned of the Battle of Abu Klea on 21 January. He was delighted with the success but the loss of Burnaby increased his anxiety about Stewart and he wrote to his wife: 'I am nervous about Stewart, for his loss – even his being badly wounded – would really, at this moment, be a national calamity.' After burying the dead and building a small fort to protect the wounded, the rest of the Desert Column marched on. Seven miles from the Nile it became apparent that the Dervishes intended to attack again and Stewart halted the column and ordered the making of a zariba of thorn bushes. The Dervishes began a harassing fire and the bullet Wolseley feared struck Stewart in the groin.

It was difficult to get word back to the fretting commander-in-chief at Korti and Wolseley said, 'I don't show it, for I laugh and talk as usual, but my heart is being consumed with anxiety about Stewart's Column. It is now nine days since I heard from him.' Stewart was dying but he wrote to his mother: 'I know you are proud of my being hit like this.'

With Burnaby dead and Stewart mortally wounded, the command of the Desert Column fell on Sir Charles Wilson, a good engineer, a fine staff officer, but an inexperienced commander. Nevertheless, he managed to defeat the Dervishes in another battle and to reach the Nile with his thirsty, tired, battle-worn and saddle-sore soldiers. There, on 21 January 1885 four of Gordon's Nile steamers reached him. Wilson must have learned then of the frightful conditions existing inside the besieged Khartoum, where the inhabitants were eating gum, hides and palm trees and men and women were dying in the streets. Gordon from the roof of his palace spent hours looking down the river through his telescope, watching for the relief force. Yet Wilson now waited three days.

There had been other and longer delays in the great attempt to rescue Gordon, but Charles Wilson was to be blamed for the rest of his life for this one. He delayed because he felt that he had to take care of his wounded and exhausted men and to prepare an adequate defence for the force he would leave waiting. 'At any rate,' he said later, 'there was nothing to show . . . that a delay of a couple of days would make any difference.' On 24 January he loaded two steamers with troops and set off up the river for Khartoum, arriving there four days later – to be greeted by fire from El Mahdi's guns. After holding out for 317 days, Khartoum had fallen and Gordon had been killed only forty-eight hours earlier.

By Nile steamer, camel messengers and then faster by telegraph and cable, the news went back from the heart of the Sudan to El Metemma, to Korti, to Wadi Halfa, and on to Cairo and London: 'Too late!' In England there was despair, dismay and angry recriminations. Wilson, Wolseley and Gladstone were indiscriminately blamed. The Queen in an open, uncoded telegram to Gladstone which began, 'These news from Khartoum are frightful

. . .' blamed him for not acting sooner. Although he was indeed the prime cause of the expedition's failure, Gladstone, after falling with his Government the following year, lived to be prime minister again, while Wolseley, although not yet fifty-two, was never again entrusted with an army in the field, and Wilson was never given another command.

Wolseley was in despair. On 4 February he wrote to his wife that Gladstone alone was to blame:

Had he been a statesman, this misfortune could never have fallen on us. . . . If – always an if – Stewart had not been wounded, the steamers with Wilson would have started for Khartoum on the 22nd instead of the 24th January . . . [El Mahdi] has won, and we all look very foolish. Indeed, if it were not that I have to think over the fate and position of the gallant Gordon, I should be lost in pity for myself and this little army generally. To have struggled up here against immense difficulty and at the cost of great labour and the expenditure of vast energy and thought, and then, when the goal was within sight to have had the prize snatched from one, is indeed hard to bear.

And again, two days later:

My mind keeps thinking of how near a brilliant success I was, and how narrowly I missed achieving it.

There was, however, some consolation: the Queen was 'very kind and gracious'. She invited Lady Wolseley to Windsor for three days and Lady Wolseley told her husband all about it: 'After dinner, the Queen talked to me most of the evening – very kindly and simply and intelligently, knowing more about Egypt and every detail of every officer than all of us put together.' Ever the politician, Lady Wolseley made the most of the occasion to further her husband's interest, sometimes to the point of being fulsome: 'She gave me a photo, framed for Frances [their daughter], which I was really touched at, and her little hand was so near me – we were sitting together – I ventured to take it up and give it a kiss! I think she liked it.'

In addition to the Desert Column, Wolseley had dispatched another part of his army to take the easier but longer route that

followed the great bend of the Nile. This force, commanded by
Major-General William Earle with the ugly, brilliant Brackenbury
as his chief of staff, encountered a large force of Dervishes at a
place called Kirbekan and successfully attacked it, but at the
cost of General Earle's life. He was shot in the forehead while
leading his troops. It was a hard war on generals.

Wolseley was terribly depressed when he thought of all his
dead comrades, and particularly Stewart and Colley, who had been
his best friends. Both had been killed in action, a gallant and
honourable death such as he himself wished for someday, but he
found it 'terrible to contemplate' that both had been atheists.

For a while it appeared that the war would go on until El
Mahdi was crushed, Khartoum was taken and Gordon avenged.
Wolseley made plans to continue the war. Buller was sent to take
Stewart's place and Wood was brought up to replace Buller as
chief of staff. Wolseley had thought Stewart

out and away the ablest man all round I had here. Redvers Buller in
some respects and in some qualities ran him close, but, all round,
Buller was not by a long way Stewart's equal. Buller is far the best
man we have now. His manner is against him, but as a fighting soldier
and an organizing staff officer he is A 1.

Wood, accident prone as always, reported to Wolseley with a
bandaged finger and his arm in a sling: 'Two days previously I
had sat down in a fold-up chair with my finger between the
joints,' he said, 'crushing the top so that it was in a jelly-like
condition.' Wood was also growing so deaf that soon Wolseley
complained to his wife that 'I have begun already to roar at
every one from talking to Wood'.

Graham was again sent to the eastern Sudan with a sizeable
little army to try to defeat Osman Digna and throw a railroad
across the desert to Berber.

The 13,000 men assembled under Graham contained elements
even more diverse than the usual hotchpotch of a nineteenth-
century British army in the field: there were elite troops such as
the Grenadier, Coldstream and Scots Guards as well as some of

the best regiments of the line, and Sikhs and sepoys from Madras and Bengal; there was also a contingent of infantry and artillery from New South Wales, and this was the first time in British history that white colonial troops had been used outside their own part of the world. Graham even had a balloon detachment, but it was not a great success. Graham wrote in his diary: 'April 2, Thursday. . . . Inflated balloon, which got torn in the bush, and soon ignominiously collapsed.'

There was only one notable battle in this short campaign. On 20 March there was a fight with Dervishes at a place called Hashin. Two days later there was a major attack on forces under Sir John McNeill (he who had had his wrist shattered in the Ashanti War). He was encamped with a strong force in a zariba when Osman Digna launched a furious attack. Some men were caught outside the zariba and the total British loss was 150 killed and 298 wounded. On 5 May Graham made a raid on Thakul. It was successful and without loss of any soldiers, but the result was only the capture of 2,000 sheep and goats. Then Graham's force was withdrawn.

The politicians, particularly Gladstone, wanted an excuse for withdrawing all the troops, and this was found in, of all places, the northern border of Afghanistan. It was called the Penjdeh Incident. A small Russian force seized the remote village of Penjdeh on the ill-defined northern Afghan frontier and the British became, or pretended to become, greatly alarmed. Gladstone called it 'unprovoked aggression' and asked Parliament for an £11 million credit. The Russians were going to invade Afghanistan, cried the politicians, and this was a threat to India. On the pretext that every soldier would be needed if this dreadful event took place, all further military operations were discontinued in the Sudan and the withdrawal of the troops began.

Gladstone later confessed that the Penjdeh Incident was a heaven sent device for getting the British out of the Sudan. One MP said, 'I don't so much object to the Grand Old Man always producing the ace of trumps from up his sleeve, but I do object to his saying that the Almighty put it there.'

There was no further campaigning on the Nile – at least not for now, and never again by Wolseley. 'I turn my back on Khartoum with a sinking heart,' he wrote to his wife from Cairo. The race to save Gordon had been exciting, both for the soldiers participating and for the gallery of spectators in England. So much effort had been expended that somehow no one expected it to end in failure. The disappointment was keen; there was much finger-pointing at the blameable; and, of course, everyone felt very sorry about Gordon. William Butler told his wife that the campaign was 'the very first war in the Victorian era in which the object was entirely worthy'. Tennyson wrote a poem about Gordon and newspapers referred to him as the soldier-saint, but blunt Redvers Buller, speaking for the minority, said, 'the man was not worth the camels'.

26

TROUBLES ON THE EMPIRE'S FRINGES:
MANIPUR AND CHITRAL

1890–95

WHILE Wolseley was leading his last expedition, Louis Riel, the cause of his first one, was back in western Canada leading another revolt. An expedition was sent against him and this time he was caught and hanged. Also at this time, in Africa, Sir Charles Warren was leading an army into Bechuanaland and an Englishman named Digby Willoughby was, without official sanction, leading Malagasy forces against the French in Madagascar. There was yet another war in Burma. But none of these aroused much enthusiasm or even attention in England. Continual little wars had by now become an accepted way of life.

The dozens of small wars and campaigns that followed attracted scant attention, but occasionally there would be some particularly unusual event, some remarkable instance of bravery or endurance which would briefly stir the public's interest in the series of dramatic events that were taking place on the edges of the Empire. One such event occurred in Manipur in 1891.

Manipur was a small hill state on the North-East Frontier, tucked in between Burma and Assam. Imphal was its capital and chief town. Although only 400 miles from Calcutta, it was cut off from India by mountains, rivers and jungles, and before 1900 there were no roads leading into it. Burma had conquered it in 1813, but it was restored as a separate state under British protection after the Burma War of 1826 and a British political officer was stationed there, guarded by 100 soldiers of the 43rd Gurkha Light Infantry. In 1891 the political agent was Frank St Clair Grimmond, and he had with him his beautiful wife, Ethel.

When in September 1890 a palace coup overthrew the raja, the British decided to treat the matter as a rebellion. They planned to intervene and to banish one of the former raja's brothers, the Sennaputti, or commander-in-chief of the Manipur army, who was suspected of engineering the coup. In March 1891 James Wallace Quinton, chief commissioner in Assam, marched to Manipur with 400 Gurkhas commanded by Lieutenant-Colonel Charles Skene to carry out the British decision. The attempt to capture the Sennaputti miscarried and the Gurkhas were attacked by the Manipuri army. When Grimmond, Quinton and Skene went to the palace at Imphal to parley, they were seized and killed.

There appears to have been no capable junior officer to take command of the situation, so the widowed young Ethel Grimmond, dressed in a white silk blouse, black patent leather shoes and a blue skirt that came well below her knees, led the Gurkhas and their British officers out of Imphal and through the jungle towards Assam. They had climbed 3,000 feet above the Manipur plain, but they were exhausted, without food, and Ethel Grimmond had just sprained her ankle when they met 200 Gurkhas on their way to Manipur for a tour of normal duty. Only then did Ethel Grimmond, filled with grief, anxiety, and pain sit down and cry.

On 26 April 1891, when a British expedition consisting of 4,000 men marching in three columns converged on Imphal they found it deserted. A determined search was made for the Sennaputti and he was finally found disguised as a coolie and brought in to face British justice. He was duly tried and publicly hanged. Ethel Grimmond, 'the heroine of Manipur' as the *Illustrated London News* called her, was given the Royal Red Cross and a pension for life; the British officers in command of the Gurkhas whom she led to safety were cashiered. The British installed a six-year-old boy, a great-grandson of the former raja on the throne of Manipur and then ruled in his name.

Four years later, on the North-West Frontier, there was another dramatic military episode. Again, it was brought about by British interference in the politics of a small tribal state.

In 1893 the governments of India and Afghanistan agreed, more or less, on a boundary between the two countries. This boundary, called the Durand Line after Colonel Sir Mortimer Durand, the chief representative of the British on the boundary commission, was the cause of a great deal of unrest in the most northern part of the North-West Frontier for the next decade. The difficulty was not with Afghanistan – with whose restless tribes there was always trouble, boundary or not – but with several independent states which had been divided by the line but which did not belong either to India or Afghanistan.

Most of the states left on the Indian side of the boundary believed – rightly, of course – that the British would eventually try to extend their control up to the Afghanistan border. The khanate of Asmar had been put on the Afghan side of the Durand Line, but it had been seized and was claimed by Umra Khan, the ruthless ruler of Jandol, whose state was on the Indian side of the line. Not unnaturally, he did not think kindly of the British. The feeling was mutual: one British official described Umra Khan as 'one of that well-known class which is invariably less placable towards helpers, who eventually fail them in some wild dream of ambition, than to those who have always been consistent enemies'. He probably was such a person, although it is doubtful if he considered the British to be the helpers they considered themselves to be. Besides, it was a prudent attitude for a ruler in this wild country.

Just north of Jandol was Chitral, a sparsely populated little country slightly smaller than Wales, about the size of Connecticut, located in a long valley up in the Himalayas where China, Russia, Afghanistan and today's Pakistan come together. It is divided into two parts by massive mountain ranges through which there

297

are three passes. The scenery is spectacular. Ian Hamilton described Chitral in a letter to his brother:

A hot little valley just stuffed with olives, pomegranates, walnut trees and mulberries. Above, the mountains shoot up sheer precipices in the most giddy and dramatic profusion. And down below the Chitral river spins along, huge and inky black, straight from the glaciers of the Hindu Kush. . . . When there are clouds on the tops of these mountains you see nothing more. But if perchance the clouds lift, the astonished traveller beholds towering in the background, darting skywards, the most stupendous bulk of a pure snow mountain.

Surgeon-Major George Robertson, the British Agent in neighbouring Gilgit who also looked after British interests in Chitral, gave a desolate picture:

All colour is purged away by the sun's glare; and no birds sing. Life is represented by great eagles and vultures, circling slowly or poised aloft, and by the straight business-like flight of the hawk. The dull ceaseless roar of the distant river changes, whenever you listen fixedly, to a sound as of supernatural voices shrieking in agony; but too remote for human sympathy.

The valley was dotted with small mud forts with towers at the four corners, resembling overturned footstools with their legs in the air. One such fort was at the town of Chitral, a village actually, which served as the capital of the country. It was here that Surgeon-Major Robertson came in late January 1895 with an escort of 100 men of the 14th Sikhs and 300 Kashmiri light infantrymen under the command of six British officers to bring order and stability to the chaos of Chitral. He had very little time to do anything, for his very presence in the country increased the uproar.

Robertson, forty-two years old, was a remarkable man. The son of a London pawnbroker, he was educated at Westminster Hospital and entered the Indian Medical Service at the age of twenty-six. During the Second Afghan War of 1879–80 he served with the Kabul Field Force, but he had seen no action since. When Colonel Durand was appointed British Agent at Gilgit he took Robertson with him as his surgeon. On a visit to Chitral with Durand, Robertson became fascinated with the country and later, in 1890–91, he spent a year travelling in the area, studying the people and their customs. When Durand went home on leave, Robertson was chosen to succeed him, passing from the medical to the political service, an unusual event.

The Chitralis were a cruel and charming people, treacherous and fun-loving. They were not Pathans but a separate breed. Robertson felt that he knew them well: 'They have a wonderful capacity for cold-blooded cruelty, yet none are kinder to children. . . . All have pleasant and ingratiating manners, an engaging light-heartedness . . . a great fondness for music, dancing and singing. . . . No race is more untruthful or has a greater power of keeping a collective secret.' Colonel Durand formed a similar impression: 'It is impossible not to be taken with the Chitralis. Putting aside their avarice . . . their cruelty and treachery among themselves. . . . The people were bright, cheery, impervious to fatigue, splendid mountaineers, fond of laughter and song, devoted to polo and dancing.' Food was always scarce in Chitral and none of its inhabitants was fat; even the noblemen looked underfed, and Robertson found that the best bribe was a full meal.

The Chitralis had long been independent, but, according to Robertson, their history was 'a monotonous tale of murder and perfidy – the slaying of brother by brother, of son by father. No gleams of generosity or magnanimity illuminate the lurid pages, but naked treachery, wholesale betrayals, and remorselessness are only varied by the complicated and mean intrigues which cement them into a connected story.'

In 1876, pressed by larger and more powerful neighbours, the Chitralis had sought the protection of the Maharaja of Kashmir, who was in turn under the protection of the government of India. Thus the British got their fingers into the sticky Chitrali pie. Once in, they experienced some difficulty in extracting them. In 1892 the Mehtar (ruler) of Chitral died and there ensued the usual series of murders and complicated intrigues among the relatives, who scrambled for the vacant throne. Umra Khan, the most important chief between Peshawar and Chitral, saw opportunity in the confusion and moved an army into the country. The British had just ordered him to get out when Robertson arrived. Either the British naïvely thought he would obey or, even more naïvely, they thought Robertson and his 400 Sikhs and Kashmiris would deter him.

The Kashmiri soldiers were little better than tribal levies, but the Sikhs were splendid soldiers and fine specimens of manhood – and they knew it. On the march to Chitral one of them had remarked to his officer: 'I suppose these folk, after seeing us Sikhs, always ask, ''Whence come these splendid, handsome young men?'' ' If the Sikhs were vain, the British were hardly less so: Robertson said, 'The country people were delighted with us.'

Shortly after his arrival Robertson held a durbar at which he, in the cavalier fashion typical of the British in Asia in this era, dethroned the ruling Mehtar – a son of the last Mehtar whom he described as 'a dull, stupid-looking youth', one who 'neither spoke himself nor listened to what was said', – and installed on the throne his twelve-year-old younger brother, Shujah-ul-Mulk, which the British quickly corrupted to 'Sugar and Milk'. Unfortunately the boy's uncle, Sher Afzal, also wanted to be Mehtar, and he had an army of sorts and the backing of Umra Khan, who had used his support as an excuse to invade.

Knowing that Sher Afzal was lurking in the neighbourhood of Chitral town, Robertson sent out 250 Kashmiri troops to make a reconnaissance. They found Sher Afzal's men. And the Kashmiris were badly trounced: fifteen were killed and about forty wounded, including one British officer mortally wounded and Captain C. P. Campbell, the senior line officer, badly wounded in the knee. Some of the Kashmiris were brave, but most fled back to the fort in confusion, their retreat covered by the Sikhs. Robertson complained that the Kashmiris' musketry was 'atrociously bad', as well it might be, for most were armed with 'gas-pipe rifles' – Sniders with the grooves worn away. The next day, 4 March 1895, the siege of Chitral began, a siege which Robertson later described as 'anachronistic'. It was indeed a quaint, colourful and bizarre siege, but none the less very real.

The ramshackle fort of Chitral, only eighty yards square, was on the right bank of the Chitral River. Its walls were a cradlework of wooden beams which held together a crude masonry of mud and stone. They were about twenty-five feet high and eight feet thick. Against the north and west faces of the walls were stables and other outhouses. At each corner were towers rising twenty feet above the walls. There was a garden on the east side of the fort and about forty yards from the south-east tower there was a summer house. There was no water inside the fort but a covered way led to the river thirty yards away and another tower had been built to protect this. Into this small fort were squeezed 543 people and a pet monkey which, from the annoyance it caused, was thought to be in the employ of Sher Afzal. In addition to Robertson and the soldiers there was young 'Sugar and Milk' and his followers, together with a collection of servants and other non-combatants. Putting sanitation and comfort over safety, Robertson ordered the latrines to be dug *outside* the walls.

At the start of the siege there were only 343 riflemen who were not in the hospital. Of these, eighty-three were Sikhs, 'good shots and trustworthy soldiers', fifty-two were untrustworthy Chitralis, and the rest were the badly armed and ill-trained Kashmiris. The fort's only artillery consisted of two seven-pounders without sights and eighty rounds of ammunition. There was, however, a fairly ample supply of rifle ammunition: nearly 30,000 rounds for the Martini-Henrys, with which the Sikhs were armed, and nearly 70,000 rounds for the Sniders.

There was enough food in the fort to last for ten weeks if rations were cut in half. The most plentiful article of food was pea flour, and there was pea soup on the menu every day of the siege. The distribution of the rations was controlled by an able Bengali commissariat agent. He was an avowed coward, but he did his job well in trying circumstances. Robertson said later, 'How we should have got on without this feeble-bodied, weak-nerved individual, it is hard to say.'

With Captain Campbell wounded and helpless, command of the troops fell upon Captain Charles V. F. Townshend (1861–1924) of the Central India Horse: a man with a curious, unlikeable personality. He was at this time a thirty-four year-old bachelor and the heir presumptive of Lord Townshend. His father, although a great-grandson of a marquess, had spent his life as a minor railroad official and young Townshend had spent an unhappy childhood in genteel poverty. He never seemed to fit in or to belong, wherever he was. As a youth he had turned down an opportunity to join the Royal Navy and at the age of twenty he took a commission in the Royal Marine Light Infantry. He served in Egypt and the Sudan with the Gordon Relief Expedition and had fought with Stewart's column at Abu Klea and Gubat. In 1886 he transferred to the Indian army and made a number of exchanges that took him from the 7th Madras Native Infantry to the 3rd Sikhs and finally into the Central India Horse. He had been posted to Gilgit four years before to command a contingent of the Kashmiri army and had taken part in the Hunza-Naga Expedition.

In spite of his active service and having been twice mentioned in dispatches, promotion had not been rapid: he had only received his captaincy three years earlier at the age of thirty-one. He had been in command of a miserable little Himalayan fort halfway between Gilgit and Chitral when called upon to join Robertson's escort. This remote part of the world was a curious place for a man with Townshend's personality and interests to find himself. He loved to associate with actors and actresses and regarded himself as a great entertainer and raconteur, but others did not always find him so amusing: his cutting quips often alienated his associates and his delight in French quotations was seldom shared by his colleagues. In short, he was not the sort of person with whom most British officers would care to be shut up in a cramped and isolated mud fort – even though he did play the banjo.

Unlike almost all other British officers, Townshend never developed a sentimental attachment for any regiment or corps. He was an ambitious, restless man who appeared to care for no one but himself. He was this way throughout his life. When the

Chitral episode was over he transferred to the Egyptian army and commanded a Sudanese battalion in Kitchener's campaign to reconquer the Sudan. He then married the daughter of a French count, who presumably enjoyed his French quotations, resigned his appointment in Egypt, and returned briefly to India to take up a staff appointment. When war broke out in South Africa he begged to be transferred there. He went, but not liking his post he obtained a transfer to England and joined the Royal Fusiliers. Restlessly he moved back to India, then to Paris for a year as military attaché, and then he transferred to the Shropshire Light Infantry; to India again, to South Africa again, and then to India once more. He was at Rawal Pindi when World War I started. After badgering his superiors for an active command he was finally made a major-general and given a division in Mesopotamia. Here before too long Townshend again found himself in command of a besieged garrison. This time at Kut in what is today Iraq.

In April 1916 after a siege of 147 days Townshend was forced to surrender 10,000 men to the Turks. It was the largest British force ever to surrender to an enemy. The Turkish treatment of Townshend's officers and men was barbaric and appalling; they were forced to make a death march of 1,200 miles: two-thirds of the British and half of the Indian troops died. Townshend himself was treated with courtesy and respect. He got on very well with the Turks – better, in fact, than he ever had with his own countrymen. He appears to have made little or no protest regarding the treatment of his men. The Turks liked him so well and trusted him so much that they released him after a year to plead on their behalf for the best possible terms of surrender. Neither the British government nor the British people – and certainly not the surviving officers and men who had served under him at Kut – ever forgave him. He never received another military appointment and, after the war, his repeated offers to serve as a negotiator between Britain and Turkey were curtly declined. He died in 1924 believing himself a much misunderstood man.

Such was the man now in military command of the garrison at Chitral. He and Robertson frequently disagreed. Robertson in his account of the siege omitted all mention of their quarrels, but Townshend was the only officer he did not praise.

The siege was carried on much as sieges have always been conducted since the early Middle Ages: the soldiers in the fort worked to improve its defences and Sher Afzal's men outside worked their way ever closer to the walls. In this instance the besieging force used sangers, breastworks of stones which they erected at night. There was almost daily contact between the two forces, several truces and exchanges of envoys. Sher Afzal offered the British a safe conduct out of the country if they would give up the fort, but this was refused. Such exchanges helped to pass the time but were hardly taken seriously by either side. However, it was by these exchanges of messages that Robertson and the officers in the fort learned of the strange fate of two young British subalterns.

On 5 March Lieutenant S. M. Edwardes and Lieutenant John Fowler set off from Mastuj, about sixty miles north-east of Chitral, with sixty soldiers and 150 porters carrying ammunition and engineering stores for Chitral. They were both young and handsome men; Robertson described them as 'admirable examples of the best type of fearless, open-hearted, single-minded soldiers'. They had not gone far when Captain C. R. Ross, their commanding officer at Mastuj received word from Edwardes that hostile tribesmen were gathering to oppose them. Ross at once set out with Lieutenant J. J. Jones and sixty Sikhs to help them. He was ambushed and his force was nearly annihilated: Ross was killed and only Lieutenant Jones and thirteen men, ten of them badly wounded, managed to escape.

Edwardes and Fowler, ignorant of Ross's fate and of the siege at Chitral, continued on until they were attacked near the village of Reshun, about halfway between Mastuj and Chitral, by a force under the command of Sher Afzal's foster brother. The young lieutenants and their men beat off the attackers and threw themselves into the village of Reshun where they prepared to defend themselves. Seeing that it would be difficult and costly to overcome them by force, the Chitralis tried treachery. In this they were experts, and certainly more proficient than the young

British officers, who were, understandably, confused about the political situation, and thought that the British were helping the Chitralis keep Umra Khan out of their country. When the tribesmen protested that the attack had been a horrible mistake and that the Chitralis and British were really friends, the officers were half inclined to believe them.

The Chitralis announced they were going to have a polo match just outside the village and invited the young officers to come and watch. Edwardes and Fowler could not resist. Besides, they thought, they would be protected by the rifles of their men on the walls of the village. The polo match was played, the soldiers on the walls became less vigilant; the polo match ended and the Chitralis began to dance; the crowd drew closer. Suddenly the young officers were seized. The leaderless soldiers in the village were soon overcome, and the affair was quickly ended. Most of the soldiers were slaughtered, but Edwardes and Fowler were carried off as prisoners to Umra Khan.

Meanwhile, in Chitral, Robertson was disturbed because they did not have a flag to fly over their mud fort; 'It seemed almost improper, not to say illegal, to fight without the Union Jack over our heads.' So they made one. It gave them something to do. On 22 March they started to eat the horses with their pea soup. As an officer might be squeamish about eating his own horse, a system was contrived so that no man knew whose horse was being eaten.

Reports of their predicament had been sent out and Robertson knew that 'the long arm of the Government of India must be stretching itself forth to rescue us'. It required a long stretch to reach Chitral, but the Government of India was indeed making the effort. A massive relief force under Major-General Sir Robert Low was being assembled at Peshawar. It took several weeks to collect the troops and find the transport, but eventually Low marched out with three infantry brigades, two cavalry regiments, four batteries of artillery and three companies of sappers and miners – 15,000 men and 20,000 animals. The force contained not only ordinary native infantry but some of the best regiments of the British army in India: Gordon Highlanders, King's Own

Scottish Borderers, Buffs, King's Royal Rifle Corps, 4th Sikhs, Gurkhas and the Guides. Low's army was a sledgehammer to smash a gnat. Only by some piece of gross mismanagement could this force be defeated by the likes of Umra Khan and Sher Afzal, but whether this huge force could crawl its way to Chitral in time to save Robertson, Townshend, Sugar-and-Milk and the others was very much in doubt.

On 6 April, in the fifth week of the siege, there was excitement at the Chitral fort when one of the towers was set on fire. There was so much timber used in the construction that fire was always a danger. It was finally put out with great difficulty by the Sikh under constant fire from the besiegers, but in the process Robertson was wounded in the shoulder. The beleaguered garrison also used fire: to keep the besiegers away at night, Robertson designed fireballs – pine chips and straw in a kerosene soaked bag – which were thrown down at the enemy.

The next day, in another part of the mountains, General Low's Chitral Relief Expedition fought its first major battle. The army had easily forced the Malakand Pass: the Guides' infantry and the 4th Sikhs had climbed mountains to outflank the defenders of the pass and Gordon Highlanders and the King's Own Scottish Borderers, supported by sixteen guns, had charged the crest with bared bayonets. On 7 April about 4,500 of Umra Khan's men made a determined effort to prevent the British from building a bridge at Chakdara and a vicious engagement took place there. After the battle, which of course the British won, some relatives of Umra Khan and some fanatics from Swat were found dead on the battlefield. For Umra Khan the British were coming too close to home.

While General Low's army was fighting its slow way through the mountains towards Chitral, another smaller force was also on its way to the relief of Chitral from a different direction. Lieutenant-Colonel James G. Kelly of the 32nd Sikh Pioneers marched from Gilgit on 27 March with 382 of his own pioneers, thirty-four Kashmiri sappers, some reluctant local porters and two ancient seven-pounder mountain guns, determined to relieve

Chitral himself. He stopped at Mastuj long enough to pick up 100 Kashmiri infantrymen and 100 Hunza and Punyal levies and marched out of there on 13 April. It was a small and unlikely force for such a task, but Lieutenant-Colonel Kelly was a brave and determined man.

Commissioned in 1863 in the 94th Foot, it had taken Kelly twenty years to obtain his majority. He had never been a particularly distinguished officer. Although he had now been thirty-two years in the service, almost all of it in India, he had seen no action except in 1891 when he had taken part in two small frontier expeditions. His regiment, which had only been raised eight years earlier, had never seen action. And a pioneer battalion was hardly an inspiring command. It was, therefore, an ordinary, middle-aged regimental officer who set off on his own initiative with his scratch force of Sikh pioneers (more accustomed to handling picks and shovels than rifles), half-trained Kashmiris and tribal levies on one of the most arduous and dangerous expeditions ever undertaken by a unit of the British army.

The most difficult part of the march was across the Shandur Pass, actually a mountain plateau 12,400 feet high, ninety miles from Chitral. Here there was heavy snow, three to five feet deep, and Kelly's men could not average more than one mile an hour. It was particularly difficult to bring through the mountain guns and their ammunition. The men were neither accustomed to nor equipped for such severe weather. Many suffered from frost-bite and snow blindness, including two of the British officers, Lieutenant H. A. K. Gough and Lieutenant C. G. Stewart. The officers still able to see watched over their men like mothers. The temperatures were below freezing at night and there were no tents; the men simply bedded down in the snow by sixes as directed by their officers.

Kelly had to fight two sharp battles against Sher Afzal's men, both in narrow gorges with the enemy in strong defensive positions. Every bridge he needed had been destroyed by the Chitralis. When at last he was within one day's march of Chitral he found himself faced with a deep gorge with a fast-flowing stream at the bottom, the bridge burned and the enemy entrenched on the opposite side.

It was at about this time that the besiegers of Chitral tried to blow up the fort with a mine. It was seen from the fort that the enemy had started their tunnel from the summer house just outside the walls. Lieutenant Henry Harley, commander of the Sikh detachment and described by Robertson as 'a melodious person of gregarious instincts', volunteered to lead a sortie. He dashed out at the head of forty Sikhs and sixty Kashmiris. There was a furious but brief scrap, but the enemy were taken by surprise and Harley was able to blow in the tunnel. Harley himself was unhurt but he suffered twenty-one casualties: eight killed and thirteen wounded. Nevertheless, the mine threat was ended, forty or fifty of the enemy had been killed and two more were taken prisoner.

The destruction of the mine took place on 17 April. Three days later Chitral was relieved. Apparently losing hope, the Chitralis had retreated from their position facing the gorge that separated them from Colonel Kelly's force, allowing Kelly to build a bridge and cross without opposition. As he advanced on Chitral the enemy withdrew from around the fort and Kelly marched in to find five Englishmen, white-faced and strangely quiet. The little garrison had lost forty-one killed and there were sixty-two wounded; five of those killed and four of the wounded were non-combatants.

Robertson described his feelings on being rescued: 'My mind was weary and my life seemed fatigued also.' Knowing the topography of the country as he did, he understood thoroughly the tremendous effort made by Kelly and his men, who had marched under such appalling conditions for 220 miles and fought two battles in twenty-eight days. Robertson called it 'one of the most remarkable marches in history'. General Low and all the officers with him were impressed too, of course, when they arrived one week later, but they were also disappointed. It was, after all, an obscure lieutenant-colonel with a batch of pioneers and Kashmiris who had saved Chitral rather than the grand, elite force Low had assembled. Still, they had played their part. Perhaps Kelly would not have got through had it not been for the pressure put on Umra Khan by General Low's army.

Low had marched over the Malakand Pass, across the Swat River, then over another pass to the Panjkora River. Here the road became a mere camel track which they followed over the Jambati Pass to Dir, a country ruled by Umra Khan. Then they marched sixty miles to the Lowari Pass, which was then under snow, and down a steep descent, where nearly 500 years earlier Tamerlane had had to be lowered on a rope, and then finally on to Chitral. It was difficult country for a large, clumsy army, and they had to fight much of the way. The disappointment of some of the officers that Chitral was already relieved after all their trouble is understandable.

One thing which Low's army did accomplish was the rescue of Edwardes and Fowler. In an attempt to appease the invaders, Umra Khan sent the two young officers unharmed to the British camp. Unappeased, the British marched on and seized Umra Khan's principal fort. Umra Khan might have been captured as well except for the timidity of General William Gatacre, a brigade commander who thought it was too risky to attack with the force available. Sir Bindon Blood, Low's chief of staff, came up and ordered an assault, but Gatacre was senior to Blood on the army list and so they argued until Low arrived and sided with Gatacre. Umra Khan and his men slipped away. Among the debris scattered about the hastily deserted fort the soldiers found a letter from a British firm in Bombay advertising its wares: 'Our price for Maxim guns is Rs 3,700 each and our revolvers are Rs 34 a piece.'

The campaign ended, as one of the officers with General Low said, 'with one of those gracious messages with which Her Majesty the Queen never fails to acknowledge the gallantry of her Army'. There were rewards all around: Robertson was knighted, Townshend was given a CB and a brevet majority, three officers of the Chitral garrison were given the DSO (then a new decoration, having been instituted in 1886), and one officer was awarded the

Victoria Cross. Kelly for his efforts, was given a CB, promoted to full colonel and made an aide-de-camp to the Queen. One cannot help feeling that had Kelly been commanding, say, the Gordon Highlanders instead of the lowly 32nd Sikh Pioneers his rewards would have included the knighthood he deserved.

Before his army had moved out of the Peshawar Valley towards Chitral General Low had sent proclamations to the tribesmen ahead of him saying that the British had no intention of acquiring new territory or of interfering with the independence of the tribes. The tribesmen, quite rightly, did not believe a word of this. Although angry, they were not surprised when at the end of the campaign the British decided that after all they would build a fort and maintain a garrison at Malakand. This garrison was one of the first to be attacked in the next great uproar on the North-West Frontier.

27

THE FRONTIER AFLAME

1897

THE year 1897 was Diamond Jubilee year: Queen Victoria had sat on the throne for sixty years. In those years there had been many a war, many a bitterly fought campaign, many a punitive expedition, but to the people living in Britain it had seemed a long period of peace and prosperity. All the little wars scarcely caused a ripple in their lives. Only a European war could have seemed near enough and real enough to bring the thrill of fear, could have seemed a threat to Britain and the British way of life. But Britain had not fought a battle in Europe since Waterloo, eighty-two years before – not a real European battle, for the Crimea was a remote place, only technically in Europe, and even the Crimean War had ended more than forty years ago. And since then, except for those unfortunate skirmishes with the Boers, the Empire's enemies had all been 'natives': black, brown and yellow men, not white Europeans, not civilized people.

The Empire was a going, growing concern in which every Englishman, whatever his social class, took immense pride. It was an accomplishment: all that vast territory coloured red on the map of the world. It was grand and wonderful and seemingly enduring, in spite of Kipling's half-believed warning that someday, doubtless in the very distant future, it would all crumble away as had other empires before it. This moment then, when the

Empire appeared to be strong, unconquerable and resolute, seemed to the British to be the moment to celebrate both the long reign of their great Queen and the nation's imperialistic achievements.

On 22 June 1897 London was ablaze with pomp and colour. Representatives of all the colonies, dominions and protectorates gathered to pay homage to the Queen and to enjoy the glory of the Empire. The army had assembled samples of the heterogeneous tribes and races of whose young men it had made soldiers for the Queen. Formed into colourful, often bizarre, regiments led by British officers, they had been used to add to the glories of the army and the Empire. Now many of these were on display in a gorgeous parade, exciting the wonder and admiration of Londoners and visitors. On that particular day, when Britain seemed so secure and powerful, it also appeared at peace. Less than sixty days later the North-West Frontier erupted in violence and was aflame with rebellion from Swat to Beluchistan.

A month earlier, Colonel Robert Warburton had retired from his post as political officer in the Khyber Pass. It seemed an insignificant event. He was but one of thousands of officers who had spent their lives on remote frontiers. Who, even today, has heard of Robert Warburton? Yet his was the greatest name on the North-West Frontier. He was called 'the warden of the Khyber' and, more grandly but perhaps more accurately, 'the king of the Khyber'. His fame, such as it is, is based not on his deeds in war, although he was a soldier, but on his character, personality and diplomatic abilities, which enabled him to keep the peace in an area famous for its absence.

His father was an officer in the Royal Artillery and he was educated in India and England, attending Addiscombe and Woolwich. In 1861 he was commissioned in the Royal Artillery and went to India, as had his father before him. This much of his life was in the conventional pattern of those born in the Anglo-Indian military caste. But Robert Warburton's mother was an Afghan, a niece of Dost Muhammed, and he had been born during the First Afghan War in a Ghilzai fort near Gandamak while his mother was fleeing from Akbar Khan's men and his father was a hostage.

Warburton spoke fluent Persian and Pushtu and the last eighteen years of his military career had been spent as a political officer in the Khyber. His influence over the Afridis and other unruly tribes was phenomenal. In an area where every male was habitually armed at all times, he went about with only a walking stick. Not even blood feud enemies dared to fight in his camp. He raised the Khyber Rifles from Frontier tribes and it was they who manned the forts which kept the Khyber British. His reputation on the Frontier was great – and surprisingly lasting.

One day in 1933, thirty-five years after Warburton had left the Frontier, British officials were startled to find crowds of Afridi tribesmen at the railroad station at Landi Kotal just before the arrival of a troop train carrying a battalion of the Cheshire Regiment. The tribesmen had learned somehow that Warburton's grandson was an officer in this battalion and they had come to see him.

Warburton, like many an able officer who did his work quietly and well, was taken for granted by the government of India and his services were underrated until he had gone. For years he had pleaded for an assistant who could be trained to take his place when he retired, but his pleas had been ignored. Whether even Warburton would have been able to hold the Afridis in check during that wild summer of 1897 will never be known, but the fact is that he had no sooner left the Khyber than all that he had established on that portion of the Frontier was swept away on a tide of fanaticism.

The trouble seems to have started in Swat. There a persuasive mullah roused the latent hatred of the tribesmen for the British and persuaded them that they could throw off the detested yoke of British imperialism. The mullah was called the Mad Mullah, of course. All religious leaders who preached rebellion were called mad by the British; there were many mad mullahs in the days of the Empire, not only in Asia but in Africa as well. This time, however, it was not just the Mad Mullah of Swat starting a local rebellion; other mullahs ranged the villages and valleys calling for action.

The story which the mullahs spread was that Britain was in trouble throughout the world. Christendom itself was trembling. In the war between Turkey and Greece, Britain had sided with Greece. In retaliation, the Sultan of Turkey had sent his agents into Afghanistan and the Frontier districts to spread the tale, easily believed, that the British had lost Aden, the Suez Canal and various seaports; that she would not now be able to reinforce her garrisons in India. Officially, the Amir of Afghanistan supported Britain, but it was widely believed, perhaps rightly, that he hated the British, would welcome their downfall, and was ready to support any attempt to overthrow them. Now was the time to attack, said the mullahs.

Rumours of unrest among the tribes on the Frontier reached the ears of the Government of India, but then rumours of this sort were always prevalent. In June there was a 'disturbance' in the Tochi Valley: a political officer and his escort were attacked. On the evening of 26 July there was an attack on the garrison in the Malakand Pass, an attack which nearly succeeded. Some of the officers, tired from a day of polo, were still in their polo clothes when they rushed out, sword in hand, to beat back the attackers. But by early August things seemed to be in hand again. Sir Bindon Blood had hurried from Agra to take command at Malakand.

When I rode in I saw a string of litters bringing in casualties and everybody looked rather melancholy. I knew exactly what I intended to do, from the notes I had made eighteen months earlier; so after a rapid look at one place, I rode up to the Fort, where Colonel Meiklejohn was holding a meeting of his officers. I assumed command at once, cleared everybody out of the office, and had the orders out in less than an hour for a sortie at daylight next morning. The plan of operation was quite simple, and quite obvious to everyone after they had been told it.

A tough, no-nonsense soldier was Sir Bindon Blood. Now fifty-five years old, he had served in a campaign against the Jowaki

Afridis, the Zulu War, the Second Afghan War, the campaign against Arabi in Egypt and the Chitral Relief Expedition. On his arrival at Malakand he at once led a successful attack on the tribesmen who were besieging the fort at Chakdara and then went on to lead an expedition into Upper Swat, where his exploits against the Swatis and Bunerwals were later described by a young officer who accompanied the Malakand Field Force as a war correspondent and wrote a book about it. The author was prime minister of Britain in the midst of a far greater war when Bindon Blood, the longest-lived Victorian soldier, died in 1940 at the age of ninety-seven and a half. His name was on the army lists for eighty years.

The attack on the Malakand was only a part of the vast uprising that rocked the Frontier. The trouble quickly swept down from Swat to the Khyber Pass and along the border of the Kohat district up to the Kurram Valley and south to Beluchistan. On 8 August the Mohmands descended from their hills and attacked the fort at Shabkadr; a field force was organized and sent out against them. But on 17 August Sir Richard Udney at Peshawar telegraphed to Simla: 'Everything quiet. Reliable sources indicate that Afridis are unaffected.' Sir Richard was soon to eat those words. With Warburton gone, the British had no reliable source of information on Afridi activities. 'Disturbances' when successful become 'outrages', and now there were outrages from one end of the Frontier to the other as isolated forts and garrisons fell before the attacks of the Pathans; 25 August 1895 has been called the blackest day in the history of the Frontier: the British lost the Khyber.

The authorities were astonished. They never understood what had happened or why. 'Under an exceptionally pure and unselfish administration, it would appear strange that there should exist such a large body of disaffected individuals', wrote two young lieutenants who took part in suppressing the uprising. Even the official history spoke of 'that sudden and, at the time, almost unaccountable display of hostility towards the British Government'. The British could never understand why the fiercely independent tribesmen should so hate them for trying to give them Anglo-Saxon justice and introduce Whitehall style efficiency.

Queen Victoria telegraphed Lord George Hamilton, Secretary for India, from Balmoral: 'These news from the Indian Frontier are most distressing . . . am most anxious to know the names of those who have fallen. What a fearful number of officers!'

Someone had the good sense to telegraph Warburton, who was still in India, asking if he would agree to be re-employed 'with reference to Afridi affairs'. He at once accepted, but he was not recalled until the end of September, and by then it was too late. He wrote to a friend: 'My mind is very heavy over this hideous disaster, which I feel could have been staved off even up to the day of mischief. It makes me quite sad to think how easily the labour of years – of a lifetime – can be ruined in a few days.'

By the end of summer there were three field forces in action simultaneously: one in the Swat Valley, a second in the Tochi Valley and a third operating against the Mohmands. The situation was confusing, and on 15 September the Queen complained to Lord George Hamilton: 'I never receive any telegraphic news from the India Office as to what is going on, on the Frontier, and would wish to hear from you [of] what the forces now are composed, and who are the officers in command. . . . All I know is from Reuter and the newspapers.' Lord George Hamilton was as confused as the Queen; he obviously had difficulty understanding the situation himself, for he confessed to the Queen that the fighting 'has been of so desultory a nature, and the various operations so disconnected with one another' that he thought it best to let the newspapers try to make the news intelligible.

In spite of all the field forces already in action, more troops were needed. The loss of the Khyber was such a blow to British prestige that it was decided that a massive effort must be made, not only to recover the Khyber, but to punish severely the Afridis and Orakzais who were the principals responsible for the worst outrages and who were the greatest threat to British rule on the Frontier. This meant still another, larger field force.

Towards the end of September army headquarters at Simla

issued a directive to 'exact reparations for the unprovoked attacks of the Afridi and Orakzai tribes on the Peshawar and Kohat borders, for the attacks on our frontier posts, and for the damage to life and property'.

The Afridi tribe, with its numerous clans, was the largest and most turbulent on the Frontier. As individual fighters, the tall and wiry Afridis were the finest warriors in Asia, and perhaps in the world. There were 30,000 of them. They had light complexions and high cheek-bones, and wore their dark hair long. They wore grass sandals and loose clothes of white or blue cotton which, as they were rarely washed, assumed the colours of the hill slopes on which they lived. They were relatively wealthy and could afford to buy modern rifles, which were highly prized and with which they were exceptionally proficient.

The Orakzai was a similar neighbouring tribe, slightly smaller, not quite so well armed, and not quite so warlike or resolute. The British had led a number of expeditions against these tribes in the past fifty years, and after the last expedition against the Orakzais in 1891 they had built forts in their territory and garrisoned them with Sikhs, traditional enemies of the Pathans.

The territory inhabited by these tribes included both the Khyber and the Kohat passes. They also controlled a mountainous area south-west of the Peshawar Valley called Tirah. This was the summer home of the Afridis, who occupied the northern part, and the Orakzais, who claimed the southern part. Tirah was a region with no well-defined boundaries but it was roughly oval in shape, about forty-five miles long from east to west and twenty miles wide. It was a land of narrow gorges, jagged hill tops and hidden nullahs. No Englishman had ever entered Tirah; no European traveller had ever visited the country; the Afridis and Orakzais considered it inviolate and inviolable.

Into this unmapped and unknown land the British decided to throw an army. Since nothing was known of the topography or the towns, the expedition's objective was given as simply 'the heart of Tirah'. Its aim was to punish. The British sought vengeance.

28

TIRAH
1897-98

Sir William Lockhart, recalled from home leave in England to command the Tirah expedition, issued a proclamation in which the intent of the British was nakedly announced with no nonsense about improving the lot of the tribesmen or installing good government. It said, in part: 'The British Government has determined to despatch a force to march through the country of the Afridis and Orakzais and to announce from the heart of the country the final terms which will be imposed. The advance is made to mark the power of the British Government to advance if and when they choose.'

The British did not under-estimate the size of their task. While waiting for Sir William Lockhart to arrive on the scene and for the other field forces to complete their work, Major-General Arthur Godolphin Yeatman-Biggs was put in charge of the preparations. Vast quantities of supplies had to be brought up and, as usual, there was at first insufficient transport. It was the same old problem faced over and over again: Britain's armies were always ready to fight but unless they could be moved by sea they always had trouble getting to the battlefield. Ways and means of moving troops and supplies had always to be found after the decision to move had been made. Eventually 60,000 transport animals –

318

camels, mules, elephants, bullocks and donkeys – were assembled. And eventually, too, an army was put together: 44,000 troops to fight the Afridis and Orakzais. It was a larger force than the British had sent to fight the Russians in the Crimea.

Lieutenant-General Sir William Stephen Alexander Lockhart (1841–1900), the commander of this army, was a very distinguished soldier, noted, according to a fellow officer, for his 'uncompromising firmness and inexhaustible patience'. Like many a Victorian soldier, he was a clergyman's son. His two older brothers had already entered the Army and had served in the Crimean War when, at the age of seventeen, he was commissioned in the Indian army. One brother, John, was now a major-general, whilst the other, Laurence, now dead, had left the Army to become a novelist.

Lockhart first arrived in India in 1859, just as the last of the mutineers were being run down. He was doubtless disappointed to have missed both the Crimean War and the Mutiny, but he lived to see more than his share of small wars. He took part in the Bhutan campaigns of 1864 and 1866, the Abyssinian War of 1867–68 and the Hazara Black Mountain Expedition of 1868. From 1875 until 1877 he was military attaché to the Dutch army and saw action with them in the East Indies. He served in the Second Afghan War of 1878–80; he led a brigade in the Burma War of 1885–87; he commanded the Miranzi Field Force in 1891 and a brigade of the Hazara Field Force in the same year; he commanded the Isazai Field Force in 1892 and the Waziristan Expedition in 1894–95. His chest was covered with medals and clasps as a result of his active life. In addition, he had the bronze medal of the Royal Humane Society for saving two women from drowning in a Gwalior lake in 1896.

There were so many wars during Victoria's reign that most long serving officers fought in at least one of them. But it was possible to live through this period as a British officer and see no action at all. Major-General Johnson Wilkinson was a contemporary of Lockhart. He joined the 15th Foot (East Yorkshire Regiment) in 1840 at the age of seventeen and, except for taking part in suppressing a very short-lived rebellion in Ceylon in July 1848, he saw no action at all in forty-two years of service.

Lockhart in his youth had broken one of the rules for military success by marrying when he was only twenty-three years old while still a lieutenant, even though he was the youngest son in the family and thus without prospects. His bride, however, was the daughter of a major-general. Again, his life can be contrasted with that of Johnson Wilkinson, whose love life was unfortunately more typical. Wilkinson was, as a young officer, once stationed on the Isle of Man. There he fell in love with a beautiful girl of good family, but as poor as himself. When the colonel's lady heard of it (she was the daughter of the Duke of Wellington's son) she kindly had arrangements made for him to be posted elsewhere. The girl subsequently married an officer in the 93rd (Sutherland) Highlanders, 'a fellow with bare legs who had come to relieve me', said Wilkinson bitterly of the man who relieved him of both his military and his amorous duties.

Although he died a bachelor, Wilkinson later had no regrets. He realized that 'the alliance of that dear young thing with me, an ensign in a marching regiment, however delicious, was not a promising nor a prudent speculation'. Fortunately, Wilkinson loved hunting; the Army gave him time for plenty of sport, and so he spent his life chasing game instead of girls. Lockhart, on the other hand, found time in his active career to marry twice. After the death of his first wife he married, at forty-nine, the daughter of a Coldstream Guards officer. Lockhart not only had ability, he had luck in both love and war. He needed both his ability and his luck in the Tirah campaign.

The jumping off point selected for the invading British army was Shinwara on the southern edge of Tirah and the concentration of troops and supplies there began in October 1897. George MacMunn, then a gunner subaltern, has described the scene on the route from Kohat to Shinwara:

The roads in every direction were full with gathering troops, Highland regiments, Gurkhas, Sikh corps . . . long lines of Indian cavalry, their lances standing high above the acrid dust that they stirred. By the side of the roads strings of laden camels padded on beside the troops, the jinkety-jink of the mountain guns, the skirling of the pipes . . . all contributed to the wild excitement and romance of the scene.

There was a sense of urgency in the preparations, for the British had decided they could not wait for spring to begin their campaign and there were only an estimated seven or eight weeks before the first snowfall. No Indian army was equipped or trained to carry out operations in cold weather; although for this campaign each man was issued with a 'British warm coat', no tents were taken. Baggage was restricted to fifty-four pounds for officers and twenty-six pounds each for other ranks.

The path of the army through Tirah went from Shinwara to the Khanki River, to the Sempagha Pass, to the Arhanga Pass and then into the fertile Maidan Valley. From there the expedition withdrew in two columns down the Mastura and Bara valleys. It was neither an easy nor a painless march. Trouble began almost immediately.

Yeatman-Biggs led the advance from Shinwara to the Khanki River. A gunner, he had seen much service in China, South Africa and Egypt, but he was fighting his first campaign on the North-West Frontier. The first clash with the Pathans came on 18 October when they were found in force on top of a bluff on which stood the village of Dargai. Although the route to the top of the bluff was precipitous, the 3rd Gurkhas and the King's Own Scottish Borderers dashed up and dispersed the enemy at a cost of only nineteen casualties. Once there, however, they found themselves isolated and without supplies, and so they were withdrawn that same afternoon. This proved to be a tragic mistake. The enemy quickly reoccupied the heights in great numbers and two days later the crest was covered with tribal standards. As the heights dominated the gorge through which the army had to pass, it was decided that the position had to be retaken. The second attack on the Dargai heights proved to be the most dramatic event of the campaign.

When on 20 October the 2nd Gurkhas, the Derbyshires and the Dorsets moved up towards Dargai there were an estimated 12,000

Pathans above them. The number seems exaggerated; perhaps there only seemed to be that many to the unfortunate soldiers who were ordered to attack them. To reach their objective the troops had to mount a glacis slope about 300 yards long completely exposed to Pathan musketry. At the end of the glacis was a cliff with a narrow footpath leading up to Dargai. For nearly five hours the British tried to rush groups up that glacis slope. Most were shot down before they reached the foot of the cliff. Those that did reach the cliff were pinned down there by enemy fire. The Pathans shot from the cover of stone sangars – and they were the best marksmen in Asia.

The general in charge of the operations at Dargai was an experienced but unpopular brigade commander named F. J. Kempster. Faced with what appeared to be an almost impossible situation, he sent back a message explaining the difficulty and asking if it was really necessary to take Dargai. Yeatman-Biggs thought it would be disastrous for them to acknowledge defeat in the first real battle of the campaign. British prestige would certainly suffer in the eyes of the Afridis and Orakzais if they gave up now. Dargai must be taken at all costs, he said, so Kempster ordered up the Gordon Highlanders and the 3rd Sikhs.

Now came the proudest moment in the history of the Gordons. Although historians might forget, 'Dargai Day' is still celebrated annually by the Gordon Highlanders. Lieutenant-Colonel Henry Mathias, in command of the Gordons, led his men to the protected depression below the deadly slope. It was crowded with stretchers, wounded, ammunition mules, and tired, dispirited Dorsets and Gurkhas. Mathias called his officers and pipers to the front. Lieutenant George MacMunn was a witness: 'The swagger with which the pipe major threw his plaid and his drones over his shoulder was magnificent,' he said. Mathias made a brief speech: 'The general says this hill must be taken at all costs. The Gordon Highlanders will take it.'

The attack was preceded by a three-minute artillery barrage. Then the Gordon pipers struck up 'Cock o' the North', and 600 cheering Highlanders dashed up that 300-yard slope raked by the murderous fire of the Pathans above them. It was one of the most magnificent charges in British military history.

Over the dead and wounded English and Gurkha soldiers who had earlier in the day tried and failed to climb this slope ran the kilted Highlanders, a cry in their throats. First one officer fell, then a second and a third. Thirty men were knocked over in a matter of minutes. Among those wounded was Piper Findlater, shot through both legs. But he pulled himself to a rock and propped himself against it. Seizing his pipes, he resumed his playing of 'Cock o' the North'. Lieutenant-Colonel Mathias was wounded but kept on. The Gordons cleared the slope and started to climb the cliff. The 3rd Sikhs followed in a second wave and then the broken units of Dorsets, Derbyshires and 2nd Gurkhas. The Pathans on the crest fled in the face of this furious onslaught, and in forty minutes the British were masters of Dargai.

The Gordons won two Victoria Crosses in this gallant charge. One went to Piper Findlater whose deed caught the popular imagination and he found himself briefly a national hero. Later, when he had retired from the army, he performed in the music halls, playing 'Cock o' the North' as he had done on the slope of Dargai. Lieutenant-Colonel Mathias was also recommended for a vc, but, except for mentions in dispatches, his only rewards for the entire campaign were a brevet colonelcy and the honour of being made an aide-de-camp to the Queen. Total losses for the retaking of Dargai were thirty-eight men killed and 161 wounded.

Two days after the battle the Queen telegraphed a message to Lockhart from Balmoral: 'Please express my congratulations to all ranks, British and Native troops, on their gallant conduct in actions 18th and 20th. Deeply deplore loss of precious lives among officers and men in my army. Pray report condition of wounded, and assure them of my true sympathy.'

The army now continued its march into Tirah. The next obstacle in its path was Sempagha Pass. The Pathans had constructed an excellent defence system of well-placed stone sangars, but the tribesmen's resistance was feeble and the pass was easily carried on 29 October. Perhaps the gallant charge of the Gordons at Dargai had indeed impressed the Pathans. Two days later the Arhanga Pass was carried by a frontal assault with slight loss and the army passed through it into the fertile Maidan Valley.

The kind of stand up slogging match which the British favoured was not to the Pathans' taste. After Dargai they took to fighting the rest of the campaign in their own way, and it was more effective. Colonel C. E. Callwell rightly said of the Tirah tribesmen:

It is in concealing themselves, in conducting fleet movements through difficult ground, in appearing suddenly in threatening force at points where they are least suspected and in dispersing without necessarily losing tactical cohesion when they find themselves worsted, that the masters of this art [partisan warfare] single themselves out and display their warlike qualities. Such methods are bewildering to the commanders of disciplined troops opposed to them.

It was to these kinds of tactics that the Afridis and Orakzais now resorted: they attacked supply trains, continually sniped at the main body of the army and, above all, they pressed heavily on the rear of any marching column.

In the Maidan Valley, however, a number of Orakzai chiefs came in to tender their submission. Lockhart, when he saw them, was surprised to see how many had served in the British army and still proudly wore their campaign medals. One old chief had five, including medals for service in Burma and Egypt. In spite of these submissions, British foraging parties were always attacked. Several reconnaissances in force were made into the surrounding hills, and always as they withdrew they were attacked from the rear, giving each withdrawal the appearance of a retreat.

The Maidan Valley, where the British now found themselves, was the heart of Tirah. It consisted of a large oval plateau, about 6,000 feet above sea level, fifteen miles long and six or seven miles wide. It was fertile and well watered, populous and prosperous. The slopes were terraced for cultivation and there were many farms, each in the shape of a fortified blockhouse. The valley was well stocked with grain, fodder and fruit; there were great storehouses of walnuts, red beans and dried apricots. Into this pleasant, thriving valley marched the British army, sowing fire and destruction.

Lionel James, the Reuter's correspondent accompanying the expedition, found the British army's retribution exhilarating:

> One of the most magnificent sights one could wish to see was the destruction by 'fire and sword' as the evening waned into night. The camp was ringed by a wall of fire – byres, outhouses, homesteads, and fortresses one mass of rolling flame, until the very camp was almost as light as day. The actual fury of the fire subsided, and the wooden structures of the houses and the uprights of the towers stood in outline, glowing in the pitchy blackness.

This destruction of private property and of food supplies by Lockhart's army was the most devastating vandalism ever perpetrated by the British in India. But this sort of thing was part of British policy on the Frontier, and always had been. It was a policy which had been condemned by both Charles Napier and Colin Campbell, but many Frontier fighters had thought it essential, including Sir Neville Chamberlain, who said:

> To have to carry destruction, if not desolation into the homes of some hundreds of families is the great drawback to border warfare; but with savage tribes to whom there is no right but might, and no law to govern them in their intercourse with the rest of mankind, save that which appeals to their own interests, the only course, as regards humanity as well as policy, is to make all suffer, and thereby, for their own interests, enlist the great majority on the side of peace and safety.

It was a civil rather than a military policy and it was favoured by Indian administrators because it seemed to work. As Sir Richard Temple said, 'In almost all cases, the aggressive tribes behaved badly before, and well after, suffering from an expedition.' It was not, of course, designed to make the tribes love the British. Lord Roberts pointed out in a speech to the House of Lords after the Tirah campaign: 'Burning houses and destroying crops, necessary and justifiable as such measures may be, unless followed up by some form of authority or jurisdiction, mean starvation for many of the women and children . . . and for us a rich harvest of hatred and revenge.'

Having turned the Maidan Valley into a smoking ruin, having, as Lionel James gleefully said, 'unearthed and consumed the grain and fodder supply of the country, uprooted and ringed the walnut groves, prevented the autumn tillage of the soil, and having caused the inhabitants to live the life of fugitives upon the exposed, bleak and bitterly cold hill tops', Lockhart was anxious to conclude negotiations with the tribesmen and to leave Tirah. Although a number of the Orakzai chiefs had paid their fines of money and rifles, very few of the fierce Afridis had submitted.

It was now nearly the end of November and the cold weather was beginning. Lockhart anxiously watched the sky; he did not want his army to be caught in the mountains when the snows began. He decided to withdraw to the Peshawar plain by dividing his force: the 1st Division to move down the Mastara Valley and the 2nd Division to go down the Bara Valley. On 7 and 8 December the Maidan Valley was evacuated. The 1st Division had little difficulty getting out of Tirah; the 2nd Division had a great deal of trouble indeed. The holocaust of destruction in the Maidan Valley had not softened the Afridis. They seemed more eager than ever to attack the invaders.

The movement of the 2nd Division down the Bara Valley was the running of a gauntlet. From both sides of the valley the Afridis fired on the column and made sorties when there were opportunities to do so. From 10 December onward it was, as Lionel James said, 'a general engagement not only of the rearguard, but all down the line of advance of both brigades from front to rear'. Although James euphemistically called it an advance, it was, in fact, a withdrawal which with each passing day looked more and more like a retreat. The march would have been miserable enough without the Afridis, for the weather was cold and rainy, and there were many streams to be crossed. The rearguard and the long lines of transport animals and camp followers suffered the worst.

11 December was the most disastrous day of the campaign. It

was bitterly cold. There was rain and sleet all day. The river had to be forded several times. The 4th Brigade was in the lead and after a ten-mile march reached its bivouac area early in the afternoon without great difficulty. The 3rd Brigade, under the unpopular Kempster, brought up the rear, but they had not been able to begin their march until eleven o'clock in the morning. The enemy started swarming around the rearguard from the start. The Indian camp followers, who tended the transport animals and carried the sick and wounded, were ill-prepared for the cold weather. Numbed by the icy winds and the sleet, they abandoned their animals and their sick and wounded charges. Soldiers had to be detailed for these duties and the effective fighting force was thus weakened.

The leading units of the 3rd Brigade reached their bivouac at dusk, but there had been a great deal of confusion on the line of march and the Afridis had managed to get between the rearguard and the main column. Major George Downman of the Gordon Highlanders, an experienced veteran of twenty-one years' service, was in charge of the rearguard. As night fell he found himself with a mixed force of Gordons, Dorsets, Gurkhas, and a company of the 2nd Punjabis. He was encumbered by twenty-one wounded, the toll of the day's fighting by the rearguard. Deciding that he would not be able to reach the bivouac area safely in the dark, he threw his force into a small village and made it defensible. Here he was comparatively safe, but the transport and camp followers who did not make the bivouac area or did not find shelter in Downman's village were badly cut up by the Afridis. The total casualties among the combatants this day were forty-one. No one kept account of the losses among the non-combatants, but the official history said that 'upwards of 100 followers and about 150 animals seem to have been lost that night'.

It rained all the next day, but the entire division halted to try to pull itself together. The rain stopped during the night, but on the following morning snow could be seen on the tops of the mountains around them. The march was resumed with the 4th Brigade now in the rear. Three of the best battalions – the King's

Own Scottish Borderers, the 3rd Gurkhas and the 36th Sikhs –
were detailed for the rearguard. They fought desperate actions all
day. The division only marched eight miles, but there was chaos
among the transport and followers. In misery from the cold and in
terror of the Afridis, drivers, hospitalmen and servants melted
into an amorphous, terrified mob. Some of the drivers opened
kegs of rum and got drunk. Some deserted their animals and
doolies. Some, seized by ungovernable panic, ran straight for the
hillside campfires of the Afridis.

Again, the rearguard was unable to reach its bivouac before
dark and camped out on a ridge. The Afridis launched a savage
attack on them, but the troops' discipline remained firm and the
Afridis were driven off. There were twenty-five killed and eighty
wounded this day among the soldiers and more uncounted losses
among the camp followers.

The following day the 2nd Division reached Swaikat and safety.
There was a road from Peshawar to Swaikat and a strong force
had been sent up to meet the 2nd Division when it emerged from
the Bara Valley. The soldiers who came out were 'drawn, pinched,
dishevelled, and thoroughly worn'. It hardly looked like an army
returning from a successful campaign. It was, however, the first
and last foreign army ever to enter the Tirah.

The British had by this time suffered 1,300 casualties on the
Frontier since the attack on the Malakand. As for the Afridis,
only a few clans had paid token fines and only eighty-nine of
the 1,907 rifles demanded had been surrendered. Queen Victoria
wondered if it was all worth while. She wrote to Lord Elgin, the
Viceroy:

The fighting on the frontier continues very severe, and causes the
Queen much pain and anxiety, as the loss of life is so great and distressing and the loss of officers most serious. Can nothing be done to make
the officers less conspicuous? As we do not wish to retain any part of
the country, is the continuation and indefinite prolongation of these
punitive expeditions really justifiable at the cost of many valuable
lives? It seems to the Queen a great question whether it is quite
justifiable. . . . The Queen cannot help fearing that there was a want of

preparation, of watchfulness, and of knowledge of what the wild tribes were planning, which ought not to have been.

The fighting on the Frontier continued until spring. A field force was sent into the Bazar Valley, another to operate around Swaikat, and a formidable blockade was imposed on the Afridis. On 7 March 1898 the Khyber Pass was retaken, and later that month the bitter Afridis gave in and agreed to pay the fines imposed on them. They did not become tame, though, and nine years later the British had to admit that 'on the whole their attitude towards Government is much the same as it was prior to 1897'.

Sir William Lockhart returned to England to finish his interrupted leave. He found when he got there that the public was no longer interested in him, the Tirah or the North-West Frontier. The eyes of all were now fixed on the Sudan.

29

BACK TO THE SUDAN

1896–98

Since the failure of Wolseley's expedition to reach Khartoum in time to save Gordon in 1885 the Sudanese had been left to pursue their own way of life unhampered by Europeans or Egyptians. El Mahdi had died not long after his capture of Khartoum and his place as spiritual and political leader was taken by his righthand man, the Khalifa.

The failure of the effort to save Gordon rankled in the proud British mind, and the feeling that his death should not go unavenged disturbed the British conscience. It was easy enough to find excuses for invading and conquering the Sudan, for there was always trouble on the Egyptian–Sudanese frontier, and when, fourteen years after Gordon's death, the means for doing so became available, it was done. But it was not easy.

The success of the Sudan campaign of 1897–98 was due in the main to the special abilities of three soldiers who were found to be in the right places at the right times. One man was given the lion's share of the credit, but had any one of the three failed in his duty the campaign could not have succeeded.

The first requirement for the reconquest of the Sudan was an army of 'natives', and this was raised through the exertions of Horatio Herbert Kitchener (1850–1916). The son of an army officer and a vicar's daughter, Kitchener was educated in

Switzerland. He returned to England to enter Woolwich and was commissioned in the Royal Engineers in 1871. Although he became the very symbol of the British army, he had seen remarkably little active service before he led an army into the Sudan. In fact, he had very little actual military experience with troops. Shortly after he was commissioned he was loaned to the Palestine Exploration Fund for several years; then he served briefly as a vice-consul in Turkey and did survey work in Cyprus. He tried to join Wolseley's expedition against Arabi in 1882, but was refused permission. He took leave and went there anyway, but he did not see battle.

When, at the end of the Arabi campaign, Evelyn Wood was made sirdar of the Egyptian army and set about remaking it into an imitation of the British army, Kitchener, then a thirty-two-year-old major, joined him as second in command of the Egyptian cavalry. During the Gordon Relief Expedition Kitchener did not have a command but served as an intelligence officer.

After the withdrawal of Wolseley's army from the Sudan Kitchener resigned from the Egyptian army and returned to normal duty with the regular establishment, serving in 1885 on an international commission which delimited the territory on the African mainland claimed by the Sultan of Zanzibar. Then, the following year, he was appointed governor-general of the Eastern Sudan. The title was grander than the territory, for his sphere of influence hardly extended beyond the small town of Suakin. This was Egypt's (Britain's) tiny foothold on the Sudanese shore of the Red Sea; the desert beyond it was controlled by Osman Digna, the best of the Dervish generals.

In January 1888 Kitchener fought his first battle. It was not very glorious, being badly directed, but perhaps it was the best that could be expected of an engineer officer who was commanding troops in action for the first time. He led his Egyptian and Black Sudanese troops out to attack Osman Digna's camp. He managed to surprise the enemy with his cavalry, but as he had left his infantry three miles behind, he had some difficulty extricating himself. That his troops did retreat in good order was due to the exertions of his second in command, for Kitchener was severely wounded in the jaw and unable to handle the retirement.

After leave in England to recover from his wound, Kitchener returned to Egypt as adjutant-general of the Egyptian army. In the summer of 1889 when the Dervishes launched an ill-planned invasion of Upper Egypt, he commanded the cavalry at the battle of Toski, where the invaders were defeated and thrown back. Then, in 1892, he became sirdar of the Egyptian army and made his major contribution to the conquest of the Sudan by his development of this army into an effective and efficient fighting force.

He was above all an organizer, a planner, a calculator. Sir Evelyn Baring, the British proconsul in Egypt, thought he possessed 'a good head for business'. It was a rare quality in a British officer and in this instance, it was just what was required. Kitchener was a cold, methodical, humourless bachelor, never well liked by his brother officers; to others than Baring he seemed colourless and undistinguished. But he had the qualities needed to prepare, with unpromising material and scanty funds, a native army for a formidable enterprise. His greatest success was in increasing the number of Black Sudanese battalions and improving their training. These battalions of Blacks from the southern Sudan, mostly ex-slaves and only partially civilized, made splendid soldiers and the Sudanese battalions were the finest fighting unit in the Egyptian army.

A commander of one of these Black battalions was Hector Archibald Macdonald (1853–1903), the crofter's son who enlisted in the Gordon Highlanders and won his commission on the battlefields of Afghanistan. To be of lowly origin and rise from the ranks was a rare event in the Victorian era, and it was rarer still for rankers to become general officers. Still, it could and did happen. Macdonald left no record of his feelings on becoming an officer, but doubtless they were similar to those of a contemporary, William Robertson (1860–1933), who rose from being a trooper in the 16th Lancers to become a field-marshal and chief of the Imperial Staff – and a baronet too.

Robertson, one of seven children of a village tailor, won his commission by virtue of his brains rather than his bravery after nearly eleven years in the ranks. It was, though, a traumatic experience to make the transition from troop sergeant major to officer and gentleman. The differences in education between a trooper and an officer were not great: Robertson was born with a good intellect and he cultivated it; most Victorian officers were poorly educated. The financial problems were formidable, and particularly so for Robertson, who accepted a commission in the cavalry, although he joined a regiment serving in India where the pay was higher; his tailor-father made gentleman's clothes for him; and there were, after all, other officers who, although born gentlemen, were also poor. It was the social barrier, the vast difference in social position and all that this meant in terms of accent, manners, habits, interests and attitudes, which stood as the greatest obstacle for a ranker trying to become a gentleman. As Robertson wrote to his father:

I'm afraid I do not remember how often I *must* feel cut off from *all* friendship. So far as I know, not *once* has any one in my present sphere taken offence at being in my company, but there is much difference between this and sincere mutual interest; this cannot naturally be between a born gentleman and one who is only now beginning to *try* to become one.

Throughout his life he remained sensitive to the differences between his origins and those of his fellow officers, and he attributed every setback in his career to prejudice against him as a ranker. He never tried to hide his background – indeed, in British society this was almost impossible to do – and he always hastened to inform acquaintances of his past. He told his mother: 'You see I feel that I am acting under a false flag if they do not know my previous life.' Hector Macdonald must have experienced the same feelings. The life of a ranker officer was a lonely one.

Macdonald, 'Fighting Mac' as he was called, was what Kitchener was not: a superb and experienced fighting soldier. In addition to his battles in Afghanistan as a sergeant, he was with the

Gordons on Majuba Hill, where he distinguished himself but was captured by the Boers, and he fought in the battles of Gemaizah, Toski, Tokar, Firket and Hafir. He trained and led the 11th Sudanese Battalion in Egypt, and when in 1898 Kitchener ordered the advance towards Khartoum he was given command of a brigade of Egyptian and Sudanese infantry. It was thanks to this ranker that Kitchener became a hero and was made a peer of the realm. Macdonald's part in the Sudan drama came at the end of the campaign in the final battle.

The first major problem which faced the British in reconquering the Sudan was that of getting into the heart of the country to face the Dervish army. More than a thousand miles separated Cairo from Omdurman, the Dervish capital just across the river from Khartoum, and most of the distance was filled with desert. The man who provided the means for moving the Anglo-Egyptian army into the Sudan was a young French-Canadian officer named Edouard Girouard (1867–1932).

Girouard was the son of a distinguished judge of the High Court of Canada. He was educated at the Royal Military College of Canada and spent two years in the service of the Canadian Pacific Railway before he was commissioned in the Royal Engineers. For five years he was railway traffic manager at the Royal Arsenal, Woolwich, and then he was seconded to the Egyptian army. The Sudan campaign has been called the River War, yet it was not the Nile but the railway built by Girouard which made the campaign possible and helped ensure its success. Certainly it proved a better means of transport than Wolseley's whale boats, but Kitchener and Girouard had time to build the railway; time denied to Wolseley.

The problems involved in building a railway into a desert inhabited by hostile tribesmen were formidable. Railway experts and experienced soldiers alike agreed that it was an impractical idea, but Kitchener disagreed and Girouard made it a reality. Eventually, forty engines of varying ages moved men and supplies into the Sudan, bypassing the Nile cataracts which had caused Wolseley and Butler such heartaches.

Back to the Sudan

In 1896 Kitchener's army advanced south of Wadi Halfa on the start of a slow, methodically planned invasion. On 7 June the Dervishes were defeated in the battle of Firket. In September the British moved further south and occupied Dongola. The British Government was still reluctant to commit itself completely to the reconquest of the Sudan in spite of the urging of the soldiers and the popularity of the idea with the British public. In 1897 a force under Sir Archibald Hunter seized Abu Hamed and then pushed on to occupy Berber. It had now been demonstrated that the Dervishes could be reached and defeated in their own country and Kitchener was at last permitted to proceed with the conquest of the Sudan.

By the end of January 1898 most of the Egyptian army plus a brigade of British troops were concentrated at a point south of Berber where the Atbara River joins the Nile. The Dervishes sent a strong force to attack the invaders here, but instead of attacking they made camp a few miles away and waited. The British waited too. After a few days of this, the British attacked: the Dervish army was routed and their commander and 4,000 of his men were captured.

Kitchener asked for and obtained additional British troops. Slowly, surely, carefully he moved deeper into the Sudan. Finally, on 2 September he had 8,200 British and 17,000 Egyptian and Sudanese troops assembled in a great half circle on the Nile only seven miles north of Omdurman, his back protected by armed steamers on the river. Here he waited for 50,000 fanatical Dervishes to attack him. They obligingly did. Fortunately for Kitchener, the Dervish units were uncoordinated and their attacks badly timed.

Sir Evelyn Baring later said that once the Anglo-Egyptian army had overcome the exceptional supply and transport problems involved in moving an army to Omdurman the result of the battle was a foregone conclusion. It was not quite so simple. True, it had been due to Kitchener's careful planning and his 'good head for business' and Girouard's railway which had made the advance possible, but battle is always a chancy event. Every general needs luck. The battle with the main Dervish army had yet to be fought and won.

Kitchener and his army were fortunate that the Dervishes chose to attack by day, for in a night attack the Anglo-Egyptian army might well have been overwhelmed. In the first phase of the battle thousands of Dervishes charged across an open desert in plain sight, waving their spears and screaming. Kitchener's howitzers, machine guns and rifles cut them down. Not a single Dervish reached the Anglo-Egyptian lines. Few even came as close as 500 yards. It was, as war correspondent G. W. Steevens said, 'not a battle but an execution'. An estimated 10,000 Dervishes fell, and few of the wounded survived, for the British used vicious dum-dum bullets.

On the right flank, the British commander of the Egyptian cavalry and camel corps cleverly diverted the Dervish cavalry away from the main battlefield and led them under the guns of the steamers on the river. On the left flank there was a bold, useless charge by the 21st Lancers in which Lieutenant Winston Spencer Churchill took part. The commander of the 21st Lancers, Lieutenant-Colonel Rowland Hill Martin, like all of his officers, was over-eager to prove the valour of his regiment, for this was the only regiment of regular cavalry in the British army without a single battle honour. Mockers maintained that their motto was 'Thou Shalt Not Kill'. So Martin led his men in a charge over unreconnoitred ground against an enemy of unknown strength, and they were almost overwhelmed. The charge proved conclusively that his regiment was brave and that he was foolish. This was a minor action which did not affect the course of the battle in any way, but it accounted for most of the forty-eight Anglo-Egyptian casualties sustained in the battle and resulted in the award of three Victoria Crosses. Martin was rewarded with a CB.

After the mass slaughter of Dervish infantry, it seemed to Kitchener that the battle was over and he had won. He gave orders for the march to Omdurman. As the word was carried to the various commanders, the Anglo-Egyptian army began the cumbersome swing from their fighting formations into a line of march, and the battalions, each in turn, began to move south. In doing this, Kitchener was unwittingly marching his troops across the front of the main Dervish army, which had not yet attacked, and was exposing an entire flank to the enemy.

Colonel Hector Macdonald, the crofter's son, was commanding a brigade consisting of one Egyptian and three Sudanese battalions, perhaps 2,000 men, on the right of the fighting line. He would thus have been in the rear of the army as it moved south. The movement of troops left his brigade nearly a mile from the next brigade. It was at this moment that he was hit by a charge of 20,000 Dervishes led by the Khalifa's brother. With cool skill he swung his troops by half battalions into an arc to meet the attack. His method of accomplishing this was later much studied at the Staff College. His splendid Black battalions remained steady and bravely faced the charging Dervishes. Had Macdonald been less skilful and less calm, his brigade would easily have been overrun and the enemy would have fallen upon the unprepared Anglo-Egyptian army like a whirlwind. In the event, Macdonald stopped the Dervishes in their tracks.

In contrast to Macdonald's cool handling of this dangerous situation, Kitchener almost panicked. He dashed about, excitedly shouting orders and trying frantically to bring his troops into fighting formations again to support Macdonald. Thanks to Macdonald's abilities and bravery, Kitchener won the battle of Omdurman. Macdonald saved the day. Literally. Still, it was almost a disaster in spite of his skill: when the battle ended it was found that Macdonald's men had an average of only two rounds per man for their rifles.

Kitchener was created an earl and went on to acquire still more honours, gaining a place of power and prestige which had not been reached by a British soldier since the death of the Duke of Wellington. Edouard Girouard was only twenty-nine when he built the railway that carried Kitchener's army into the desert. He went on to build more railways in South Africa and Nigeria. He became governor of Northern Nigeria and, during World War I, director-general of munitions supply. The last years of his life were spent in private business.

The fate of the crofter's son was sadder. Macdonald further distinguished himself in the Boer War and he eventually became a major-general, but in 1903, while commanding the British forces in Ceylon, he was charged with being a practising homosexual. He went to London to defend himself, but was ordered back to Ceylon to face a court of inquiry. He got no further than Paris. There in a hotel room this officer, so brave under the fire of Afghans, Dervishes and Boers, shot himself.

30

THE BOER WAR I: 1899

FOR most Englishmen the war with the Dutch farmers of the Transvaal and the Orange Free State broke what was frequently called 'the long peace' – the eighty-four years between the battle of Waterloo and the outbreak of the Boer War. So little did all of Queen Victoria's little wars penetrate the consciousness of most of her subjects.

The Boer War, or South African War (the Afrikaners called it the English War) was not the usual little war fought by professional soldiers with armies largely composed of native troops, but a major war, a serious war, in which the general public became intimately involved. The Boer War had many of the characteristics of the later world wars: it involved large armies and masses of ill-trained volunteers; it affected large numbers of civilian noncombatants and drew rather heavily on the civilian resources of the countries involved; it was affected by technological changes in warfare and presented great logistical problems; and it lasted longer than any previous conflict since the Napoleonic Wars.

The Boer War was disturbing for the British, though it began in the conventional style of British military dramas: In Act I the Boers beat the British; in Act II the British beat the Boers; then in Act III it all became very messy and the final scene was unsatisfactory: the Boers refused to believe that they were beaten and took to guerrilla warfare; the British retaliated by burning farms and forming concentration camps. By the time the final curtain fell Queen Victoria was dead and so was an era. For those with vision, the end of the British Empire was in sight.

Throughout the winter months of 1899 – June, July, August and September in South Africa – both sides prepared for war and waited: the Boers for the spring grass to maintain the horses and oxen of their commandos; the British for reinforcements of Imperial troops. William Butler, blunt, brilliant and outspoken, one of the Wolseley gang, former commander of the flotilla of Nile whaleboats, described by Sir Alfred Milner as 'that brilliant but impossible Irishman', was commander-in-chief in Cape Colony while the trouble between Boer and Briton was brewing. He saw his fellow countrymen push the Boers towards war, and he thought that British policies were foolish and that an Anglo-Boer war would be a calamity. He did what he could to avert it and was damned as pro-Boer and recalled for his efforts. As a result, he became, in his own words, 'the best abused man in England'.

When the spring grass covered the veldt, Paul Kruger demanded that Britain give up her claim to suzerainty over the Transvaal, and he issued an ultimatum. When this expired at 5.00 p.m. on 11 October 1899 the Boers moved on their British neighbours, across the border from the Transvaal and the Orange Free State into Cape Colony and Natal. The first act of the war had begun.

As usual, the British were not quite ready. There were only 14,750 regulars in South Africa, but a field force of 47,000 men under General Sir Redvers Buller was on its way. This was a very sizeable portion of the British Army, which then consisted of only 250,000 regulars, 70,000 of whom were in India while 60,000 were scattered about the rest of the Empire. It was not enough. Estimates of the size of the Boer forces vary wildly, but it is doubtful that they ever had more than 45,000 men under arms at one time and usually fewer than 30,000. To subdue these tough, stubborn men the British were eventually forced to raise a large volunteer army from social classes other than the lowest – fortunately, it was a popular war – and eventually to commit nearly half a million men to the South African struggle, 21,000 of whom died from bullets or diseases.

It was, for the British, the first war in which brains and skill on the part of the generals were more important than bravery and endurance on the part of the soldiers and junior officers. Unfortunately, brains were in rather short supply in the British army just at this time. As Wolseley told the Queen's private secretary, 'What we are now most in want of is good Generals.' Britain's Boer War generals have often been portrayed as stupid. Certainly many of them did a number of incredibly stupid things. But most of the senior officers were not stupid; they were simply average Victorian officers who found themselves in positions where what was required of them was a rather high degree of intelligence, initiative and imagination, and they were found to be somewhat deficient in these qualities.

Perhaps no more typical Victorian soldier could have been chosen to lead the forces of Empire against the Dutch farmers than sixty-year-old Sir Redvers Buller, v c, described by one war correspondent as 'a stern-tempered, ruthless man, with a gift of grim silence'. The most successful member of the Wolseley gang, he had in his forty years of service taken part in the China War of 1860, the Red River Expedition in Canada, Wolseley's Ashanti War, the Gaika War, the Zulu War (where he won his Victoria Cross for saving the lives of two officers and a trooper under heavy fire), the First Boer War, the Arabi rebellion in Egypt, and the Gordon Relief Expedition. He was now to fight his last war as the commander of a splendid army that included many of the finest regiments in the service. Success would ensure a peerage. But the brave and popular Buller had unfortunately risen to a level of command that was too high for his abilities. There was to be no peerage for him, only defeat, demotion, and a distinguished reputation irretrievably lost.

By the time Buller and his army arrived in South Africa the Boers were already besieging a number of towns. Boer commandos had bottled up British forces at Ladysmith, Kimberley and Mafeking. The first phase of the war involved the gallant defence of these towns – although pressing home an attack on a fortified town was not the Afrikaner's forte; the besieged towns were rarely in danger of being overwhelmed – and the inept attempts by the British army to relieve them.

Strategically, the relief of Kimberley was not at the top of the list of military priorities. But politically it was, for Cecil Rhodes, the most important man in South Africa and the richest Briton alive, was in Kimberley and demanding the immediate relief of the town. Reluctantly, Buller dispatched 8,000 men to raise the siege. He told the Queen he did 'not anticipate that the force will meet with very serious difficulties'. In command was fifty-four-year-old Lord Methuen, 'a burly man with a large drooping moustache, a strong, purposeful chin and steady but not unkindly eyes'. He had served in a number of campaigns but always as a staff officer; this was his first important command. He exhibited considerable bravery but few brains, and he made a hash of it.

Methuen first encountered the Boers on a hill at Belmont on 23 November 1899 and decided on a frontal assault. When a staff officer suggested that perhaps this was not the best way to attack an entrenched enemy, Methuen replied, 'My good fellow, I intend to put the fear of God into these people.' The Brigade of Guards (Grenadier, Coldstream and Scots) moved up close to the Boer positions at night and charged at dawn. The Boers coolly sighted down the barrels of their modern Mauser rifles and knocked over 291 British soldiers; then they mounted their horses and rode off, suffering little loss to themselves.

Two days later Methuen again encountered entrenched Boers at Graspaan (or Enslin). When the officers and men of the Naval Brigade learned that they had been selected to lead the assault the sailors were overjoyed. One naval officer later said that 'the news seemed almost too good to be true, and it was some time before we could believe it and realize our luck'. It was the Naval Brigade's luck to suffer 50 per cent casualties, including nearly all their officers, when they led the frontal attack Methuen had ordered. *The Times* described the charge of the sailors as 'an attack that will live to all times as one of the most splendid instances of disciplined courage'. It was that, of course. It was also tragic. Boer losses were negligible. They had again bloodied the British nose and bolted.

Three days after the Battle of Graspaan Methuen reached the Modder River where 2,500 Boers were entrenched and, as a new refinement, had stretched barbed wire in front of their position. It was a blistering hot day, the thermometer reaching 110°F. The Boers had anticipated that the British would again make a frontal attack and did not bother to protect their flanks. Methuen did not disappoint them. He launched another frontal attack. The Guards charged and were shot down. The entire attacking force was soon pinned to the ground in the hot sun by the fast, accurate fire of the Boers' Mausers. And they stayed on their stomachs all day. Some of the Guardsmen actually fell asleep and the kilted Highlanders got sunburned on the backs of their knees. Methuen personally led a small party in a charge and was slightly wounded. The Boers inflicted 483 casualties, waited until dark and then retreated. Methuen, whose knowledge of military history was obviously deficient, called it 'one of the hardest and most trying fights in the annals of the British Army'.

As a result of these Pyrrhic victories Methuen had lost 10 per cent of his original force, but he had been reinforced by a Highland Brigade (Black Watch, Gordons, Seaforths and the Highland Light Infantry), the 12th Lancers, more artillery and some Canadian and Australian troops. The Boers, led by Piet Cronjé, had also been reinforced and now mustered 8,500 men, including a foreign legion of Americans and Europeans.

The next battle was at Magersfontein on 10–11 December. Here even Methuen could see that the key to the Boer position was a hill which the Boers would be forced to defend. On the evening of 10 October the British laid down a splendid artillery barrage on the crest of this hill. It would have had a devastating effect had any of the enemy been there, but none were. Jacobus De La Rey, a brilliant Boer leader who had been averse to beginning the war but was determined to win it, had convinced Cronjé that the Boers should not entrench on the crest but at the foot of the hill – a bold and original idea. De La Rey did not stay to see the successful working of his plan, for he left to go and tell his wife of the death of their son, killed by the British at the battle of the Modder River.

A thunderstorm rolled overhead as the Highland Brigade, commanded by popular, experienced, much-wounded Andy Wauchop (known as 'Red Mick'), moved by night into attack positions. At dawn they charged. It was, of course, another frontal attack and under the intense fire of the murderous Mausers the Highlanders wilted. Red Mick was killed. There was a stampede to the rear by the pride of Scotland. The Highland Light Infantry panicked and trampled on their colonel in their retreat. And the Boers shot them in the back as they ran. A few stayed to fight, charged the Boer trenches and were caught on the barbed wire. Officers managed to stop the rout of the Highlanders, but then the Boer artillery opened on them and they fled again. Methuen's only order was 'Hold on until nightfall'. He assumed that the enemy would again retreat under cover of darkness. But this time they stayed.

One Highlander, speaking of Magersfontein, said that his regiment had been 'led into a butcher's shop and bloody well left there!'

A poetic Highland private in the Black Watch wrote of his regiment's experience:

> 'Tell you the tale of the battle, well there's not much to
>   tell;
> Nine hundred men went to the slaughter, and nigh four
>   hundred fell.
> Wire and Mauser rifle, thirst and a burning sun
> Knocked down by hundreds ere the day was done.

When details of this battle reached Edinburgh there was general mourning. All dances were cancelled and there were crying women in the street. For Scotland, Magersfontein was a calamity. It was also a disaster for Methuen and for the Empire's reputa-

tion. Methuen had led the flower of the British infantry to defeat –
and at the hands of an inferior force of Dutch farmers! The next
day he began a retreat to the Modder River.

The force opposing the British was composed of Boers from the
Transvaal and Methuen estimated that there were 17,000 of them.
Cecil Rhodes in Kimberley was scornful:

Look at the census reports. Men cannot be made in a minute. It takes
twenty years to make a man, and we know how many they had at the
beginning of the war. The Transvaal only polled a little over 17,000
voters at the last election. No, we are exaggerating their numbers
simply because by doing so we account for bad generalship without
confessing it.

The week of 10–17 December 1899 was known as 'black week'.
It was, said Conan Doyle, 'the blackest one known during our
generation, and the most disastrous for British arms during the
century'. During this week, in addition to the disaster at
Magersfontein, a force under General William Forbes Gatacre
(known to his men as General Back-acher) was routed at Stormberg
and Buller himself, leading a large force towards Ladysmith, was
repulsed at Colenso on the Tugela River.

The failure of Buller to get across the Tugela River was the
greatest setback of the war. Gatacre's disaster was the most
disgraceful. On the night of 9 December General Gatacre set off in
the dark from Molteno in northern Cape Colony with 2,700 men –
three battalions of infantry, some mounted men and two guns – to
surprise the Boers at the Stormberg railway junction. He lost his
way. Some of his men bumped into an enemy outpost; there was
firing and a Boer commando arrived on the scene and began to cut
them up. Gatacre beat a hasty retreat. It was too hasty. Only
when he got back to Molteno did he discover that he had accidentally left some 600 of his men behind! They were surrounded
and forced to surrender. Total losses at Stormberg were 719
officers and men, of whom only twenty-nine were killed. 'Hope
better luck next time', telegraphed Buller to Gatacre.

Less than six weeks later occurred the bloody but curious

battle of Spion Kop. The British seized a ridge and then the troops lay there on the crest all day under intense fire, suffering heavy casualties. When night came, the British withdrew, feeling that their position was untenable. The Boers, discouraged by their failure to dislodge the British, were about to give up the fight and retreat when they discovered that the British had retreated first. They reoccupied the ridge and claimed a victory.

Black week was too much for the people at home. 'Our generals,' said Asquith, 'seem neither able to win victories nor to give convincing reasons for their defeat.' The failure of Buller was a personal disappointment to Wolseley, who told his wife that Buller, his protégé, 'had not shown any of the characteristics I had attributed to him: no military genius, no firmness, not even the obstinacy which I thought he possessed when I discovered him. He seems dazed and dumbfounded.' It was time to change generals.

31

THE BOER WAR II: 1900

'Very bad news for Buller, my dear child,' wrote Wolseley in
London to his wife in the country. 'I am in despair at all our
misfortunes. God seems to be with the Boers and against us. I am
not easily depressed, but what a hopeless condition one is in here –
7,000 miles away from the actual seat of war. Yet I feel I have no
right to blame men at a distance.'

The old war horse wanted nothing better than to go to South
Africa himself. In succeeding the Duke of Cambridge as commander-in-chief at the Horse Guards, he had finally achieved his
heart's desire, but the post had been stripped of much of its
authority and power. Wolseley was undoubtedly the most
brilliant general of the Victorian era, perhaps the most brilliant
general in British history, but it was his misfortune never to have
commanded in a major war. He was born at least twenty years
too soon. Now, sadly, this most intelligent of soldiers was losing
his memory; often he could not even remember the faces of his
best friends. When a new general was being selected to take over
the top command in South Africa, he was not only not considered
but he was not even consulted. He was not alone in feeling
slighted: the Queen had not been consulted either, and she
thought it 'very wrong'.

347

It was 'Britain's other general', Lord Roberts, known affectionately as 'little Bobs', who was chosen to take command in South Africa. Wolseley was bitter indeed. In another letter to his wife he called Roberts a 'cute, little jobbing showman' and 'a snob as regards Dukes and Earls'. Although Wolseley and Roberts were about the same age, Roberts was at the height of his power and his star was in the ascendant; Wolseley's great career was over and at the end of November 1899 he retired. He died fourteen years later.

Roberts was elated when he was called to the War Office and told that he was to lead the largest British army to take the field since the Peninsular War and an army which was to grow into the largest army Britain had ever put in the field. It must have been the happiest moment in his life when he was given this splendid command, the pinnacle of his career. A few hours later, he was plunged into grief by the news that his only son, Freddy, a lieutenant in the King's Royal Rifle Corps had been killed while trying to save a gun at Colenso. Young Roberts was awarded the first Victoria Cross ever to be given posthumously; the gun he had tried to save was later presented to his father. It was a poor exchange.

In spite of Roberts's record of success and undoubted abilities, it is remarkable that he was selected, for he was an 'Indian officer', and there was still a snobbish prejudice against officers of the Indian army. Even when thousands of volunteers were being taken in and there was fear that there would not be enough men left in Britain to defend it in case of attack, and even when officers were scarce and badly needed, officers of the Indian army found it difficult to get into the war. In addition to prejudice in England, the Government of India was reluctant to release officers for service in South Africa, for this was a home army war.

In part, Indian and other native troops were not sent to South Africa because of a feeling that it was unseemly to use Asiatics to fight against white men. It also seemed improper to both sides to arm Africans. They were used in non-combatant roles but, in spite of charges to the contrary levelled by both sides against the other,

black Africans were not made into fighting soldiers by either Boer
or Briton, except towards the end of the war when the British
armed native scouts and guards. In the desperate struggle of the
Great War fifteen years hence such niceties would disappear, but
now Britain felt compelled to find her soldiers at home and in the
'white colonies'.

Kitchener, fresh from his conquest of the Sudan, was selected
to be Roberts's second-in-command. It is difficult to imagine two
more different men than the tall and haughty Kitchener and
Little Bobs Roberts.

Their personality (*sic*) methods, and manners were entirely different
[said General George Younghusband]. Yet they both rose to be great
soldiers. Lord Roberts was the modern Bayard, *chevalier sans peur et
sans réproche*. Lord Kitchener was fashioned more on the lines of Bis-
marck. Both were born British, but one developed into the highest type
of English gentleman, the other acquired more Teutonic characteristics.
It would therefore be somewhat difficult for an honest admirer of Lord
Roberts to be an equally honest admirer of Lord Kitchener.

Roberts reached Cape Town on 10 January 1900 and Act II of
the war began one month later when he took the offensive.
Methuen's force lay, still licking its wounds, on the Modder River
when Roberts joined it. There he received a message from Cecil
Rhodes in besieged Kimberley: 'There is no fear our surrendering,
but we are getting anxious about the state of the British Army. It
is high time you did something.' Roberts did not need this advice.
By the middle of February he had flanked the Boers and relieved
Kimberley. The *Daily Mail* crowed: 'Kimberley is won, Mr Cecil
Rhodes is free, the De Beers shareholders are full of themselves,
and the beginning of the war is at an end. It is a great feat to have
accomplished, and the happiest omens for the future. There is no
one like Bobs!' On 27 February, the nineteenth anniversary of the
battle of Majuba Hill, Roberts captured Cronjé and 4,000 Boers
at Paardeberg. On 13 March he entered Bloemfontein, capital of
the Orange Free State.

Meanwhile Buller was still trying to relieve Ladysmith, and the day after Cronjé's surrender to Roberts he finally made it. It had been a long and arduous siege. Captain Hubert Gough was the first officer of the relief force to ride into town. General Sir George White, Commander of the Ladysmith garrison, greeted him on the main street: 'Hello, Hubert, how are you?'

Ladysmith was relieved, but many were still bitter at the length of time it had taken Buller to accomplish it. Lord Rawlinson, a staff officer in Ladysmith, said, 'The British infantry has once more saved their generals.' The Queen, naturally, had been following the course of events in South Africa with great interest. She was so impressed by the gallantry of her Irish troops that she permitted them to wear the shamrock, previously forbidden in the army, on Saint Patrick's Day.

Roberts had achieved almost instant success. He had seen at once that failure had resulted from bad management and lack of mobility, and he had promptly set about to correct both. In less than three months after his arrival he got rid of five generals (including William Gatacre), six brigadiers and nearly two dozen colonels commanding regiments. Buller, no longer commander-in-chief, was allowed to stay on as a subordinate of Roberts and Kitchener. Roberts collected all of the horses he could find and formed units of mounted infantry; every infantry battalion in the field was ordered to form one mounted company; cavalry regiments were raised from local volunteers and a cavalry division was formed and placed under the command of Lieutenant-General John French.

On 17 May Mafeking was relieved. British troops had in their history relieved dozens of forts and towns and won dozens of brilliant victories, yet no event in British history, either before or since, ever created such wild jubilation in England as did the news that Mafeking had, after a siege of 217 days, been at last relieved. In London there was a spontaneous outburst of joyful hysteria. *The Times* published a description of the scene at Piccadilly Circus:

The walls around the big open space were alive with cheering and gesticulating figures. The pavements and the streets blocked with them, and motionless among them the streams of omnibuses and cabs, all crowded with persons waving hats, umbrellas, flags, anything . . . and over it all and throughout it all, the cheers thundered on in a continuous roar like the sound of a heavy surf on a rocky shore.

For years afterwards, 'Mafeking night' was a yardstick against which all celebrations were measured. Even in far off Pekin, the British ambassador and his staff, soon to be besieged themselves, celebrated the relief of Mafeking.

The names that the London crowds shouted most often were 'Mafeking' and 'Baden-Powell', the officer in charge of the town's defence. Neither the wretched little town nor the somewhat ridiculous and vain little colonel who defended it seems worthy of such ardour.

Robert Baden-Powell (1857–1941) – he always pronounced his name as rhyming with 'maiden noël' – was the eighth child by the third wife of an Oxford don. After trying unsuccessfully to enter Oxford, he joined the army and was gazetted straight into the 13th Hussars without benefit of any military instruction. He loved to draw caricatures, do imitations, act in amateur theatricals, and play practical jokes. He was a very amusing fellow. He also wrote articles for newspapers, and books on pig-sticking and cavalry instruction, and about the Matebele and Ashanti wars in which he was a participant. His most famous book was *Reconnaissance and Scouting*, and, of course, today he is less known as the 'Hero of Mafeking' than as the founder of the Boy Scouts.

Colonel Baden-Powell was a forty-three-year-old bachelor when he found himself in command of a small force shut up by the Boers in Mafeking, the northernmost town in Cape Colony. It was, as he described it, 'a very ordinary-looking place. . . . Just a small tin-roofed town of small houses plumped down on the veldt.' Besides about 7,000 Africans, who were bystanders and victims in the clash of white men, there was a European population of 1,074 men, 229 women and 405 children. The Boers besieged the town but never completely invested it or made an all-out attack on it. As Emerson Neilly, correspondent for the *Pall Mall Gazette*, who was on the scene, later said: 'Frankly, our defender's pluck did not save Mafeking, great and heroic though that pluck was. The cowardice of the enemy saved us.'

When Mafeking was relieved, Queen Victoria wrote to Lord Salisbury (22 May 1900): 'It is indeed a most blessed termination of a long and wearying anxiety. . . . The strain of their long hardships and exertions must have been very severe.' It was not really as bad as that. Messengers and other individuals had little difficulty getting in and out and, thanks to the foresight of a wealthy staff officer who had procured vast stocks of supplies with his own credit, there was enough to eat throughout the siege: meat, bread and vegetables.

For Baden-Powell it was something of a lark. He employed his energies less in fighting the Boers than in arranging amusements. There were polo matches, teas, concerts and plays. The commander himself took part in these with gusto, singing cockney songs and acting in the plays. He once put a mop on his head and did an imitation of Paderewski at the piano. It was, as Brian Gardner has said, 'the most casually conducted and jauntily withstood siege in modern history'. Life in the town proceeded almost normally: there were the usual births, deaths and weddings. When a soldier who spoke no Afrikaans married a Dutch girl who spoke no English, the local newspaper, the *Mafeking Mail*, reported the event, adding, 'This celebration is another proof of the pluck and courage which, in the garrison, is available for any event'. It was a delightful siege, marred only by a handful of casualties, and Baden-Powell was rewarded for his gallantry by being made a major-general, the youngest in the British army, and eventually a peer.

On 5 June 1900 victorious British troops occupied Pretoria, capital of the Transvaal, and Paul Kruger fled to Europe. But it was not until October that all organized Boer resistance came to an end and Roberts sailed for England, leaving Kitchener to deal with the numerous guerrilla bands of stubborn Boers who refused to quit. As all the world knows, the children and grandchildren of these proud, brave, bigoted men at last won their fight and in 1961 carried the Republic of South Africa out of the British Commonwealth.

The Boer War II: 1900

On 2 January 1901 the Queen, although ill, welcomed home Lord Roberts. He was created an earl and given the Order of the Garter. Less than three weeks later, at 6.30 p.m. on Tuesday 22 January, Queen Victoria died. She had lived for 81 years, 7 months and 2 days. Fittingly, she who so dearly loved her Army was given a military funeral.

When the great Queen died, her soldiers were still fighting, not only in South Africa, but in West Africa (the Ashantis again), in the Sudan (where some Dervishes in the provinces were still causing trouble) and in China. The little wars of empire continued to occur in remote places: Borneo, Waziristan, Tibet, Arabia, Venezuela, Somaliland. Thirteen years after her death much of Victorian military thinking and many a Victorian soldier perished in mud and blood in Flanders.

Those who created the great British Empire believed they were creating an enduring edifice, but many had read their Gibbon and knew that all empires come to an end; that proud rulers of the world change; and that shifts in world power are accompanied by war. Lord Wolseley, his memory of the past fading, could still look into the future, and in 1903 he made an astonishing and chilling prediction: The Chinese, he said,

are the most remarkable race on earth, and I have always thought, and still believe them to be, the coming rulers of the world. They only want a Chinese Peter the Great or Napoleon to make them so . . . and in my idle speculation upon this world's future I have long selected them as the combatants on one side of the great Battle of Armageddon, the people of the United States of America being their opponents. The latter nation is fast becoming the greatest power of the world. Thank Heaven, they speak English, are governed by an English system of laws, and profess the same regard that we have for what both understand by fair play in all national as well as in private business.

THE BRITISH REGIMENT

THE most distinguishing feature of the British army has always been its regimental system. Unlike regiments in other armies, a British regiment is not a unit of a relatively fixed size. It can be as small as a weak battalion or as large as twenty-five or more battalions or, as is the case with the Royal Regiment of Artillery, include an entire arm of the army.

It is in the cavalry and infantry that the British regimental system is seen in its most peculiar and characteristic form. Basically medieval in concept, each regiment of cavalry and infantry, even today, is much like a separate army, with its own distinctive uniforms, customs, unique characteristics, and sometimes even its own marching pace. It does its own recruiting and selects its own officers. It is also like a clan or tribe; or like an enlarged family, a tightly knit family, with its own quarrels, perhaps, but ever united against attack from the outside, be the outsiders the War Office, another regiment or enemies of the monarch. Each has its own sense of honour, its own history with glorious deeds to which it points with pride, and often, too, skeletons in the regimental closet.

Real families identify themselves with particular regiments, sons following fathers as officers into the same regiment for generations. There have been family quarrels when a son has decided to join the navy or another regiment, and even, in at least one case, there was a family scene when a daughter married an officer not in the Gordons, to which the family felt allied. In some regiments it is, or was, almost impossible for an officer to serve unless some relative was or had been a member.

An officer whose father and perhaps grandfather were in a particular regiment was said to have been born into it. In the case of children of some other ranks this was quite literally true, and children born in the barracks whose mother and soldier father had died were often raised by the regiment: the boys to be first buglers or drummers and then soldiers; the girls to marry soldiers of the regiment when they came of age. Private Robert Waterfield told of the young daughter of a quartermaster-sergeant killed in the Second Sikh War, who was raised by the regiment and at sixteen married a thirty-four-year-old colour sergeant. 'I really think that some women belonging to the army would marry the devil himself if he had a scarlet jacket with three stripes on the sleeve,' he said.

Each regiment has its own distinct personality and its own friends and enemies among other regiments. Typical of regimental friendships is that which exists between the Worcestershire and the Lincolnshire regiments, formerly the 29th and 10th regiments. It started during the Napoleonic wars and was cemented when the regiments fought side by side at Sobraon (1848) in the First Sikh War. To this day, sergeants and officers are honorary members of each other's messes and the adjutants of the two regiments address each other as 'My dear cousin' in official correspondence.

The old regiments grew mossy with history, and regimental memories are long and do not forget comrades who came to their aid in time of need. The Royal Norfolk Regiment is also a friend of the Worcestershires, for when it was the 9th Regiment of the line it came to the aid of the 29th at the Battle of Rolica in 1808. The Berkshire Regiment and the 15th Sikhs became friends when the Sikhs saved several Berkshires at the Battle of McNeill's Zariba in the eastern Sudan in 1885.

The friendships among individuals of different regiments is not confined to the officers. Private Waterfield of the 32nd Regiment during the 1840s spoke of how the men of his regiment and the men of the 67th were 'on the most intimate terms'. Mountaineers from widely separated mountain homes became friends during the Second Afghan War when the 72nd (Seaforth) Highlanders and the 5th Gurkhas formed a lasting friendship. When General Frederick Roberts was made a peer he took as supporters for his coat of arms a representation of a soldier from each of these two gallant regiments.

Traditional friendships exist not only between British regiments, but between British regiments and units of foreign armies; telegrams and sometimes gifts are exchanged on important regimental anniversaries. Such a friendship developed between the Royal Welch Fusiliers and the United States Marine Corps during the Boxer Rebellion in China in 1901.

British regiments also have traditional enemies. Some regiments will not stand side by side on parade and generals must be careful not to bivouac uncongenial regiments together. Scots and Welsh regiments generally have little love for each other. Although only four other regiments in the entire British Army have more battle honours than the Highland Light Infantry, its members are not popular with other Scots regiments who maintain, rightly, that for the most part its recruits are not really Highlanders at all.

Sometimes regiments experience divorces – one battalion leaving the other to become a regiment of its own – and, more frequently in this century, there are marriages of regiments – two regiments being combined, usually in the name of economy, to form one. Not all of these mergers have been happy ones and many were very much shotgun marriages. Such amalgamations have sometimes created crises of conscience among the officers, some of whom have resigned their commission rather than become a part of the joined regiment, refusing to 'soldier with that lot!' In some officers' messes of merged regiments the two groups of officers, forced now to mess together, have refused to associate with each other socially, have clung to their old designations, insignia and regimental ties, and have tried not to recognize their new regimental names and badges.

In truth, some of the regimental marriages were curious combinations: in the early 1880s, when the territorial system was introduced, the 3rd Bombay European Infantry was merged with the 100th Royal Canadian Regiment to form the Leinster Regiment. Sometimes, though, regiments long separated were remarried. In the eighteenth century the 2nd Battalion of the 24th Regiment was

divorced and became the 69th Regiment; in the nineteenth
century it was married to the 41st Regiment to become the Welch
Brigade (taking pride in the eccentric spelling of 'Welsh'); in the
twentieth century the first battalion of the Welch Brigade was
remarried to the 24th (then called the South Wales Borderers) to
become the Royal Welsh Regiment.

It has been 100 years since regimental numbers for British
infantry regiments were replaced by names, usually county
designations, but most officers even today know the old number
by which their regiment was formerly known. This is perhaps not
so unusual as the old numbers designated, as they still do, each
regiment's order of precedence in the army. This takes on importance at parades, where the senior regiment is always on the right
of the line and the junior on the left. There is, however, a quarrel
between the Coldstream Guards and the Royal Scots as to which
regiment is Number One and they can for this reason never be
placed side by side on parade. This love of the old numbers is
stronger in some regiments than in others. The Black Watch and
the Green Howards, for example, have always been better known
by their names than their numbers, but men of the Somerset Light
Infantry could never forget that they were the 13th regiment of
the line, and the King's Royal Rifle Corps (originally formed as
the Royal Americans) cannot forget that they were the 60th.

Regiments also acquired nicknames, some of which have stuck
and some have not. The 17th Lancers were known as the 'Death
or Glory Boys', and the 29th Foot, who in American histories are
the villains of the so-called Boston Massacre, were known as 'The
vein openers'. The Northamptonshire Regiment used to be called
'The Steelbacks' because the men took pride in not flinching while
being flogged. Because one of the ornaments of the King's Royal
Rifle Corps is a Maltese Cross they were unkindly called 'The
Kaiser's own' in World War I. The Middlesex Regiment was known
as the 'Diehards' because at Albuera in 1811, their colonel called
out to his men, 'Die hard, my men, die hard!' and at Inkerman
the colonel called out 'Diehards, remember Albuera!'

When temporary regiments of 'natives' were formed they were

usually, following the ancient British practice, named after their commanding officer. Thus, there was 'Wood's Regiment', 'Wilde's Rifles' and 'Hodson's Horse'. Sometimes these temporary regiments were taken into the regular establishment, at least in the Indian army: Wood's Regiment existed for only a few months during the Ashanti War, but Wilde's Rifles became the 4th Punjab Infantry.

An exception to the rule of naming irregular regiments after their commanders was the curiously named 'Guides'. There are conflicting accounts of how this regiment acquired its name, but it bore no relation to the function of this famous fighting unit. Raised on the North-West Frontier, it consisted of both cavalry and infantry, and was composed of men from an exceptionally wide variety of races and religions, but it was always officered, of course, by Britons.

Each regiment has its own official march. Several adopted 'The British Grenadiers', but many of the marches are not very martial. It is natural that the Lincolnshire Regiment should use 'The Lincolnshire Poacher' and that Highland regiments should use Highland songs, but the official regimental march of the King's (Liverpool Regiment) was 'Here's to the Maiden of Bashful Fifteen', and the Royal Irish Rifles marched to the tune of 'Off, Off, said the Stranger'. Although every Scottish regiment had bagpipes, the regiment had to buy them; the regulations only provided for fifes to be issued to these regiments, but only the Scots Guards ever drew them.

Regiments take great pride in the special privileges given them. The Northumberland Fusiliers, the Buffs, 3rd Grenadier Guards and Royal Marines are the only units entitled to march through the City of London with 'fixed bayonets, colours flying and drums beating' without first obtaining the permission of the Lord Mayor and the Aldermen. Regiments which fought in the battle of Minden in 1759 wear roses in their headgear on the anniversary of this battle. The Cheshire Regiment wears oak leaves in its headgear on all Royal Ceremony parades in honour of the battle of Dettingen in 1743 when the King sought shelter under an oak tree and was protected by the regiment. All Welsh regiments have a goat as a mascot, usually a gift of the sovereign, and it appears on parade with them.

Regiments usually have their own homes: barracks they can call their own and where they keep the regimental museums and hold reunions of old soldiers. Pride is taken in the regimental silver, the drums and colours with the battle honours of the regiment on them, and in officers who rose to fame as distinguished generals or in any soldier of the regiment who won the Victoria Cross. The commercial value of a bronze Victoria Cross is now more than £1,000 because medal collectors must compete with regiments whose officers, both serving and retired, club together to contribute money to purchase the medal and return it to the regiment.

Even when an officer is not serving with his regiment – and he may be absent from it on staff duties for most of his career – he retains his identification with it, wears its uniform and takes pride in it. If his regiment goes on active duty, he often begs to return and serve in it. Positions on the staff were much sought for, but many felt like Lieutenant William Hargood of the 1st Madras Fusiliers who while serving as aide-de-camp to General Havelock during the Mutiny wrote home that 'I very often long to be back with the Regiment, for, after all, next to your home, there is no place like your Regiment'.

In the last century, and up until World War II, an officer could hold a rank in his regiment that was different from his rank in the army. Sometimes an officer would hold three ranks, depending upon where he was and the circumstances. In 1854 Neville Chamberlain was only a captain in his regiment but he held a brevet lieutenant-colonelcy in the army and a local rank of brigadier on the North-West Frontier. The title of brigadier-general was never a substantive rank in the nineteenth century but always local and temporary. Officers in Guards regiments always held a rank in the army two grades above their regimental rank and when the British took command of the Egyptian army officers seconded to it were given ranks two grades higher than their rank in the British army.

An officer reverted to his rank in the army whenever he served outside his regiment or when his own unit was brigaded with another unit, though it be but a battery of artillery. This sometimes created embarrassing situations. During World War I, when the retreat from Mons began, the Gordon Highlanders, together with some of the Royal Irish and a detachment of the Royal Scots found themselves abandoned. The orders to retreat had not reached them. Lieutenant-Colonel Francis Neish commanded the Gordons, but his second-in-command, William Gordon, v c, was a brevet colonel in the army and assumed command of all of the troops in the area, becoming the commanding officer of his own regimental commander. As Colonel Gordon did not like the plans of Neish, he changed them. The result was that almost the entire force was killed or captured, including Colonel Gordon, who spent the remainder of the war in a German prison.

Regiments with snob appeal are not unique to the British army, for even the armies of republican countries often cannot resist forming elite units, but surely the British army has always been the most class conscious of all armies. Socially, the Guards regiments, both cavalry and infantry, are the elite. Yet, for the professional officer seeking active service and hoping for high rank, service in the Guards is not, and has never been, the preferred road. Few Guards officers have become distinguished generals.

In 1899 the Royal Horse Guards (The Blues) contained twenty-five officers, not counting the Prince of Wales who was Colonel-in-Chief and Lord Wolseley who was Colonel, both largely honorary posts; of these twenty-five, seven were peers and six were the sons of peers. Others had aristocratic names such as Arthur Vaughan Hanning Vaughan-Lee. None had attended the Staff College. In contrast, the Northamptonshire regiment had sixty-two officers, excluding the colonel (who was not even a knight), but none were peers or sons of peers. However, one had the Victoria Cross and three had passed the Staff College.

The Northamptonshire officers took their profession seriously and they were in a fighting regiment. Soldiers in Guards regiments were splendid physical specimens and subjected to a ferocious

discipline, but they were rarely absent from England and until the
end of the century saw little action. They were never involved
in the little wars in India, Burma, Afghanistan or New Zealand;
even during the Mutiny, the Guards stayed at home.

When most old soldiers in Britain think of the army, they think
of their regiment. In the last century the regiment was even more
self-contained than it is today. It gave men of whatever rank and
of whatever background a respectable home and an honourable
family. It gave men a sense of belonging and a sense of pride – *we*
are better than 'those others'. It also gave them a sense of purpose
and a harsh but effective code of conduct. It served better than
any nationalistic crusade or pat patriotism to make meaningful
their life of killing and dying. As Wolseley, speaking of the
'uneducated private soldier', said: 'The Regiment is mother,
sister and mistress. . . . It is a high, an admirable phase of
patriotism, for, to the soldier, his regiment is his country.' Men
died for the honour of their regiment. 'Forward the 53rd!' was a
more potent cry than 'Forward for Britain!' And, of course, it was
possible to instil love of regiment into Sikhs, Gurkhas and Pathans
who would never have learned to love England.

Officers and other ranks certainly saw life from different angles,
but for both the regiment was a home. Other ranks usually served
their entire careers in one regiment. It was an isolated and insulated
society of its own. This was particularly true of the tribal regiments (Scots, Welsh and Irish). Scottish regiments, particularly
in Victorian times, carried Scotland with them. Each regiment
was a movable parish in a sense, its members, bound together by
ties of kinship, tradition, religion and speech, passing through
exotic lands without leaving home and returning to their High-
lands after years in India, Afghanistan and Africa untouched by
pagan customs or foreign ways to take their place by the peat fires
in their cottages almost as if they had never left them.

The mercenary or native regiments were allowed the freedom
to develop their own character and characteristics, and this was
one of the strengths of the British regimental concept. The
British officers in these regiments were usually successful in

engendering the same fierce regimental pride in their sepoys and sowars as they themselves felt. Officers in the 4th Gurkhas or the 32nd Sikhs felt no less pride in their regiments than officers in the Guards or the Gordons, and many of these mercenary regiments survived long enough to develop traditions, customs and a list of accomplishments to justify their pride.

The most important single factor contributing to the success of British arms in Asia, Africa and elsewhere in the last century – more important than superiority of weapons, which did not always exist, and certainly more important than the professional training of the officer corps or the generalship of commanders – was the spirit engendered in all ranks by the regimental system.

The value of this British regimental concept in modern warfare is questionable, but it has the advantage, a tremendous advantage in the last century and always an essential element in any army, of creating a splendid *esprit de corps*. 'It can be argued that other nations do without the regimental system,' said R. L. V. ffrench Blake. 'Other nations are not the same as Britain. The Briton likes to be part of a small family group – not a cog in a state machine, not a number in a vast card index system.' Being costly and administratively inefficient, the regimental system has been under attack by politicians for generations, but it has always been fiercely defended by every soldier from the Duke of Wellington to Lord Montgomery. 'Keep your hands off the regiment, ye iconoclastic civilian officials who meddle and muddle in Army matters' thundered Wolseley. And Field-Marshal Montgomery has warned, 'We must be very careful what we do with British infantry. They are the people who do the hard fighting and the killing. . . . Their fighting spirit is based largely on morale and regimental *esprit de corps*. On no account must anyone tamper with this.'

But politicians did tamper with the British infantry. Beginning in 1957, disaster began to overtake the regiments. Old and distinguished regiments of the line started to disappear from the order of battle of the British army. They were no longer needed 'somewhere east of Suez' – or so it was thought. What the Sikhs, Afghans, Zulus, Boers, Dervishes, Germans and other enemies of

Appendix I. The British Regiment

the sovereign were unable to accomplish the British did to themselves in the systematic destruction of some of their finest regiments, amalgamated or disbanded. Many were more than 200 years old. Some remain still, but many famous names are now gone, their colours laid up, their drums inscribed with battle honours now silent, the regimental silver, pictures, medals and mementos sold or put in museums, cellars and attics, and the old hunting trophies burned.

Britain is littered with monuments to regiments and to battles long forgotten by all but the members of the regiments who fought in them, and many a village church has its plaques and commemorative windows to local soldiers who died in remote parts of the Empire for the honour of their regiments. For a while the memories of the lost regiments will be preserved in associations of old soldiers and in little regimental museums, each carefully tended by some retired officer. But as the survivors die, so will the museums and the memories. Only the scattered monuments will remain (unless they are in the path of a new motorway) as reminders of what the British army once was.

THE LITTLE WARS

IT is curious that no complete list exists of the Victorian wars, military expeditions, campaigns; all the revolts, uprisings and mutinies that were suppressed. The list below, although long, and including all the major actions and most of the minor ones, is still incomplete. Some of the dates are probably inaccurate, for, although in every case an attempt was made to obtain dates given by participants themselves, in some cases two participants listed different years for the same event. Of some of the small affairs, only the name and date are known, for the details were lost when the participants with their memories died. This list, then, is a partial record of the conflicts in those years of the 'long peace' and an indication of the cost of the *pax britannica*.

1837   Insurrection in Canara, India

1837–38 Mackenzie's rebellion in Ontario
        Second Goomsore campaign

1839   Operations in the Persian Gulf
        Kurmool campaign
        Capture of Aden
        Jodhpur campaign

1839–42 First Afghan War
        Opium War

1840   Expedition into Kohistan
        Marri uprising in Sind
        Operations on the coast of Syria

1841   Expedition into Zurmatt
        Expedition against dacoits in Shahjehanpore district

1841–42 Expedition against Walleng hill tribes on the Arracan frontier

Appendix II : The Little Wars

1842 Expedition against Shinwaris
Pirara expedition
Insurrection in Shorapore district, India
Bundlecund campaign
Industrial disturbances at Leeds
Military occupation of Natal

1842–43 Operations in the Saugor and Nerbudda territories

1843 Rebecca riots in Wales
Sind campaign
Gwalior campaign
Pirates of Borneo chastised
Disturbance in Malabar, India

1843–48 First Maori War

1844 Mutiny of two native regiments on Sind frontier

1844–45 Campaign in southern Mahratta country
Campaign against hill tribes on northern frontier of Sind

1845 Expedition against Boers
Suppression of pirates in Borneo
Naval action against Argentines on Parana River

1845–46 First Sikh War

1846 Aden besieged

1846–47 Kaffir War (War of the Ax)

1847 Capture of the Bogue forts, China
Rebellion in Golcondah and Darcondah in the Golcondah Zemindary

1847–48 Expedition to Goomsore

1848 Sherbo expedition
White Cloud expedition against the Braves
Expedition against King of Appolonia on Gold Coast
Rebellion in Ceylon
Action at Boomplaats against disaffected Boers

1848–49 Second Sikh War

1849 Expedition against Baizai

1849–50 Expedition against Afridis

1850 Mutiny of 66th Native Infantry, India
Expedition against Kohat Pass Afridis

1850–53 Kaffir War

1851 Expedition against Miranzai
Occupation of Bahadoor Khail
Bombardment of Lagos
Siege of Dhasore
Operations against Umarzai Waziris

1851–52 Two expeditions against Mohmands
First Basuto War (actually two separate affairs, one in 1851 and another in 1852)

1852 Expedition against Umarzai Waziris
Expedition against Ranizais
Expedition against Afridis

1852–53 Expedition to Black Mountains to punish Hasanzais
Second Burma War

1853 Expedition against Kasranis
Expedition against Hindustani Fanatics
Expedition against Shiranis
Expedition against Bori clan of Jowaki Afridis

1854 Expedition against Mohmands
Battle of Muddy Flat
Rebellion of Burmese in Bassein district
Operations against Rohillas, India
Relief of Christenborg on Gold Coast
Riots of Chinese in Singapore
Eureka Stockade incident, Australia
Operations against rebels in Tondiman Rajah's country, India

1854–55 Malageah expeditions
Crimean War

1855 Expedition against Aka Khel Afridis
Expedition against Miranzai
Expedition against Rubia Khel Orakzais
Insurrection of Bedeers of Deodroog
Storming of Sabbajee

Appendix II : The Little Wars

1855-56 Insurrection of the Sonthals suppressed

1856   Expedition against Turis
Fights with hill Kareems in Burma

1856-57 Persian War

1856-60 Arrow War in China

1857   Operations on Canton River
Operations against Shans and Kareens of the Younzareen
district, Martaban Province
Expedition against Beydur Beluchis
Expedition to the Bozdar hills
Expedition against hill tribes in Rajahmundry district
Expedition against villages on the Yusafzai border
The island of Perim in the Strait of Bab-el-Mandeb (near
Aden) occupied

1857-59 Indian Mutiny

1858   Expedition against Khudu Khels and Hindustani fanatics
Expedition against the Crobboes

1858-59 Expedition against Singhbhum rebels

1859   Great Scarcies River expedition
Bundlecund campaign
Expedition against Kabul Khel Waziris
Expedition against the Dounquah rebels

1859-62 The 'Blue Mutiny' in Bengal

1860   Expedition against Mahsud Waziris

1860-61 Baddiboo War on the Gambia
Maori War
Sikhim expedition
Quiah War in Sierra Leone

1861   Storming and capture of Rohea
Disturbances in Honduras
Attack on Madoukia
Expedition against Porto Novo, Dahomey
Bombardment and destruction of Massougha on Sierra Leone
river

1862–63 Cossiah Rebellion

1863   Umbeyla campaign
         Action against Malay Pirates

1863–64 First Ashanti War

1863–66 Maori War

1864   Operations against shore batteries in Japan
         Bhutan expedition
         Expedition against the Mohmands

1865   Insurrection of freed slaves in Jamaica
         Bombardment of Cape Haitian in Haiti

1865–66 Expedition into interior of Arabia from Aden

1866   Fenian raids from United States into Canada

1867   Fenian troubles in Ireland
         Expedition to Honduras
         Expedition to Little Andaman Island

1867–68 Abyssinian War

1868   Expedition against the Bizoti Orakzais
         Hazara expedition against Black Mountain tribes
         Basuto War

1868–70 Maori War in New Zealand

1869   Expedition against Bizoti Orakzais

1869–70 Red River expedition in Canada

1870   Fenian raid from United States into Canada

1871–72 Lushai campaign

1872   Expedition against Dawaris

1873   Town of Omoa in Spanish Honduras bombarded

1873–74 Second Ashanti War

1874–75 Daffla expedition on North-West Frontier

1875   Naga Hills expedition
         Bombardment of villages on Congo river
         Rebellion in Griqualand

Appendix II : The Little Wars

1875–76 Rebellion of slavers against British-imposed anti-slavery laws
in Mombasa and Kilwa
Operations in Malay Peninsula

1877–78 Kaffir War
Expedition against Jawaki Afridis

1878 Pirate strongholds in Borneo bombarded
Gaika War in South Africa
Expedition against Zakha Khel Afridis

1878–80 Second Afghan War

1879 Expedition against Zakha Khel Afridis
Expedition against Suliman Khel Pawindahs and others
Punitive expedition against Zaumukts
Expedition against Mohmands
Zulu War
Expedition against Sekakuni

1879–80 Naga expedition

1880 Expedition against Batanis
Expedition against Marris
Expedition against Mohmands
Expedition against Malikshahi Waziris

1880–81 The Gun War or Fifth Basuto War
First Anglo-Boer War

1881 Expedition against Mahsud Waziris

1882 Arabi rebellion

1883 Bikaneer expedition, India

1883–84 Akha expedition, India

1884 Rebellion of Metis in Western Canada
Zhob Valley expedition

1884–85 Expedition to Bechuanaland
Gordon Relief expedition

1885 Bhutan expedition

1885–87 Third Burma War

1885–98 Wars with Arab slave traders in Nyasa

369

1888   Black Mountain or Hazara expedition

1888–89 Sikhim expedition

1889   Tonhon expedition
        Expedition to Sierra Leone

1889–90 Chin Lushai campaign

1890   Malakand campaign
        Mashonaland expedition
        Vitu expedition
        Punitive expedition in Somaliland

1891   Manipur expedition
        Hunza and Nagar campaign
        Samana or second Miranzai expedition
        Hazara expedition

1891–92 Operations in Uganda
        Campaign in Gambia

1892   Isazai expedition
        Tambi expedition
        Chin Hills expedition

1893   British and French shoot at each other by mistake in Sierra
          Leone
        First Matabele War
        Expedition to Nyasaland

1893–94 Third Ashanti War
        Arbor Hills expedition

1894   Gambia expedition
        Disturbances in Nicaragua
        British expedition to Sierra Leone
        Expedition against Kabarega, King of Unyoro, in Uganda

1894–95 Punitive expedition to Waziristan
        Nikki expedition

1895   Chitral campaign
        Brass River expedition

1895–96 Second Matabele War
        Jameson Raid
        Fourth Ashanti War

Appendix II : The Little Wars

1896   Bombardment of Zanzibar
Rebellion in Rhodesia
Matabele uprising

1896–98 Reconquest of Sudan

1897   Operations in Bechuanaland
Operation in Bara Valley, India

1897–98 Punitive expedition into Tochi Valley
Tirah campaign
Uganda mutiny

1897–
1903   Conquest of Northern Nigeria (capture of Benin City in 1897)

1898   Riots in Crete, bombardment of Candia

1898–
1902   Suppression of the Mad Mullah in Somaliland

1899   Campaign in Sierra Leone
Bebejiya expedition, North-East Frontier

1899–
1902   Anglo-Boer War

1900   Boxer Rebellion
Aden field force supported Haushabi tribe fight off Humar
tribe from Yemen
Rebellion in Borneo

1900–01 Ashanti War

SOME BRITISH ORDERS

KG	Knight of the Order of the Garter
GCB	Knight Grand Cross of the Order of the Bath
KCB	Knight Commander of the Order of the Bath
CB	Companion of the Order of the Bath
GCSI	Knight Grand Commander of the Star of India
CSI	Companion of the Star of India
GCMG	Knight Grand Cross of the Order of St Michael and St George
KCMG	Knight Commander of the Order of St Michael and St George
CMG	Companion of the Order of St Michael and St George
GCIE	Grand Commander of the Indian Empire
KCIE	Knight Commander of the Indian Empire
CIE	Companion of the Indian Empire
GCVO	Knight Grand Cross of the Victorian Order
KCVO	Knight Commander of the Victorian Order
CVO	Companion of the Victorian Order
DSO	Companion of the Order of Distinguished Service

BIBLIOGRAPHY

ADAMS, JACK. *The South Wales Borderers.* Hamish Hamilton, London, 1968

ADYE, GENERAL SIR JOHN. *Recollections of a Military Life.* Smith, Elder, London, 1895

ALDERSON, BREVET LIEUTENANT-COLONEL E. A. H. *With the Mounted Infantry and the Mashonaland Field Force.* Methuen, London, 1898

ALFORD, HENRY S. L. and SWORD, W. DENNISTOUN. *The Egyptian Soudan, its Loss and Recovery.* Macmillan, New York, 1898

AMERY, L. S., ed. *The Times History of the War in South Africa 1899–1900.* 7 Vols., Sampson Low, London, 1900–09

The Army in India, a Photographic Record 1850–1914. Hutchinson in association with the National Army Museum, London, 1968

ARTHUR, SIR GEORGE, ed. *The Letters of Lord and Lady Wolseley, 1870–1911.* Heinemann, London, Doubleday, New York, 1922

ATKINS, JOHN BLACK. *The Relief of Ladysmith.* Methuen, London, 1900

ATTERIDGE, A. HILLIARD. *Towards Khartoum.* A. D. Innes, London, 1897

AUSTIN, HERBERT H. *With MacDonald in Uganda.* Edward Arnold, London, 1903

BAIRD, WILLIAM. *General Wauchope.* Anderson & Ferrier, Edinburgh and London, 1901

BARAT, AMIYA. *The Bengal Native Infantry.* Firma K. L. Mukmopadhyay, Calcutta, 1962

BARCLAY, SIR THOMAS. *Thirty Years, Anglo-French Reminiscences (1876–1906).* Houghton Mifflin, Boston and New York, 1914

BARNES, R. MONEY, *A History of the Regiments and Uniforms of the British Army.* Seeley Service, London, 1950

BARNETT, CORRELLI. *Britain and Her Army 1509–1970.* Allen Lane The Penguin Press, London, 1970

BELHAVEN, LORD. *The Uneven Road.* Murray, London 1955

BENNETT, ERNEST N. *The Downfall of the Dervishes.* Methuen, London, 1899

373

BENTLEY, NICOLAS. *Russell's Despatches from the Crimea.* Hill & Wang, New York, 1967

BLAKE, R. L. V. FFRENCH. *The 17th/21st Lancers.* Hamish Hamilton London, 1968

BLAKE, ROBERT. *Disraeli.* St. Martin's, New York, 1967

BLUNT, WILFRID SCAWEN. *Secret History of the English Occupation of Egypt.* Knopf, New York, 1922

BOLT, DAVID. *Gurkhas.* Weidenfeld & Nicolson, London, 1967

BOND, BRIAN. *Victorian Military Campaigns.* Praeger, New York, 1967

BONHAM-CARTER, VICTOR. *Soldier True, The Life and Times of Field Marshal Sir William Robertson Bart, GCB, GCMG, KCVO, DSO, 1860–1933.* Muller, London, 1963

BRACKENBURY, HENRY. *The River Column.* Blackwood, London, 1885

BRADDON, RUSSELL. *The Siege.* Viking, New York, 1970

BRANDEN, MICHAEL. *The 10th Royal Hussars (Prince of Wales Own).* Leo Cooper, London, 1969

BRETT-SMITH, RICHARD. *The 11th Hussars (Prince Albert's Own).* Leo Cooper, London, 1969

BRUCE, GEORGE. *Six Battles For India. The Anglo-Sikh Wars, 1845–6, 1848–9.* Arthur Barker, London, 1969

—— *Retreat From Kabul.* Mayflower-Dell, London, 1967

BURLEIGH, BERNET. *Two Campaigns, Madagascar and Ashanti.* Fisher Unwin, London, 1896

—— *Khartoum Campaign, 1898.* Chapman & Hall, London, 1898

BUTLER, LEWIS. *Sir Redvers Buller.* Smith, Elder, London, 1909

BUTLER, WILLIAM. *A Narrative of the Events Connected with the Sixty-Ninth Regiment.* W. Mitchell, London, 1870

—— *The Campaigns of the Cataracts.* Sampson Low, London, 1887

—— *The Life of Sir George Pomeroy-Colley.* Murray, London, 1899

—— *Sir William Butler, An Autobiography.* Constable, London, 1911

CALLWELL, C. E. *Tirah, 1897.* Constable, London, 1911

CAMPBELL, DAVID. *General Hector A. MacDonald.* Hood, Douglas & Howard, London, n.d.

CAREW, TIM. *The Royal Norfolk Regiment.* Hamish Hamilton, London, 1967

CARLYLE, THOMAS. *On Heroes, Hero-worship and the Heroic In History.* Chapman & Hall, London, 1840

Bibliography

CARTER, M. E. *Life of Baden-Powell*. Longmans, London, 1956

CARTER, THOMAS FORTESCUE. *A Narrative of the Boer War: Its Causes and Results*. John MacQueen, London, 1900

CHICHESTER, HENRY M. and BURGES-SHORT, GEORGE. *The Records and Badges of Every Regiment in the British Army*. Gale & Polden, Aldershot, 1900

CHURCHILL, WINSTON. *A History of the English-speaking People*. Vol. 7, Dodd, Mead, New York, 1958

—— *My Early Life*. Scribner's, New York, 1960

—— *River War*. Eyre & Spottiswoode, London, 1899

CLARK, CUMBERLAND. *Britain Overseas*. Kegan Paul, London, 1924

CLARK, G. KITSON. *The Making of Victorian England*. Methuen, London, 1962

COATES, THOMAS F. G. *Hector MacDonald or the Private Who Became a General*. Partridge, London, 1900

COLBORNE, J. *With Hicks Pasha in the Soudan; Being an Account of the Senaar Campaign in 1883*. Smith, Elder, London, 1884

COLVILLE, COL. H. E. *History of the Sudan Campaign*. 2 Vols, H.M.S.O., London, 1889

COMPTON, PIERS. *Colonel's Lady and Camp-Follower*. Hale, London, 1970

COOPER, LEONARD. *Havelock*, Bodley Head, London, 1957

CREIGHTON-WILLIAMSON, DONALD. *The York and Lancaster Regiment*. Leo Cooper, London, 1968

CROMER, EARL OF. *Ancient and Modern Imperialism*. Murray, London, 1910

CROSS, COLIN. *The Fall of the British Empire, 1918–1968*. Hodder & Stoughton, London, 1968

DAVIS, JOHN. *The History of the Second, Queen's Royal Regiment, Now the Queen's (Royal West Surrey) Regiment*. Vol. V. Eyre & Spottiswoode, London, 1906

DeWATTEVILLE, COLONEL. *The British Soldier*. Putnam, New York, 1955

DUPUY, R. ERNEST and DUPUY, TREVOR. *The Encyclopedia of Military History*. Harper & Row, New York, 1970

EDWARDES, MICHAEL. *The Necessary Hell, John and Henry Lawrence and the Indian Empire*. Cassell, London, 1958

—— *Battles of the Indian Mutiny*. Batsford, London, 1963

ELLIOTT, J. C. *The Frontier 1839–1947*. Cassell, London, 1968

ELTON, LORD. *Gordon of Khartoum*, Knopf, New York, 1955

FEATHERSTONE, DONALD. *At Them with the Bayonet! The First Sikh War*. Jarrolds, London, 1968

—— *All For a Shilling a Day*. Jarrolds, London, 1966

FINCASTLE, VISCOUNT and ELIOTT-LOCKHART, P. C. *A Frontier Campaign*. Methuen, London, 1898

FLEMING, PETER. *Bayonets to Lhasa*. Harper & Row, New York, 1961

—— *The Siege at Peking*. Harper, New York, 1959

FLINT, JOHN E. *Sir George Goldie, and the Making of Nigeria*. Oxford University Press, 1960

FORBES-MITCHELL, WILLIAM. *The Relief of Lucknow*. The Folio Society, London, 1962

FORTESCUE, JOHN. *The Empire and the Army*. Cassell, London, 1928

—— *Military History*. Cambridge University Press, 1923

FOSS, MICHAEL. *The Royal Fusiliers*, Hamish Hamilton, London, 1967

Frontier and Overseas Expeditions from India. Vols. I and II. Government Monotype Press, Simla, 1907 and 1908

FORNEAUX, RUPERT. *The Zulu War: Isandhlwana and Rorke's Drift*. Weidenfeld & Nicolson, London, 1963

GARDNER, BRIAN. *Mafeking, a Victorian Legend*. Harcourt, Brace, Jovanovich, New York, 1966

—— *The Lion's Cage*. Arthur Barker, London, 1969

GATACRE, BEATRIX. *General Gatacre*. Murray, London, 1910

GERMAINS, VICTOR WALLACE. *The Truth About Kitchener*. Bodley Head, London, 1925

GIBBS, PETER. *A Flag for the Matabele*. Vanguard, New York, 1956

GIBSON, TOM. *The Wiltshire Regiment (The 2nd and 99th Regiments of Foot)*. Leo Cooper. London, 1969

GOPAL, RAM. *How the British Occupied Bengal*. Asia Publishing House, London, 1963

GREW, E. S. and others. *Field-Marshal Lord Kitchener, His Life and Work for the Empire*. 3 vols. Gresham Publishing Co., London, 1916

HAGGARD, H. RIDER. *The Last Boer War*. Kegan Paul, London, 1899

HAKE, A. EGMONT, with additions by HUGH CRAIG. *The Story of Chinese Gordon*. Worthington, New York, 1884

HAMILTON, IAN B. M. *The Happy Warrior, a Life of General Sir Ian Hamilton G.C.B., G.C.M.G., D.S.O.* Cassell, London, 1966

—— *Listening for the Drums*. Faber, London, 1944

Bibliography

HARROP, A. J. *England and the Maori Wars*. Whitcombe & Tombs, Australia and New Zealand, 1937

HASWELL, JOCK. *The Queen's Royal Regiment (West Surrey)*. Hamish Hamilton, London, 1967

HIBBERT, CHRISTOPHER. *The Destruction of Lord Raglan*. Little, Brown, Boston, 1961

HILTON, MAJOR-GENERAL RICHARD. *The Indian Mutiny*. Hollis & Carter, London, 1957

HODSON, MAJOR W. S. R. *Twelve Years of a Soldier's Life in India*. *George H. Hodson*. John W. Parker, London, 1859

HOLT, EDGAR. *The Opium Wars in China*. Putnam, New York, 1964

HOWARD, PHILIP. *The Black Watch*. Hamish Hamilton, London, 1968

INGLIS, LADY. *The Siege of Lucknow, A Diary*. Tauchnitz, Leipzig, 1892

INNES, J. J. MCLEOD. *The Life and Times of Genera Sir James Browne*. Murray, London, 1905

JAMES, DAVID. *Lord Roberts*. Hollis & Carter, London, 1954

JENKINS, L. HADOW, *General Frederick Young*. Routledge, London, 1923

JERROLD, WALTER. *Sir Redvers H. Buller, V.C.* Partridge, London, 1900

JOCELYN, LORD. *Six Months with the Chinese Expedition; or Leaves from a Soldier's Note-book*. Murray, London, 1841

KAYE, JOHN WILLIAM. *Lives of Indian Officers*. 3 Vols. Strahan, London, 1869

KIERMAN, V. G. *The Lords of Human Kind*. Weidenfeld & Nicolson, London, 1969

KNAPLUND, PAUL. *The British Empire 1815–1939*. Hamish Hamilton, London, 1942

KNOLLYS, HENRY, ed. *Life of General Sir Hope Grant*. 2 vols. Blackwood, Edinburgh and London, 1894

LAMBRICK, H. T. *John Jacob of Jacobabad*. Cassell, London, 1960

LAWRENCE, ROSAMOND. *Charles Napier*. Murray, London, 1952

LEHMANN, JOSEPH. *The Model Major-General*. Houghton Mifflin, Boston, 1964

LLOYD, ALAN. *The Drums of Kumasi*. Longmans, London, 1964

LOCKHART, J. G. and WOODHOUSE, C. M. *Cecil Rhodes*. Macmillan, New York, 1963

LONGFORD, ELIZABETH. *Victoria R. I.* Weidenfeld & Nicolson, London, 1969

LUMSDEN, GENERAL SIR PETER S. and ELSMIE, GEORGE R. *Lumsden of the Guides*. Murray, London, 1899

LUNT, JAMES. *Bokhara Burnes*. Barnes & Noble, New York, 1969

LUVAAS, JAY. *The Education of an Army 1815–1940*. University of Chicago Press, 1964

MCCALMONT, SIR HUGH. *The Memoirs of Major-General Sir Hugh McCalmont K.C.B., C.V.O.*, edited and completed by Major-General Sir C. E. Callwell. Hutchinson, London, 1924

MCCOURT, EDWARD. *Buckskin Brigadier, The Story of the Alberta Field Force*. Macmillan, Toronto, 1955

—— *Remember Butler*. Routledge & Kegan Paul, London, 1967

MACDONALD, ALEX. *Too Late for Gordon and Khartoum*. Murray, London, 1887

MACMUN, SIR GEORGE. *The Romance of the Indian Frontiers*. Cape, London, 1931

MACRORY, PATRICK. *The Fierce Pawns*, J. B. Lippincott, Philadelphia, 1966

MAGNUS, PHILIP. *Gladstone*. Dutton, New York, 1954

—— *Kitchener, Portrait of an Imperialist*. Murray, London, 1958

MALLESON, G. B. *Ambushes and Surprises*. W. H. Allen, London, 1885

—— *The Indian Mutiny of 1857*. Seeley, London, 1891

MARJOURAM, SERGEANT WILLIAM. *Memorials of Sergeant William Marjouram, Royal Artillery*, ed. Sergeant William White. Nisbit, London, 1863

MARTIN, W. A. P. *The Siege in Peking*. Revell, New York, 1900

MAURICE, SIR FREDERICK, *The Life of General Lord Rawlinson of Trent From His Journals and Letters*. Cassell, London, 1928

MICHAEL, FRANZ (in collaboration with CHUNG-LI CHANG). *The Taiping Rebellion, History and Documents*. Vol. I. University of Washington Press, Seattle, 1966

MILLER, MARGARET and MILLER, HELEN RUSSELL, eds. *A Captain of the Gordons, Service Experiences, 1900–1904*. Sampson Low, London, n.d.

MILNER, ALFRED. *England in Egypt*. Edward Arnold, London, 1892

MITFORD, MAJOR R. C. *To Caubul with the Cavalry Brigade*. W. H. Allen, London, 1881

MOIR, GUTHRIE. *The Suffolk Regiment (The 12th Regiment of Foot)*. Leo Cooper, London, 1964

Bibliography

MORRIS, DONALD R. *The Washing of the Spears*. Simon & Schuster, New York, 1965

MORRIS, JAMES. *Pax Britannica, The Climax of an Empire*. Harcourt, Brace, Jovanovich, New York, 1968

MUTER, MRS. *My Recollections of the Sepoy Revolt (1857–58)*. John Long, London, 1911

MYATT, FREDERICK. *The March to Magdala, The Abyssinian War of 1868*. Leo Cooper, London, 1970

—— *The Royal Berkshire Regiment*. Hamish Hamilton, London, 1968

—— *The Golden Stool*. William Kimber, London, 1966

OATTS, L. B. *The Highland Light Infantry*. Leo Cooper, London, 1969

OUTRAM, J. *A Refutation of Certain Calumnies Cast on the Author by Major-General W. F. P. Napier, in his recent work entitled 'The Conquest of Scinde'*. Part I, privately printed, 1845

PARR, SIR HENRY HALLAM. *Recollections and Correspondence*, edited by Sir Charles Fortescue-Brickdale. Fisher Unwin, London, 1917

PEARMAN, JOHN. *Sergeant Pearman's Memoirs*, ed. The Marquess of Anglesey, Cape, London, 1968

PEARSE, H. H. *Four Months Besieged, The Story of Ladysmith*. Macmillan, New York, 1900

PEMBERTON, W. BARING. *Battles of the Boer War*. Dufour, Chester Springs, Pa., 1964

PETRIE, SIR CHARLES. *The Victorians*. Eyre & Spottiswoode, London, 1960

POLLOCK, J. C. *Way to Glory, The Life of Havelock of Lucknow*. Murray, London, 1957

POLLACK, SAM. *Mutiny for the Cause*. Leo Cooper, London, 1969

POPHAM, HUGH. *The Somerset Light Infantry*. Hamish Hamilton, London, 1968

POWELL, GEOFFREY. *The Green Howards*. Hamish Hamilton, London, 1968

PRESTON, ANTONY and MAJOR, JOHN. *Send a Gun Boat*. Longmans, London, 1967

RAIT, ROBERT S. *The Life and Campaigns of Hugh First Viscount Gough Field-Marshal*. 2 Vols. Constable, London, 1903

—— *The Life of Field-Marshal Sir Frederick Paul Haines*. Constable, London, 1911

Regimental Nicknames and Traditions of the British Army. Gale & Polden, London, 1915

ROBERTS, FIELD-MARSHAL LORD. *Forty-One Years in India.* 2 Vols. Richard Bentley, London, 1897

ROBERTSON, SIR GEORGE S. *Chitral, The Story of a Minor Siege.* Methuen, London, 1899

ROBERTSON, SIR WILLIAM. *From Private to Field-Marshal.* Constable London, 1921

ROBINSON, CHARLES N., ed. *Celebrities of the Army.* Newnes, London, 1900

ROYLE, CHARLES. *The Egyptian Campaigns 1882 to 1885.* Hurst & Blackett, London, 1900

SALE, LADY. *The First Afghan War,* edited by Patrick Macrory (Military Memoirs Series) Longmans, London, 1969

SCHREINER, OLIVE. *Trooper Peter Halket of Mashonaland.* Fisher Unwin, London, 1897

SELBY, JOHN. *Balaclava: Gentlemen's Battle.* Atheneum, New York. 1970.

SHEPPARD, ERIC WILLIAM. *A Short History of the British Army,* Constable, London, 1926

—— *Military History for the Staff College Entrance Examination.* Gale & Polden, Aldershot, n.d.

SINCLAIR-STEVENSON, CHRISTOPHER. *The Gordon Highlanders.* Hamish Hamilton, London, 1968

STANLEY, HENRY M. *Coomassie and Magdala.* Harper, New York, 1874

STEVENS, G. W. *With Kitchener to Khartum.* Dodd, Mead, New York, 1899

STEINBERG, S. H., ed. *A New Dictionary of British History.* St. Martin's, New York, 1963

STEPHENSON, SIR FREDERICK CHARLES ARTHUR. *At Home and on the Battlefield, Letters from the Crimea, China and Egypt, 1854–1888.* Collected and arranged by Mrs Frank Pownall. Murray, London, 1915

STRACHEY, LYTTON. *Eminent Victorians.* Chatto & Windus, London, 1918

—— *Queen Victoria.* Harcourt Brace, New York, 1921

SUTHERLAND, DOUGLAS. *The Argyll and Sutherland Highlanders. (The 91st and 93rd Highlanders).* Leo Cooper, London, 1969

Bibliography

SWINSON, ARTHUR. *North-West Frontier*. Praeger, New York, 1967

SYMONS, JULIAN. *Buller's Campaign*. Cresset Press, London, 1963

—— *England's Pride*. Hamish Hamilton, London, 1965

TAYLOR, DON *The British in Africa*. Dufour, Chester Springs, Pa., 1962

THOMAS, HUGH. *The Story of Sandhurst*. Hutchinson, London, 1961

THOMPSON, EDWARD and GARRATT, G. T. *Rise and Fulfilment of British Rule in India*. Central Book Depot, Allahabad, India, 1962

TISDALL, E. E. P. *Mrs. Duberly's Campaigns, An Englishwoman's Experiences in the Crimean War and Indian Mutiny*. Rand McNally, Chicago, 1963

TREVELYAN, G. M. *British History in the Nineteenth Century and After: 1782–1919*. Longmans, London, 1922

TROTTER, LIONEL J. *A Leader of Light Horse, the Life of Hodson of Hodson's Horse*. London, 1901

—— *The Life of John Nicholson*, Murray, London, 1904

TURNER, E. S. *Gallant Gentlemen*. Michael Joseph, London, 1956

VERNEY, MAJOR-GENERAL G. L. *The Devil's Wind*. Hutchinson, London, 1956

VETCH, COLONEL R. H. *Life, Letters and Diaries of Lieutenant-General Sir Gerald Graham*. Blackwood, Edinburgh and London, 1901

VIBART, H. M. *Addiscombe, Its Heroes and Men of Note*. Constable, Westminster, 1894

VICTORIA, QUEEN. *The Letters of Queen Victoria*, 1st Series, 3 Vols. Eds. Arthur Christopher Benson and Viscount Esches. Murray, London, 1902

—— 2nd Series, 3 Vols. Ed. George Earl Buckle. Murray, London, 1926

—— 3rd Series, 3 Vols. Ed. George Earl Buckle. Murray, London, 1930

WAHL, PAUL and TOPPEL, DONALD R. *The Gatling Gun*. Herbert Jenkins, London, 1968

WALEY, ARTHUR. *The Opium War Through Chinese Eyes*. Allen & Unwin, London, 1858

WATERFIELD, ROBERT. *The Memoirs of Private Waterfield*, ed. Arthur Swinson and Donald Scott. Cassell, London, 1968

WATERS, W. H. H. *The War in South Africa*. Murray, London, 1904

WHITMORE, SIR GEORGE S. *The Last Maori War in New Zealand Under the Self-Reliant Policy*. Sampson Low, London, 1902

WILKINSON, OSBORN and WILKINSON, JOHNSON. *The Memoirs of the Gemini Generals*. A. D. Innes, London, 1896

WILSON, SIR CHARLES W. *From Korti to Khartoum*. Blackwood, Edinburgh and London, 1886

WOLSELEY, VISCOUNT. *The Story of a Soldier's Life*. 2 Vols. Westminster, 1903

WOOD, SIR EVELYN. *Winnowed Memories*. Cassell, London, 1917
—— *From Midshipman to Field-Marshal*. 2 Vols. Methuen, London, 1906

WOOD, HERBERT FAIRLIE. *The King's Royal Rifle Corps*. Hamish Hamilton, London, 1967

WOODHAM-SMITH, CECIL. *The Reason Why*. McGraw-Hill, New York, 1953

WOODRUFF, PHILIP. *The Men Who Ruled India*. 2 Vols. St. Martin's, New York, 1954

WRIGHT, H. C. SEPPINGS. *Soudan, '96. The Adventures of a War Artist*. Horace Cox, London, 1897

WRIGHT, THOMAS. *The Life of Colonel Fred Burnaby*. Everett London, 1908

WYKES, ALAN. *The Royal Hampshire Regiment*. Hamish Hamilton, London, 1968

WYLDE, A. B. *'83 to '87 in the Soudan*. 2 Vols. Remington, London 1888

WYLLY, H. C. *The Military Memoirs of Lieutenant-General Sir Joseph Thackwell*. Murray, London, 1908

YOUNG, PETER and LAWFORD, J. P., ed. *History of the British Army*, Putnam, New York, 1970

YOUNGHUSBAND, G. J. *The Relief of Chitral*. Macmillan, London, 1895
—— *A Soldier's Memories in Peace and War*. Herbert Jenkins, London, 1927
—— *The Story of the Guides*. Macmillan, London, 1909

ZETLAND, MARQUESS OF. *Lord Cromer*. Hodder & Stoughton, London, 1932

INDEX

Index

Index

Index

Index

Index

Index

Index